D0536789

Hugh Johnson

The Story of Wine

New Illustrated Edition

Hugh Johnson

The Story of
Wine

New Illustrated Edition

MITCHELL BEAZLEY

The Story of Wine – New Illustrated Edition
by Hugh Johnson

Published in Great Britain in 2004 by Mitchell Beazley, an
imprint of Octopus Publishing Group Ltd, 2–4 Heron Quays,
London E14 4JP

First published in 1989 as *The Story of Wine*
First published in this edition in 2005

Copyright © Octopus Publishing Group Ltd 1989, 2004, 2005
Text copyright © Hugh Johnson 1989
Condensed text copyright © Hugh Johnson 2004

Reprinted 1996, 1998 (twice), 1999, 2002

All rights reserved. No part of this work may be reproduced
or utilized in any form by any means, electronic or mechanical,
including photocopying, recording or by any information storage
and retrieval system, without the prior written permission
of the publishers.

A CIP catalogue record for this book is available from the British
Library.

ISBN 1 84000 972 1

The author and publishers will be grateful for any information
that will assist them in keeping future editions up-to-date.
Although all reasonable care has been taken in the preparation
of this book, neither the publishers, editors nor the author can
accept any liability for any consequences arising from the use
thereof, or the information contained therein.

Commissioning Editor: Hilary Lumsden
Executive Art Editor: Yasia Williams
Senior Editor: Julie Sheppard
Editor: Margaret Rand
Designer: John Round
Proofreader and Indexer: Laura Hicks
Picture Research: Giulia Hetherington
Production: Julie Young

Typeset in Gill Sans and Berkeley

Printed and bound in China

CONTENTS

FOREWORD

Farmer and artist, drudge and dreamer, hedonist and masochist, alchemist and accountant – the wine-grower is all these things, and has been since the Flood.

The more I have learned about wine in the course of a quarter of a century of enjoyment, the more I have realized that it weaves in with human history from its very beginnings as few, if any, other products do. Textiles, pottery, bread… there are other objects of daily use that we can also trace back to the Stone Age. Yet wine alone is charged with sacramental meaning, with healing powers, indeed with a life of its own.

Why is wine so special? Partly because for most of its history, and mankind's, it has been his one source of comfort and courage, his only medicine and antiseptic, his one recourse to renew his tired spirits and lift him above his weary, saddened self. Wine was the foremost of luxuries to millennia of mankind. Yet at the same time wine is unpredictable, and hence its value is variable: so variable, in fact, that no two seasons nor two vineyards will ever give identical results.

It was the convention, when I began to read and write about wine, to provide each famous growth with a little flourish of history. This one was the favourite of Charlemagne; that of Henri IV; and the other the wine that cured poor Louis XIV of the ague. Classical scholars in particular were fond of referring to the apparently great wines of the ancients, yet never quite explained why their idea of fine wine and ours never matched. I remember thinking how little these anecdotes added to my enjoyment and understanding of what I was drinking, and in my first book, *Wine*, gave them rather short shrift. It was the taste of this mysterious, infinitely varied, infinitely subtle and perpetually inspiring drink that captivated me as a writer, owing, first of all, to its utter elusiveness to words.

Words were not the ideal instrument, either, for exploring the relationships between vineyards adjacent on a hillside or opposite each other across a valley; this was geography, and maps were needed. Once I had plotted a vineyard on a map, I found, not only was I able to remember where it was, but even flavours seemed to organize themselves around something so graphic and so demonstrably true.

Maps in their turn were not enough, I later found, to bring into focus the modern world of wine: its goals, its methods, its plant of vineyards and cellars – and above all its practitioners. An encyclopedia was the only way to answer the immediate questions wine buyers ask – except for the recurring question, why?

To try to fathom the causes and origins of things is a different discipline. It requires reading on a scale I had never undertaken, and a system of enquiry that I had to try and learn. It asks for leaps of the imagination into ages whose traces are few, and places that have disappeared. It demands ruthlessness with rumour, but an ear for clues that ring true. In short it takes a historian – and that I do not pretend to be. That is why I have called this book *The Story of Wine*: it is my interpretation of its history, my attempt to place it in the context of its times, and to deduce why we have the vast variety of wines that we do – and why we don't have others.

The aura around wine in all its aspects is so potent that even the humdrum operations of the cellar have been romanticised. What exactly is this dreamy youth supposed to be doing?

Of course it is, before all else, a human story. It begins with the worship of wine as a supernatural being: the bringer of joy. It climbs to the heights of dramatic inspiration, and descends to the depths of fraud, drunkenness, betrayal, and murder. It involves passionate spiritual convictions: none more so than the Islamic belief that wine is too great a blessing for this world. It visits the physician at his task of healing, the politician in the act of cheating, the monk in his cell, and the sailor at sea.

Wine, one might say, gave man his first lessons in ecology. It was at the birth of biochemistry. It has urged man forwards in knowledge, and at the same time degraded him in stupor.

Only forty years ago wine was in the doldrums, battered by disease, war, and poverty; profitless and depressed. Today there are more fine wines in the world, and in greater variety, than ever before in history. Wine is a vast international business, a cultural network that spans more than half the globe, an art form with followers in almost every country – and with a vocal minority of enemies.

All in all, wine is a force to be reckoned with: and never has it been more topical than today. The time is ripe, if ever it was, to see it in its historical perspective.

I n acknowledging all those whose help has made this book possible, the name that must go first is that of the late James Mitchell, my dear friend, and the co-founder of Mitchell Beazley, who encouraged me to write it. Faced with the research for such a vast subject, I turned to a young Cambridge historian, Helen Bettinson, who has been the most dogged and ingenious, dedicated and loyal partner that an author could hope for, during four years in the library, on location, and in tracking down illustrations from around the world.

The project was interrupted – if that is the word – by two years' work on a thirteen-part television documentary series which used the same material in an appropriately different way. *Vintage – A History of Wine* was co-produced by Malone Gill Productions, W.G.B.H., the Boston Public Broadcasting Service, and Channel 4, London, and sponsored by the Banfi Charitable Foundation. To John and Harry Mariani, the benefactors of the Banfi Foundation, I offer a sincere tribute: they are the world's most dedicated and liberal lovers of wine.

Travelling for television led me to explore and explain, first to my patient producers, Michael Gill and Christopher Ralling, aspects of wine and its culture I would not have questioned without. The subject became broader as well as deeper as we worked. Cameramen see things others miss (and sound recordists have very sharp ears).

My colleagues at Mitchell Beazley have had a less exciting but no less demanding job. They have made editing and designing the book another journey in creative self-discipline. To Di Taylor and Diane Pengelly, my original editors, to Margaret Rand, who helped me to distil this new edition, to Julie Sheppard and Laura Hicks who polished it, and to Yasia Williams who gave it its brave new look, I offer the thanks of a grateful author.

CHAPTER 1

THE POWER TO BANISH CARE

It was not the subtle bouquet of wine, or a lingering aftertaste of violets and raspberries, that first caught the attention of our ancestors. It was, I'm afraid, its effect.

In a life that was "nasty, brutish, and short", those who first felt the effects of alcohol believed they were being given a preview of paradise. Their anxieties disappeared, their fears receded, ideas came more easily, lovers became more loving when they drank the magic juice. For a while they felt all-powerful, even felt themselves to be gods. Then they were sick, or passed out, and woke up with a horrible headache. But the feeling while it lasted was too good to resist another try – and the hangover, they found, was only a temporary disease. By drinking more slowly, you could enjoy the benefits without suffering the discomforts.

Wine provided the first experience of alcohol only for a privileged minority of the human race. For the great majority it was ale. Most of the earliest cities grew up in the grain- rather than grape-growing lands of the Near East: Mesopotamia and Egypt. Although ancient Egypt made strenuous efforts to grow good wine, only a minority had access to it.

But wine was always the choice of the privileged. Mesopotamia imported what it could not make itself. Why should this be? A simple and cynical answer is that wine is usually stronger than ale. It also kept longer, and (sometimes) improved with keeping. One can hardly state categorically that it always tasted better. All we can say for sure is that it was valued more highly.

Other foods and drinks had mind- (and body-) altering effects. Primitive people are acutely aware of poisons. But whatever spirit was in this drink, mysterious as the wind, was benevolent; was surely, indeed, divine. Wine, they found, had a power and value far greater than ale and quite unlike hallucinatory drugs. Its history pivots around this value.

What is wine, and what are its effects? What has made men from the first recorded time distinguish between wines as they have done with no other food or drink? Why does wine have a history that involves drama and politics, religions and wars? And why, to the dismay of young men on first dates, do there have to be so many different kinds? Only history can explain.

The polite, conventional definition of wine is "the naturally fermented juice of fresh grapes". A more clinical one is an aqueous solution of ethanol with greater or lesser traces of sugars, acids, esters, acetates, lactates, and other substances occurring in grape juice or derived from it by fermentation. It is the ethanol that produces the obvious effect. What is ethanol? A form of alcohol produced by the action of yeasts on sugar – in this case, grape sugar.

Ethanol is clinically described as a depressant, a confusing term because depression is not in the least what you feel. What it depresses ("inhibits" makes it clearer) is the central nervous system. The effect is sedation, the lifting of inhibitions,

LEFT Wine has always been more than mere fermented grapes, and more than mere alcohol. *The Sense of Taste*, the title of this allegory by Jan Breughel and Peter Paul Rubens, finds properties in wine that have been considered divine.

the dulling of pain. The feeling of well-being it brings may be illusory, but it is not something you swallow with your wine: your wine simply allows your natural feelings to manifest themselves.

What is true of wine is true of other alcoholic drinks – up to a point. Ethanol is the principal active component in them all. Its effects, though, are significantly modified by other components – in other words, the differences between wine and beer, or wine and distilled spirits. Little that is conclusive about these differences has yet been discovered by scientific experiment. We are talking about tiny traces of substances whose precise effect is very difficult to monitor through the complexities of human responses. But much that is clearly indicative has accumulated over centuries of usage.

W ine has certain properties that mattered much more to our ancestors than they do to ourselves. For 2,000 years of medical and surgical history it was the universal and unique antiseptic. Wounds were bathed with it; water made safe to drink.

Medically, wine was indispensable until the later years of the nineteenth century. In the words of the Jewish Talmud, "Wherever wine is lacking, drugs become necessary." A contemporary (sixth century BC) Indian medical text describes wine as the "invigorator of mind and body, antidote to sleeplessness, sorrow and fatigue… producer of hunger, happiness and digestion". Enlightened medical opinion today uses very similar terms about its specific clinical virtues, particularly in relation to heart disease. Even Muslim physicians, as we shall see in a later chapter, risked the wrath of Allah rather than do without their one sure help in treatment.

But wine had other virtues. Not only does the natural fermentation of the grape produce a drink that is about one-tenth to one-eighth alcohol, but its other constituents, acids and tannins in particular, also make it brisk and refreshing, with a satisfying "cut" as it enters your mouth, and a lingering clean flavour that invites you to drink again. In the volume of its flavour, and the natural size of a swallow (half the size of a swallow of ale), it makes the perfect drink with food, adding its own seasoning, cutting the richness of fat, making meat seem more tender, and washing down dry pulses and unleavened bread without distending the belly.

Because wine lives so happily with food, and at the same time lowers inhibitions, it was recognized from earliest times as the sociable drink, able to turn a meal into a feast without stupefying (although stupefy it often did). But even stupefied feasters were ready for more the next day. Wine is the most repeatable of mild narcotics without ill effects – at least in the short or medium term. Modern medicine knows that wine helps the assimilation of nutrients (proteins especially) in our food. Moderate wine drinkers found themselves better nourished, more confident and consequently often more capable than their fellows. It is no wonder that in many early societies the ruling classes decided that only they were worthy of such benefits and kept wine to themselves.

The catalogue of wine's virtues, and its value to developing civilization, does not end there. Bulky though it is, and often perishable, it made the almost perfect commodity for trade. It had immediate attraction (as soon as they felt its effects) for strangers who did not know it. The Greeks were able to trade wine for precious metals, the Romans for slaves, with a success that has a sinister echo in the activities of modern drug pushers – except that there is nothing remotely sinister about wine.

In this sense it is true to say that wine advanced the progress of civilization. It facilitated the contacts between distant cultures, providing the motive and means of trade, and bringing strangers together in high spirits and with open minds. Of course, it also carried the risk of abuse. Alcohol can be devastating to health. Yet if it had been widely and consistently abused it would not have been tolerated. Wine, unlike spirits, has long been considered the drink of moderation.

E ven at its most primitive, wine is subject to enormous variations. Climate is the first determining factor; then weather. The competence of the winemaker comes next; then the selection of the grape. Underlying these variables is the composition of the soil and its situation. The key word is selection: of grape varieties, yes, but also of a "clone", a race of vines propagated from cuttings of the best plants in the vineyard. Then restraint in production: to produce only a moderate number of bunches, whose juice will have more flavour than the fruit of an overladen vine. In the ancient world such practices probably first developed in the sheltered economy of royal or priestly vineyards. But the principle has not changed. Selection of the best for each set of circumstances has given us the several thousand varieties of grape which are, or have been, grown in the course of history.

T aking this panoramic view, the discovery that must have done most to advance wine in the esteem of the rulers of the earth was the fact that it could improve with keeping – and not just improve, but at best turn into a substance with ethereal dimensions seeming to approach the sublime. Beaujolais nouveau is all very well (and most ancient wine was something between this and vinegar), but once you have tasted an old vintage burgundy you know the difference between tinsel and gold. To be able to store wine, the best wine, until maturity performed this alchemy was the privilege of pharaohs.

It was wonderful enough that grape juice should develop an apparent soul of its own. That it should be capable, in the right circumstances, of transmuting its vigorous spirit into something of immeasurably greater worth made it a god-like gift for kings. If wine has a prestige unique among drinks – unique, indeed, among natural products – it stems from this fact and the connoisseurship it engenders.

H ow can a rare bottle of wine fetch the price of a great work of art? Can it, however perfect, smell more beautiful than a rose?

No, must surely be the honest answer. But what if, deep in the flushing velvet of its petals, the rose contained the power to banish care?

CHAPTER 2

WHERE GRAPES WERE FIRST TRODDEN

It is late October in the steep-sided valleys of Imeretia. A mist hides the slow windings of the Rioni, gorged with the noisy waters of Caucasian streams.

At intervals all through the subtropical summer, fogs have invaded the Black Sea coastline, the afternoons of hot still days, softening the air in the tree-choked gulleys where the streams run, and shading the rambling grapevines from the burning sun. Grapevines are everywhere: in stream beds, thick as dragons climbing forest trees, flinging themselves over pergolas, through orchards and against the walls of every wooden balconied farmhouse.

Shaded by laurels among the vines beside the house each farmer keeps his *marani* – his wine cellar. It is a mystery: there is no sign of wine, of barrels or vats or jars. A series of little molehills in the well-trodden earth is the only clue.

The family brings the grapes here, in long conical baskets, and empties them into a hollowed-out log beside the fence. When the log is half full the farmer takes off his shoes and socks, carefully washes his feet with hot water from a bucket, then slowly and deliberately tramples the bunches until his feet feel no more resistance.

The molehills cover his wine jars, his *kwevris*, buried to their rims in the laurel-shaded ground. With a hoe he carefully opens one, chipping at the molehill until it reveals a solid plug of oak under the clay. Into the *kwevri*, freshly scoured with a mop made of corn husks, he ladles the crushed grapes until they almost reach the brim. They will ferment in there, in the cool of the earth.

In the spring he will ladle the wine out again, into another scoured-out *kwevri*, leaving the skins behind. Then, sealed up under its molehill, cool in the shaded *marani*, it will keep almost indefinitely. When the time comes to open it there is no need to send out invitations: the heady perfume leaps from the freshly opened well. The neighbours come, bringing their wine cups: shallow pottery bowls that the ancient Greeks would recognize. And a long banquet begins, stately and full of toasting and old epic songs.

Little has changed in Imeretian custom since the time of Homer; and in the way wine is made, almost nothing since prehistoric times. A Greek or a Roman would call a *kwevri* a *pithos* or a *dolium*: the vessels in which the wine of the ancient world fermented. Transcaucasia, the land of the Georgians and Armenians, is one of the native countries of the wine-grape vine. This could be the place where grapes were first trodden, and man discovered the joys of wine.

We cannot point precisely to the place and time when wine was first made any more than we can give credit to the inventor of the wheel. Wine did not have to wait to be invented; it was there, wherever grapes were gathered and stored, even briefly, in a container that would hold their juice. There have been grapes, and people to gather them, for more than two million years. It would be strange if the accident of wine never happened to primitive nomadic man.

Archaeologists accept accumulations of grape pips as evidence (of the likelihood at least) of winemaking. Excavations in Turkey (at Catal Hüyük, perhaps the first of all cities), at

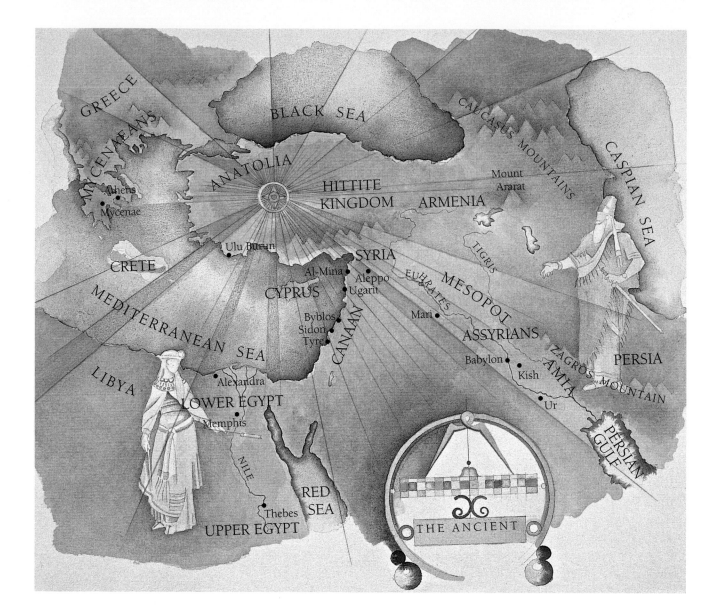

The map shows the ancient Near East and Mediterranean region, with labels including GREECE, MYCENAEANS, Athens, Mycenae, CRETE, MEDITERRANEAN SEA, LIBYA, LOWER EGYPT, Alexandra, Memphis, NILE, UPPER EGYPT, Thebes, RED SEA, BLACK SEA, ANATOLIA, HITTITE KINGDOM, Ulu Burun, Al-Mina, CYPRUS, SYRIA, Aleppo, Ugarit, Byblos, Sidon, Tyre, CANAAN, CAUCASUS MOUNTAINS, Mount Ararat, ARMENIA, TIGRIS, EUHRATES, MESOPOT, Mari, ASSYRIANS, Babylon, Kish, Ur, ZAGROS MOUNTAIN, AMIA, CASPIAN SEA, PERSIA, PERSIAN GULF, THE ANCIENT

Damascus in Syria, Byblos in the Lebanon, and in Jordan have produced grape pips from the Stone Age known as Neolithic B, about 8000BC. But the oldest pips of cultivated vines so far discovered and carbon dated – at least to the satisfaction of their finders – were found in (then Soviet) Georgia, and belong to the period 7000–5000BC.

You can tell more from a pip than just how old it is. Certain characteristics of shape belong unmistakably to cultivated grapes, and the Russian archaeologists were satisfied that they had evidence of the transition from wild vines to cultivated ones some time in the late Stone Age, about 6000BC. Recent researches using DNA analysis have done nothing to contradict these ideas. If they are right, the archaeologists have found the earliest traces of viticulture, the skill of selecting and nurturing vines to improve the quality and quantity of their fruit.

T he wine-grape vine is a member of a family of vigorous climbing woody plants with relations all over the northern hemisphere, about forty of them close enough to be placed in the same botanical genus of *Vitis*.

Its specific name, *vinifera*, means wine-bearing. Cousins include *Vitis rupestris* (rock-loving), *Vitis riparia* (from river banks) and *Vitis aestivalis* (summer-fruiting), but none of them has the same ability to accumulate sugar in its grapes up to about one-third of their volume (making them among the sweetest of fruit), nor elements of fresh-tasting acidity to make their juice a clean and lively drink. The combination of these qualities belongs alone to *Vitis vinifera*, whose natural territory (since the Ice Ages, when it was drastically reduced) is a band of the temperate latitudes spreading westwards from the Persian shores of the Caspian Sea as far as western Europe.

The wild vine, like many plants (willows, poplars and most hollies are examples), carries either male or female flowers: only very rarely both on one plant. The female plants therefore can be expected to fruit – given the presence of a male nearby to provide the pollen. Males, roughly equal in number, will always be barren. The tiny minority of hermaphrodites (those which have both male and female flowers) will bear some grapes, but about half as many as the females.

The first people to have cultivated the vine would naturally have selected female plants as the fruitful ones and destroyed the barren males. Without the males, though, the females would have become barren too. The only plants that would fruit alone or together are the hermaphrodites. Trial and error, therefore, would in time lead to hermaphrodites alone being selected for cultivation. Their seedlings tend overwhelmingly to inherit the habit of bearing both male and female flowers. So eventually the cultivated vine becomes distinguished from the wild one by being consistently hermaphrodite.

Botanists have labelled the two as separate subspecies of *Vitis vinifera*: the wild one as *sylvestris* (woodland), the form resulting from man's selection as *sativa* (culivated). (Strictly, by botanical definition, *sativa* is a cultivar, or cultivated variety, not a subspecies.) The earliest grape pips found in Georgia can be identified as *Vitis vinifera var. sativa* – the basis of the argument that vines were cultivated, and wine presumably made, in the country south of the Caucasus mountains at least 7,000 years ago, and maybe long before that.

T o put this era of human history in some sort of perspective, it was when advanced cultures, in Europe and the Near East, had changed from a nomadic to a settled way of life and started farming as well as hunting, when speech and language reached the point where "sustained conversation was possible and the invention of writing only a matter of time", when technology was moving from stone implements to copper ones, and just about the time when the first pottery was made, in the neighbourhood of the Caspian Sea.

It seems, from what faint traces we can see, that it was a peaceful time, which has left us images of fertility rather than of power and conquest. The *kwevri* is the other evidence of this very early date. In the museum of Tbilisi, the capital of Georgia, is a clay jar that they call a *kwevri* which archaeologists have dated as early as 5000 or even 6000BC. In fact its squat, pot-bellied shape resembles even more the *pithos* of the Greeks and the Roman *dolium* than the more slender and amphora-like *kwevris* of today. But it even has, as decoration, a delta-shaped bunch of little knobs on each side of the wide mouth, which could be interpreted as a bunch of grapes.

The same museum contains some rather baffling objects, which, if they have been interpreted and dated correctly, are the oldest indication we have that wine (or rather the grapevine) was held in special regard: perhaps veneration, perhaps affection – although why not both? They are simply cuttings from a vine, about as long as your little finger, which have been given close-fitting silver sleeves, moulded around them so that the characteristic vine-bud shape shows through like a breast through a blouse. There is no mistaking what they are; the vine wood is perfectly preserved. What they are for is another matter. Apparently they were part of the accoutrements of a burial. The simplest conclusion is that the vine was given a precious setting to symbolize its worth, perhaps even to carry it over into the world of the dead where it could be planted and give pleasure again.

The civilization of China was well advanced in the Bronze Age, and some sort of wine was an important part of it. Inscriptions on oracle-bones from the Shang and Chou dynasties describe the religious rituals of the time, all of which involved wine. Wine drinking, moreover (in the words of the curator of the great National Palace Museum at Taipei), "has been a favoured pastime of heroic figures and poets since ancient times, and has contributed to the creation of countless masterpieces in the history of human culture".

China has native vines, but *Vitis vinifera* is not among them. The first import of the wine vine to China is well documented. It took place from Persia, in 128BC, when the Chinese general Chang Chien made a famous expedition and spent a year in Bactria. From Fergana, the country east of Samarkand, the general took seed of vines and alfalfa (the horse fodder of the Persians) back to the Chinese emperor. In Fergana, he reported, the wealthy stored grape wine in quantities of up to 45,500 litres, keeping it for several decades without risk of deterioration.

No distinction is made in ancient Chinese records between wine made of rice and wine made of grapes or other fruit, nor between wine and what we would call spirits.

The development of the Silk Route across Central Asia introduced more and different varieties of vine to China. At various times the growing of vines had the most influential support of all, that of the emperor. Kían-hi, who was contemporaneous with Louis XIV, was a positive Thomas Jefferson of an emperor, experimenting with vines in different parts of his realms, finding that they did well in the North, but rapidly degenerated in the subtropical South. One can almost hear the voice of Jefferson in his declaration: "I would rather procure for my subjects a novel kind of fruit or grain, than build a hundred porcelain kilns."

A note from the thirteenth century is intriguing for several reasons. Grape wine in glass bottles was sent as tribute from Islamic countries to the Mongol Khan. It was an orange liquid, and each bottle contained ten small cups. It was said to be intoxicating – but it was also clearly very rare. Perhaps it was distilled.

Marco Polo's account of wine in China in the late thirteenth century sounds authoritative: "In Shan-si province grew many excellent vines, supplying a great deal of wine, and in all Cathay this is the only place where wine is produced. It is carried hence all over the country."

These unique objects were found in Trialeti in southern Georgia. Carbon dating puts them at 3000BC – which was about the time that the rich cities of the Sumerians were developing in Mesopotamia far to the south.

T he grape vine is a native of more southerly regions, too. All it asks is moisture in the growing season, and a winter rest to make new buds. Persia had its own vines. Although Mesopotamia is vineless, the Zagros mountains curve south from the Caspian Sea down towards the Persian Gulf, providing just the kind of country the wild vine enjoys.

Botanists, perhaps in desperation with such a vagabond plant, have given names to several different strains or sub-species. Vines from the Caucasus and Anatolia have been called *Vitis vinifera pontica*. According to one theory, this strain was distributed as far as Europe by the Phoenicians from what is now the Lebanon, and is the ancestor of many of our white varieties of grape. *Vitis vinifera orientalis* is a strain from the valley of the river Jordan whose descendants in Europe (they say) include the Golden Chasselas – Germany's Gutedel and the Fendant of Switzerland.

biomolecular archaeology Until very recent years a potsherd was just a piece of clay, perhaps interesting for its shape or its context or where it was found, but otherwise mute. No one could tell what its contents might have been. The invention of new ways of examining such inert materials began with the advent of radiocarbon dating. In the 1990s the development of higher and higher-resolution microscopes allowed archaeologists to scan individual molecules. If the smallest trace was left on the clay it could be analysed. And since 1998 the DNA revolution has meant, among other things, that the parentage of vine varieties has been open to investigation.

A conference on the Origins and Ancient History of Wine at the Robert Mondavi Winery in Napa in 1991, when researchers in the field met for the first time, stimulated the use of these new tools. The University of Pennsylvania Museum and its Applied Sciences Center for Archaeology took the lead. The head of the Center, Patrick E McGovern, published the first book on the subject in 2003.

The Jurassic Park scenario is still far-fetched, but the contents of neolithic cellars are less of a mystery than they were, and the grapes of the ancients may one day be identified.

Most historians are happy with the idea that Egypt received its first vines from the lands to the north, Canaan or Assyria (it is difficult to know what names to use when one is talking about such vast stretches of time, long before countries in the modern sense existed). But it is also possible that vines came to Egypt down the Nile from African highlands to the south in Nubia, or from the west, along the coast of North Africa (according to one set of legends the route taken by the race who became the Egyptians). In any case, the vines of the Nile valley are said to constitute another subspecies, *Vitis vinifera occidentalis*, a proposed ancestor for many of our red varieties of grape.

W hether these differences are real or supposed is academic. What matters is the adaptability of the vine. No other plant has adapted itself so effectively to the enormous range of climates and latitudes where man has introduced it. It is one of the most variable of all domesticated plants. Its genes (it has an unusually large number) are readily reshuffled to produce a marginally different variety. But it is also remarkably prone to mutation in the plant itself. Suddenly a bud will develop as a branch with greater vigour, or leaves of a different size or shape, or even grapes of a different colour. The famous Muscat vine of enormous size at Hampton Court near London is an example of spectacular mutation.

Moving a plant to a different region, with a different climate, tends to encourage such mutations. All of this makes the genealogy of grape varieties a Sisyphean labour, scarcely to be contemplated before the discovery of DNA, and the confident tracing of their remote history impossible.

Compared with such shifting sands, legends have a reassuring solidity. There are plenty about where wine was first made – starting, of course, with Noah.

The ninth chapter of Genesis tells how, after Noah had disembarked the animals, he "began to be an husbandman, and he planted a vineyard". Theology apart, there are other interesting aspects to Noah's story. First, it was "the mountains of Ararat" on which the Ark grounded. Ararat (in Turkish, Buyuk Agri) is the climax of the lesser Caucasian ranges that stretch in pleats and folds down between what is now Turkey and Armenia, a vast double-peaked cone, ice-capped and forbidding, that reaches 16,946 feet (Mont Blanc, the summit of the Alps, reaches 15,771 feet).

The Bible thus supports the thesis that the general area of the Caucasus was the original home of wine – unless, of course, one asks the awkward question: where did Noah live before the Flood? Wherever he built the Ark he already had vineyards, and knew how to make wine. Vines, clearly, were among the Ark's cargo.

M uch more imposing than all this speculation (and much older than the Book of Genesis) is the Babylonian Epic of Gilgamesh, which in part tells the same story of a deluge. Gilgamesh is the oldest literary work known, dating from perhaps 1800BC, but treats, like all epics, of a much earlier time of heroes.

Winemaking is the theme of tablet ten, in which the hero,

Gilgamesh, setting out in search of immortality, enters the realms of the sun, where he finds an enchanted vineyard whose wine (if he had been allowed to drink it) would have given him the immortality he sought.

The divinity in charge was a goddess, Siduri. (In Babylon, as we shall see, women usually seem to have been in charge of the wine supplies.) But if, like the deluge story, and most legendary incidents, some remote historical event lies behind it, could it have recalled an expedition from vineless Mesopotamia to regions that were the source of wine, whether they were in western Syria (as some authorities on the text believe) or in the mountains to the north?

The most quoted of all the legends about the discovery of wine is surely the Persian version. Jamsheed – there are many spellings – was a semi-mythical Persian king. Some legends about him seem to relate him to Noah: he is said to have saved the animals by building a great enclosure for them. To Omar Khayyam he represented heroic antiquity:

ABOVE The fertile foothills of these inhospitable mountains in Georgia are one of the homelands of the wild vine, and may be where vines were first cultivated.

LEFT The story of Noah's disembarkation from the ark, his planting of the first vineyard, and its unhappy aftermath, is told in this illumination from the fifteenth-century Bedford Hours.

"They say the lion and the lizard keep
The courts where Jamshid gloried and drank deep."

At his court, the story runs, grapes were kept in jars for eating out of season. A jar with a strange smell, in which the grapes were foaming, was set aside as unfit to eat, possibly poisonous. A damsel of the harem sought surcease from "nervous headaches", and tried to take her life with this reputed poison. Instead she found exhilaration and refreshing sleep.

Dutifully she told the king, whereupon "a quantity of wine was made, and Jamsheed and his court drank of the new beverage".

CHAPTER 3

THE PHARAOHS AND THEIR WINE

The Egyptians were not the first to grow wine, but they were certainly the first we know of to record and celebrate the details of their winemaking in unambiguous paintings. Vintage time in ancient Egypt is an image no more remote to us than the medieval harvest in France depicted in tapestries and illuminations. What is hard to register is that the activities we can witness so clearly took place between 3,000 and 5,000 years ago; that the technology of winemaking had by then been thoroughly mastered. There were experts in Egypt who discriminated between qualities of wine as confidently and professionally as a Bordeaux broker of the twenty-first century.

Mesopotamian citizens of the same time were wine drinkers too, but they make a much more shadowy picture: we have no time-capsule tombs to bring their existence to life for us. Mesopotamia is the land between the two great rivers, the Euphrates and the Tigris, that rise in the mountains south of the Caucasus and flow south to join the Persian Gulf. It is flat, hot, and (until irrigated) arid: the very antithesis of natural vine country. The Sumerian race settled here from the North or East some time between 4000 and 3000BC and founded the cities of Kish and, later, Ur. Kish has provided us with the earliest form of writing that we know: stylized pictures known as pictograms, drawn with a stylus on moist clay. Among them is a recognizable vine leaf. Ur, dating from about 3000BC, offers much clearer evidence of the enjoyment

RIGHT Stages of the Egyptian grape harvest, from picking, through sealing in jars for fermentation, to shipping; from the tomb of Kha'emwese at Thebes, c.1450BC.

of what is presumably wine in a famous inlaid box known as the Standard of Ur, representing serried courtiers who appear to be toasting their ruler.

It can be argued that their drink was more probably beer in a land where wine was then rare and exotic. On the other hand, who would drink wine if not courtiers?

The cities of Mesopotamia knew wine and used it, but where did they get it from? In later times they tried growing it for themselves, but originally it must have been an import from a country where vine-growing was already well established. It could have been the hills to the east in Persia (we don't know if vines were grown there then), but the readiest answer is provided by the Greek historian Herodotus, respectfully known as "the father of history". Two and a half thousand years later he gave an account of the use of the Euphrates for shipping wine to the great city that succeeded Kish and Ur, Babylon:

"But the thing that, next to the city, seems most wonderful to me is this: the vessels that go down the river to Babylon are round and made all of skins. For they make ribs of the willows that grow in Armenia, above Babylon, and cover them with hides stretched over the ribs on the outside to serve as a bottom, making no distinction of stem or stern. The vessels thus made like shields they fill with reeds and use for carrying merchandize down the river, generally palm-wood casks of wine."

There are several surprises in this graphic account – not least that the vessels to hold the wine were not earthenware jars but barrels. The Romans are reputed to have learnt about

barrels from the Gauls, and the Greeks not to have used them at all. But Herodotus, a native of Halicarnassus in Asia Minor, then part of the Persian Empire, speaks of wine casks as a matter of course. Can he be right, though, about the wood being palm wood? Palm trunks are almost impossible to saw into planks. If the wine came from Armenia, where there are better trees, why use palms?

Archaeology, with its revolutionary new tools of DNA analysis and infrared spectrometry, which can quiz molecules for meaning, brings to light new evidence each year of ancient enthusiasm for wine in every culture from Persia to Phoenicia. Where tartaric acid residues are found, often on shards of pottery, it is prima facie evidence that grapes were involved. They are the only fruit that contains it in quantity. Traces of yeast are evidence of fermentation.

W e know everything and nothing about ancient Egyptian wine. The available detail is almost overwhelming. It is most graphic in the tomb paintings of high officials whose business it was to supervise it, and more lowly craftsmen who so delighted in vines and their fruit that they decorated the ceilings of their tombs as arbours heavy-laden with grapes. Luxor, the ancient capital Homer called "hundred-gated Thebes", at its height the greatest city in the world, and near which pharoahs and nobles were entombed, is where most of the evidence is to be found.

We know where wine was made and precisely how, and how it was named, stored, served and drunk. What we don't know is what it tasted like. It would not be difficult to reproduce the wines of ancient Egypt. What grape varieties to use would be the principal problem. But if we were to plant a vineyard in the Nile delta country on the antique model (which means in fertile silt, irrigated and manured with dung), train the vines as they did on a high pergola, tread the grapes and ferment their juice in clay jars, we would not expect wine of any quality. Certainly no wine of quality is made in modern Egypt. Yet to dismiss what people of such culture as the Egyptian aristocracy described as good, very good or excellent, and took such trouble in making and pleasure in drinking, clearly cannot be right.

Already in some of the earliest pictures of winemaking there are signs of technical ingenuity which was not to be reproduced by any other civilization until modern times. Some of it is just applied common sense. Treading grapes in an open tank is trickier than it looks: to keep your footing in the deep, slippery mass you need something to hold on to. The Egyptians had a marvellously simple idea: bars across the treading floor just above head height. Workers steadied themselves as they trampled, like strap-hangers on an airport bus.

We can be sure the grapes they picked were fully ripe. Under the Egyptian sun they would have been honey-sweet. Most pictures show us black grapes. They also show us dark juice running from the press into the fermenting jars, which suggests (since treading alone extracts little colour from grape skins) that fermentation began in the trough where the grapes were trodden.

It is strange that, according to the pictures, they did not bury the jars as the Georgians bury their *kwevris*. None of the pictures shows any efforts at keeping the jars cool as they fermented – a fundamental precaution in a hot country, where the transition from juice to wine to vinegar can be disastrously quick. The final sealing with clay was undoubtedly as effective as any cork, but if the wine did keep well (or keep at all) it must have been due to its high alcohol content more than to hygienic making or inherent stability. It may also have leant on the preservative qualities of resin – that of the terebinth tree (and, more expensively, myrrh) was certainly sometimes mixed with wine in the ancient world. Not, though, one would think, with precisely identified vintages from the best vineyards. *Grand cru* retsina is an improbable idea.

How the Egyptians drank their wine is even better known to us than how they made it. Egyptians feasted in an atmosphere of brilliant colour, powerful perfumes (they put scented ointment on their heads which slowly melted and trickled down their braided hair and wigs): and garlands of flowers and vine branches, lotus blooms and lotus buds. Sometimes they drank from wine cups, sometimes through straws directly from wine jars. Wine from different jars was sometimes siphoned into a fresh one, presumably to be blended. When wine was poured from an amphora it was often sieved (which confirms that solid matter was left in it after fermentation). There is not much evidence of self-restraint in these feasting scenes: ladies are occasionally sick, although nobody is seen under the table or being carried out.

The 5,000-year-old panel known as the Standard of Ur shows peace on one side and war on the other. Peace is represented by the first known illustration of wine drinking, by courtiers in the royal presence.

grave goods When the tomb of the nineteen-year-old King Tutankhamun, who died in 1352BC, was opened by the great Egyptologist Howard Carter in 1922, he found among the treasures around the golden mummy the wine jars that were to accompany the royal spirit on its journey.

Twenty-six of the thirty-six amphoras were labelled, seven of these with the seal of the king's personal estates, and sixteen with the name of the royal house of Aten: both "on the Western River" (the western arm of the Nile delta, always considered Egypt's best wine country).

Twenty-three of the wines came from three vintages: "year four", "year five", and "year nine". Whether these are the years of the king's reign, or whether they simply indicate the age of the wine, is unclear, but they show that top-quality wine was appreciated at a considerable age. One amphora is even dated "year thirty-one" – which cannot refer to the king's short reign. The name of the chief vintner is recorded on every amphora except the three oldest. One chief vintner, Kha'y by name, made five of the wines of Tutankhamun's estate,and also one of the House of Aten, which suggests either that the royal officials ran both estates, or that Kha'y was such a gifted vintner that, like Professor Peynaud in Bordeaux today, he was responsible for several top estates at the same time.

Two wines (both labelled Sdh, which seems to mean new or fresh) are labelled "very good quality". The others are only described in any way if they are sweet (four out of the twenty-six). By this analysis the most telling piece of information (apart from the vintage) on each label is the name of the chief vintner. What could be more realistic? Nothing matters more than the man who makes the wine.

The Greek writer Athenaeus believed that "among the Egyptians of ancient times, any kind of symposium was conducted with moderation… They dined while seated, using the simplest and most healthful food and drinking only as much as would be sufficient to promote good cheer." But Victorian schoolmasters would have their pupils believe that all Greeks were sober, upright, and honourable men.

The wine left in tombs, even from the earliest dynasties, is designated by origin, even if only vaguely. By 2470BC (the fifth dynasty), six different "appellations" were in use. Whether they

The Hittites occupied the heart of Anatolia for most of the second millennium BC. Like generations after them, they lavished their most precious metal and finest craftsmanship on drinking vessels. This silver *rhyton* dates from 1400–1200BC.

signified distinctly different sorts of wine, or merely where they came from, we don't know. "Wine from Asia", an import, probably from Syria or Canaan, is also mentioned. Egyptian ships regularly visited Byblos in Canaan to buy timber. The cedars of Lebanon were one of Egypt's chief imports; palm trees are no better for building than they are for barrel-making.

By the time of the "New Kingdom", which came into being in 1550BC, and whose most famous monument is the tomb of Tutankhamun, the labelling of wine jars was almost as precise as, say, Californian labelling today – with the exception of the grape variety. It specified the year, the vineyard, the owner, and the head vintner. The leading vineyards were on the "West River" (the western arm of the Nile delta), at Sile, Behbeit el-Hagar, Memphis, and the oases – all in Lower Egypt. Wine-growing was not attempted, it seems, in Upper Egypt until the rule of the Greek-inspired Ptolemies from 300BC.

Insofar as the Egyptians ascribed wine to one particular god it was usually to Osiris, the god of life after death, who was also responsible for plant life. He was addressed as "lord of the wine at flooding" and "lord of carousing at the festival". Later Greek writers were apt to associate Osiris with Dionysus, the Greek wine god, but there is little evidence that he was held responsible in a direct way with wine and its effects on the spirit, as Dionysus was.

The great pharaoh Ramses III, in the eleventh century BC, recorded his gifts to Amun, the god of Thebes, and in a sense Egypt's national god. They included "vineyards without limit for you in the southern oasis and also in the northern oasis, and others in great number in the southern region… I equipped them with vintners, with the captives of foreign lands and with canals from my digging…" From the same period a letter has survived that gives a precise picture of the scale of operations on a fairly small delta wine estate:

"Another communication to my lord. I have arrived at Nay-Ramesse-miamun on the edge of Ptri-waters with my lord's scow and with two cattle-ferries… and found that the vineyard keepers were seven men, four lads, four old men, and six children, total twenty-one persons. For my lord's information, the whole of the wine which I found sealed up with the master of the vineyard-keepers Tjatroy was: 1,500 jars of wine, fifty jars of sdh-wine… and sixty krht-baskets of grapes. I loaded them into the two cattle-ferries belonging to the 'Mansion of Millions of Years of the King of Upper and Lower Egypt', and sailed downstream from Pi-Ramesse-miamun… I have written to let my lord be cognizant."

The elements of this picture are still in place. The Nile slides majestically on among its palms. The *shaduf* raises water for the irrigation channels. The same brown faces smile, and quick-footed donkeys run. White-winged feluccas are not precisely the boats that this accountant sailed in, but the Egypt of today matches its ancient records at so many points that only a little imagination is needed to visit the pharaonic world. It is a different matter with the world of the ancient Greeks.

CHAPTER 4

GREECE:
THE WINE-DARK SEA

"The peoples of the Mediterranean began to emerge from barbarism when they learnt to cultivate the olive and the vine." It was Thucydides, the Greek historian, who wrote this at the end of the fifth century BC, when Athens had become the centre of the most cultivated and creative society the world had known.

Oil and wine were powerful stimulants to trade; trade led to the exchange of ideas, and wine in particular brought a new dimension to social intercourse. Wine led naturally to festivities, to confidences, to a sense of occasion (which also had religious significance). The gold and silver drinking vessels that appeared in the Aegean at this time would hardly have been created for water. So wine feeds on its success, good wine fetches a premium, therefore more good wine is made. The better it is, the greater the demand, and the more stimulus for trade.

Homer, telling the story of the siege of Troy and the travels of Odysseus, the half-remembered epics of the Mycenaean era, gives us detailed information about at least some of the sources of its wine. On his voyage Odysseus took wine from his own island, Ithaca, but also extra-high-strength wine he had extracted as a ransom from Maro, the priest of Apollo at Imarus in Thrace, the mainland to the north of the Aegean. The priest's Maronean "red wine, honey-sweet" was supposedly so strong that it was usually drunk diluted 1:20 with water.

Odysseus used this as his secret weapon. On the coast of Sicily the Cyclops Polyphemus, the one-eyed monster, captured him and devoured his companions. Odysseus offered him Maronean wine by way of a digestif. Polyphemus was accustomed to weak Sicilian wine – presumably made from unpruned wild grapes. Good Greek wine overwhelmed him. "Thrice in his folly he drank it to the lees", and sank into a deep sleep, during which Odysseus put out his single eye. The boulders that the blinded giant threw at the fleeing Odysseus are still to be seen, half-submerged, in the sea near Mount Etna.

Through Homer's *Iliad* the image of the "wine-dark sea" runs like a refrain. The poet's description of the shield of the hero Achilles has the ring of a favourite scene remembered: "… a vineyard laden with grapes… was beautifully wrought in gold… and the delicious fruit was being carried off in baskets by merry lads and girls, with whom there was a boy singing the lovely song of Linus in a treble voice to the sweet music of his tuneful lyre. They all kept time with him and followed the music and the words with dancing feet." It is a vision of vintage time, of autumn's gilded haze, of labour and laughter that has never faded.

Growth of population, in time, intensified economic activity. Greece became ready to emulate the Phoenicians in voyages of exploration, and the founding of new cities outside the "Greek lake" that the Aegean had become. And very soon such thriving colonies as Syracuse had their own litters, so that Sicily and the toe of Italy were called Magna Graecia – Greater Greece. They were also called Oenotria – the land of (staked) vines.

Various theories are in circulation about why the vines of Italy at this time were described as "staked" – presumably in contrast to Greece, where they were grown either in trees or

prone on the ground. One is that Magna Graecia was colonized by a new kind of capitalist entrepreneur whose farming methods were more intensive than the old ways; that a vineyard became for the first time a monoculture, tidily staked, and so presented a very different appearance.

To the same new era of energetic searching for more land belongs the first Greek colonization of southern France, when the Phocaeans from Lydia in Asia Minor, under threat from the Persian invasion of their homeland, founded Massalia where Marseilles stands today, and also settled in Corsica.

By 500BC Massalia was making its own wine, and its own amphoras to export it. According to the Roman historian Justinius, "from the Greeks the Gauls learned a civilized way of life... to cultivate the vine and the olive. Their progress was so brilliant that it seemed as though Gaul had become part of Greece." A more modern historian points out that the first wine drunk in Burgundy was probably Greek wine from Marseilles (or indeed from Greece, shipped by the Etruscans).

What can we say about the qualities of Greek wine? The Aegean islands were the main exporters, possibly because they were more prone to specialize. They lacked trees (except sometimes olives), and the wind forced them to grow their vines low against the stony soil, where the grapes would reach much greater ripeness than bunches hanging in rich swags between arching trees, the Arcadian picture of an idyllic vineyard.

Of the islands, Chios in the eastern Aegean, off the coast of Ionia in "East Greece", was the biggest exporter, and by most accounts had the best wine. It has been called the Bordeaux of ancient Greece. Its characteristic amphoras, easily identified by their design and the quality of their pottery, and usually stamped with the Chian emblem of a sphinx, an amphora, and a bunch of grapes, have been found in almost every country where Greeks traded from the seventh century BC onwards.

Equally famous was the wine of Lesbos, the large island due north of Chios, the home of the poet Sappho (whose brother, it seems, combined the trades of wine merchant and procurer at Naucratis, a city famed for the "looks and easy virtue of its women"). Lesbian wine was highly rated under the island's name, but Lesbos may also have been a source (or the source) of Pramnian, the Greek equivalent of the rarest and most luscious of all wines, Tokaji Eszencia.

Sweetness is praised in contemporary accounts of many Greek wines. Most often it was probably achieved in exactly the same way that the Cypriot Greeks make, and always have made, their Commandaria. The grapes are picked fully ripe, then laid out on straw mats (plastic today) in the vineyard for a week or so for the sun to concentrate their sugar. A similar method is used in Spain at Jerez for sherry-making. Homer describes the sun-drying of grapes in this manner. Surprisingly, one writer, Archestratus, describes a Lesbian wine as having "its liquid locks thickly overgrown with white flower", which is a fair enough poetic description of the growth of the yeast called *flor* that sherry-makers depend on for the special savour and longevity of their wine. One vase painting shows a long dipper,

"the canaanite jar" The standard wine container of the ancient world was the amphora, a clay vase with two handles, ranging in shape from the Don Quixote to the Sancho Panza, but generally rather like a root vegetable with a long neck. Its bottom end was either pointed like a root or formed into a knob, but never flat. Size varied widely. Greek amphoras averaged about forty litres; Roman ones about twenty-six litres – or nearly three dozen modern wine bottles.

The amphora was an invention of the Canaanites, the forebears of the Phoenicians, who introduced it into Egypt before 1500BC. The name (which is Greek) means something which can be carried by two; one on each side. So useful was the invention of a strong, inexpensive, disposable or reusable, easily lifted and stored container that amphoras were used for any substance that could be poured. Although wine was their usual contents, oil, grain, water, and the favourite seasoning of the Romans, the *garum* made of the fermented remains of fish, were often transported in amphoras.

Some ended their working life as funerary urns, as children's coffins, or even as roofing materials. Herodotus tells the story of how one Greek clan, the Phocaeans, even set an ambush with them. They dug a pit in a narrow mountain road, filled it with empty amphoras, then covered them with earth. When the enemy cavalry arrived the pit caved in and the horses were trapped.

A potter makes an amphora on his wheel in two or three sections; it is too big to turn all at once, and he cannot reach inside the neck to shape it. The sections are moulded together wet; then the amphora is turned upside down, and its original flat base is pared down to a point (or knob). It seems curious to remove the base, but in practice the amphora is much easier to lift and tip with its bottom forming a third handle.

Properly sealed, an amphora was as airtight as a bottle and, like a very big bottle, kept good wine in good condition for an immensely long time. Without amphoras the ancient world would have had no knowledge of the splendour of matured wine.

To archaeologists, amphoras have unique value as evidence of ancient trading patterns. Each district, town or island had its own slightly different model, which developed over time. With the help of a computer, even a relatively small shard, a piece of neck or handle, can be accurately classified. Shards are virtually indestructable. Biomolecular analysis of what remains of the contents has now added organic dimensions to amphora archaeology. So many millions of amphoras were made that even today in trading centres such as Delos, in the Aegean, entire beaches consist of nothing but a mixture of white marble from ruined monuments and the red, sea-smoothed shards of broken wine containers.

remarkably like a sherry-shipper's *venencia*, ideal for plunging through the scum of *flor* (in an amphora?) to extract a clear sample of wine.

Certainly the Greeks of Homer's time already recognized many different varieties of wine. Laertes, the father of Odysseus, whose vineyard was his pride and joy, boasted that he had fifty rows, each of a different vine, so that he had ripe grapes in a long procession from summer to late autumn.

Were the ancient wines treated with resin to taste like modern retsina? Certainly not, say some scholars, although others point to the pine cone that was part of the wine god's sceptre, and the resin of the terebinth tree was used in ancient Egypt. The practice of adding pitch from pine trees was only

LEFT By 2000BC Minoan Crete had evolved a rich and complex civilization. This fresco of a man carrying a drinking vessel is from Knossos, c.1700–1400BC.

the great vase of vix Ideas about the connections between the world of the Greeks and the Celtic world of northern Europe were transformed in 1952 by the discovery, between Paris and Burgundy, of the most magnificent Greek vase that has ever been found. It lay in the tomb of a Burgundian princess at Vix, near the trading centre of Mont Lassois on the river Seine, where Phocaean Greeks, and probably Etruscans too, went for shipments of tin from the mines of Cornwall.

The vase, or *crater*, of Vix is a wine-mixing bowl in the finest bronze, standing 2.1 metres (seven feet) high and with a capacity of 1,200 litres, or about forty-five amphoras of wine. The princess died in about 600BC, and at that time in Gaul one amphora of wine was traded for one slave. Almost more astonishing than the opulence implied is the vase's carriage, from either southern Italy or Greece, either up the Rhône and Saône valleys or over Alpine passes. Expert opinion differs as to where it was made. Sparta is one theory; another is south-central Italy, where Etruscan and Greek cultures mixed. So huge and fragile an object must have been taken to pieces for transport, its great bronze shell cut up and then welded together again. But whether it travelled on pack animals over the Great Saint Bernard Pass, or by ships and barge and wagon via Massalia, today Marseilles, its presence in the heart of France tells us that the Greeks had no monopoly of power even at the height of their colonizing period. It also tells us that the French loved their wine.

mentioned in ancient Greece in connection with the already undrinkable wines of Galatia in Asia Minor. It seems to have been rare in Greece but common in Italy. On the other hand, the Greeks did mix their wines – and in fact they rarely drank them straight. It was normal to add at least water (usually seawater), and the more formal the occasion and elaborate the food, the more spices and aromatics were added to the wine. The mixing was done in a vase of pottery or bronze called a *crater*, which could be of any size. The wine was scooped out with a dipper, a *kythos*, and drunk from a shallow, graceful, usually two-handled cup, a *kylix*.

The Greeks loved their wine and rhapsodized over it, but their literature does not leave the impression that they were hard drinkers. Water in the wine had two obvious purposes: it stretched the supply of a commodity which may have been too expensive for some citizens, and it meant you could go on drinking longer. Their word "symposium" means nothing more or less than "drinking together".

The justification of its modern meaning, a learned conference, lies in the Greek practice of long after-dinner

conversations between men over their wine. They reclined on couches, propped up on their elbows – a habit learned from the Assyrians in about 600BC, and an attitude then and now associated with nomadic peoples. The dining room was called the men's room and was appropriately plumbed. Women, if they were present (and not as dancers), sat on the edge of the couch or on a chair. A symposium had a chairman in just the same way that Georgian banquets have a *tamada*, although his job was to stimulate the conversation rather than to elaborate long toasts.

No one pretends that all Greeks were philosophers. Symposia came in all degrees of seriousness or laxity, and it was common for flute girls and dancing girls to perform. But according to (the admittedly straitlaced) Plato: "Wherever men of gentle breeding and culture are gathered together at a symposium, you will see neither flute girls, nor harp girls; on the contrary they are quite capable of entertaining themselves without such nonsense and childishness, but with their own voices, talking and listening in turn, and always decently, even when they have drunk much wine."

Plato's views on the minimum drinking age are remarkably severe: "Boys under eighteen shall not taste wine at all, for one should not conduct fire to fire. Wine in moderation may be tasted until one is thirty years old, but the young man should abstain entirely from drunkenness and excessive drinking. But when a man is entering his fortieth year… he may summon the other gods and particularly call upon Dionysus to join the old men's holy rite, and their mirth as well, which the god has given to men to lighten their burden – wine that is, the cure for the crabbedness of old age, whereby we may renew our youth and enjoy forgetfulness of despair." It is a sobering thought that to Plato old age began at forty.

Hippocrates, who was born on the island of Kos in about 460BC and lived, it is said, for nearly a century, is called the father of medicine. Wine played a part in almost every one of his recorded remedies. He used it for cooling fevers, as a diuretic and a general antiseptic, and to help convalescence. But he was completely specific, occasionally advising against any wine at all, and always recommending a particular wine for a particular case.

Hippocrates also had strong views on how wine should be drunk: neither too warm nor too cold. The prolonged drinking of warm wine, he claimed, led to "imbecility", while the excessive use of very cold wine led to "convulsions, rigid spasms, mortifications, and chilling horrors, terminating in a fever".

We can leave the conclusion to the wisest of all Greek philosophers, Socrates. "Wine", said Socrates, "moistens and tempers the spirits, and lulls the cares of the mind to rest… it revives our joys, and is oil to the dying flame of life. If we drink temperately, and small draughts at a time, the wine distills into our lungs like sweetest morning dew… It is then the wine commits no rape upon our reason, but pleasantly invites us to agreeable mirth."

Kottabos About the year 600BC some light-headed Sicilian colonist from Greece, leaning on his elbow at an after-dinner symposium, bet his friends that he could hit the lamp on top of its stand with the dregs in his shallow, two-handled wine cup.

Whether he put out the lamp or not, it was just the sort of Drones-Club idea that would catch on among the lighter element. Throwing bread rolls loses its magic after a while. The new game was baptized as *kottabos*, and a crafty bronze merchant designed a special stand, like a lampstand but with a tiny statuette on top with its arm held aloft. On the hand, precariously balanced, went a faintly concave bronze disc. Halfway up the stand the merchant fixed a much larger bronze disc. The idea now was to dislodge the top disc, called the *plastincx*, so that it fell and hit the lower one, the *manes*, which when hit rang like a bell.

Kottabos became the rage. It spread back to Athens and Sparta, and for no less than 300 years, during the whole period of Athenian ascendancy, it remained the fashionable after-dinner game. It is portrayed on countless Greek vases (the only graphic depiction of Greek domestic life we have) and the rules are known from literature.

The best illustration is on an Athenian wine cooler dating from the first half of the fourth century BC, which shows four ladies of the town, whose names might be rendered Slinky, Wriggly, Couchy and Sexy. Slinky, naked on a couch, is flicking her wine cup with the index finger of her right hand. The caption by the cup reads: "I'm throwing this for you, Leagros." Other paintings show more decorous players in action, but leave no doubt at all how *kottabos* was played, nor how popular it was.

I have had a *kottabos* stand made, and practised assiduously. From personal experience I can say that it is not at all easy. The best trainers advise a very high arching shot, so that the wine falls onto the *plastincx* from above. But liquid does not easily dislodge bronze, however delicately balanced, easily. And it makes a terrible mess on the floor.

(An authentic game needs a dedicated young servant, who for economy wears nothing but a garland, to rebalance the *plastincx* and recharge the wine cups.)

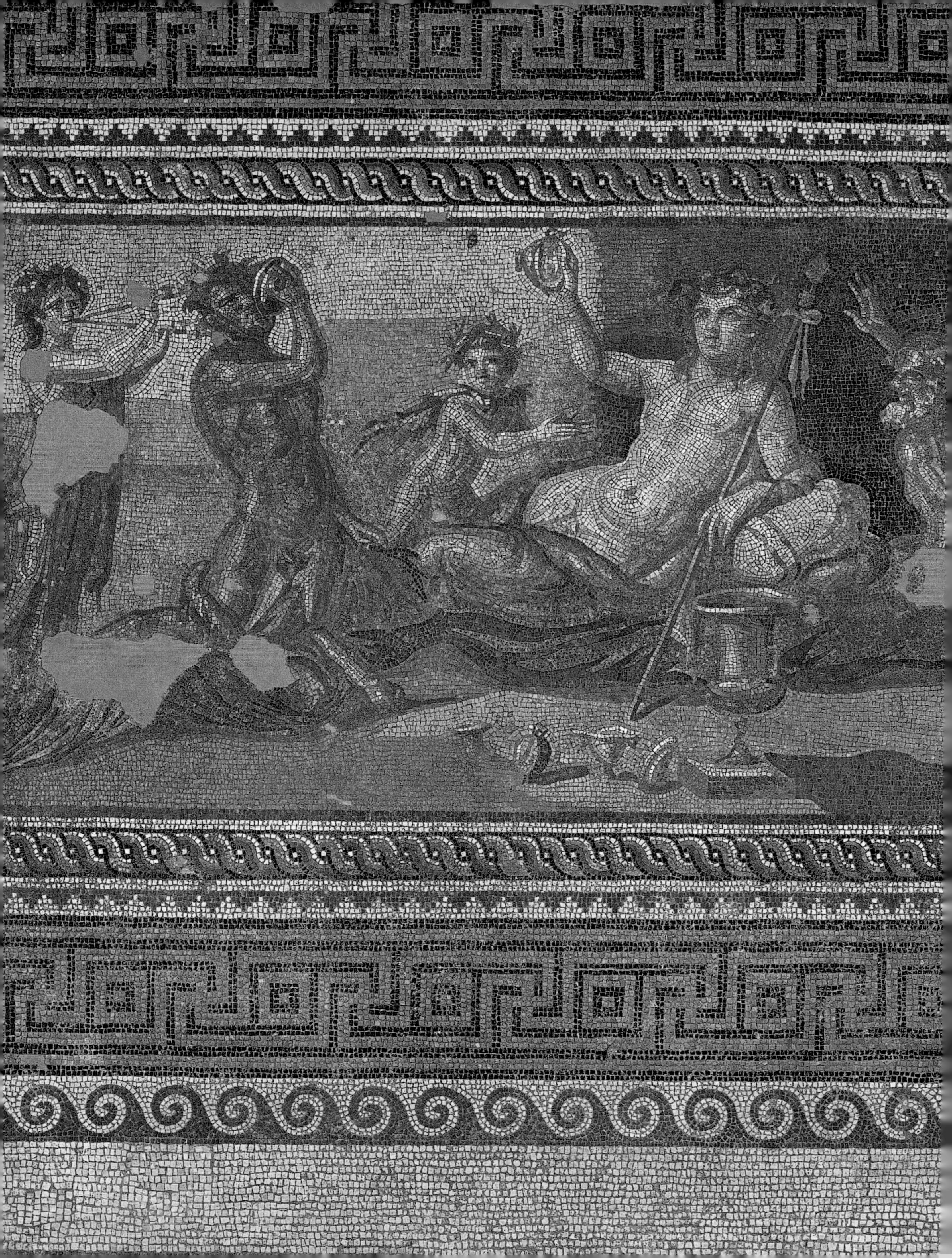

CHAPTER 5

DRINKING THE GOD

The Greeks had every reason to be enthusiastic about wine. It had provided the impetus for the economy of their strange country, half land, half sea. It gave them a pleasure they could find in no other form. But there was more to it than either business or pleasure: a mystical element that they expressed through their worship of the wine god, Dionysus.

Of course, wine was not alone in having a deity. All the elements, every concept, each crop, even a forest or a spring had its sponsoring senior god or junior guardian spirit. Zeus, the father of the gods, lived on Mount Olympus in Thessaly, surrounded by, and constantly intriguing and quarrelling with, eleven gods of cabinet rank, while a great civil service of gods milled about in complicated and frequently incestuous relationships, seducing hapless humans, causing accidents, and interfering in battles, altogether more like a hippy colony than a responsible superior order of beings.

The only personal relationships between Olympians and men belonged in the realm of mythology. Myths must sometimes have appeared to thinking Greeks to be handed out with the rations. This is where Dionysus was different. Dionysus was not a myth but a very palpable fact. You actually drank the god of wine, and having the god inside you took away care.

One morning in March in the year 404BC, 14,000 of the people of Athens packed the huge theatre on the east flank of the Acropolis for the first day of drama of the annual Great Festival of Dionysus. The day before there had been sacrifices of bulls, so many of them that the stink of blood still filled the city, mingled with the sharper smell of wine. Most of the crowd were carrying wine skins, swaying as they swigged their *trimma*, wine flavoured with an unknown formula of herbs, and joking that their wobbling goat skins were softer to sit on than the hard theatre benches.

Last into their seats in the huge theatre were the senior magistrates of the city and the army commanders, and then the priests of Dionysus Eleutherus, the wine god from Eleusis on the road north to Thebes. They took stone thrones on the edge of the vast semicircular marble stage, where dancers were already weaving in elaborate patterns, chanting, and beating tambourines. The women dancers wore only soft fawn skins, with wreaths of ivy, and carried long hollow stalks of wild fennel tipped with pine cones and wreathed with more ivy. The men jiggled about absurdly with preposterous leather phalluses flapping in front and long horse-tails sticking from the back of their breeches. Each time one of these *satyrs* tried to catch one of the *maenads* she would scamper away, prodding him with her wand, her *thyrsis*: the sceptre of the wine god and the symbol of his powers.

All this was entirely familiar to the Athenians. The various festivals of Dionysus went on at intervals throughout the winter, starting in December with the Country Dionysia in the villages, when the emphasis was more on the phallus and less on the wine god. He, after all, was symbolically dead. His body (in the form of grape clusters) had been dismembered and crushed at vintage time, and now his vines stood bare and apparently

LEFT Gods at their most human: Dionysus and Heracles compete to out-drink each other, in a mosaic of c.100BC from Antioch.

lifeless. Only ivy remained as a wintry substitute, producing its hard little fruit in winter among its shiny but vine-shaped leaves. The word for the dance around a giant phallus was *komos* – the root of the word "comedy".

Every second winter, though, a large crowd of women of all ages set off on a pilgrimage, taking the road via Eleusis and the sacred city of Thebes to the holy shrine of the oracle at Delphi. Delphi, sacred to Apollo for nine months of the year, became the shrine of Dionysus from December to February. His priestesses there were joined by housewives, maidens, and grandmothers from all the cities around, who dressed as *maenads,* and were sworn to secrecy. There were plenty of rumours about what went on. All agreed that the *maenads* went up into Mount Parnassus above Delphi and stayed there all night. In his *Antigone*, the playwright Sophocles describes the scene: "Surrounded by the light of torches, he stands high on the twin summits of Parnassus, while the Corycian nymphs dance around him as *Bacchantes*, and the waters of Castalia sound from the depths below. Up there in the snow and winter darkness Dionysus rules in the long night, while troops of *maenads* swarm around him, himself the choir leader for the dance of the stars and quick of hearing for every sound in the waste of the night."

This chilly picnic had many meanings. (The summit of Parnassus is at more than 2,438 metres (8,000 feet), and there are very believable reports of snow storms cutting off the worshippers, of rescue parties and *maenads* suffering from frostbite, "their clothes frozen stiff as boards".) The simplest, perhaps, was to encourage the god to return from the dead. Greek historians said that it was a very ancient practice, kept up in their own times simply as an antique custom. Certainly the death and rebirth of a god, symbolizing the renewal of nature, is one of the oldest and most common of religious themes. But others, modern doctors among them, believe that *maenadism* really was mass hysteria. *Maenads* were always depicted with their heads thrown back: a clinical indication, they say. In this state, people commit acts they would normally shrink from: handling snakes, carrying fire or killing and eating raw flesh. There are other historical instances of dances turning to near-madness. Some point out that Greek womenfolk (respectable ones, that is) were virtual slaves to their men, and that permission to congregate for worship in the wilds was their unique psychological release.

One distinct possibility is that the secrets of the mountain involved taking drugs other than wine. The *thyrsis* itself can be seen as a symbol of drug-taking. The fennel stalk, known as a *narthex*, was what Greek herbalists stored their plants in to keep them fresh. The pine cone came from a tree whose resin, fermented, makes a powerful intoxicant (and was perhaps added to Greek wine, as unfermented resin is today). Some *maenads* wore coronets woven with the seed heads of the opium poppy. And the berries of the ivy are intoxicating even without fermentation.

Winter, moreover, is the season of mushrooms in Greece. The Indian god Soma, some of whose myths are so similar to those of Dionysus that they must have common roots, produces his narcotic effect through the common fungus *Amanita muscaria*, or fly agaric. The effect of fly agaric is to destroy inhibitions, lead to powerful sexual desire, induce hallucinations, and finally lead to total lethargy.

Another fungus that was readily available, and was possibly used in the *maenads'* mysteries, is the parasite on barley and other grasses known as *ergot*. Its psychoactive alkaloids are better known today as LSD. We should remember that the Greeks rarely drank their wine unmixed. Even the *trimma* in the audience's wine skins was brewed with herbs. Syrian frankincense was another ingredient with narcotic properties. To sophisticated Greeks, at least in early times, it may be that wine more often meant one of a range of mildly narcotic cocktails.

Dionysus had a second festival, a perfectly unmysterious one, in February when it was time to open the fermenting jars and taste the new wine. This was the Anthesteria, the Flower Festival (from *anthos*, a flower: an image wine lovers still use today in talking of the bouquet of a wine).

Drinking seems to have been the main attraction of the February festival, with amphora parties, competitions for the greatest and longest drink, and such side-shows as trying to sit on a bulging wine skin smeared with grease without falling off.

The Great (or City) Dionysia was the March meeting in Athens, based on the ancient Eleutherian cult but with far more ancient ancestry still. Back in Babylon, the spring equinox, in March, was celebrated as the New Year. In that era the equinox coincided with the sun's entry into the constellation of Taurus. Bulls were ceremonially set to the plough. Babylon's chief god, Marduk, was represented as a bull. So, in many rites, was Dionysus.

By the fifth century BC the City Dionysia had been adapted and expanded by the government into one of the main public events of the city calendar. It was a remarkable instance of authority bowing to popular demand. Far back into history, the cult of Dionysus had been regarded as disreputable or worse; an excuse for the underdogs in society, women and slaves, to kick over the traces. In the sixth century BC this former minority cult suddenly became a force to be reckoned with. The shrewd tyrant Pisistrates, who ruled Athens from 546–527BC, recognized that the best way to control a popular movement is to make it official. If the Dionysiacs were going to dress up and dance in the streets, let them be organized into a popular spectacle. Thus the first of all theatres came to be built, in the heart of Athens, to accommodate and control an ancient rite that had acquired too much importance, and too many adherents, to be ignored.

The play that won the day in the competition of 404BC was a posthumous work. Its author, Euripides of Salamis, had died of old age in exile two years before, after a long and triumphant theatrical career. His last play, *The Bacchae*, took one of the foreign names of the wine god, the name he was known by across the Aegean in Lydia, and told the story of his arrival in Greece at the city of Thebes in Boeotia, not far north of Athens.

Everyone in the theatre knew the story. The lives of gods

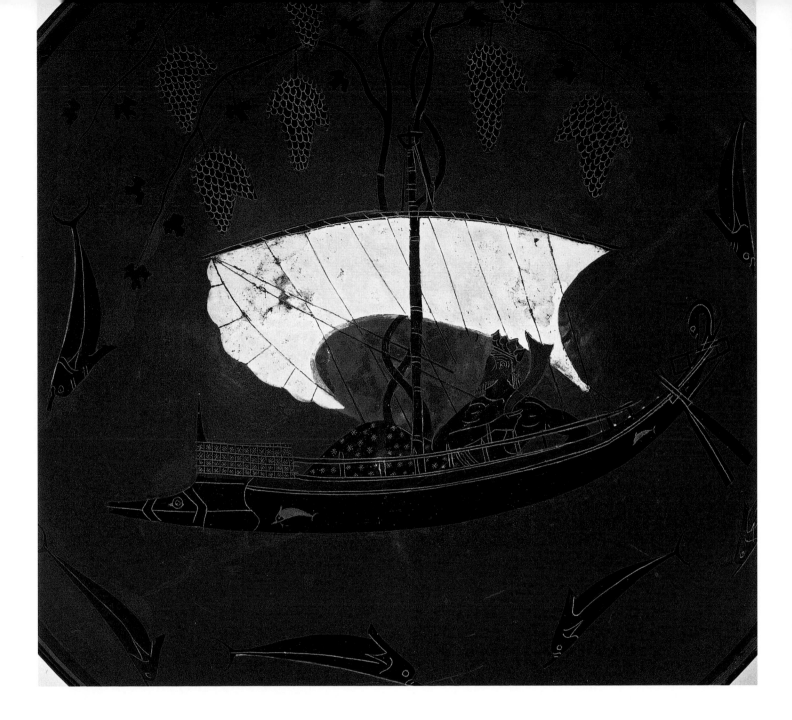

and men in Greece were a tissue of legends, layer upon layer of them, often contradictory, usually with local variations. The more important the god, the more versions there were of his or her adventures. It is also certainly true that the more myths attached to a god, the older he or she was. Dionysus is larded with legend. He was born and reborn, of different parents in different places, again and again.

His Theban legend is best known, partly owing to Euripides' play, but it is still hard to make intelligible. His father was Zeus, his mother the mortal Semele, daughter of Cadmus the king of Thebes. Semele, pregnant with Dionysus, dared to ask Zeus to show himself in glory. Reluctantly, he turned on his full voltage, Semele was fried alive, but the immortal infant in her womb was saved by Zeus, who opened his thigh and kept the foetus there until it was ready to be born. (Soma's story is very similar. He was born from the thigh of Indra, the Indian Zeus.)

The fate of Semele is a sort of prologue. *The Bacchae* starts

When Dionysus was captured en route to Italy, he turned the Etruscan pirates into dolphins and made a grape vine climb the mast. From a Greek *kylix*, or wine cup, by the Athenian painter Exekias, c.550BC.

years later when Dionysus returns to Thebes to bring it the gift of wine. He specifically says that he brings wine from the East, on the face of it a simple and true historical statement:

"From Lydia have I come and Phrygia
The golden lands
From sun-drenched plains in Persia
From the walled cities of Baktria
From the dreaded land of Media.
And I have passed through the whole of happy Arabia
And all of Asia Minor's coast…"

He appears in disguise, an effeminate youth rather than a god.

Nobody in Thebes, he discovers, believes the story of his divine birth. Even Semele's sisters, the mother and aunts of the present king, Pentheus, believe she had had a mere mortal lover.

The first half of the play makes the audience laugh. King Pentheus personifies indignant authority. How dare the women leave their household duties and go gallivanting on their own? But the mood changes. Dionysus tempts the king to go and spy on the women, to watch "their obscene acts". Only by dressing up as a woman, the god argues, can he creep up on them. Watching the scene in which the king minces up the mountain in the equivalent of high heels, the audience is tense. Drunk, in the brilliant sunshine, with their eyes riveted to the unblinking masks, strangely hypnotic, that the actors wear, they become intensely involved.

All scenes of violent action in Greek drama happen off-stage and are reported by a messenger. What the messenger now tells freezes the blood. The women of Thebes, possessed by Dionysus, tear their king down from his tree and, led by his mother, rend him limb from limb. Agaue, his mother, finally wrenches off his head. They return to the city with no idea what they have done. Whatever effect the god has had upon their minds, they believe they have hunted and killed a mountain lion. Agaue shows her son's head to her father Cadmus and tells him to nail her trophy to the palace wall.

As Cadmus cries in horror, we must believe the audience cried too. As Agaue comes to her senses the sense of desolation is absolute. Dionysus alone remains unmoved. Gods punish men for disbelief.

What are we to make of *The Bacchae*? It is one of the strangest of plays. Its poetry puts it on a level where literal meaning may be secondary, yet myth has meaning, and Dionysus is perfectly specific about where he comes from and why.

His purpose is to bring wine to Greece. He also brings a form of religion which threatens (and actually destroys) the state. But both are paradoxes. Wine, described as a blessing, apparently becomes a curse; and he is presented as a new god, while in reality he is among the oldest gods of all.

What is new about the god, and perhaps the crux of the play, is his direct relationship with wine. The old all-purpose god of growing things has become specific to the vine – and at the moment in history when the vine had become the economic motor of the expanding Greek empire.

How ancient then is Dionysus? He can be traced so far back that he first appears as the consort (or the child) of the earth-mother herself. He is probably the little figure in the most ancient representations (sometimes uncannily similar to the Virgin and Child) which go back at least 9,000 years, to Stone Age shrines in Catal Hüyük, the first of all known cities.

To Orpheus, the mythical singer, long before the age of Homer, Dionysus (with the surname Zagreus) was a son of Zeus and Persephone, the goddess of death, who was torn apart and eaten by the Titans, a race of primitive giant men. In Orpheus' story, the goddess Athena saved Dionysus' heart, from which he

was reborn – another resurrection story. (The clear parallel between this and the Egyptian story of Osiris, whose body was torn apart and scattered all over Egypt, then reassembled by Isis, explains why Osiris was identified with Dionysus by the Greeks.)

There is no end to these early legends surrounding Dionysus. He belongs firmly in the most ancient mythology, but strikingly not in the Olympian religion propounded by Homer, which is the "established" religion that, in *The Bacchae*, is represented by Pentheus and his beliefs.

The metamorphosis of Dionysus from god of vegetation and fertility to god of wine took place gradually over perhaps a thousand years. It did not stop there, but continued with more and more elaborate and mystic rites to embrace a whole system of beliefs about spirituality and the afterlife: an immediate forerunner of Christianity.

During the sixth century BC the worship of Dionysus was officially accepted into the Greek Pantheon. His portrait, followers and attributes – *maenads* and *satyrs*, *thyrsis*, and vines, and ivy – became the most popular of all subjects for vase-painting. The most famous of these paintings, recalling a legend of his capture at sea by Etruscan pirates on the way to Italy, was painted by the master Exekias in 550BC. A place was even made for him among the twelve Olympians by the retirement of the modest Hestia, the goddess of the hearth. In 530BC Pisistratus sanctioned his rites in Athens and built his first theatre. *The Bacchae* was first performed in 404BC. A century later the present vast stone theatre, reaching right up the flank of the Acropolis, was built. Dionysus had an active following that outdid those of all the other gods.

The nature and scope of the Greek world changed completely in the late fourth century BC. The royal house of Greece's northern neighbour Macedonia, Philip and his son Alexander, ended the loose confederation of free city-states led by Athens and Sparta. Under Alexander, the Greeks became an irresistible force that carried before it all the ageing empires of the east. Anatolia, Assyria, Babylonia, Persia, Egypt fell. Alexander marched right to the frontiers of India, and even over the Oxus into central Asia.

At his death this enormous, ungovernable realm split into three: Macedonia and Greece, Egypt under the Ptolemies, and a vast kingdom from Anatolia to India that took the name of its founder Seleucus. The influence of Greek thought was felt throughout the Middle East, as it already was in the rapidly expanding sphere of influence of Rome to the west. Yet within 200 years, by the middle of the first century BC, Rome had inherited, by conquest or secession, the entire Greek world, with the exception of Persia. The last to fall was Cleopatra's Egypt, in 31BC.

Rome was wary at first of the powerful cult of Bacchus (the Romans knew Dionysus by his Lydian name). The Etruscans, whom they had not so long ago subsumed into the new Roman Italy, had had a similar god, who rejoiced in the name of Fufluns. The followers of Fufluns found Bacchus very much to their liking, and the two gods soon became one.

But the martial spirit of Rome in its Republican days was not in tune with nature worship, or with personal enthusiasms of any kind. Bacchus' rites, the Bacchanalia, were a hole-and-corner affair where respectable citizens would never be seen. The state, like Pentheus in *The Bacchae*, was nervous and disapproving.

Matters came to a head in 186BC. The Bacchanalia were banned, on the evidence of a courtesan. In the witchhunt that followed, some 7,000 people all over Italy were accused of conspiracy against the state. It is clear from the speech for the prosecution that the Roman establishment felt threatened by a popular movement that might undermine its stern and warlike values. Such people would never make Roman soldiers.

But Bacchus was not so easily dismissed. His cult continued to flourish in secret, fed by the doctrines of Orphism, the gospel according to Orpheus, which were effectively transforming cult into religion. By the first century BC Bacchus had outgrown the role of wine god and become a saviour figure, the god of the underworld with the power to grant an afterlife. His connection with the theatre remained, so that masks of the characters in famous plays were buried with the dead. He even acquired a military past, including a victorious expedition to India which identified him with, of all people, Alexander the Great.

The ban on the Bacchanalia was lifted by Julius Caesar in response to popular pressure. The temper of Rome had changed with the enormous wealth of its empire. In the past, Bacchus had been the favourite god of the common man. Now he had followers among the rich and powerful. One of the most devoted of them was Mark Antony, who saw himself, on Cleopatra's couch in Alexandria, as a new Dionysus. His austere rival Octavius, predictably enough, identified himself with Apollo.

The influence of Bacchus and his cult on Christianity, when it arrived in Rome, is beyond question. Orphism had already anticipated the concept of spiritual salvation, with Bacchus/Dionysus as the saviour. Returning from the dead was commonplace among the ancient gods. Eating the god's flesh was a familiar idea to the Orphics. And Bacchus' blood, of course, was wine.

Like the followers of Bacchus, the Christians were at first persecuted, then tolerated, before they were fully accepted. In the fourth century the Emperor Constantine made Christianity the official religion of Rome and its Empire. By this time it was so confused with the old Bacchic cult that Constantine's

The cult of Dionysus had been a minority one until it became official in the sixth century BC. This theatre, on the eastern slope of the Athens Acropolis, became its home.

daughter, building her mausoleum in the church of Santa Costanza, covered its ceiling with a mosaic of conventional Bacchic symbols, and herself appears on it wreathed in vines.

The Emperor Theodosius banned the old pagan cults in an edict of 392. The followers of Bacchus, now a small minority, adopted Christian symbols, just as the Christians had borrowed theirs. Bacchus wears a halo, and appears (as he did thousands of years before at Catal Hüyük) as an infant on his mother's knee.

Yet at the same time Christian theologians rediscovered Euripides' work, and were unable to ignore the clear parallels between *The Bacchae* and their gospels. Dionysus was the son of god and a mortal woman. He worked miracles and was persecuted. Euripides, they supposed, had been divinely inspired to prepare the way for Christianity.

H as the wine god ever been snuffed out? His worship gradually dwindled, discouraged by the Christian authorities. An edict published at Constantinople in 692 strictly forbade women's public dancing ("the root of all evils and ruin"), chorus singing, and mysteries: "ancient customs altogether alien to Christian life". It was forbidden to dress as the opposite sex or impersonate comic or tragic characters. It was also decreed that when wine-growers tread the grapes:

"Nobody should invoke the name of the infamous Bacchus, and when wine is poured into casks, nobody should provoke laughter by actions which bear the imprint of lies and madness." The punishment was excommunication. Evidently the Bacchic rites still had their followers.

They exist still in much modified form. Velazquez painted Bacchus as a real being among the peasants of Castile. Rhinelanders dressing up as satyrs at a Weinfest may be self-conscious, but there is no ignoring the graven image that the Soviet Georgians set up outside the Palace of New Ritual in their capital, Tbilisi. It is Dionysus, a modern bronze instantly recognizable as the Greek god. The Palace is where secular weddings are held. Georgia is one of the oldest Christian countries, yet its Communist authorities chose the wine god as their symbol of celebration and blessing.

Sometimes his worship survives as a riotous note in a Christian ceremony. Each year on San Pedro's day at Haro in Rioja, his madness breaks out again. Thousands of people throng to Mass at dawn at a hillside chapel. The moment it is over a howl goes up from the crowd, and every man uses his wine skin to soak everybody in reach with pale red wine. The dancing churns up a mud of wine and earth under the olive trees.

There is no stage management here; no violence, either. But the Bacchae are there: a distant voice, a faint echo of the ecstasy that devastated Thebes.

The infant Dionysus, in a fifth-century Cypriot mosaic reminiscent of the Adoration of the Magi. Confusion between Christianity and the Bacchic cult was common.

CHAPTER 6

DE RE RUSTICA

Wine-growing in southern Italy arrived in a rush from Greece. There may have been earlier, Mycenaean, Greek settlements, but those we are sure about happened from 800BC onwards. The vine was the anchor the Greeks dug into the Sicilian and Italian shores. It took hold and so did they; within 300 years Syracuse in Sicily had outgrown Athens to be the most populous of all Greek cities.

Were there no vines in Italy before they came? Indeed there were, and wine-growers, too. The country just north of centre on the long boot shape of Italy, Tuscany today, was the land of the Etruscans. They in turn had probably come from the East, but we know little more. The Etruscans grew wine, making it and using it very much after the fashion of the Greeks, and traded with it, right up into Gaul beyond the Alps. They were almost certainly in Burgundy before the Greeks; selling wine, not growing it. They may have brought their vines with them from the East, had them from earlier Greek expeditions, or even found them in Italy. The wild vine was growing in the peninsula prehistorically. Who first used it in Italy for wine has not emerged from the night of time.

The Etruscans' vineyards reached up well into northern Italy; the earliest amphora yet found with a cork stopper is Etruscan, of 600BC. In the South, the Greeks enjoyed "the land of staked vines", but vineyards were a low priority to the stern and martial people who were steadily enlarging their dominion outwards from Rome. Their womenfolk were forbidden wine; a husband finding his wife drinking was at liberty to kill her for the offence (although it is hard to imagine that many husbands would). Divorce on the same grounds was last recorded in 194BC.

The turning point in Roman attitudes was the long-drawn-out struggle with the empire of Carthage in North Africa for control over the western Mediterranean. Victory, quickly followed by others over the Macedonians and the Syrians, changed the mood of Rome. From 200BC, wine-growing began to interest its increasingly worldly citizens; the security and wealth of empire brought a market for luxuries which would have shocked the founding fathers.

The first author to write in detail about wine-growing was Cato. In his eighties he set down, in *De Agri Cultura*, exactly how a country estate should be run – including cold-blooded calculations about how much slaves could do without dropping dead.

Romans were beginning to invest capital in farming enterprises with serious business intent, and wine-growing came top for profitability – partly because there were few commercial vineyards, and Rome had become a big city with a big thirst. Cato's textbook was, one might say, slavishly followed by new proprietors, many of them absentee landlords whose only concern was output.

Ironically, the author whose farming manual was the most widely read was a long-dead Carthaginian, Mago. Mago had set down the Phoenician and Canaanite traditions of agriculture as perfected and practised in Carthage in 500BC. When Carthage was defeated, Mago's ancient manual was the one book in all the city's libraries that the Romans rescued. More than any other work, it stimulated the growth of commercial wine-growing, and the swallowing-up of small estates by big ones. According to Pliny, by the time of the Emperor Nero, 200 years later, only six proprietors owned the whole of Roman North Africa.

Not only was Rome growing fast, but it was drawing in people of talent and cunning from all over its empire, and with them cosmopolitan tastes that led to a higher standard of living. A date that helps us pin down their progress is 171BC, when the first commercial bakery opened in Rome. The old Roman diet was porridge. Now Rome ate bread, it has been reasonably suggested, its thirst for wine was bound to increase. At the time, Rome was extending its control over the great Greek vineyards of southern Italy. They were boom years in the wine trade. It is no coincidence that the first mention of a Roman "first-growth", the top-quality wine of a particular vineyard, is in this era. The occasion was the miraculous "Opimian" vintage of 121BC (Opimius was the consul that year), and the vineyard in question was Falernum.

Once the concept of a "first-growth", or "*grand gru*" (there is no precise Latin term), had been introduced, a clear division could grow up between wines produced for quality, and the great bulk where quantity was all that mattered. The Romans loved rarity. Now wine joined the catalogue of conspicuous consumption.

T he vine that made Falernian, and was to make all the wines rated "first-growths" in this first Golden Age of Italian wine, was the Amineum. It is surprising to learn that all of these wines were white – until you also learn that they were all sweet. The taste of the Augustan age (Augustus reigned from 27BC to AD14) was for wine that was sweet and strong, and very often cooked in much the same way as madeira is today. Usually it was drunk diluted with warm water – even with seawater. Madeira and water, whether cold, warm or sea, is not exactly to your taste or mine. And yet there is no doubting the Romans' discrimination between one kind and another, or the technical refinement they put into making their best wines. Nor were they alone in appreciating them: the wine trade with Greece became a two-way affair, with ships passing at sea carrying Greek wine to Italy and vice versa.

By Augustus' time, the wine industry was established over the length of Italy. All the most famous wines came from between Rome and Sorrento, but the production of the Adriatic coast was important (it exported to Dalmatia, Macedonia, and Greece); the region of Aquileia (today's Venezia Giulia and Friuli) sent its wine east and north, using the river Sava to reach the Danube, and Pliny, our great source of information on all such matters, mentions notable wines in Liguria, Umbria, Emilia, and Rhaetia (at Verona), besides old Greek colonial vineyards in Calabria and Apulia in the extreme South. If Tuscany is surprisingly missing from this list, it is because it was (as it still largely is) forest; the Via Chiantigiana north from Siena still seems to find it difficult to pick a way through the oak-clad hills.

One town besides Rome had a dominant position as a wine port: the Bordeaux of Roman Italy, producing and shipping vast quantities of all qualities of wine. It so happens that it is the one Roman town we can visit almost as though it still lived – Pompeii.

T here are some 200 bars still recognizable among the ruins of Pompeii. In one street near the public baths, eight bars line one block not seventy-three metres (eighty yards) long. Outside one quite simple establishment you can still read the price list painted on the wall: wine on offer by the carafe, or *cucumas* (what today is known in Naples as a *cucumella*), at one, two or four *as* – call it a shilling:

"For one as you can drink wine,
For two you can drink the best,
For four you can drink Falernian."

The last price argues a pretty gullible public. Genuine Falernian, the wine of emperors, would certainly have cost more than four times the price of the house wine.

The counter only needs a good scrub down to bring back the colour into the marble. Behind it in a rack lie a dozen amphoras, their bungs gone, as though a weekend's drinking had left the owner waiting for the morning's delivery. Two porters with a sling between them carried each amphora along the crowded narrow street, lifted it into the rack and took away the empty. That was the problem with amphoras: they weighed as much as the wine they contained – and twenty-six litres could be drunk up in an hour or two by a party from the baths across the street.

Pompeii not only supplied Bordeaux; it seems in many ways to have foreshadowed what Bordeaux was eventually to be. There is a clear analogy between the Roman town, centre of the international wine trade, surrounded by splendid villas, and Bordeaux 1,700 years later, when its merchants began investing in wine-growing châteaux in Graves and the Médoc. Of thirty-one villas so far discovered in the countryside around Pompeii, twenty-nine seem to have been wine producers. They were the châteaux of their day, their vineyards lapping their walls, their cellars full of maturing wine.

P ompeii was destroyed in AD79 by a massive eruption of Mount Vesuvius that laid waste the countryside for many miles around. Rome's principal source of wine went with it: the 78 vintage was destroyed, the 79 never made. The immediate consequence was a mad scramble to plant vines everywhere within reach of Rome. Cornfields became vineyards, the balance of supplies to the capital was seriously disrupted; established wine-growers, who benefited from the wine famine of 80 and the next few years by higher prices, soon found themselves instead in a glut of wine.

It seems likely that it was this situation that precipitated a famous edict of the Emperor Domitian. In AD92 he banned the planting of any new vineyards in Italy, and ordered the grubbing up of half the vines in Rome's overseas provinces. In a separate edict he also banned the planting of small vineyards (presumably by such as tavern keepers) within towns in Italy.

The map shows labels including: Aquileia, Milan, RHAETICUM, Venice, Verona, PO, HADRIANUM, Ravenna, LUNENSE, PRAETUTIUM, ARNO, Florence, TIBER, SABINUM, TIBURTINUM, Rome, ALBANUM, SETINUM, SIGNINUM, CAECUBUM, FALERNUM, CAULINUM, MASSICUM, TREBELLICANUM, GUARANUM, Naples, Pompeii, SURRENTIUM, MAMERTINUM, Syracuse

THE GRANDS
CRUS OF ROME

Scholars have accused Domitian's government of strangling the infant wine industries of Gaul, Spain and the other provinces. There is very little evidence, though, that his edict, a political measure to placate big business and public concern about food prices at the same time, ever resulted in the uprooting of many provincial vines. It remained on the statute book for almost 200 years, until it was repealed by the Emperor Probus in 280. During that period, most of the principal vineyard regions of Gaul were either begun or steadily developed.

The writer who gives us most information about the actual mechanics and economics of Roman wine is Lucius Columella, a Spaniard from Cádiz. His comprehensive farming manual appeared in about AD65. Roman authors did not cast about for original titles. His book, like Mago's, is called *De Re Rustica*, or *On Country Matters*.

Everything you could want to know about viticulture is in Columella, starting with the proposition that it can be the most profitable form of agriculture, and yet people lose fortunes at it. Why? Because it is fashionable, and people rush into it without worrying about the soil, the situation, or whether they know what they are doing. They then neglect their pruning, ruin their

One of the many *thermomopalia*, or wine bars/cafés that lined the streets of Pompeii. Hot food was served at all hours, and wine was mixed with water, often seawater.

vineyards with heavy crops that make miserable wine, and wonder what went wrong. Columella sets everything out in detail. His costings can be followed to the last vine stake and slave's breakfast. We learn from him that a good Roman vineyard produced about the same amount of wine per acre as a first-class French vineyard today (in French terms, sixty hectolitres per hectare: the Roman measure of surface was a *jugera*, equal to one quarter of a hectare. Production was measured by the notional whole cattle skin, called a *culleus*,

holding twenty amphoras, or about 500 litres. Three *cullei* per *jugera* = sixty hl/ha).

Columella recommends a staked vineyard, with vines planted two paces apart each way, each tied to a chestnut stake the height of a man with withies of willow. This is more or less the method used, with variations, both on the Mosel and in Beaujolais today. (One man, Columaella calculated, can cut and sharpen 100 stakes in a January day, plus ten before dawn and ten after dark by lamplight.) But staked vineyards were probably in the minority. Alternatives included everything from letting the vines trail along the ground, layering as they went (mice tended to eat the grapes), to training them up tall trees, a method still common in central and southern Italy. In between came every variation from "head-pruning" (*en gobelet* in French), which turns the vine into a small self-supporting pollarded tree, to various forms of trellis, ranging from a simple T-bar to a full-scale pergola. The only element of a modern vineyard that was missing was wire.

Oddly, there was marked disagreement among authors about growing vines up trees. Earlier writers scarcely mention it; later ones go into great detail. To Pliny, slightly younger than Columella, it was the method that (in Campania) produced the finest wines of all, which by modern standards is certainly not the case. Poplars were recommended by some authors, elms by others. Working up tall trees was left to casual labour; no prudent slave owner would risk a valuable asset on such a dangerous job. "A hired vintager", says Pliny, "expressly stipulated in his contract for the cost of a funeral and a grave."

The first question for anyone planting a new vineyard was which grape variety to choose; colour, flavour, the size of the crop, and its ability to age all depend on it. By the first century AD, varieties exercised Roman minds almost as much as they do Californians or Australians today. The best wines were still in the Greek tradition, and the Aminean vines (there were five kinds), whose wines Pliny describes as full-bodied and vigorous, improving with age, were unchallenged for quality.

Vines from the overseas provinces, on the other hand, were being increasingly planted for greater fruitfulness. Of these the most promising were the Balisca and the Biturica, respectively (according to Columella) from Spain and Bordeaux. More of this in Chapter Eight.

The Roman vintage was cut with a knife like a miniature sickle, brought in baskets to the press-house, and trodden in shallow tanks, like the *lagares* still used for port-making. The wine press was developed by the Romans up to the point where it remained almost until modern times: great beams were used for weight, capstans for adding pressure, and rope wound around the "cake" of pressed grapes to keep it in place.

Fermentation took place in earthenware *dolia*, like the Greek *pithoi* (and the Georgian *kwevri*), sunk up to their necks in the floor of the cellar. *Dolia* were also used for maturing wine and in later times for transporting it. As the seaborne wine trade grew, the amphora, weighing as much as its payload, gave place to the much more economical bulk of a *dolium* – even if the *dolium* could not be moved and had to be filled from wine skins. The archaeological evidence for wine shipments by sea becomes scarcer and scarcer after about AD250; only recently has it been realized that the reason is the gradual introduction of the much stronger and lighter barrel. Pieces of pottery are immortal; barrels usually disappear in time without trace.

The sweet tooth of the Romans meant that the vintage was left as late as possible. The poets Virgil and Martial both advised leaving the grapes on the vine until November, or until they were "stiff with frost". A Greek technique was to pick them slightly underripe (presumably to keep a relatively high acidity) and to leave them in the sun for three or four days to shrivel and

the grape archaeologist The most respected winemaker in Campania today is Antonio Mastroberardino of Avellino, a town thirty-two kilometres (twenty miles) inland from Vesuvius. Mastroberardino is a viticultural archaeologist. All his wines are made from grapes that were used in the region by the Romans, and two of them were reputed (in Pliny's account) to be imports from Greece in pre-Roman times. Their names, Greco and Aglianico (or Ellenico), both mean, simply, "Greek".

The highest rank among Greek vines, said Pliny, is given to the group called *Aminea*, whose wine has body and vigour, and improves with age. The Greco is easily identified as Pliny's "twin sisters", the *Aminea gemina*, because its (white) bunches are always divided into two distinct parts. Its modern wine, Greco di Tufo, does indeed have body and vigour, although it is rarely given a chance to age today.

The Aglianico is not so easily identified in classical references, but makes the best modern red wine of Campania, Taurasi: wine with a firmness and depth of colour and flavour that outshines anything else from the South. The so-called Falernian (or Falurnum) of today is also made from Aglianico, in what is reputed to be the original area on the borders of Campania and Latium north of Naples, but the modern product has no qualities that confirm, or even hint at, its past glory.

Mastroberardino also grows three grapes of identifiable Roman origin. The best is the Fiano, originally called Latino to distinguish it from the Greek varieties. "Fiano" is said to derive from *appianum* – although this name, which means attractive to bees, is given by Pliny to what seems to be the Moscadello of Tuscany. To confuse matters more, *musca*, its Latin root, is a fly, not a bee. Fiano, in any case, is certainly not a Muscat vine, but gives pale white wine with an aristocratic, even austere, firmness: Campania's best today.

The name of another white variety, the Coda di Volpe, or foxtail, suggests Pliny's Alopecis, "which resembles a fox's brush" – although to Pliny this was a table grape, not for wine. This and the Piedirosso ("red-stem") are still grown on Mount Vesuvius. Pliny certainly would not recognize the name their wine goes by today: Lacryma Christi. The Galilean was only about twenty-five years old when Pliny was born.

to concentrate their sugar. Another, a speciality of Crete, was to twist the stalks of the bunches and leave them on the vine to shrivel deprived of sap. *Passum* was the term for these wines concentrated by drying. In Italy today they are called *passiti*.

Reduction and concentration of the juice (the must) by boiling was another technique for making stronger and sweeter wine. *Defrutum* was the general term, although different degrees of reduction were called by different names. *Defrutum* was often used for blending with thin vintages. A third method for sweetening was simply to add honey – as much as three kilograms to twelve litres. The sticky result, called *mulsum*, was drunk as a *gustatio*, an aperitif, with the hors d'oeuvres. The Romans also knew how to make what they called "permanent must" (and the Germans today call *Süssreserve*). They prevented fermentation by submerging the amphoras in cold water (the sea or a well) and keeping them there until winter. This *semper mustum* was another way of sweetening wine that had fermented too dry for their liking.

Reading Roman recipes gives a strong impression that the seasoning was more important than the primary flavour. Powerfully savoury tastes, fermented fish sauce, garlic, and most of all asafoetida – a strange onion-smelling root that to some modern sensibilities is a byword for nausea – were regularly combined with every sort of sweetening from raisins to honey, including a drench of the sweetest wine. Meat was regularly cooked and served with such fruit as apricots (an introduction from the Caucasus), and dishes of fig or plum sauce were used as all-purpose dips.

Pliny gives an alarming list of the flavourings that were added to make the forefathers of our vermouths. The whole class of wines cooked up with infusions, or the maceration of, herbs, spices, resin, and other flavourings was often referred to as "Greek", since the Greeks rarely drank wine without seasoning. Adding seawater was a Greek idea that was followed in Pompeii (Pliny shrewdly advises that it be collected well out to sea).

Absinthe was a popular flavouring for a "Greek" wine; rose petals, violets, mint, and pepper were others. The famous cookbook of Apicius gives a recipe for a "marvellous brew" involving resin, ground pepper, saffron, malobathre, and grilled dates in a reduced mixture of wine and honey. Travellers often carried with them a flask of some such *conditum*, perhaps just honey mixed with pepper, to drown the taste of the local wine along the way.

It was the mark of fine wine with the Romans, as it is with us, that it improved with age. Horace, in one poem contemplating his end, seems more concerned about parting from his cellar of wonderful old wine than from his wife. Very sweet wines will usually keep well without turning to vinegar, but the Romans had no means of increasing their alcoholic strength to preserve them. No yeast will continue to ferment when the alcohol level reaches fifteen or sixteen per cent of the wine. Distillation was unknown. This, then, was the strongest drink they knew. They made a clear distinction, though, between heavy sweet wines that they aged in the open air, "exposed to the sun, moon, rain and wind", and weaker wines that should be kept in jars sunk in the ground. The great Campanian wines came into the first category; like sherry and madeira they were intentionally oxidized – a process accelerated by changes of temperature. About these wines, Pliny anticipated a discovery of seventeen centuries later: "With wines shipped over sea… the effect of the motion on vintages that can stand it is merely to double their previous maturity."

Another practice with the same aim in view – to speed oxidation and the symptoms of maturity – was the *fumarium*, a smoke chamber in which amphoras were stored above a hearth. The heat and the smoke both affected the wine. Apparently it eventually emerged with a smoky flavour and, curiously, paler in colour and sharper in acidity. Pliny and Columella both give the impression that smoking was not something you do to first-growths.

P liny also noticed that the thinner a wine is, "the more aroma it has". The taste of the Romans was to change, with their experience of more "thin" wines, from the north of Italy and from Gaul. The first Gallic wine arrived in Rome during Pliny's lifetime. A century later it accounted for one-third of all the amphoras found by archaeologists in their excavations at Ostia, the seaport of Rome.

Our best source of information about the wines of the second century is Galen, a Greek physician from Pergamon in Asia Minor, who became the personal doctor and adviser of the Emperor Marcus Aurelius. His name is still known to every doctor; his observations succeeded those of the great Hippocrates as the medical reference point which was not entirely superseded until the nineteenth century.

Galen made his reputation curing (or at least treating) wounded gladiators. In AD169 he became the emperor's physician. An important part of his duties was to protect the imperial person from poisons. Concoctions of wine and drugs for this purpose were called *theriacs* (whence the English 'treacle'). *De Antidotis* was the title of Galen's treatise on the subject. It contains a characteristically thorough and well-observed account of the wines drunk in Rome in his day, both Italian and Greek: how they should be judged, stored, and aged.

The word "austere" continually enters Galen's descriptions of his choice of wines. Roman taste was clearly shifting away from the thick, sweet wines that had made Campania the most prestigious region. Galen and other doctors were recommending drier and lighter wines. The vineyards closer to Rome, dismissed in earlier times because their wine was "harsh" and acidic, are among Galen's favourites. Sabine and Tiburtine, from districts north of the capital on the Tiber, are promoted to "first-growths". Setinum, from south of Rome, had made its name as the favourite of Augustus (the very opposite of a voluptuary). Galen describes these wines as "fluid but strong, and fairly astringent", and variably full-bodied or lighter. All of them, like the first-growths of previous generations, are white. It seems that red wine that was not expected to age remained the daily drink of taverns. The concept of full-bodied, tannic red wines, aged in barrel and then in bottle, was still in the distant future.

A fter Galen we have no commentator on the progress of Roman taste in wine. The same first-growths apparently continued to fetch the highest prices. Imports from the provinces certainly increased, but there was room for all on the insatiable Roman market. With over one million inhabitants, Rome was by far the greatest city the Mediterranean world was to know until our own century. A hundred years ago even Naples, the most populous Mediterranean city of its time, had only half a million inhabitants.

Obviously most of the demand was for cheap wine, which was most easily brought by sea (unless it came down the river Tiber). Spain and Gaul obliged with huge amounts – although the increasing use of the wooden barrel means that we have no evidence to estimate how much. One effect of the growing provincial vineyards was that mass production became less profitable in the Italian regions that traditionally supplied Rome. A wine estate tended increasingly to become a gentleman's pastime – or even an emperor's; one emperor, Julian, is said to have planted a vineyard with his own hands and bequeathed it to a friend as the highest compliment he could pay him – "a modest souvenir of my gardening".

A positive disincentive to Italian growers was a tax in kind imposed on them from about AD250. They were obliged to deliver a proportion of their wine to Rome and other centres, for the rations of the army, and to supply the populace with subsidized drink. Only carriage was paid; not surprisingly, many wine-growers gave up.

It may have been partly to remedy this situation that in AD280 the Emperor Probus, whose principal concern in his short reign was to face the onslaught on the Empire of barbarians from the North, repealed the widely ignored edict of Domitian against the planting of vines. He even set the army to work to make new vineyards in Gaul and along the Danube (where, ironically, he was murdered in a vineyard). By now the decline of Rome had begun, the city's population was falling, and the future lay in the provinces of the Empire it had so spectacularly created.

Amphoras are a source of precise information about trade: certain forms, curves of the lips, and shapes of handles, can place even tiny shards in a recognized category. Molecular analysis even makes it possible to say what they contained.

CHAPTER 7

JEWISH LIFE AND CHRISTIAN RITUAL

"**The various modes of worship, which prevailed in the** Roman world, were all considered by the people as equally true; by the philosopher, as equally false, and by the magistrate, as equally useful." This was Gibbon's cynical dismissal of Roman religion. He saw in it none of the fervour and mystery of ancient Greece: simply the opiate of the people.

Cults came and went; some of their own accord, some with a push from the magistrates. To educated Romans there must have been little to distinguish the early Christians – Jews, apparently, following what they called the cult of the Nazarene – from the followers of Bacchus – and indeed there were enough parallels and points of contact to justify confusion. Both were performed in secret (or at least in private) and apparently involved a cannibalistic meal. The followers of Bacchus had claimed to be eating their god's flesh and drinking his blood. So did the Christians. But to understand the Christian rites, we must see them in the context of Jesus' Jewish faith and upbringing.

Wine was no less important in Israel than it was in Greece, but there is no parallel between its meaning to a Jew and its meaning to a follower of Dionysus. In Israel the idea of a libation, or any sort of sacrifice in the Greek or Roman sense, was sacrilegious – indeed, the horror of the thought still lies behind the definition of what is "clean" and what is "defiled". To Greeks, wine was the bringer of liberation and ecstasy: drunkenness could be sacred. To Jews it was a blessing fraught

RIGHT "Christ in the grape press", underlining the association of wine and Christ's blood, was a popular motif in medieval Central Europe. This is Bavarian, c.1500.

with danger that had to be kept under strict rabbinical control.

For Moses' followers, the first sight of the Promised Land was a prodigious bunch of grapes. He sent spies into the land of Canaan, "And they came unto the brook of Eshcol, and cut down from thence a branch with one cluster of grapes, and they bare it between them upon a staff." The Israelites' interest in wine-growing is a continual theme of the prophets. Indeed, in the whole of the Old Testament only the Book of Jonah has no reference to the vine or wine.

Joseph, when he interpreted the dreams of Pharoah's chief butler, talked as a man who had watched vines grow – and so did Jesus, when he called himself "the true vine": "Every bunch in me that beareth not fruit he taketh away; and every branch that beareth fruit, he purgeth it, that it may bring forth more fruit…" is a reasonable account of the process of pruning. "A householder", in one of his parables, "digged a wine-press" – an expression that remained mysterious to me until I found, near the Sea of Galilee, an ancient wine-press that had indeed been dug, in three separate pits at different levels, for treading the grapes, straining must, and fermentation.

The book of laws known as the Babylonian Talmud contains an idea for distinguishing the terroir that I have only come across elsewhere in Burgundy: "The Hurites used to smell the smell of the earth, while the Hivites… used to lick it like snakes." The Cistercian monks of Citeaux, it is said, tasted the soil before deciding where to mark their vineyard boundaries.

Jewish devotion to wine runs right through their law and literature. To the Jews there is no communal, religious, or

kosher wine The rules defining a Jewish (or kosher) wine have the simple aim of ensuring (by strict rabbinical supervision) that no Gentile has tampered with it in any way. They are carried to extreme lengths. At the Quatzrin winery near the Golan Heights in northern Israel, a young worker dashed forward to prevent me from even brushing against the stainless-steel valve on a huge insulated vat. He steered me right away from the hose snaking across the floor; if I had touched either (or anywhere where the wine is or might be in transit), I could have defiled it. It would no longer be kosher. Even in the bottling room, even when the bottle was corked, I was not allowed to touch a bottle – until it was sealed with a capsule.

The harm that I might do, I was told, was to dedicate the wine to an idol: to perform a libation with it, if only in my mind. The fact that this sanction has survived long past the last hint of Baal worship confirms the underlying reason: a Gentile must be kept at a distance to ensure the integrity of the Jews. With a typically pragmatic touch, the law allows a Jew to drink wine that a Gentile has defiled with the intention of causing damage; this is in order to discourage other Gentiles from following suit.

family life without it. Jesus' first miracle, at Cana, was simply to make good the lack of wine as a necessity at a marriage feast. He ordered the servants to draw six pots of water from the well (which can still be seen in the crypt of the little Franciscan church now on the site). When it was poured out it was wine – and better wine than the apparently rather meagre supply that the bridegroom had provided.

Each Sabbath starts with an act of blessing, the *kiddush*, or "sanctification", chanted over a cup of wine which the whole family shares. Four cups of wine must be drunk at the Passover, two cups at weddings, and one at circumcisions. At a funeral, in ancient times, the "cup of consolation" offered to the bereaved was ten glasses of wine. When three or more men recite the grace after meals their leader pronounces the blessing over a cup of wine, which all present then sip. The law is wholly specific about these ritual uses. They introduce the joy of wine into each act of worship, but reject any Dionysiac idea that intoxication is a good thing in itself. In the words of one rabbi, wine "helps to open the heart to reasoning". Reason is the goal, not inspiration.

Lying behind the ancient rules is a much stricter injunction still that reveals the fundamental fear behind them all. More important than what you drink is who you drink it with. Jews should not accept wine from Gentiles. Such social intercourse may lead to intimacy, intimacy to intermarriage.

Whatever the historical causes of Jewish law and custom in relation to wine, one point stands out strikingly. Its excessive use in Jewish communities is remarkably rare. Looking for an explanation, researchers have fallen back on the fact that Jewish children from the earliest age are initiated into wine-drinking in their families, in a religious context, where drinking is always moderate.

S t Paul's First Epistle to the Corinthians provides the first reference to Christians remembering Christ's Last Supper as a formal observance: "… the Lord Jesus the same night in which

RIGHT The use of wine in the Passover, from a fourteenth-century haggadah from southern France. Haggadahs are explanatory parables that accompany the Talmud.

he was betrayed took bread: And when he had given thanks, he brake it, and said, Take, eat: this is my body, which is broken for you: this do in remembrance of me. After the same manner also he took the cup, when he had supped, saying, This cup is the new testament in my blood: this do ye, as oft as ye drink it, in remembrance of me." Paul wrote this before any of the gospels were compiled.

The symbolism of sacrifice in Christianity has never been easy to understand. It developed in a Greek, rather than a Jewish, tradition. (The New Testament was written in Greek, not Hebrew.) In pagan Greece it was a sacred act to burn meat on an altar to feed the gods with its smoke, and then eat the meat. The very word for god in Greek, *theos*, derives from the word for smoke. The same root, *thusia*, is still preserved in the word enthusiasm, which thus means "filled with god". A similarly sacred act, going back thousands of years, was to drink blood, or blood mixed with wine, or wine as a symbol for blood. It was called *eucharistia*. The Greek word was used for such ceremonies when they were formal acts of thanksgiving. Thus the Christians' word for their act of worship linked it directly to pagan sacrifices.

As soon as Greek thought touched Christ's teaching, it took on a meaning that was impossible for Jews to accept. Christ's sacrifice of himself was far too close in its symbolism, or in the symbolism that the church put on it, to the ancient pagan rites. The clearest connection was to the Orphic followers of the wine god. Originally, Dionysus had merely liberated the spirit. The Orphics turned him into a god who saved the spirit and could grant it eternal life. This was no different in concept from what the Christians taught.

The image of these first celebrations of what was to become the Eucharist is preserved in wall paintings in the catacombs of Rome, where the persecuted Christians met in secret. In the catacomb of Priscilla, seven men and women are at a table set with a single cup, and plates with bread and fish. One of the figures is breaking bread. In another scene, more like a banquet, the six participants, sitting around a table with bread, fish and wine, and with an amphora beside them, are calling to their servants, whose names are Irene (Peace) and Agape (Love), for wine. One says, "Mix it for me"; another, "Give it to me warm."

By the second century the Christians in Asia Minor had been able to build their first churches; by the fourth, when Constantine became a deathbed convert, the Eucharist had become the ritual that remains with us to this day, although now interpreted in ways as different as a High Mass and a plain Baptist Communion Service.

The precise phrases of St Thomas Aquinas, the great Italian friar-philosopher of the thirteenth century, sum up the significance of wine in the Mass:

"The Sacrament of the Eucharist can only be performed with wine from the vine, for it is the will of Christ Jesus, Who chose wine when He ordained this Sacrament… and also because the wine of grapes is in some sort an image of the effect of the Sacrament. By this I mean spiritual joy, for it is written that wine makes glad the heart of man."

CHAPTER 8

A GREENER COUNTRY

No one disputes that France was to become the motherland of wine, but the circumstances of its insemination are a battleground between historians. In brief, there are those who believe what Roman writings, backed up by Roman remains, tell them, and those whose Gallic pride leads them to look much further back, and to claim that it was the forgotten predecessors of the Celts who established wine-growing in France. Some even argue that Stone-Age Frenchmen were *vignerons*.

The Celts of Gaul were certainly an active and aggressive race. They dominated almost the whole of Europe north of the Alps in the time when Athens dominated Greece. They invaded Italy, occupied Lombardy (founding Milan) and reached Rome, settled briefly in Asia Minor, and in the aftermath of Alexander the Great they even penetrated his Macedonian kingdom, reaching as far as Delphi, and founded a settlement on the Danube at Belgrade.

There is no arguing with the fact that they appreciated wine. The ancient Gauls had extensive contacts with the Mediterranean wine world over a long period, and they were a ready market for Greek and Etruscan wine; if the wine-vine was a native plant in France, as it certainly was, then surely they must have made wine for themselves.

The Roman evidence says not. The account from the classics is that Greeks from Asia Minor, the Phocaeans, established the colony of Massalia (Marseilles) in 600BC, planted vines, and traded with the natives. The Celts from the interior of Gaul had not even reached the south of France by this time; the inhabitants were Ligurians and Iberians, respectively from northern Italy and Spain.

The enormous success of Massalia was due to the natives' thirst for wine, but it is even doubted (by some authorities) that it had its own vineyards. Some say the Greeks taught the natives wine-growing, others that all "Massaliote" wine was imported from Greece or the Greek colonies in Sicily and southern Italy.

If there were vineyards in Celtic Gaul, they were not down on the Mediterranean coast, where the Gauls began to arrive in about the fifth century BC. They must have been in the interior, attached to such tribal settlements as Bourges, Chartres, Metz, Reims, Amiens, Troyes, and Bibracte (of which more in a moment), growing native grapes (the climate would have excluded Mediterranean vines), and moreover, subject to the disapproving looks of the Druids, who anticipated certain sects of Christianity in their moralistic stance towards wine. It is easier to believe the authors who say that France had no wine – and difficult otherwise to understand the enormous prices Gallic chieftains would pay for it. Diodorus Siculus, admittedly writing rather later, about the time of Christ, ensured himself fame with the statement that "Italian merchants, prompted by their usual cupidity, regard the Gauls' thirst for wine as a godsend. They take the wine to them by ship up the navigable rivers or by chariot overland and it fetches incredible prices: for one amphora of wine they receive one slave, thus exchanging the drink for the cupbearer."

RIGHT Bacchus reached the furthest outposts of the Roman empire. He is depicted on the handle of a bronze wine jug from the late first century, found in Britain.

Massalia became part of the expanding territory of Rome in about 125BC, but continued to be regarded as a Greek town. The magnificence of the Roman buildings, monuments, theatres, and aqueducts of Provence, in masonry as fine as any in the Empire and far ahead of anything in Gaul, is said to be due to the Greek tradition of craftsmanship in Massilia, as the Romans called it. Young Romans even came here to be educated in preference to making the longer trip to Athens.

The first true colony of the Romans in France was founded a few years later, along the coast to the west at Narbo, near the mouth of the river Aude. Narbo (Narbonne) became the capital of the province of Narbonensis. Like all Rome's great colonial cities, it was based on veterans from the army (who did not have to be native Romans; army service conferred the coveted rights of citizenship on Roman and barbarian alike). It was the period after the destruction of Carthage when wine-growing was spreading like wildfire in Italy. Some of the soldiers would have been the sons of wine-growers and known all about vineyards. They planted the hill slopes near Narbonne, today's Corbières, Minervois, and the Coteaux du Languedoc. These are the first extensive vineyards in France that we can be certain about. They provided the trading strength of a province that was to control all of France south of a line from the Spanish border to Geneva.

Rome's war to the death with the Carthaginians had already given it another prize. The coastal parts of Spain became the first two great overseas provinces of what became the Roman Empire. The northern province, eventually extending right to the Atlantic, became Tarraconensis, based on what today is Tarragona. The southern province, modern Andalusia, was called Baetica, from the river Baetis, now the Guadalquivir, at whose mouth the town of Gades (Cádiz) had been founded a thousand years before by the Phoenicians.

Wine was no stranger to these provinces. It was the Carthaginians' wine-growing skills, inherited from the Phoenicians, that caused Cato's envious outcry, which Pliny quotes as *Delenda est Carthago* – Carthage must be destroyed. Columella was a native of Cádiz. Wine from the coastal parts of Spain soon became commonplace in Rome. Pompeii traded with Tarragona, both buying and selling wine, which argues the quality of the Spanish product. Enormous quantities of Baetic wine reached Rome (the voyage normally only took a week). Most of it was described as ordinary, but one wine, Ceretanum, picked out by the poet Martial (who, although poor, had expensive tastes), was apparently highly regarded. If it came from Ceret, which seems probable, Martial was the first writer to write about sherry. The modern name of Ceret is Jerez de la Frontera.

The Phoenicians had not stayed on the seacoasts, but used the navigable rivers to go far inland. In Portugal (Lusitania to the Romans) they had sailed up the Tagus and the Douro (where Greek, although not Phoenician, coins have been found). In Spain they used the Baetis and the one considerable river of the Mediterranean coast, the Iberus – to us the Ebro. They left traces up the Ebro as far as Alfaro in Rioja. The Roman legions went farther, and colonized what today is the wine region of the Rioja Alta. The towns of Calahorra, Cenicero, and Logrono were all Roman veteran colonies (Cenicero means "crematorium"). In a field near the Ebro at Funes, no more antique or dramatic looking than any long-abandoned agricultural building, is the entire layout of one of the wine bodegas that must have dotted the region to supply the troops. Its sizeable cisterns, beside the four *lagos* for treading the grapes, indicate that it could produce and store as much as 75,000 litres, or nearly 3,000 amphoras of wine.

In the middle of the first century BC the Gauls step from the twilight of illiterate barbarism, however gleaming with jewelled armour and ringing with battle cries, into the full light of history. It was their fortune to meet one of the greatest commanders and administrators of the ancient world, and one of its most lucid chroniclers – Julius Caesar.

Caesar's Gallic War was over in only seven years, but even before the Romans had subjugated Gaul there was a wine-trade network, beginning with the Rhône Valley as the route from the Provincia Narbonensis northwards. In Chalon-sur-Saône, Caesar found two Roman wine merchants already in business. Caesar took note that a couple of northern tribes refused to be lured. Wine, they said, was a Roman trap. It dulled their fighting power. They might have noticed that it didn't dull the Romans'.

Under Augustus, Gaul entered an era of peaceful prosperity and varied industry it could never have imagined under the old tribal system. His great general Agrippa founded and fortified towns (often on the sites of old Gallic settlements), and drove straight no-nonsense Roman roads through forests, across rivers and over mountains. The heart of Agrippa's road network was Lyons, where the waters of the Rhône, draining the Alps, merge with the broad slow-moving Saône that Caesar had described as "a great river of incredible tranquillity". Lyons was Roman Gaul's second capital, succeeding Narbonne in the South. It rapidly became the second-greatest wine port in the world, after Rome.

Up to this time, the beginning of our era, there is no clear evidence of any vineyards in France north of the Mediterranean zone, defined by the Alpes-Maritimes in the east and the Cévennes in the west. The wine trade, though, was enormous – pouring up the narrow corridor of the Rhône Valley to reach central and northern France and Germany, and trundling by caravan, rather more laboriously, northwest up the valley of the Aude, which is not navigable much above Narbonne, through the lowland gap past what is now Toulouse, or over the shoulder of the Cévennes and down the rivers Tarn or Garonne to the west coast at Burdigala – Bordeaux.

Bordeaux, with its almost perfect situation on the estuary of the Gironde, had customers in Ireland, Britain (a *negotiator Britannicus* was identified on the waterfront in the first century BC), around the north coast of France to Holland, and even as far as the Baltic. Gallic seamen were not timid. We know from the Greek geographer Strabo, who made the first mention of "Burdigala" in the reign of Augustus, that it had no vines of its own. An *emporium* he called it: a store.

There were two rival routes north into Germany, where the

garrison legions were an important market; one went down the river Mosel and one down the Rhine. Everything possible was done to avoid the cost of overland freight. The Romans even planned to dig a canal to link the Saône to the Mosel.

Who were the customers in these unexpected northern markets? In Ireland the king's court was famous for its feasting. Britain had an active maritime trade, concentrated in Cornwall where the tin mines supported an unusually wealthy society. And of course there were thirsty Gauls at all stages in between.

The much respected French historian Roger Dion has postulated a credible scenario for the advance of wine-growing north into central and western France from its suntrap in the Midi. Dion believes Gaillac is where the Romans thought vine country stopped. If they could make wine here, why cart it all the way up from the coast? Save the carriage and supply Bordeaux from the watershed above it, using the river Garonne. If this is what happened, Gaillac, in what became known as the High Country, was supplying Bordeaux with wine before the latter had a vineyard of its own. (Later generations in Bordeaux never entirely lost their jealousy of High Country wine, and did

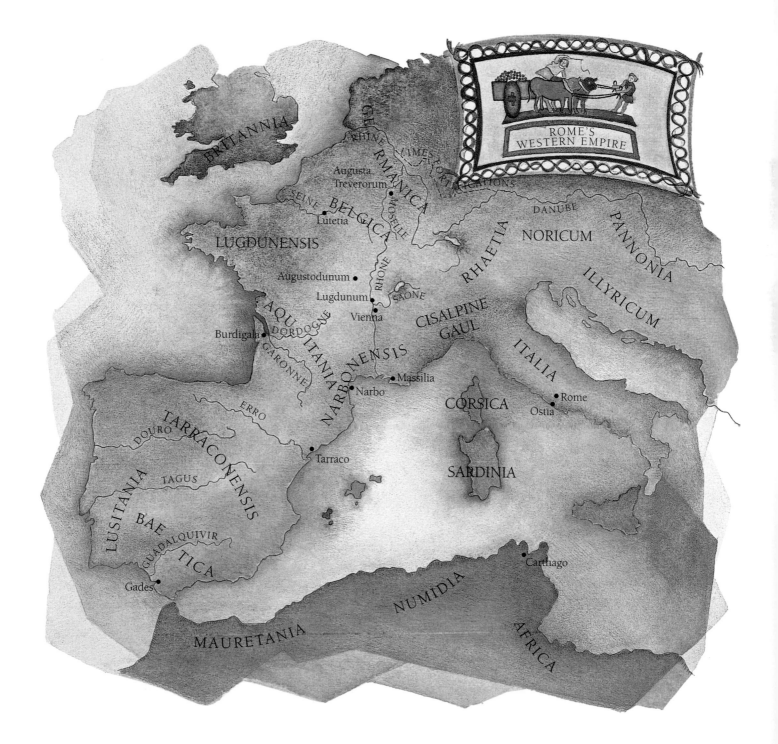

celts and casks
The amphora was superseded by the barrel for the transport of wine in the course of the third century AD; when, that is, the flow of wine from Rome to its northern colonies was reversed, and it was the Celtic races who began to furnish Italy.

The barrel as we know it was a Celtic invention: exactly as we know it, since hardly any changes have taken place in the art of the cooper, the barrel maker, for 2,000 years. Wood and metal were the Celts' favourite materials. So skilful were they with roof beams that some of the more ambitious of the stone vaults of Rome could not have been achieved without Celtic carpenters to make the templates. Iron wood-working tools have been found from the La Tène culture of Switzerland in the fifth century BC which would be familiar in a cooper's shop today. The earliest barrels even had iron hoops, which gave way to wooden encircling bands in Roman times, only to be reinstated in the barrels of the seventeenth century. The historical trend has been for barrels to become shorter and fatter – otherwise there has been almost no change in form.

The Romans soon realized the superiority of the light, resilient, rollable barrel over the cumbersome, fragile amphora, particularly in cooler northern climates with high humidity. The one advantage of the amphora that the barrel did not possess was that it could not be made airtight. Wood "breathes"; wine cannot be "laid down" to mature for years in a barrel, as it can in an amphora.

their best to suppress it.) To this day, Gaillac has vine varieties peculiar to itself: the Fer-Servadou, Ondenc, L'en de l'Elh, Duras (perhaps what Cato called the Duracina). Their wine is of no very special quality by today's standards. But why should this remote spot have ancient indigenous grapes unless it is a survivor from before the time that the great mainstream vineyards of Aquitaine began?

Bordeaux's first vineyards of its own must have been planted very soon after Strabo's visit – indeed, in the very generation when (in AD43) the Romans under Claudius invaded Britain. In 71, Pliny recorded not only the fact of vineyards in Bordeaux but also what he knew about their grapes – which was not very much. There is no question of there having been wild vines growing at Bordeaux already. In fact, Bordeaux is an unpromising location for any sort of agriculture except pasture. The site of the town was chosen for a port because a respectable bank of gravel fronts the river here on the outside of a wide crescent curve, with marshes or low alluvial land, subject to flooding, almost all around. It lies shortly above the confluence of the Garonne and the Dordogne, where the Garonne is still not too wide – but these are the thoughts of a trader looking for a safe and convenient haven, not a farmer.

It is rare, in fact, to find any ancient settlement in a place so unsuitable for growing its own food. Bordeaux's gravel is mean and hungry. It can only have been with a good deal of industry and recourse to manure that its first vines were persuaded to grow. The commercial argument was the overriding one. There was a well-established market for wine, and ships were coming from the north to fetch it. If Bordeaux could supply the wine itself, without the expense and risk of bringing it down-river from Gaillac and beyond, all the profits would stay in Bordeaux. From its inception, Bordeaux was destined to be linked to the British Isles.

It was a rather different story over on the other trade route, the Rhône Valley. There was apparently no need to bring up vines from the Mediterranean to grow here. All the indications are that the vine they chose was already growing in their woods. The grape vine, always a variable plant, is most variable near the limits of its natural habitat. Perhaps a mutation produced a clearly superior vine that they baptized as Allobrogica.

In any case its wine, sold at Vienne, had within ninety years of Virgil's death (as Pliny points out) become a challenger to the first-growths of Rome. It was particularly appreciated for its sharp flavour of pitch, or burnt resin, which seems a rather unreverential addition to a particularly fine wine.

Rome's first allies among the Gauls were the Aedui, whose stronghold of Bibracte lies in the Morvan hills not very far to the west, behind the range of the Côte d'Or. Under Augustus, they abandoned Bibracte on its hilltop to found, with Imperial blessing and Roman help, the new city of Augustodunum, or Fort Augustus. Augustodunum has long since been shortened to Autun. In Roman days it was one of the principal cities of Gaul, but too high and cold to grow vines. On the other hand, its *civitas* (county would be the approximate modern equivalent) included and ended with the Côte d'Or: a magnificent opportunity for the Aedui to plant vineyards and make wine in, as it were, a shop window on the principal north–south artery. A river would have been better, they had to admit. The Côte d'Or, indeed, is the only great vineyard of ancient foundation without the benefit of a river at the door.

The first clear account we have of the Pagus Arebrignus, which the vine-growing Côte was then called, is in a plaintive address to the Emperor Constantine delivered when he visited Augustodunum in 312. The palmy days of the Empire were already past. The later years of the last century had seen catastrophic incursions deep into Gaul by barbarians from beyond the Rhine.

The vineyards of the Côte, the orator told Constantine, although envied by all, are in a sorry state. They are not like those of Bordeaux which have limitless space to expand. They are squeezed in between the rocky hilltop and the marshy plain where frosts ruin the crop. In this narrow strip (which anyone who knows the Côte will recognize), the vines are so old, he said, that they are exhausted, and the soil cannot be worked owing to the tangle of ancient vine roots. Also the main roads, even the great military road, were so potholed that half a load was enough to break a wagon. The bottom line, unsurprisingly, was that the loyal citizens were having difficulty with their taxes.

How old is old? How long had it taken the vineyard to reach the state described (allowing for hyperbole) by the worthy orator? It sounds as though the vines were cultivated on the system of *provignage* – not one recommended in the Roman textbooks – which consists of laying the trunk along the ground to form new roots by layering. Each year the new shoots and their fruit are supported above the ground by a temporary light stake. *Provignage* would account for a surface tangled with old roots – but in how long, who can say?

Suppose the trouble started with the barbarian invasions, and the vineyard was well established before that, it seems reasonable to date the planting of the Côte d'Or in the first half of the third century. The great city of Lyons went into decline at this time, although whether this was cause, effect, or coincidence we don't know. Those who argue an earlier date point out that the town of Beaune was flourishing a century before that; even remains of pruning knives and effigies of Bacchus have been found. Amphoras stopped being delivered to Augustodunum in the second century, which argues the use of barrels. It seems probable that they were barrels of the local wine.

We are frustrated when we try to find precise starting dates for France's other vineyards, too. Their sites follow a clear logic: the nearness of an important town, almost always a river, and in every case, especially as we move north, a good steep hill. The Romans knew how cold air runs like water down slopes to form, like water, pools at the bottom. The pools are frost pockets, fatal to a good crop.

Certain prominent hilly outcrops in otherwise relatively flat country are known to have been among the first vineyards of the Gallo-Romans. The chalk hill of Sancerre, almost as much a landmark on the Loire as Hermitage on the Rhône, is a good example. Another is St-Pourçain-sur-Sioule, at the confluence of the rivers Allier and Sioule near the Roman road from Lyons to Bourges and the Loire. Auxerre, on the way north to Paris, is a probable Gallo-Roman vineyard, and Paris itself a certainty. The Emperor Julian, known as the Apostate, who rejected the Christianity of his predecessor Constantine and tried to return the Empire to the old true gods, stayed for two years at Lutetia, the little proto-Paris on the Ile-de-la-Cité, and enjoyed the wine grown on, presumably, the hill of Montmartre.

The mountain of Reims is another obvious candidate. Reims, the capital of Champagne, is hollow with chalk quarries cut by the Romans for building stone. The south slope of its "mountain", overlooking the river Marne, has all the right qualifications.

Most of these Gallic vineyards, with the probable exceptions of Bordeaux and the Rhône, were planted when the edict of Domitian, banning planting in the provinces, was still theoretically in force. We do not know whether they had special permission from Rome, or (as seems more likely) if local needs and desires overcame any scruples (and means of enforcement). There was, in any case, a convenient dodge available: any land owned by a Roman citizen could be described as "Roman" – and hence eligible for planting. Nonetheless, when the beleaguered Emperor Probus repealed the edict in 280 ("Citizens", he said, "plant vines and grow rich."), it gave a powerful new impetus to wine-growing. It seems likely that many of the vineyards of the Loire were planted in the fourth century. The Loire completed the process that had started with the Biturica in Bordeaux and the Allobrogica in the Rhône Valley – western and eastern grape varieties invaded the valley from their respective ends. Today along the Loire, the Cabernet lies down with the Pinot, and the Gamay of Burgundy with Bordeaux's Sauvignon Blanc.

The turbulent times of the later Empire concentrated more power in the North than ever before. Far from spelling the end for Roman power in the North, barbarian pressure intensified Imperial commitment. Cologne, and then Trier, were made Imperial capitals.

Roman officers at these northern outposts must have been at least as eager for a supply of wine as their friends at home. At the end of such a long journey, though, the price would have been high, and the quality far from certain. The historian Tacitus tells us that the people of the country drank an inferior sort of beer. The prospects for vineyards in the darkness of the North must have seemed remote – unless, as seems perfectly possible, there were wild vines here, too. There are those who believe that the Riesling is a selection from a native German vine.

Probably Germany's first vineyards were planted in the same spirit as those of Bordeaux. Trier was a flourishing emporium for Imperial wine: what if vines could be made to grow on the steep forest slopes around? The three elements were present: city, river, and hills. Only here the choice of hill made all the difference. A steep south-facing slope not only caught all the meagre warmth the sun provided, but also sheltered vines from the north winds, rapidly drained off the excessive rainfall, and by tilting the surface at the sun's rays received them perpendicularly rather than low-angled and diffuse.

Trier was surrounded by suntrap vineyards hanging from improbable slopes, perhaps from as early as the second century. Our evidence, when it comes, is of a long-established and flourishing vineyard scene in the second half of the fourth century: the scene described in a much-quoted poem by the Imperial tutor Ausonius.

The Mosel reminds Ausonius of his native Bordeaux, where grapevines are reflected in the river Garonne. He speaks of rich villas with smoking chimneys, of boatmen calling out insults to the workers among the vines, of the delicate fish playing in the river, and, in a famous passage, of the hillsides mirrored in it.

Ausonius was one of the last Roman citizens to see the Mosel as a vision of peaceful fecundity. When he died in 391, the defences of the Empire needed only a determined push to bring them down. His grandson, on his own estate near Bordeaux, was reduced to a landless labourer by the invaders.

There remains the question of Roman Britain. The logical probability is that the Romans would certainly have planted vines, even in this misty outpost of their Empire. Enough grape pips have been found, in London, in Gloucestershire and Wiltshire, to suggest that wine was made. But proof is lacking, and we are left only with the certainty that Britain was a voracious market for imported wine.

Excavations near Colchester, Britain's Roman capital, have identified at least sixty apparently different sorts of wine – or rather their containers. In the earlier years of Roman Britain they came principally from Italy and Spain, and included both Falernian and Baetican. Later, the principal source of amphoras is the Rhine, with less evidence of wines from Bordeaux than the known history of Bordeaux would lead us to expect. But barrels rarely leave traces, and all the indications are that from the start the barrel was the standard container of Bordeaux.

Trier is a good place to study the effects of the barbarian invasions. It bore the full brunt. Roman writings are bound to give us the view that the best you could hope for from a barbarian was a speedy death on a sharp sword. True, there were pillaging tribes whose attentions were always messy and usually terminal. But the Germans, the Franks, and the Alamans were not only old foes of Trier; they were also old neighbours, and undoubtedly customers for Trier's wine. Of all the misguided and forlorn attempts to stave off barbarian invasion, the most ill-conceived was an edict forbidding the sale of wine and oil across the frontiers. It was as good as an invitation to break down the door.

Having despatched Roman authority from the city, they are unlikely to have destroyed houses that would shelter them better than their own. Trier is magnificently preserved; not only its immensely solid stone Porta Nigra but also the soaring brick walls

of its baths, and what is known as the Palace of Constantine, have clearly not been put to the sack with any conviction.

The same is true of the vineyards. The wisest move was to encourage the wine-growers, not to butcher them. There is no certainty about what happened as we enter the "Dark Ages", but patchy records show that life, at least in favoured places, went on as before, but without the Roman soldiers.

Gibbon described Rome's decline and fall as "the triumph of barbarism and religion". The Age of Emperors was succeeded by the Age of Saints. Constantine had made the

Empire Christian, and established the Imperial capital at Constantinople. Rome had little power left. Franks, Vandals, Goths, and Visigoths moved into an almost unresisting Europe, and it was the Franks who controlled – and gave their name to – northern France. All that was left of the administration of the Empire was its church.

In a real sense the Church was a creation of ancient Rome, was organized in the Roman fashion, but it had no army to rout, nor troops to be pulled back to headquarters for a last-ditch stand. Its early bishops were members of the Romanized upper or learned classes of the provinces of the Empire. When Rome's temporal power was gone, those who survived continued as far as possible the Roman pattern of life in the vestments of priests or bishops.

Saintly bishops are credited with many miracles, but perhaps their greatest was the maintenance of organized agriculture (of which wine-growing was an important part) through the three centuries when it must have seemed that hell's legions were massing in the East, to bring yet another wave of sackings and pillage.

Many early bishops are associated in legend with wine-growing, starting with St Martin, a soft-hearted legionary from Hungary (the story goes that he divided his cloak with a shivering beggar), who in 371 became Bishop of Tours. He is credited with starting wine-growing in Touraine, and also with the discovery of pruning, by watching a donkey – which is some measure of the dimness of the records of the fading Roman Empire.

The bishops were soon rivalled by the growing power of the monasteries. They dominate the Middle Ages, and we shall discuss them in their appropriate chapter. But all the struggles of the Franks are dwarfed in historical perspective by their great successor and first Holy Roman Emperor, Charlemagne.

Trier was an Imperial capital – these are the ruins of the Imperial baths – and a centre both of wine-growing, on the banks of the Mosel, and of the wine trade.

in a glass (lightly)

Wine was first drunk from pottery, occasionally and ceremonially from gold, but by as early as the late Bronze Age, about 1500BC, also from glass.

The technique of firing a glassy or "vitreous" substance onto solid objects was discovered in about 4000BC. In about 1500BC the idea of a hollow glass vessel appeared – possibly in Egypt. It was made by dipping a cloth bag of sand into a crucible of molten glass, then modelling it by rolling it on a *marver*, a flat stone bench, then when the glass had cooled, emptying out the sand. The technique was known all over the Near East until about 1200BC, then apparently lost in the first "Dark Age", to re-emerge in the eighth century BC, with Egypt, Phoenicia, and Syria as glassmaking centres, but also with workshops in Italy and Celtic Europe.

The idea of glassblowing originated in Syria in the first century BC. It spread rapidly around the Roman Empire, with Syrian or Alexandrian craftsmen setting up workshops, especially in Italy, Gaul, and the Rhineland. Glassmaking survived the fall of the Empire, with the Rhineland as a continuing centre. It tended to be concentrated in forested areas where there was plenty of fuel for the furnaces. Wine glasses, however, remained objects of luxury until the eighteenth century.

CHAPTER 9

THE HOPE OF SOME DIVINER DRINK

The man who was to have the most profound effect of any individual on the history of wine was born as the Roman Empire finally disintegrated, far from any vineyards, in what is now Saudi Arabia. Mohammed was born into one of the Middle Eastern cultures that from earliest times had been grateful for the gift of wine. If Arabian vintages can never have been other than unsubtle, wine, locally grown or imported from Syria, Iraq or the Yemen, was part of the daily life of sixth-century Mecca.

Within ten years of Mohammed's death in AD632, it was totally banned not only from Arabia but also from every country which listened to his words, or which the armies of his followers had conquered. So vigorous was the thrust of Islam that its empire already included Egypt, Libya, Palestine, Syria, Mesopotamia and Armenia, besides the whole of Arabia. Within a century of Mohammed's death, western North Africa, Spain and Portugal, Sicily, Corsica, Sardinia and Crete, and western Asia as far as Samarkand and the river Indus were ruled by his successors, the caliphs, first of Damascus, then of Baghdad.

Mohammed did not write. The angel Gabriel dictated to him, and he repeated what he had been told to his disciples, who committed it to memory. Later his revelations were written down, although not in any particular order. When an authorized version was compiled, some fifteen years after his death, it was a jumble without sequence, and with many disputed meanings. It was accompanied, however, by a body of commentary that makes it possible to unravel which parts were revealed while the Prophet lived at Mecca, his birthplace, and which belong to the period of the *hegira*, the eight years when he and his disciples

were in exile in the city of Medina, 300 miles to the northeast across the desert. This is how we know that the prohibition of wine in the Koran was the result of a change of heart – perhaps even a measure of desperation.

In one of the early verses, wine is part of a catalogue of the good things of the earth, with water, milk and honey: "We give you the fruits of the palm and the vine, from which you derive intoxicants and wholesome food." Its next mention is cautionary: "They will ask you concerning wine and gambling. Answer, in both there is great sin and also some things of use unto men: but their sinfulness is greater than their use." This revelation, we are told, was not considered as a prohibition. It is interesting to note that wine and gambling are linked – both in sin and in "usefulness". The usefulness of gambling is a matter the Koran does not explain. There followed a very reasonable admonition, similar to one in Jewish law: "Believers, do not approach your prayers when you are drunk, but wait till you can grasp the meaning of your words; nor when you are polluted – unless you are travelling the road – until you have washed yourselves."

The single verse on which the prohibition of wine is based was dictated, we are told, as a result of an incident in Medina when Mohammed's disciples were drinking together after dinner. One of his Meccan followers began to recite an uncomplimentary poem about the tribe of Medina, whereupon one of his Medinite followers picked up the meat bone from the table and hit the ribald Meccan on the head. It was only a flesh wound, but Mohammed was distressed and asked the Almighty how to keep his disciples in order. The reply came, "Believers, wine and games of chance, idols and divining arrows, are abominations devised by Satan. Avoid them, so that you may prosper. Satan seeks to stir up enmity and hatred among you by means of wine and gambling, and to keep you from the remembrance of Allah and from your prayers. Will you not abstain from them?"

The believers' answer, according to Islamic scholars, was such a resounding "yes" that all the wine in Medina was immediately poured into the streets. Thus one of the principal characteristics of the Muslim way of life arose as a result of a quarrel (which may or may not have been drunken). It will immediately strike any observer of the Muslim world that Satan is not so easily foiled. The evil one does not need the help of wine and games of chance, nor of idols and divining arrows.

Are we to imagine that moderate, healthy wine drinking was unknown in seventh-century Arabia? Indeed, it was known, and widely practised, even among Mohammed's own followers, who justified their action with another Koranic verse: "No blame shall be attached to those that have embraced the faith and done good works in regard to any food they have eaten, so long as they fear Allah, believe in him and do good works." Mohammed's successor, the Caliph Umar, had them flogged.

Even the Prophet's favourite wife, Ayesha, quibbled with the injunction: "She quoted him as saying 'you may drink, but do not get drunk'." Mohammed, it is said, drank *nabidh*, a sort of wine made from dates. There was plenty of room here for ingenious sophistry. Was it only wine that was forbidden, or intoxication? Did date wine count? How was wine to be defined? Before long the poets and courtiers at the Caliph's court were debating every hint of a more liberal interpretation of the law with the fervour of schoolchildren looking for a way around school rules. It has been said that the theological spirit of Islam was drowned in quibbling casuistry – and not only, of course, on the question of wine.

Certainly in the eighth century a school of Arabian Bacchic poetry grew up in which wine became the focus of a romantic, rebellious philosophy. Prohibition took on quite a different aspect as Islam conquered lands whose wines had long been their pride and joy. It was one thing to give up the headache mixture of Arabia, quite another to throw away a cellar of treasured vintages from Syria or the Lebanon.

Much the most famous of the great poets who rebelled against Islamic domination of their heritage and their lives were the Persians: Firdausi in the tenth century, Omar Khayyam in the eleventh, Sa'di in the thirteenth, and Hafiz in the fourteenth.

No poet has ever made wine so much the hub of his universe as Omar Khayyam. His *Rubaiyat*, a long series of individual quatrains, was brilliantly linked by Edward Fitzgerald to form a single poem that sums up Omar's philosophy – Persian in its epicurean audacity, Muslim in its fatalistic resignation:

"You know, my Friends, how long since in my House
For a new Marriage I did make Carouse:
Divorced old barren Reason from my Bed,
And took the Daughter of the Vine to Spouse.
The Grape that can with Logic absolute

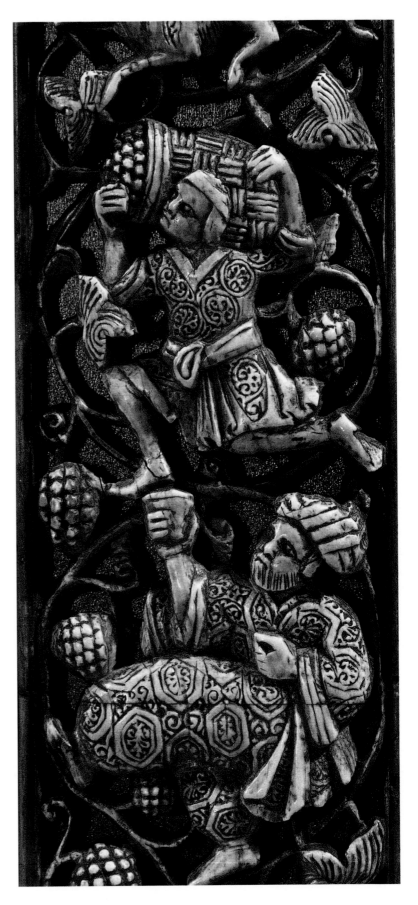

Wine-drinking was far from unknown in the early centuries of Islam. This carved ivory of a turbaned man with a wine cup is from eleventh- or twelfth-century Egypt.

The Two-and-Seventy jarring Sects confute:
The subtle Alchemist that in a Trice
Life's leaden Metal into Gold transmute."

To Omar, the promise of wine deferred until the afterlife is a sham:

"I sent my soul through the Invisible
Some letter of that After-life to spell:
And after many days my Soul return'd
And said 'Behold, Myself am Heav'n and Hell'.

I must abjure the Balm of life? I must
Scared by some After-reckoning ta'en on trust,
Or lured with Hope of some Diviner Drink
When the frail cup is crumbled into Dust!"

Omar Khayyam could, perhaps, be dismissed as a poet of little account in the history of Islam, were it not for the fact that he was also one of the greatest mathematicians and astronomers of the Middle Ages, who led the thought of his time in algebra, physics, and geography, as well as calculating the most accurate calendar yet devised, with a measurably smaller margin of error than the Gregorian calendar we use today.

Arab physicians were thrown into a quandary by the prohibition of their principal medicine. The great Avicenna, in charge of the hospital in Baghdad a generation before Omar Khayyam was born, brought together much of the medical knowledge of the ancient Greeks, with pertinent observations of his own on the effects of wine in different persons under different conditions. His Rule 860 concludes with a thought that may possibly have some bearing on the success of prohibition in desert lands: "Wine is borne better in a cold country than in a hot one." Nor did the doctor neglect the benefits of wine to his own person:

"If a problem was too difficult for me, I returned to the Mosque and prayed, invoking the Creator of all things until the gate that had been closed to me was opened and what had been complex became simple. Always, as night fell, I returned to my house, set the lamp before me and busied myself with reading and writing. If sleep overcame me or I felt the flesh growing weak, I had recourse to a beaker of wine, so my energies were restored."

This contradiction between what was known to be good and what the Koran outlawed continued in a state of variable equilibrium for at least 1,200 years. Islam is not normally a proselytizing or coercive creed, and by tolerating Jews and Christians within its boundaries it enabled the growing and distribution of wine to continue – subject to sanctions which produced a useful revenue in taxes.

As always, it was the ruling class that took most liberties, both in drinking and in selling wine (or in having the right to sell wine) to others. Even caliphs – the highest rank of ruler – showed an unseemly desire to anticipate Paradise by giving parties in gardens that closely resembled the Promised Land of the Koran: not running streams nor soft couches, not houris nor fruit and wine, were wanting.

Upper-class wine parties commonly started in the morning (working people, who had a living to earn, drank at night if at all). A meal was offered first; wine drinking came later, after the guests had washed, perfumed themselves, and put on fine garments. They formed a circle, sitting on seats or lying on cushions (young people had to stand). The first cup was taken in the right hand and drunk in one swallow, then given back to the servant who filled it for the next guest. Different wines were drunk in a prescribed order, while connoisseurs among the guests inhaled deeply and discussed the bouquets. Some accounts of the wine parties of Baghdad bring to mind a Greek symposium: long discussions over many cups, often with musicians, the proceedings measured and ceremonial to slow down the effects of the wine.

Only occasionally were specific wines mentioned, although we know that the Arabs recognized four colours: red, white, yellow, and black. The Persians were fond of yellow wine, the Byzantines of red. No great age is ever mentioned. New wine was cloudy, with little bouquet; one-year-old wine clear and ideal; older wine usually, we may imagine, spoiled, and considered less of a sin than sweet young wine. In principle, the sweeter the wine the more it was liked; it was common to add honey or spices, even drugs – and also water. The greatest luxury was snow from the mountains, or ice from deep ice-houses. Specialist snow merchants could charge a fortune in summer. Sir John Chardin, travelling in Persia in the seventeenth century, records how the centrepiece of the Shah's magnificent touring tent was a golden basin full of snow and crystal ewers of ruby wine.

From time to time public attitudes certainly hardened. Tenth-century Caliphs carried out a succession of measures to prevent winemaking, including throwing 5,000 jars of honey into the Nile, pulling up vineyards and burning raisins, and above all, raising the taxes on wine merchants. These very taxes, though, were the Jews' and Christians' insurance against their trade being prohibited altogether. It is recorded that on one occasion, feeling themselves threatened by the mood of the people, they volunteered to pay the caliph twice as much tax for his protection – which he granted.

No generalization holds good for all times and places, especially about a creed so open to interpretation as Islam, or an empire so shifting in its dynastic successions. The faith has grouped and regrouped again and again around new centres of energy and power. From the start there were schools of more liberal and more puritanical teaching. In the Turkish Ottoman Empire, which by the sixteenth century controlled the Near East from the Adriatic to Iraq and Upper Egypt, *arrack* or *raki*, alcohol flavoured with aniseed, was essential in masculine conviviality (wine was discouraged). One could say that the Ottomans took the opposite view from Mohammed, believing that it was better to let citizens drink *raki* than "melancholy" coffee.

Yet established vineyard regions from ancient times had managed to survive with few exceptions while the controlling powers of Islam were Arab, or Syrian, or Persian. It was the Ottoman Empire that finally chased wine out of some of its oldest-established strongholds.

On the eve of Ottoman rule, and indeed throughout the Middle Ages, vineyards planted by the Greeks, the Phoenicians, the Romans, the Egyptians – all the most ancient civilizations – were still, however precariously, in existence.

Spain and Portugal never lost their vineyards as a result of Islam. Wines of the eastern Mediterranean, of the Lebanon, Cyprus, and Crete in particular, were much in demand in Europe throughout the Middle Ages. Algeria maintained a Roman wine tradition – although it was to supply the hard-drinking Barbary pirates of Algiers. Coptic Christians in Egypt

A Persian drinking party, by the painter Sultan Mohammed, 1527. Guests in the garden are having the most riotous time, while the balcony on the left seems more decorous. The roof is reserved for a private party of angels.

The poet Hafiz enraptured and scandalized fourteenth-century Persia with his sensuous and Bacchic verses. Here he is imagined in a much later painting. He was born and died at Shiraz, the most famous wine centre of the Muslim world.

continued to make wine. Persia proudly produced its vintages at Shiraz and in Bactria, not only for home consumption but to supply a considerable export market.

Remotest of all were the vineyards of the High Indus Valley and Afghanistan. High in the Hindu Kush the Ismaeli sect nurtured vineyards, and vines lined the old route of the Silk Road through the Hounza Valley, north of Kashmir. Kafiristan, north of Kabul, supplied the court of the Sultan Babur, the founder of the Mogul Empire in sixteenth-century India, with his favourite wine.

How old these vineyards are no one can say. It is conceivable that they had an independent existence in prehistory; equally that they are the last memorials of Greek influence, the last echo of Alexander the Great.

The following tasting notes are almost a century out of date, but may be regarded as fairly accurate:

"The Hounza wine is not kept beyond a year, and stands underground in earthern jars... It looks like cold weak tea with milk in it, and is not unpalatable, though sourish, tasting like Norman cider of the rough sort, and containing, I should say, about the same percentage of alcohol. For the benefit of travellers, I may mention that the vintage of Baltit is best."

The underground jars are surely cousins of the Imeretian *kwevris*.

S uch outlandish regions never felt the lash of the Ottomans, but the vineyards of the eastern Mediterranean and its islands, survivors of a thousand years of coexistence with

Islam, were much more hardly dealt with by the *raki* drinkers. As the Ottomans swept through the Levant, it almost ceased to be a useful source of wine for Europe. One exception was Santorini. The only value of this windswept rock to its Turkish masters was for any taxes they could extract from it, and the only possible crop on its raw volcanic rock is the vine.

Santorini's vines crouch low on its cliff like the nests of big seabirds braced against the gale. The island's wine, fermented in caves cut into its cliffs, and manhandled down to ships waiting in the unfathomable water of its crater, became the staple Eucharistic wine of Turkey's greatest foe, Russia. Wines from Crete were similarly bought by Venetian merchants, and traded north over the Alps to market in northeast Europe. What is certain is that the coffers of the Sublime Porte were at least as much a beneficiary as either wine-growers or traders.

T here are other reasons why wine faded even from its strongholds in the Middle East. The region never entirely recovered from the Mongol invasions of the thirteenth century. The horsemen from the Steppes destroyed villages and irrigation systems and drove the population from the countryside to the cities. Wars and epidemics further reduced the population, so that Baghdad, the home of 1.5 million people at its zenith, was reduced by the mid-nineteenth century to a mere 60,000. A consequence was the departure of Jewish and Christian communities and traders, those who had kept the wine industry in being. As vineyards were abandoned, the price of wine rose, and consumption fell even further. For those who could no longer afford to buy wine, hashish became the affordable intoxicant.

women or wine In 1986, Russia celebrated the 1,000th anniversary of its foundation by the Viking Prince Vladimir at Kiev. Although Vladimir's manners left something to be desired, he was a good king, worthy of his great country. For its proper dignity and the sake of their souls, he thought, the Russes should have a religion. He therefore sent to the Jews, to the Christian churches at Rome and Constantinople, and to the Muslims to inform him of their faiths.

First he was visited by the Bulgars, who professed the Muslim faith, and who (according to the *Russian Primary Chronicle*, written by an eleventh-century monk) addressed him thus:

"Though you are a wise and prudent prince, you have no religion. Adopt our faith and revere Mahomet." Vladimir enquired what was the nature of their religion. They replied that they believed in God, and that Mahomet instructed them to practise circumcision, to eat no pork, to drink no wine, and, after death, promised them complete fulfilment of their carnal desires. 'Mahomet', they asserted, 'will give each man seventy fair women. He may choose one fair one, and upon that woman will Mahomet confer the charms of them all, and she shall be his wife. Mahomet promises that one may satisfy every desire, but whoever is poor in this world will be no different in the next.' They also spoke other false things, which out of modesty may not be written down.

"Vladimir listened to them, for he was fond of women and indulgence, regarding which he heard with pleasure. But circumcision and abstinence from pork and wine were disagreeable to him. 'Drinking', said he, 'is the joy of the Russes. We cannot exist without that pleasure.'"

CHAPTER 10

INHERITORS OF THE EMPIRE

The light at the end of the Dark Ages has a name – and it is Charlemagne. That, at least, is how he was seen, this steadfastly successful, ambitious but conservative ruler, by his contemporaries, and by the succeeding ages that credited him with every virtue, and most inventions.

Charlemagne added the whole of Germany to the Frankish crown, conquering the Saxons in the North, and extending his borders eastwards from the Rhineland to include Bavaria, as well as southeast from the Alps to include Lombardy and Rome, and southwest beyond the Pyrenees to provide a "march", or buffer, against the Moors in Spain. This was the Holy Roman Empire, of which, on Christmas Day 800, the Pope crowned him emperor in Rome.

Rome was the pope's headquarters; it was not Charlemagne's. The great palace and chapel which Charlemagne built at Aachen symbolized the shift in the centre of gravity of Europe from South to North. The eighth and early ninth centuries were a time of consolidation and relative prosperity in northern Europe. The Rhine, which had been both highway and frontier for the Romans, became the centre of activity for Charlemagne's empire. He built a palace near the river at Ingelheim, near Mainz, granted lands to nobles, bishops and monasteries, and gave rights to settlements to hold markets and become towns.

An important motor in this Rhineland activity was the Frisians, the race of seamen from what are now The Netherlands, who can be said to have initiated that country's energetic involvement in the wine trade. Their customers included not just the ports of the North Sea but also the hanse cities of the German Baltic, and indeed came from as far as Poland and Russia. Across the Channel in England, King Offa of Mercia opened a dialogue with Charlemagne which probably led to the first wine-for-wool trade with England since Roman times. The earliest post-Roman references to almost all the wine regions of Germany are found in the period between 650 and 850, the Carolingian era.

Charlemagne's energy was devoted as much to bureaucracy as to empire-building. The best-known legends about him that concern wine stress the ecologist. He observed, it is said, while passing by boat up the Rhine to Ingelheim, that the snow melted first on the steep apron of Johannisberg (or the even steeper scarp of the Rüdesheimer Berg, according to your informant). So he ordered that vines be planted there – and indeed it was during his reign (or, to be exact, three years after his death) that we know that the Rheingau had its first vineyards. In Burgundy they tell a very similar story about the hill of Corton, whose chalky upper slopes he gave to the Abbey of Saulieu in 775, and whose wine to this day is called Corton-Charlemagne. Burgundy has attached to the emperor the fairy story that he specified white grapes (in a red-wine district) because red wine stained his white beard.

It is less well known that he laid down strict laws about hygiene in winemaking, including the revolutionary (and scarcely practicable) injunction that the grapes should not be trodden with the feet. "With what other instrument?" must have been the puzzled reaction. He also banned the storage of

les enfeignemens que n
disines en le premier p
car por les enseignemens
noul distinct fesismes la
en passerons briement.

wine in animal skins, and gave wine-growers the right to hang out a green branch and sell direct to all comers. The right to do so survives, passed down by succeeding Holy RomanEmperors to the growers of Vienna. Every *Heurige* has its leafy bough – although, as the saying goes, good wine needs no bush.

I n Greek and Roman times it had been a matter of doubt whether grapes would grow at all outside their "natural" environment, a Mediterranean (or warmer) climate. The Romans had shown what you could do by planting on steep south slopes, and finding the right varieties of vine.

The Romans' Mosel was very light and low in alcohol by Italian standards, but they soon learned that the new "austere" taste had its points. At a strength of probably only seven or eight degrees of alcohol, it was treated as the all-purpose drink. (It was certainly safer than water.) In winter it was heated in a kettle and drunk as we drink tea or coffee. Vineyard workers in Germany still often keep a kettle of wine on a fire of vine prunings on cold days. With a spoonful of sugar in a plastic cup, it has much to be said for it.

N ow that northern Europe was beginning to bustle, much more wine was needed than a few privileged river bends could provide. Monasteries were springing up like snowdrops in January; each needed wine, and so did such towns as there were. Wine was needed in Britain, in Ireland, by the Frisians of course, and across the north of France. Why did the old trade routes not operate to bring it from the South? What had happened to the shipping from Bordeaux, and the long trek up from the Rhône Valley and Burgundy?

The problem, in the case of Bordeaux, was probably pirates, or at least unfriendly heathens, whose presence made the open seas too unsafe for business (but not for the Irish saints, who made the journey to the mouth of the Loire on many occasions, their ships returning with wine for Irish monasteries).

The short voyage across the English Channel or even up the North Sea was comparatively safe. At any rate, England's principal supplier at this time was Germany. German merchants kept houses in York, and in the ports of Boston and Lynn on the English east coast, and had a substantial headquarters at the Steelyard in London. French wine was shipped either down the Seine from Rouen, or down the little river Canche from the port of Quentowich – which was rediscovered in 1987 after disappearing for nearly a thousand years. As for long-distance transport overland, the road from Burgundy had been almost impassable, we were informed, during Constantine's time. So by now it had probably disintegrated altogether.

The threat of heathen raiders was not only felt at sea and along the coast. In the ninth century, Viking plunderers reached and sacked both Paris and Orleans, and virtually depopulated Normandy. In 867, the Chapter of St Martin at Tours on the Loire, a good 150 miles from the sea, appealed to King Charles the Bald for a vineyard site that was well inland and out of danger. He granted them land at Chablis on the

A thirteenth-century Benedictine cellarer does some drinking on the sly while drawing the general ration: a satire by the manuscript department on their fellow monk.

river Yonne. Picture the satisfaction of the Brothers as they discovered not only that their wine was going to be better but also that the Yonne runs into the Seine, and the Seine means Paris. Chablis began to be a name in the capital (it was the only "*vin de Bourgogne*" that reached it) – although little Chablis was only a drop in the ocean compared with the vineyards that were already planted around the cathedral town of Auxerre on the same river.

I f the North in its new mood was to have enough wine, it had to grow it, and as close as possible to its market. So vineyards were planted in places where a really ripe grape must have been a rare sight. The ninth century, for all its disruption, even saw a wave of planting in Belgium, where the river Meuse might be called a poor man's Mosel. Liège, Naumur, Brabant, Hainault, Antwerp were all wine-growing provinces in the early Middle Ages. The city of Louvain led the way, as the seat of the Dukes of Brabant (and later Burgundy). The eventual decline of the vineyards of Louvain corresponded precisely with the rise of the House of Burgundy and its Côte d'Or wines in the fifteenth century.

The true limit, it was found, to a realistic prospect of making drinkable wine was indeed the climate – although not in quite the predictable north–south sense. Northern France has a climate without great extremes, tempered (like Britain's) by the mild airs that accompany the Gulf Stream. The farther west, the more this Atlantic influence makes itself felt, but not, unfortunately, to the benefit of the sun-loving vine. Brittany has a balmy (if blowy) climate, but scarcely a single vine. The problem is the clouds that trawl eastwards up the Channel, following the north French coast and reaching inland to cover all of Brittany, and almost all of Normandy and Picardy.

Paris lies on the edge of this grey-green zone. Only a little farther east, the influence of the continent begins to be felt: winters are colder and summers hotter. Here the vineyards can edge north a little, profiting from the clearer skies. This is the Champagne region, today the northernmost under vines in France. Farther east still, the Mosel and Rhine are able to take profitable wine-growing as much as 80 miles farther north; by this point the climate is noticeably more extreme, influenced as much by the landmass to the east as by the great reservoir of grey skies to the west.

All the vineyards that the Middle Ages planted north and west of this diagonal line have since disappeared – although some of them not until the nineteenth century. Yet those just south of it (Champagne, for example) produce some of the most highly prized wines of all. The vine, as we will often be reminded, does its best work at the very margins of where it is practicable to cultivate it.

The two centuries that followed the plundering raids of the Vikings, or Norsemen (once settled, they sounded much more respectable as Normans), saw a great acceleration of

wandering scholars Besides churches and monasteries, two other great medieval institutions derived much of their income from wine: hospitals and universities. The most famous wine-endowed hospital is the beautiful Hôtel-Dieu in Beaune, which dates from the later Middle Ages. But throughout Europe it was commonplace and logical for a hospital (which in its broadest meaning catered for the sick, the poor, and the traveller, student, or pilgrim) to make wine both for use and for sale. The sick received an allowance which may well have kept their whole families: 4.8 litres a day was the ration at one hospital on the Bodensee.

The University of Paris was the forerunner and model of similar foundations throughout Europe, which in the thirteenth century set a new fashion that could almost be called tourism. Students were given safe-conducts and exemptions from customs dues to encourage their travel to other seats of learning and promote the exchange of ideas. (The "duty-free" idea appealed to merchants, too, who sent their clerks, who knew Latin and could write, on "study" trips disguised as students.)

The wandering scholars seem to have spent more time in taverns than in lecture rooms. They formed a distinct subclass of society that was both learned and irresponsible, loosely attached to the Church but principally interested in wine, women, and (ribald Latin) song. In a time when guilds controlled every calling, they called themselves the Order of Goliardi (from *gula*, the Latin for gluttony). If anyone was knowledgeable about the different wines of different parts of Europe, it was probably these Rabelaisian wanderers.

Alsace – this is Colmar – was the last part of the Rhineland to be planted, but it soon became the largest producer of the whole region. A medieval poet wrote that the people here could "drown in the bounty of their production".

growth and trade throughout northern Europe. The population may have increased by fifty per cent. Safer trade meant richer cities with more artisans to feed, which in turn demanded more farmland and a bigger population in the countryside.

As an emblem of this new prosperity, of the freedom of travel and a marketable surplus of goods, in the 1100s a pattern of regular fairs emerged, centred around the Ile de France, Flanders, and above all the towns of Troyes and Bar-sur-Aube in the open, unforested countryside of Champagne. Italian merchants even crossed the Alpine passes of Saint Bernard and Mont Cenis to trade in this marketplace. It was the first faint breath of a renaissance of the single Europe of ancient Rome.

S uddenly to plant what must have been tens of thousands of hectares of new vineyards around the towns and abbeys of newly prosperous northern Europe was a not-inconsiderable achievement. Vineyards – as both Cato and Columella pointed out – need high investment, and skilled and intensive care. The last great planting had been under the slave system of the Romans. Who undertook this new great labour?

Much of the credit is given, probably rightly, to the monks. But in France, most of the land belonged to nobles who had given the king their support, in battle or otherwise. Royal thanks took the form of great tracts of what was often virtually wilderness: forest, marsh, and mere, but not many fields, and not many peasants to take the part of slaves.

A solution was found in the new notion of partnership. A free labourer would offer to cultivate uncleared land in exchange for a share from the landowner – either of the land itself, or more often of its crop. The system of *complant,* as applied to vineyards, meant that the worker, the *prendeur,* owned the vines, and the *bailleur* the soil. The period of contract was five years; long enough to establish a vineyard and judge its produce. Sometimes the partnership went on for generations, the *bailleur* receiving anything from one-third to two-thirds of the revenue. In other cases the *bailleur* bought out the *prendeur* – effectively paying him for five years' work. The system seems to have satisfied both parties, particularly in remoter districts where labourers were scarce – so much so that it still persists, in a modified form, now known as *metayage.*

E arly medieval Britain drank more German wine than French: presumably because it was better – or at least better liked. Climatically, as we have seen, the Rhineland vineyards had the advantage over what were generically called the *vins de France* ("France" being limited to the Seine and its tributaries).

The expansion of the Rhineland vineyards (including those of Alsace) was even more rapid and impressive in the early Middle Ages than the boom in French planting. It was also more monastery-led. Two great Benedictine abbeys were founded in Charlemagne's reign that were to plant gigantically, not just along the Rhine, but in Franconia to the east, Alsace to the west, and Austria and Switzerland to the south. The names of Fulda (which is north of Frankfurt) and Lorsch (south of Mainz) appear in document after document as they spawned more and more abbeys and outlying dependencies. Fulda was founded by an Englishman, St Boniface, who is said to have stimulated the wine trade with England. It was due to them and scores of other monasteries that wine-growing villages multiplied along the Rhine from less than forty in the seventh century to almost 400 two centuries later.

Working alongside the monasteries were the churches and cathedrals. Charlemagne followed the example of his predecessors in granting churches a tax (known as a "tithe", or tenth part, although it was usually between three and five per cent) on all agricultural produce. A tithe of a peasant's haycrop was not so much use as a tithe of his wine, which could easily be turned into cash. Churches therefore gave villages every encouragement to plant vineyards, from technical help with terracing to celestial privileges for especially good results.

A great economic historian has pointed out that wine and wool were the two true luxuries of northern Europe in the Middle Ages. To be warm within and without was well-being indeed. Both were agricultural products that depended on skilled handling by the primary producer, which for wool was principally England. English wool was woven in Flanders. Trading in cloth and wine, Flanders soon became the banking centre of the North. Although town burghers could grow fat as vintners or clothiers, it was in everyone's interest that a fair

A public bathhouse, which appears to have been as much (or more) tavern and brothel, as illustrated in a manuscript written for Antoine of Burgundy in about 1476.

proportion of the price be passed back to the supplier.

Hence the wine village, in Germany the *Winzerdorf,* developed a special status, under the wing of Mother Church (and positively saturated with saints' days), but businesslike, and with a degree of independence that was unusual in feudal times. The *Winzerdorf* was usually walled like a tiny town, built beside the river road, with its own network of paths up into the terraced vineyards above. Little shrines and huts for watchmen were scattered among the vines. In the tiny square was a common hall, and often a common cellar; the growers operated as what we would call a cooperative.

No great imagination is needed to picture such a place. They still exist by the score all along the Mosel and Rhine, and their tributaries. Bernkastel on the Mosel is perhaps the finest – but it was granted town rights and a market in 1291. The tall and narrow half-timbered houses that huddle and confide over the steep streets may be more opulent, but their plan, and their attitudes, will have been much the same 700 years ago, and possibly 400 years before that. Another, and perhaps the most perfectly preserved of all late-medieval wine towns, still entirely within its fifteenth-century gated walls, is Riquewihr in Alsace.

The position of the Rheingau was particularly privileged, even among wine districts. It passed from Charlemagne's successors partly into the hands of their Imperial abbeys of Fulda and Lorsch, but also to the archbishops of Mainz, just across the river. The whole magnificent undulating landscape, sloping up to the Taunus forests, and facing south over the broad silver waters of the Rhine, was now Church ruled, and its pious proprietors set about clearing its woods and planting vines so comprehensively that since 1226 there has been no more clearing or planting to do.

The Church's way of assuring hard work and good wine was to make even the lowly toilers in the vineyards free men with equal rights to townsmen. They could take their wine to market in Mainz, and even carry arms. They were, you might say, wine-burghers, and the resulting esprit de corps can be tasted in the wines of the Rheingau to this day.

Pruning in a late-medieval vineyard, illustrated in the *Liber Ruralium Commodorum* by Pietro de Crescenzi, the standard work of the time on vine-growing.

Much the greatest part of this soaring wine production, which reached right up the Rhine, through the Palatinate to Alsace and Baden, was destined for export. Alsace, although the last to be planted, was the biggest producer and exporter of the whole Rhineland. By 1400, 100 million litres a year went through the Strasbourg market, en route for all parts of Germany, the Hanseatic towns, and England. The other great market of Alsace, Colmar, supplied huge quantities via Basel to Switzerland. The river-port towns prospered accordingly, as both merchants and producers. No potential vineyard was left unplanted. When Cologne, the chief of all the wine-trade cities, replaced its ancient battlements with a new defensive curtain-wall ninety-one metres (100 yards) farther out, the intervening space was immediately filled with vines. (But of Cologne it was said, right up to the eighteenth century, that the water was poison.)

The town of Worms still contains, beside its Gothic Liebfrauenkirche, the vineyard that gave its name to the original Liebfraumilch. Würzburg in Franconia was described as being surrounded with vineyards "like a thick wreath". They are still there, the famous Leisten and Stein slopes that have produced wines of extraordinary power and plenitude for 900 years – although unfortunately today dominated by another and thicker wreath, of concrete tower blocks. So besotted were the Franconians with their local wine that they supported their prince-bishop in actually forbidding its export for fear of going thirsty, or having to import inferior stuff.

Other wine towns formed free-trading partnerships (Frankfurt, for example, with Strasbourg) to their mutual benefit, and to avoid the ever-increasing tolls that almost every town imposed to cash in on the wine trade. In the fourteenth century there were sixty-two customs points on the German Rhine, and merchants were making laborious overland journeys to avoid them. The pattern of supplies flowing down (and occasionally up) the great rivers of Europe, the rivalries between producing regions and trading towns, the complexity of tolls and customs add up to an economic epic that it would be beyond your patience and mine to pursue.

German documents of the times build up a picture of a great bubble expanding and expanding, of wine becoming the obsession of the German race. By the sixteenth century, noble households employed professional drinkers: Falstaffian characters whose job was to jest, and swallow, and belch, and swallow again. The bubble is symbolized by the mighty "tuns" that were built to house the best vintages. The most famous of them, in Heidelberg, held 150 hogsheads, or 19,000 dozen bottles. An eighteenth-century Polish governor of Königstein took leave of his senses and ordered a tun of twenty-five times the capacity of the Great Tun of Heidelberg.

The bubble was to burst in the apocalyptic destruction of the Thirty Years War. The Rhine would never again be such a river of wine. Sheer quantity eventually had to give place to quality. In this, as in so many stages of wine's history, the Church was in the lead.

CHAPTER 11

MAKING AND TASTING MEDIEVAL WINE

Whatever difficulty we may have in imagining the circumstances, the beliefs and superstitions, the dangers, the narrowness, and what, to us, would be the privations of medieval life, we have a remarkably direct link, and real common ground, through the technology of winemaking. About the precise taste we can be less sure, chiefly because so much depends on grape varieties, and little is known for certain about which they used. Even some whose names match our own may have changed character in many centuries of cultivation. But the way wine was made in the Middle Ages persisted almost everywhere until at least the eighteenth century, and in some places has scarcely changed today. More, in most cases, has changed in the vineyard than in the cellar: changes forced by the arrival of fatal but previously unknown diseases and pests of the vine in the nineteenth century.

A medieval vineyard was, wherever possible, planted by ploughing into deep furrows, then pushing in simple rootless cuttings, short canes of the last year's growth, with a small "heel" of older wood attached. In northern Europe the cuttings were put in a mere pace apart; the vines covered the soil in a dense carpet, with up to 20,000 vines to a hectare. In the South, where drought was a problem, the spacing was much wider: perhaps only 5,000 vines.

Unrooted cuttings were the cheapest way of planting, but there was small chance of them all taking. Next year there would be gaps to be filled. The more expensive way was to grow roots on your cuttings in a nursery bed, and transplant them with a tuft of roots, and a third way was to "layer" canes on growing vines by partially burying them, then separating these *marcottes,* and planting them as soon as they had made roots of their own. Where *marcottage* was practicable, a new vineyard could be producing grapes within three or even two years. The same system, but without separating *marcottes,* and instead leaving the new plants in place to thicken up the vineyard, was called *provignage*. It eventually produced a terrible tangle of roots and shoots, but it seems to have been the system used by the Romans on the Côte d'Or. Certainly it would explain their complaint to Constantine that the land had become choked with vines.

The most fundamental decision, then as now, was which variety of vine to plant. For most simple growers there would be little choice; but for preference they would plant several different kinds in a mixture as an insurance against the crop failing in any one of them. The textbook of French agriculture of 1600, Olivier de Serres' *Théâtre d'Agriculture,* recommends planting five or six.

More important economically, and the cause of constant dispute between landlord and tenant, was the vigour and productiveness of the varieties. The eighteenth-century German author and traveller Goethe put the matter in a nutshell: "The rich want good wine, the poor plenty of wine." Even by the thirteenth century, in the Rhineland there was a clear distinction between "Hunnish wine" and "Frankish wine"; the latter at twice the price of the former. Today's terms would be bulk wine and fine wine. Eventually, in all the best vineyard sites the Frankish would prevail, but not without many generations of dispute – and not without backsliding either, even today.

The mixed varieties in the vineyard might be either red or white. Although in the early Middle Ages white wine had the greater cachet, especially in northern vineyards, in most cases its colour was a secondary consideration. Presumably most ordinary wine was either pale red (in French, *clairet*) or pink-tinged white.

The signal to begin the vintage (in French, the *ban de vendange*) was given by the landlord. To pick before it was a punishable offence. Normally one week's notice was given, and watches were set in the vineyards to guard the ripening fruit. Only the landlord was exempt from the ban: an unfair advantage he was happy to enjoy. On the announcement, by drum, trumpet or bells, all hands set to picking. Twenty pickers, it was reckoned, could harvest a hectare of vines in a day.

All the grapes were trodden. It is surprising that France and Germany have scarcely any old stone treading tanks like the *lagares* of Portugal. The familiar medieval picture is of treading in a wooden trough or shallow vat. At this stage, white juice was strained from its skins and bucketed into barrels to ferment. But if the majority of grapes were red, and red wine was what was wanted, a deep vat was needed in which juice and skins could ferment together until the colour had been leached from the skins. Red winemaking was therefore a more elaborate operation. It could also involve risk. The obvious shortcut was to tread the grapes in the vat. Once they started to ferment as the vat filled, the carbon dioxide could suffocate the treaders – as parish records show that it not infrequently did.

Only large estates belonging to nobles or the Church had wine-presses in the Middle Ages. They were massive pieces of capital equipment, cumbersome structures built of the biggest trees from the nearby forest. Their only role was to extract an extra fifteen or twenty per cent of juice from white grapes, or wine after fermentation from red. The *vin de presse* that they produced was inferior in quality to the *vin de goutte* that ran free from the vat. Its only virtue was extra tannin (and in reds, extra colour), which in any case was scarcely a virtue in wines intended for immediate drinking. Good wine could be made very well without a press. Why, then, were they built? And why did tenants pay a proportion of their crop to use the landlord's press? The only answer is that the extra wine was worth the investment, despite the fact that, according to Olivier de Serres, it was unusual to add it to the *vin de goutte*. Normally it was sold separately, and more cheaply. He mentions the fact that it was blended in Anjou as an exception to the rule.

The principal change that was to come over winemaking during the seventeenth and eighteenth centuries was the goal of durability – for which press wine was needed. Annotations in an 1804 edition of the *Théâtre d'Agriculture* specify that press wine is an essential preservative if the aim is wine that will mature.

Once the wine was fermented, the grower's whole object was to sell it before it went sour. An ordinary grower could not afford to drink wine himself; for his family he made *piquette* by adding water to the waste skins. He probably had nowhere to keep it: wine cellars were for rich establishments and town merchants. Leaky barrels, or barrels not topped up, could go off

LEFT Harvesting and treading grapes, from the fourteenth-century Italian *Codex Vindobonensis*. The vines appear to be grown up trees, in the age-old Italian fashion.

even on the way to market, particularly in a warm October.

Given that medieval wine was made in a hurry, often from a random mixture of grapes, with little or no knowledge of how to preserve it, it is surprising how much time was spent discussing it, and how much distinction was made between one wine region and another. The times, it seems, were far more preoccupied with wine than its quality can really have justified.

How was it judged? Most seriously, in the first place, by its supposed or alleged effect on the drinker's health. The first wine book ever to be printed was the *Liber de Vinis* of Arnaldus de Villanova, a physician who was probably Spanish or Catalan, but who taught medicine in the famous University of Montpellier in the south of France until his death, by drowning, in 1311. Unlike most medieval books, the *Liber de Vinis* was no rehash of the classics but a firsthand medical view of wine – perhaps the first since Galen's. Villanova is typically realistic about wine tasting: "... note that some wine dealers cheat... they make bitter and sour wines appear sweet by persuading the tasters to eat first licorice or nuts or old salty cheese... Wine tasters can protect themselves against such doings by tasting wine in the morning after they have rinsed their mouths and eaten three or four bites of bread dipped in

a whiff of brimstone A quiet revolution took place in Germany just over 500 years ago, in 1487, when a royal decree permitted the addition of sulphur to wine for the first time. It has often been asserted that this was an ancient practice. There are vague references in Homer and Pliny, but no document before 1487 stipulates how much, by what method, and why sulphur should be added.

The permitted amount was apparently 16.2 grams to 860 litres of wine, applied by soaking wood shavings in a mixture of powdered sulphur, herbs, and incense, and then burning them in the empty barrel before it was filled. It must have been known that sulphur has valuable properties in preserving wine, chiefly in killing microbes, and protecting it from the effects of oxygen, preventing spoilage and browning. (How this knowledge was acquired without royal permission is not recorded.)

From then on sulphur dioxide (which is pure sulphur burned in air) was regularly added to German wines, with immensely valuable results in keeping them fresh and allowing a slower maturing process. It has been said that before the advent of sulphuring the grape variety scarcely mattered, since all wines rapidly oxidized and thereafter smelt and tasted similar. The Germans, whose wines have little alcohol to preserve them and can contain enough sugar to make them unstable, perhaps needed sulphur more than other winemakers. Yet it is very surprising that the French did not officially allow its use until the eighteenth century – since when it has been used routinely, and often (especially in sweet white wines) seriously overused.

The original German permission was for only 18.8 milligrams per litre (or "parts per million"): an extraordinarily modest amount by today's standards, when amounts up to 250 ppm are not uncommon. The figure is so improbably low that one suspects a mistake in the records, or in their interpretation. At high modern concentrations (not, I hasten to add, found in fine wines) the smell is easily detectable as a slight stinging in the nostrils or throat (or a smell like a spent match), although it rapidly dissipates on contact with air.

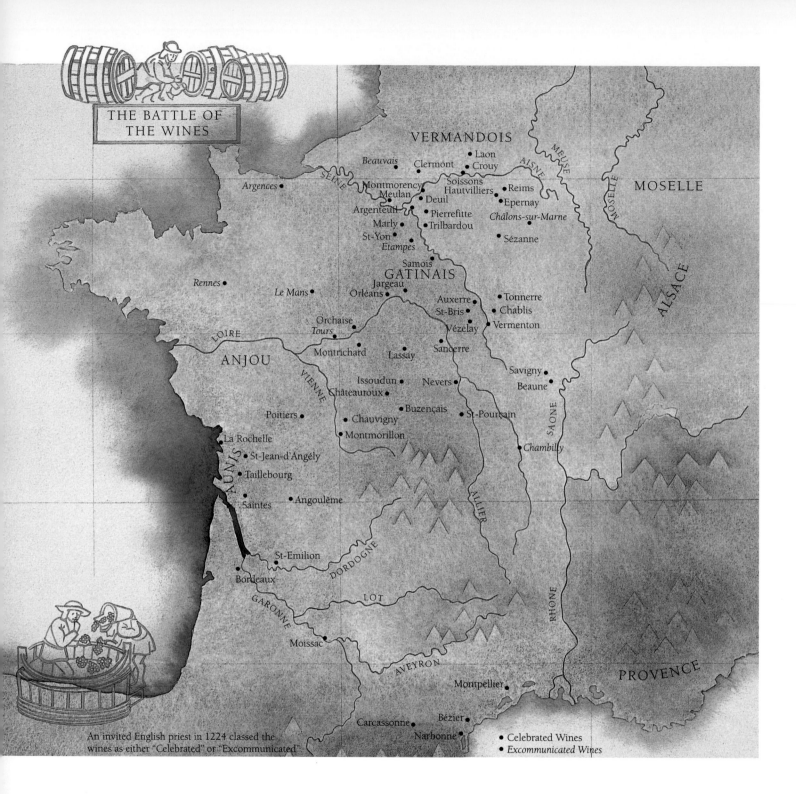

VERMANDOIS

MOSELLE

ALSACE

GATINAIS

ANJOU

AUNIS

PROVENCE

Beauvais · · Laon
Clermont · · Crouy
Argences · Montmorency Soissons
Meulan Hautvilliers · Reims
Argenteuil Deuil · Epernay
Pierrefitte Châlons-sur-Marne
Marly · Trilbardou
St-Yon · Sézanne
Etampes
Samois
Rennes · Jargeau
Le Mans · Orléans Auxerre · Tonnerre
St-Bris · Chablis
Orchaise Vézelay Vermenton
Tours
Montrichard Lassay Sancerre
Savigny
Issoudun Beaune
Châteauroux Nevers
Poitiers · Buzençais
Chauvigny · St-Pourçain
La Rochelle Montmorillon
St-Jean-d'Angély Chambilly
Taillebourg
Saintes · Angoulême
St-Emilion
Bordeaux
Moissac
Montpellier
Carcassonne · Bézier
Narbonne · Celebrated Wines
· Excommunicated Wines

SEINE · AISNE · MEUSE · MOSELLE · LOIRE · VIENNE · SAONE · ALLIER · RHONE · DORDOGNE · LOT · GARONNE · AVEYRON

An invited English priest in 1224 classed the
wines as either "Celebrated" or "Excommunicated".

water, for whoever tries out a wine on a quite empty or on a quite full stomach will find his mouth and his tasting spoiled."

The book suggests cures for wines with bad smells or poor colour, and wines that have gone flat. It gives directions for racking from one barrel to another, and lists almost as many flavoured wines as Pliny as remedies for every sort of ailment, including ox-tongue wine (for healing the insane and demented), and rosemary wine, whose "marvellous qualities" include correcting the appetite, exhilarating the soul, rectifying the sinews, making the face beautiful, and the hair grow. It also keeps you young, and cleans your teeth. Yet just as you begin to suspect that the whole book is medieval mumbo jumbo there

comes a passage of perfect good sense.

Italy produced, in the late thirteenth century, the lineal descendant of Cato and Columella in a citizen of Bologna called Pietro de Crescenzi, whose *Liber Ruralium Commodorum*, completed in 1303, established him as the great agricultural writer of the Middle Ages. Crescenzi had strong views on the right age for wine. It should be neither new (first year) nor old, which suggests that he found one- or two-year-old wine best. His *Liber* was printed and reprinted for centuries (the memorable woodcuts of a later edition are still regularly commandeered for wine lists). Yet what he was expressing was only his understanding of the classics he closely followed, applied as well as he knew how to contemporary Italian wine.

The majority of critics held that it was better simply to wait until fermentation was finally finished and then drink up. The more northern (and weaker) the wine, the more important to drink it quickly. Taillevent, the famous chef to Philippe VI of France, began to look for stronger, more southern wine from Easter onwards. Burgundy of high quality could be expected to be drinkable at two years. The only known reference from the Middle Ages to any wine being especially good at as old as four years was, remarkably enough, the exceptional Chablis vintage of 1396.

Most original and precious of all the wine critics of the Middle Ages was a particularly harsh one, the Catalan author of an encyclopedia of morals named Francesco Eiximenis. His book was called *Lo Crestia* (*The Christian*). He dedicated its third volume, called tersely *Terç*, to an immensely detailed discussion of the seven deadly sins. Under gluttony is found a complete cellar manual, treatise on drunkenness, book of table etiquette, observations on the benefits of moderate drinking, and conclusive evidence of the superiority of Catalan wines and customs. "Only the Catalan nation", he writes, "is an example to others in the way of tempered correct drinking." He is particularly censorious of the Italians, wine snobs, apparently, to a man. Every wine writer should listen to the Catalan moralist: "Those who dwell, think, and cogitate ceaselessly about wine, speaking, writing, following and moulding themselves to it, will suffer these consequences." I will spare you the list of consequences.

According to Eiximenis (who says, reasonably enough, that the French like white wines, Burgundians red, Germans aromatic, and the English beer), the English begin to drink before breakfast, and the Germans even get up in the night to drink. His own favourite wines are sweet and "Greek", from Cyprus, Crete, and Mallorca. He prefers these even to the Spanish wines he mentions (two Catalan and two Castilian) and one Italian, Tribià – which may be Trebbiano. Most of his choices, he says, are white, sweet, aromatic, and strong, which makes one commentator suspect that he hankered after Muscatel.

On the manner of drinking, Eiximenis is uniquely precise. "The drinker should hold the cup properly, with his hand, carrying it to his mouth and not the mouth to the cup… Some never raise their elbow from the table while they drink… and appear… like pigs." Not that he was in favour of fancy table manners. Those who "hold the cup curiously with three fingers" are equally censured. The Italians are commended for providing individual cups for everyone, while the rest of Europe was apparently happy to pass the glass around.

An ideal wine, for Eiximenis, should be pure, fresh, strong, odorous, fragrant, bubbly, and effervescent. It should not be weak, insipid, unctuous, smoky, iron-y, subject to change, bitter, green, or honey-like, or have the flavour of the cask. With the exception of the last remark, he could be describing the ideal of not a few Australian winemakers.

Adding water was a subject that no writer of the time could avoid. Every man, Eiximenis very reasonably says, should know his own capacity, and should, if necessary, dilute his wine accordingly. Catalan wine (he must have been thinking of the inky Priorato) is so dense and strong that it quickly numbs the mind unless water is added. But the French, he says, if they could, would even shake off the water the vine collects when it rains.

The fourteenth-century Queen Mary Psalter makes the process of medieval vinification very clear. Modern port-grape pickers, who carry the grapes in similar baskets on their backs, could vouch for the weight of a load of grapes.

CHAPTER 12

THE CLOISTER AND THE PRESS

The links between wine and worship, whether through the ancient gods, the Jewish and Christian rites, or the initiatives of monasteries and bishops, recur so often in our story that the storyteller must keep challenging himself: was it really religion that called the tune again?

With the white monks of Cîteaux there can be no mistake. For 500 years the Benedictine black monks had been the one great order, found their secure and splendid place in the scheme of things, and grown stout, and perhaps a little short of breath. Their greatest abbey of all, greater even than their mother-house of Monte Cassino, was Cluny, in the hills near Mâcon in the heart of Burgundy. Suddenly, in April 1112, in the same Saône valley, an extraordinary young zealot named Bernard de Fontaine raised the stakes. At the age of twenty-one he led a band of thirty well-connected youths into the tiny new monastery at Cîteaux, just north of Beaune, which had been founded only fourteen years before. The novice Bernard pushed them to the limits. His followers lived by the strict rule of St Benedict, but with the fervour of revolutionaries.

With these educated and fanatical volunteers, the new Order took wing. Bernard's rule of expansion was rigid. Once a monastery had sixty monks, twelve of them must set out and found another one. Within three years Bernard had founded La Ferté, Pontigny, Morimond, and the illustrious Clairvaux on the borders of Champagne, where he himself became abbot.

RIGHT The marriage feast of Duke Philippe the Good of Burgundy to Isabella of Portugal in 1430 saw the culmination of independent Burgundy.

While Bernard's influence was in full command the white monks were a formidable force. Their recruits were intelligent, even learned, young people, and like St Columbanus' Brothers of 500 years before they worked until they dropped. The life expectancy of a Cistercian in the eleventh century was twenty-eight years. Much of this work was labouring in their abbey's vineyards. They brought to wine-growing the zeal and perfectionism that Bernard demanded in everything.

On Christmas Day of the very year of their foundation the Cistercians had been given their first vineyard, by the Duke of Burgundy, in Meursault. The first Cistercians to buy vines were the monks of Pontigny, who bought land at Chablis from the Benedictines of Tours (the land they had been granted by the king in 867). One story has it that they were the first to plant Chardonnay vines in Chablis (where Chardonnay is still known by the name of Beaunois).

In 1110, Cîteaux was given some land on the Côte d'Or at Vougeot (the Vouge is the name of the stream that supplies the abbey), and set about acquiring more. The Abbot was not too proud to ask for it. The Abbey of St Germain des Prés in Paris was among the religious houses that gave at least some of their *friches*: the rough, uncultivated fringes of their land. The bargain was a sort of *complant*: St Germain was to receive one barrel of 228 litres a year. More land was soon given, bought, rented or exchanged, in Corton, Beaune, Chambolle, Volnay, Fixin, Pommard, Vosne, Nuits... eventually in almost every commune of the Côte d'Or south to Meursault. But it seems that Cîteaux at an early stage set its heart on the nearest slope

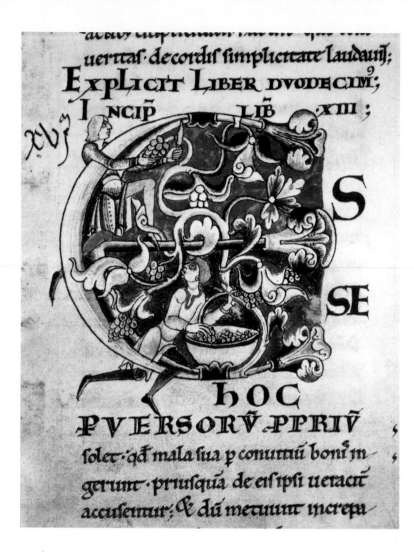

the most careful winemaking, and above all by tasting. Their greatest contribution to wine was the concept of the *cru*: a homogeneous section of the vineyard whose wines year after year proved to have an identity of quality and flavour.

They observed that differences of colour, body, vigour, and other qualities in the wine were remarkably constant from one patch to another. They made small batches of wine from separate plots, compared the scores of samples of tithe wines that came their way, and began to form a picture of the resources of the Côte: which parts made a more aromatic wine, which more robust and rough, which suffered most from frost, which needed picking early – a whole data bank of information. Then they started drawing lines on the map, even building walls around the fields that regularly produced a recognizable flavour.

They were certainly lucky with their choice of region. Not everywhere in France can you find an escarpment with the peculiarities of the Côte d'Or. Its long line of low hills, facing east across the plain of the Saône, is a complex geological fault where a chunk of the earth's surface has slipped vertically several hundred feet. The result is a layer cake of exposed rocks of different ages, all eroding and mingling to form varying cocktails of soil and subsoil according to the lie of the land.

A modern Burgundian winegrower has said she believes the Cistercians actually tasted the soil, they were so acute in their perception of its qualities and where it changed. The Professor of Geology at the University of Dijon describes them as geologists who used their noses and palates to find out the soil and subsoil structure of the region.

Their skill is measured by their success. They began the process by which the name of a *climat*, a particular named vineyard, designates a certain style and value of wine. Other monasteries and churches were not slow to follow their lead. The word *clos* means an enclosure of vines under one ownership. (For arable land the word is *couture*.) The Cistercian nuns of Notre Dame de Tart at Genlis established the Clos de Tart at Morey; the chapter of the cathedral at Langres (whose bishop had moved to Dijon for better wine) had a Clos du Chapitre, and named its Clos de Bèze after its Abbey of Bèze down near the Saône, the cathedral of Autun made a clos at Corton; the chapter of St Denis at Vergy owned the Clos St Denis; the parish church at Santenay owned the Clos St Jean; while the Abbey of Cluny, which owned most of Gevrey-Chambertin and had built a castle there to stress the point, is remembered by the Clos Prieur and the Combe aux Moines. It was this process that divided and subdivided the Côte d'Or into hundreds of separate *climats*.

There were many reasons why the Church was growing richer, of which good management was only one. A major contribution came from the Crusades. Eight generations of Crusaders set out to recapture the Holy Land between 1096 and 1290. Each parting knight had the same concern: to insure his soul against damnation if he should die in sin far from home. They bought indulgences, they endowed chantries, and they gave the monasteries parcels of land. No one knows for sure how much land Cîteaux owned in its heyday. Its fortunes began

An illuminated capital letter from a manuscript made at Cîteaux. The Cistercians were perfectionists in all they did; the modern map of the Côte d'Or owes much to them.

of the Côte, where the Vouge rises, and where the monks could quarry building stone. It was this unspectacular site, a gradual bench from the level of the plain to halfway up the hill, that they made the laboratory of their pursuit of perfection: the Clos de Vougeot. Eventually, in the 1330s, they enclosed it with the stone wall you see today.

In 1100 the vineyards of Burgundy were in stagnation. They were outside the fashionable ambit of northern France and had nothing but a local market. Nothing was really known of their potential. But the Cistercians saw the vineyards of the Côte as their God-given challenge. It has been said that in their devotion they raised agricultural labour to an art form. To supplement their saintly but limited workforce, they recruited and trained hundreds of *layots*, or lay brothers, who wore brown habits: the *layots* were another contribution to the quality of burgundy, since their painstaking methods spread by example throughout the region.

The Cistercians set about reviving a neglected vineyard, or making a new one, by careful study of the best plants, by experimenting with pruning, by taking cuttings and grafting, by to decline in the fifteenth century. When it was secularized by the French Revolution it was down to its last 25,000 acres.

More important, perhaps, for the fortunes of Burgundy, and of the Cistercians in particular, was the papal quarrel of 1308, when Pope Clement V, the former Archbishop of Bordeaux, set up a rival papacy to Rome in Avignon. The Avignon papacy lasted for seventy years – on the strength, some say, of the wines of Burgundy. Such pleasure did the Avignon popes take in the wine they knew as Beaune that in 1364 Urban V issued an edict, or "bull", forbidding the Abbot of Cîteaux to send any Beaune to Rome on pain of excommunication. They also found consolation in the vineyards they planted in the stone-strewn soil around the Pope's new château just north of Avignon: Châteauneuf-du-Pape.

P hilippe de Valois, nicknamed the Bold, son of John II, king of France, was appointed to the vacant dukedom of Burgundy in 1363. For four headstrong generations, the Valois dukes swaggered colourfully and lawlessly on France's eastern border. It was Burgundy's century of glory, and for a while it made the wine of Beaune the most famous in the world.

Philippe the Bold paid close attention to this important asset. Thanks to the popes, Beaune's reputation was already so high that in 1321 it had been used for the coronation of King Charles IV at Reims. But in 1348 and again in 1360 the Plague had terribly reduced the workforce, especially the Cistercians. Quantity was out of the question; Burgundy's policy had to be quality. (Having no river transport northwards, in any case, it always made sense for a barrel of burgundy to be worth more than the cost of carting it.) The Duke put his strategy brilliantly to the test at a conference at Bruges between England and the Pope. He offered his guests unlimited amounts of the finest white wines of France, but only a rare taste of the red wine of Beaune. His point was made – and after centuries of preference for white wines, red Beaune became the rage.

U p to this time very little mention was made of the grape variety. The best in the northeast of France, according to reports from as far apart as Burgundy and Paris, was the Fromenteau or Beurot, now known as the Pinot Gris. It has pale red berries which produce white, or faintly "grey", juice, and makes excellently "stiff", that is, full-bodied and even dense, but aromatic and delicate wine. But in Burgundy mention was sometimes also made of the Noirien, which presumably was so-called because its wine was black.

Philippe the Bold was well aware that the Noirien was essential for his red Beaune. In 1375 the name Pineau appears for the first time. The Duke himself has been credited with selecting a superior form of the Noirien and giving it this name (which may derive from pine cone, in reference to its small, tight bunches). It seems more likely that if anyone selected a new and superior grape it would be the Cistercians. In any case, the Duke took the first and most important step towards an eventual *appellation contrôlée* by specifying the Pineau and outlawing an upstart rival that had recently appeared, the Gamay.

P hilippe the Good brought the reputation of Burgundy to its height. He insisted on the independence of his dukedom from France, siding with the English (and cynically selling them his prisoner, Joan of Arc, for 10,000 gold crowns). His court could be said to have staged its own renaissance, independent of the Italian renaissance of the same time. His

Wine-presses in the vaulted hall of the Cistercian abbey of Kloster Eberbach in the Rheingau. This hall was the refectory of the lay brothers who worked the vines.

gamay: "a bad and disloyal plant"

The Gamay's appearance was mysterious and spectacular. It arrived from nowhere (or more likely as a mutation of the Noirien) in the village of Gamay, south of Beaune and one valley back in the hills from Meursault, some time in the 1360s. To the growers it seemed like a miracle; the Almighty was almost apologizing for the Black Death. The Gamay ripened two weeks earlier than the Pineau, was more hardy and reliable, and bore so much fruit that it needed a trellis to support it. One plant of Gamay gave up to four times as much wine as one of Pineau. What is more, the wine was darker and stronger.

What it did not have was the aristocratic elegance, the light texture, and the glorious fragrance that made the world – or rather the worldly – hanker after Beaune. The Duke was enraged. In July 1395 he declared the Gamay an outlaw, "a very bad and disloyal plant", whose wine was "foul" – even "harmful to human beings". All plants must be destroyed before the following Easter. In the same decree he denounced the use of manure as fertilizer, saying that it gave the wines a bad taste and smell. His subjects did not take kindly to this decree. It caused an immediate shortage of wine, a slump in sales, and the bankruptcies of leading citizens who had invested in this wonderful plant. Naturally, the growers stopped far short of pulling all the Gamay out.

The grandson of Philippe the Bold, Philippe the Good, was still issuing edicts against the Gamay sixty years later:

"It has been forbidden, time out of mind, to bring Gamay wines into Beaune. When new they flatter strangers with their sweetness [the inference being that they disappoint them later]. The Dukes of Burgundy are known as the lords of the best wines in Christendom. We will maintain our reputation."

Flemish court painters included two of the greatest artists of the Middle Ages, Jan van Eyck and Rogier van der Weyden. His Chancellor, Nicolas Rolin, founded the most famous of all hospitals, the Hospices de Beaune (where Van der Weyden's masterpiece, *The Last Judgment*, can still be seen). Philippe passed laws that brought Burgundy even closer to the concept of *appellation contrôlée* (although the term still lay five centuries in the future). He banned wine-growing from specified unsuitable land. Wine was the mainspring of the southern part of his Duchy; the *raison d'etre* of Dijon and Beaune.

The Cistercian order was Burgundy-born, and as far as wine is concerned Burgundy is where it made its greatest mark. It would be wrong, though, to give the impression that wine was the only temporal preoccupation of the Order. It rapidly grew to resemble a modern multinational corporation, transcending national boundaries. It had every sort of agricultural investment from forestry to fish-breeding. Perhaps most profitable of all were its famous flocks of sheep, whose wool, coming particularly from England and Champagne, supplied the clothiers of Flanders, and stimulated the great Champagne fairs.

Of the thousands of Cistercian monasteries that had vineyards, only one stands out in the history of wine with the same lustre as Cîteaux: the Abbey, or *Kloster*, of Eberbach, founded in the first great era of expansion in a typically tough Cistercian site: a forested valley in the hills of the Rheingau, on land granted by the Archbishop of Mainz. Its founders were Burgundians: twelve monks sent from Clairvaux in 1136 by Bernard. Their dedication and efficiency had the usual result:

within thirty years of its foundation it had a dozen satellites, and eventually became the centre of a monastic network with 200 establishments along the Rhine between Worms and Cologne. During the twelfth and thirteenth centuries, Kloster Eberbach was the largest wine-growing establishment in the world. It is the place to go both to see Cistercian splendour and to feel the pull of its asceticism. The great Abbey is completely hidden in a fold of the hills: a complex of cloisters, church, press-houses, dormitories, and cellars that seems ready for a chanting file of white-robed figures to move in and set it all in motion again.

In fact it is not quite out of motion. Today it is the ceremonial headquarters of the State Domain of the Rheingau, and although its rows of giant wooden presses, not unlike the presses of an imaginary medieval newspaper, no longer open their great jaws, its lofty Gothic cellar is still full of wine. And above it on the hill, facing south towards the Rhine, its walled Steinberg, the Clos de Vougeot of Germany, is still planted with the Riesling vines that the monks planted – eventually.

At first they probably planted vines from Burgundy: Fromenteau and Noirien, perhaps. The Rheingau was only just finding itself as a wine region. The Burgundians may well have been surprised at how good their homegrown wine rapidly became. One can imagine them swapping notes with their Burgundian brothers, and soon discovering that nothing they could do in the Rheingau could make really satisfactory red wine.

Were it just for Mass and mealtimes, they might have settled for second-best, but Cistercians were entrepreneurs from tonsure to toe. Nothing could give them a cash income so quickly as good wine. They tried white grapes, tried the steepest slopes, and found that the Rheingau was made for white wine.

Today the region is synonymous with the Riesling. Nobody is certain where it came from or whether it was the Cistercians who found it. The first documentary evidence we have is not until 1435, and then from Rüsselsheim on the Main, east of the Rheingau. There is, though, a direct link with Kloster Eberbach. Rüsselsheim was the castle of the Counts Katzenelnbogen, and their family vault, an affair of typically chivalric panache, stands at the crossing of the Eberbach Abbey church.

Riesling or not, Eberbach wine set the standards for the region. From its own little harbour, or *hof*, at Reichartshausen, the nearest point on the Rhine, the Abbey's three boats, the *Bock*, the *Sau* and the *Pinth*, relayed countless barrels to the Abbey's own gate and cellars in Cologne – passing all the customs posts with a duty-free smirk. As a measure of the importance of this trade to the Abbey, by 1500 its vines only covered 2.8 per cent of its huge domain of 23,000 acres, yet contributed three-quarters of its entire agricultural income.

Community relations, though, seem to have been poor. In 1525 the peasantry stormed the cellars, drank the wine (or a good deal of it), and plundered the Abbey. But abbeys were accustomed to occasional unpleasantness. What mattered was that, by their readiness to experiment, their reinvestment in the land, and their ability to see things on a long time-scale, they slowly but surely moved quality up notch by notch.

CHAPTER 13

ENGLAND AND GASCONY: THE BIRTH OF CLARET

Every wine lover has an inkling of the fact that Bordeaux and England were almost literally married in the Middle Ages: an oil strike for Bordeaux, and the start of the saga of claret that continues to this day. What had happened between its Roman budding and its medieval blossoming?

We left Bordeaux suffering the same sort of barbarian incursions as Trier, with the gentle phantom of Ausonius brooding over the dissolution of both these thriving Roman towns. In Bordeaux the unwelcome intruders were Goths, Vandals, and Visigoths – and in short order: Goths arrived in 406, Vandals passed through in 408, and Visigoths came to stay in 414. To make matters worse, Bordeaux was on what the Romans had dubbed "the Saxon shore", by which they meant that no amount of patrolling could prevent the Saxon longboats from landing or their crews from helping themselves.

Gothic as they were, though, the new arrivals were not unimpressed by the old Gallo-Roman establishment. Not every move they made was a violent one. Having put the town to the torch as a matter of form, they sought out its leading families, intermarried with them, and were happy to take over their rational working of land and government. The Roman Emperor Honorius was content to acknowledge local Visigothic rulers. The old university professors of rhetoric and grammar were even given high rank at their court.

This extension of the Roman system was ended by the arrival of the Franks at the close of the fifth century. In the seventh century another cut-throat tribe arrived, the Gascons, who came north from the mountainous headwaters of the river Ebro in Spain (just as, some historians believe, the Biturica grape had done six centuries before). After them came the Saracens, also from Spain. Then it was the turn of the Carolingian Franks; and after them, the Vikings. The city withstood three waves of Viking attack before it fell.

There is some evidence that wine-growing survived these centuries of changing management. The principal customers were Ireland and the western Celtic fringes of Britain. Eastern England imported wine by the shortest route, from northern France and the Rhine. But after 870 there is a silence of nearly 250 years.

The court of Duke Guillaume X of Aquitaine in 1120 was famous for its elegance, its troubadours and chivalry – and for the Duke's beautiful daughter. But its economic motor was in the North, and this is where the Duke concentrated his ambitions. His western shore, including the islands of Ré and Oléron, was one of the principal European sources of salt, evaporated from the sea in lagoons – and this in an age when salt was almost the only preservative. He promoted, with enormous success, the new port of La Rochelle, which was described as "*vicum mirabile de novo constructum*" ("a wonderful new town"). It attracted shipping from all the northern ports of Europe, and to add to its attractions its ambitious immigrant citizens planted vineyards. The area (now the Charente) is sunny and relatively frost-free. By extensive use of the crop-sharing system of *complant* they made it a sea of vines, with the deliberate intention of undercutting the *vins de France* and the Rhine wines that everyone drank in northern Europe. They created a sort of medieval Muscadet (although it would have tasted closer to modern Gros Plant) – and no one went on south to pay more in Bordeaux.

In 1130 Duke Guillaume died in Spain. As soon as he heard the news, King Louis sent his son and heir (who was only sixteen) to Bordeaux with a train of 500 knights to collect as his bride Guillaume's only daughter and her enormous dowry: Aquitaine and Poitou, the southwestern third of France. They were married in the Cathedral of St-André in Bordeaux in July 1137.

Louis the Dauphin adored his young wife. He was also devoutly pious. But Aliénor was a girl of strong character, and not at that stage either particularly pious or in love. In Paris in 1151 the court received a visit of homage from the Duke of Normandy and his eighteen-year-old son, Henry Plantagenet. Aliénor, aged twenty-nine, compared the fiery youth with her religious husband, and decided on a change. Astonishingly, after fifteen years of marriage (and two daughters) the King and Queen of France returned to Bordeaux in 1152 to be ceremonially de-wed – on the grounds that they were cousins

who should never have been married in the first place.

Eight weeks later Aliénor married Henry Plantagenet, Duke of Normandy and Count of Anjou. Two years after that, in 1154, he became King Henry II and she Queen Eleanor of England. The famous link was made.

T he fortunes of Bordeaux did not change suddenly. Eleanor followed her father in favouring La Rochelle. Her new husband was an Angevin, a man of Anjou on the Loire, and his inclinations were also towards the northern part of their duchy. It was not until the 1190s, with their second son, Richard, now ruling both England and Aquitaine, that Bordeaux began to come into the picture. With its cathedral and ducal castle, it became King Richard's base in France, although from 1190 to 1192 he was away on the third Crusade, earning himself the surname of *Coeur de Lion*. But La Rochelle still had favoured treatment. In 1190 the Queen-Duchess built it a new port, whose monumental walls still stand. New deep-draught freighters, known as cogs, were coming into use in northern ports, and needed better anchorages and deeper wharves. Bordeaux began to complain bitterly that the royal favour continued to rain on the makers of downmarket white wines around La Rochelle, while a great log-jam of old feudal

This fifteenth century illustration of the King of France riding into the harbour at Sluys in Flanders shows the rounded wine ships, or cogs, used in the wine fleets of the Middle Ages. The largest cogs could carry over 200 barrels.

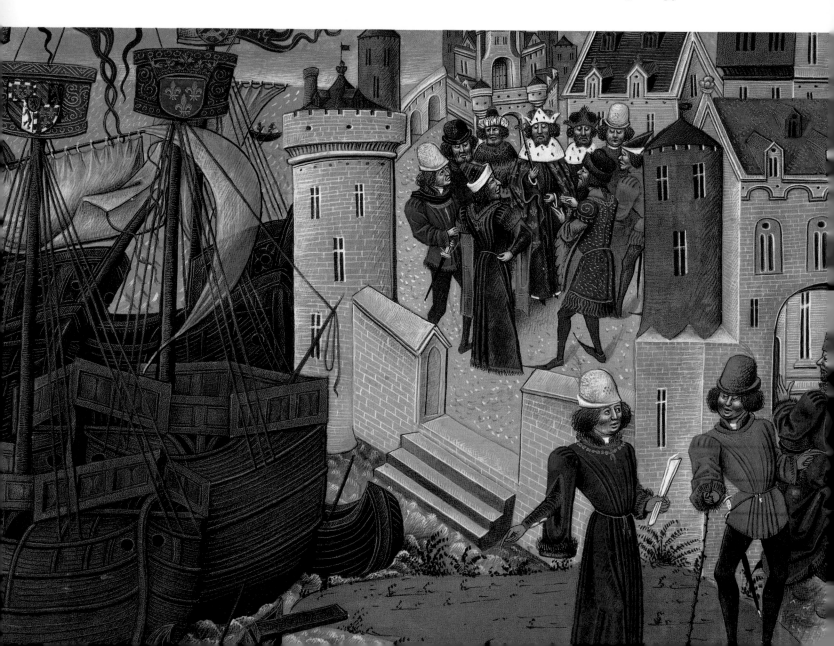

dues and customs prevented its venerable wine industry from competing at all.

Royal favour was all-important. The wine the king drank today, everybody would drink tomorrow. It was Richard Coeur de Lion who first made Bordeaux his household wine, but since he lived almost constantly in France he can hardly be said to have popularized it in England.

When he was killed, besieging a Limousin castle, his mother manoeuvred her last surviving son onto the throne. John Lackland, therefore, was the King of England who first gave Bordeaux merchants a fair chance at the English market. Gascon merchants were at last to start coming to England.

At this point the 82-year-old dowager, the grand old ex-Queen of both France and England (Shakespeare rather sourly called her a "canker'd grandam"), died. Her last matriarchal act had been to cross the Pyrenees in winter to inspect her Spanish granddaughters.

Jealous manoeuvring between Bordeaux and La Rochelle for the King's favour continued for years. What finally decided it against La Rochelle was not the acidity of its wine, but the disloyalty of its citizens. In 1224 the King of France made a determined effort to chase the English out of Poitou and Guyenne. La Rochelle capitulated to the King of France; Bordeaux stayed loyal to England. From this date Bordeaux took every advantage of the unique relationship it had gained with England. Its citizens pressed for, and in 1235 were given, the right to elect their own mayor in perpetuity (a right which Bristol had only acquired in 1217, and even London itself only in 1191).

The quantity of wine England bought, and the speed with which Bordeaux was suddenly ready to supply it, suggests that huge vineyards had already been planted in the region in readiness. In fact it was not so. Bordeaux had started out in Roman times as an *emporium*, and when its star rose in the thirteenth century was again more of a port than a producer. The area immediately around the city, especially the district of Graves to the south, was the principal vineyard of Bordeaux. There were also vineyards along the steep banks of the Garonne opposite the port (today the Premières Côtes), in Entre-Deux-Mers, between the Garonne and the Dordogne, and others along the estuary at Blaye. The Médoc had hardly any vines. The grand total was not very impressive.

It was the Aquitaine basin as a whole, reaching right up into the "high country" around, that supplied the bulk of England's needs. Most Gascon wine came down the Garonne from Gaillac (high up in the Tarn), Moissac, and Agen, and, closer to home, St-Macaire, Langon, and Barsac, or down the Dordogne from Bergerac and, although less important at first, St-Emilion. Cahors, high up the river Lot, was another provider of what were called generically High Country wines, to distinguish them from the produce of Bordeaux itself. In all probability they were often better, stronger wines than most of what Bordeaux made locally, and the Bordelais were correspondingly jealous of them and anxious to sell their own production first.

the police des vins The privileges of Bordeaux, impudently established during English rule, were still effectively in place in the eighteenth century. Louis XVI's reforming Minister of Finance, Turgot, summed them up in a document that tells the whole unworthy story:

"Languedoc, Périgord, the county of Agen and Quercy; all the provinces linked by the multitude of rivers that join beneath the walls of Bordeaux, not only cannot sell their wines to the citizens of Bordeaux who may want to buy them; these provinces cannot even freely use the river highway that nature has provided to link them with foreign trade.

"The wines of Languedoc are not allowed down the Garonne before St Martin's day; they cannot be sold [in Bordeaux] before December 1. And those of Périgord, Agen, Quercy and all the upper Garonne are barred from Bordeaux until Christmas.

"By this means the growers of the wines of the High Country are kept out of the market at its busiest season, when foreign merchants are obliged to hurry their purchases to get the wine home before ice closes their harbours. Nor are they allowed to store their wines in Bordeaux to sell them next season: no wine from outside the Bordeaux region can remain in the town after September 8. The owner who cannot sell his wine before that date has the choice of distilling it or taking it back upriver with him. By this arrangement, the wines of Bordeaux have no competition whatsoever between the vintage and December 1.

"Even in the low season between December and the following September the trade in High Country wines groans under multiple yokes. They cannot be sold immediately on arrival; they cannot be transshipped directly from one vessel to another, either at Bordeaux or any other port on the Garonne. They have to be unloaded and taken ashore, and that not even in Bordeaux itself, but in the suburbs, in specified parts of the suburbs, and in special cellars separate from the wines of Bordeaux.

"Wines from outside the region have to be kept in barrels of a certain design, whose volume is deliberately inconvenient for foreign trade. These barrels, banded with fewer and more feeble hoops, are less durable and less able to withstand long voyages than the exclusive barriques of Bordeaux. The conduct of this set of rules, most artfully devised to guarantee to the bourgeois of Bordeaux, the owners of the local vineyards, the highest prices for their own wines, and to disadvantage the growers of all the other southern provinces... is called, in this town, the *police des vins*... and it has the full authority of the Parlement."

It is hard to exaggerate how important timing was. The wine Bordeaux sold, although certainly a degree fruitier, possibly a degree stronger, and probably a more pleasant and satisfying drink than the northern whites it began to supersede, was no less perishable. It was expected to turn sour within a year at most, and tasted best within a few months of the vintage. Year-old wine was halved in price as soon as the ships with the new vintage dropped anchor. In many cases it was simply thrown away.

All the politicking that went on over the privileges of this town or that turned on this simple fact. And Bordeaux, an ideal port lying between most of its rivals and the sea, was beautifully situated to send its wines to market before allowing its rivals to offer theirs. Gradually, during the course of the thirteenth and fourteenth centuries, the city arranged for itself a code of unfair practices guaranteeing its precedence over its neighbours and rivals – a system known as the *police des vins*. This system was tolerated by the kings of England chiefly because it simplified

the vine in england The Domesday Book, William the Conqueror's acre-by-acre survey of his new English realm, gives us the first good information about the growing of wine (or at least grapes) in England. It mentions a total of forty-two vineyards, including several in London and Westminster, the greatest concentration in Essex, east of London, and the northernmost at Ely, which the Normans called "L'Isle des Vignes", much as their forebear Leif Ericsson a century before had called America "Vinland". Ely was an isolated hill in fen country, crowned with a cathedral already venerable before the Normans arrived; it is reasonable to believe that the Anglo-Saxons had been growing vines there for – who knows how long? Since the Romans?

England's vineyards were never extensive, but were an accepted accompaniment to any castle or monastery in the south. The royal Windsor Castle made its own wine in 1155. The Cistercian Abbey of Beaulieu near Southampton on the south coast naturally had a vineyard. It seems to have been the Archbishop of Canterbury who had most, but probably none was commercial, and no tasting notes have survived.

The acquisition of Bordeaux did not lead to any marked decline in English wine-growing – although it may have discouraged its extension. Nonetheless it spread through the Middle Ages, so that in 1509 there were 139 vineyards, of which eleven were owned by the Crown (on the head of Henry VIII), sixty-seven by noblemen, and fifty-two by the Church. "Theologicum" was the name given to the best (monastic) wine – whether generally or specifically is not known. At the dissolution of the monasteries in the 1530s their vineyards were appropriated by the local nobility. The antiquarian and headmaster of Westminster School, William Camden, travelled throughout the country to compile his survey *Britannia*, which appeared in 1586. His conclusion was that wine-growing had declined not owing to the climate or the exhaustion of the soil, but to the sloth of the inhabitants.

their tax collecting. When Bordeaux eventually became French again it was tolerated to prevent seditious backsliding by those who thought they had had a better deal under the English.

Not that Bordeaux had suddenly become England's only supplier. Anjou wines were still in demand, being relatively ripe and sweet, and Rhine wines were perennially popular. The wines of Burgundy, which we have seen beginning to flourish at the very same time as those of Bordeaux, scarcely reached England. But the *vins de France* that used to flow in an acidic stream from Rouen were quite outclassed by the new Bordeaux. Moreover, from Bordeaux to Bristol, London, Southampton, Hull, Berwick or any of a hundred little ports around the coast was relatively convenient door-to-door transport. By the middle of the thirteenth century three-quarters of England's royal supplies were coming from Bordeaux – and by "royal" we should understand not just the King's table, but his households, the civil service, his gifts and favours, and indeed the supplies for his entire army. In 1282, Edward I ordered 600 *tonneaux* for his campaign against the Welsh.

Both sides took advantage of the new situation. Hitherto useless royal lands in Bordeaux suddenly became valuable. King John and his successors, Henry III and Edward I, all sold, leased, or granted land for the planting and building boom that swept the region. Such newly prosperous towns as Bergerac were soon petitioning for charters – which of course had their price. King Henry III built his own walled town to control the traffic on the river Dordogne: Libourne, founded in 1270 by the King's Seneschal, his chief officer in the region, Sir Roger de Leyburn. Libourne effectively took away the trade from neighbouring Fronsac and St-Emilion's little port of Pierrefitte. St-Emilion in any case grew more grain than grapes; it was a busy little town with many mouths to feed, a sharp contrast to the wild hillside where 400 years before St Emilianus had found his lonely hermitage.

The figures for the 1308 vintage show that Libourne exported nearly 11,000 *tonneaux* of wine, or 97,000 hectolitres. Most of it would have been grown in Bergerac. But this was only one-sixth of the massive volume that all Gascony exported that year – and the other five-sixths went through Bordeaux. It helps us to realize the size of the Bordeaux–England wine trade to read that the year before, 1307, King Edward II had ordered, for his wedding celebrations in London, 1,000 *tonneaux* of claret, which the late Edmund Penning-Rowsell gleefully calculated to be 1,152,000 bottles. The Florentine bank that financed this huge purchase was the house of Frescobaldi, which we shall meet again.

In the first half of the fourteenth century we have complete records for seven years' exports. The annual average was 83,000 *tonneaux*, or 700,000 hectolitres, of which it has been calculated that the British Isles took almost half… to eke out among its population of perhaps five million. At a conservative estimate that was six bottles of claret for each man, woman, and child. To make this much wine, considering the much smaller yields of medieval vineyards than today's, it is estimated that the whole of Gascony must have had approximately its current modern total vineyard area, or about 250,000 acres.

Today the same surface produces about three times as much wine, but only after World War II was this export figure reached again. In 1900, which you might well think was a good claret-drinking year, the total was about 12,000 hectolitres less than that of 1308.

It was hardly likely that in the long run France would allow the English king to rule a substantial part of its land. Already the French had recovered Poitou. The Hundred Years War went on in fits and starts, mercilessly pursued by the Black Prince, interrupted by the Black Death: so black a chapter, indeed, that calmly to chronicle the commerce of one provincial city seems almost callous.

The flow of claret was never so great again as in the years before the war. For much of the time the High Country was in French hands. The English wine fleet convened twice a year, in October and February, to fetch the latest vintage. The east coast ships met first at Orwell, then sailing to the Isle of Wight met the Portsmouth fleet. With a favourable wind they could be in Bordeaux within a week. Waiting for the wind, though, could be a matter of months – in which case the wine must certainly have suffered. Often they had to shelter or revictual, usually at Port St-Mathieu on the western tip of Brittany where Brest stands today. They were provided with expensive passports by the Duke of Brittany. There were plenty of Breton pirates, however, who could not read.

Although the total quantity of Bordeaux wine fell, England needed a higher and higher proportion of it, as war with France in the North cut off the supplies of alternatives. In the 1390s, when a lengthy truce led to easier conditions, England still took eighty per cent of Bordeaux's exports.

Some of the best wine available came from the estates of the archbishop, who grew a little red wine at Pessac in the Graves, and much more at Quinsac, ten miles up the Garonne. Bertrand de Goth, who later, as Pope Clement V, moved the papacy to Avignon, clearly saw his chance to capitalize on the boom. His Pessac estate, now known as Château Pape Clément, was planted in 1300, when exports were at their height. That year more than 900 ships cleared Bordeaux for England. It was only a small property, but it stands within a mile of the château where the next great Bordeaux boom was to be born 350 years later.

How good even archiepiscopal wine could have been it is not easy to judge, although detailed records survive of how his estates were run. Bordeaux winemaking was no different in essence from the winemaking we have seen in Chapter Eleven, except that in Bordeaux presses were decidedly uncommon. It was a region of small producers, without lordly domains or great monasteries which would own a wine-press.

Many explanations have been put forward as to why the French word *clairet*, anglicized as claret, is applied uniquely to Bordeaux. One, of course, is that during the 300 years of its Bordeaux dominion England learned it too well ever to forget it. Strangely, though, its use is not recorded in English, as opposed to French, before the sixteenth century. But from the outset it seems almost certain that very light red or rosé was the best wine (apart from white) that Bordeaux had to offer – or at least that it suited English taste, and the demands of the voyage to England.

Claret was made as a *vin rosé* is made today – or, more precisely, like what the French call a *vin d'une nuit*: one that spends a single night in the vat. The grapes were trodden in the usual way, and the wine fermented at first in the vat on the skins – many of which in any case would have been white – but for no longer than twenty-four hours. Then the pale liquid was run off into barrels to ferment as clear juice. The wine left with the skins in the vat for longer became redder; it was known as *vin vermeilh*, or *pinpin*. It represented perhaps fifteen per cent of the crop, but like press-wine was considered too dark and harsh on its own. A little might be used to add some more colour or edge to claret; the rest was sold off for what little it was worth – when, of course, they made *piquette* with the skins alone.

It is tempting to compare claret – pale, light, highly swallowable, soft enough but with a refreshing "cut" – to modern Beaujolais nouveau. This must have been the general effect, although the flavour of Beaujolais is the pungent one of Gamay. Claret was presumably made with the ancestors of the Cabernets and the Merlot.

The end of the Hundred Years War came in 1453. In 1438 the French entered Gascony and devastated the vineyards. A truce followed: on second thoughts, this was part of France. The object was to throw the English out, not to destroy such a valuable asset. The French set about wooing the Gascons. England seemed neither able nor desperately anxious to keep its ancient possession. At home, civil war was breaking out between Yorkists and Lancastrians.

But after 300 years the English made one last effort. The following autumn the venerable John Talbot, Earl of Shrewsbury, led a fleet up the Gironde and landed in the Médoc. The people of Bordeaux opened their gates to welcome "*le Roi Talbot*". He retook Libourne and Castillon with a mixed English and Gascon force and in July 1453 set out to meet the French, commanded this time by the King himself, just outside what is now called Castillon la Bataille. It is a tale still often told in Bordeaux that the aged Talbot, having once been released as a prisoner on the promise not to bear arms against France again, led the charge at Castillon (in his eightieth year, say the true believers) without sword or lance. He and his son were both killed, and the French went on to accept the surrenders of Libourne and, in October, Bordeaux.

the mystery of vintners To be a wine merchant in Bordeaux in the Middle Ages had distinct advantages. Not only did the system of privileges known as the *police des vins* work in your favour, but wealthy and dependable Gascon merchants could also become Freemen of the City of London, and take advantage of reduced duties there too. To be a Freeman of both London and Bordeaux was a licence to print money – which is more or less what the grandest Gascons did, lending to the king in competition with the great Italian bankers.

Gascon merchants were, of course, subjects of the English king, who was ready to do almost anything to secure their loyalty against the French. Edward I was believed by Londoners to be especially partial to the Gascons. Much to the City's dismay, in 1302 he passed ordinances that exempted Gascons from the usual petty (but very expensive) regulations that applied to overseas merchants. He had good reason. Besides the throne, he had inherited his father's quite remarkable wine bill. This was his way of paying it.

The Gascons in London were even granted the right to establish their own association, the Merchant Wine Tonners of Gascoyne, later known as the Mystery of Vintners and in 1345 incorporated by royal charter as the Vintners' Company – one of the richest and most splendid livery companies throughout the Middle Ages. It still survives near its original site in the City, at Three Cranes Wharf by the Thames. A tablet on the wall of the present Hall records the "Feast of Five Kings" at Vintners Hall in 1363, when Sir Henry Picard gave a banquet to Hugh IV of Cyprus, Edward III, John the Genial of France (who was a prisoner in England), the King of Scotland, and King Waldemar of Denmark.

The French *tonneau* is the same as the English "tun" or "ton", a measure of wine described as "XII score and XII gallons"(i.e. 252 old – or American – gallons, or 900 litres). This size of cask is unmanageable, so it is broken down for shipping into two "pipes" or four "hogsheads" (now usually called "barriques") of 225 litres each. In modern terms, a *tonneau* equals 100 cases of a dozen (75cl) bottles of wine, a barrique twenty-five such cases.

In the Middle Ages all ships were gauged as to how many tons (of wine) they could carry. It was the practice in ancient times and is still in use today – although for bulk carrying a ship's "ton" is 100 cubic feet. A "metric tonne" is 1,000 kilograms weight. A hectolitre is 100 litres.

The harbour at La Rochelle. Rivalry and jealousy between La Rochelle and Bordeaux continued throughout the early Middle Ages; Bordeaux was victorious because it happened to be loyal to the winning side at a crucial moment.

Of course, what sounds like a great finale is nothing of the sort. Every year produces wine, and growers and merchants must go on living. The French gave the English six months to ship the 1453 vintage. They gave Gascons free leave to take themselves and their goods abroad. They grudgingly and selectively granted safe-conducts to English vessels coming for wine, while they invited Scots, Dutch, Flemish, Hanseatic, and Spanish to come and buy freely, hoping to widen the narrow scope of the trade. (The Scots needed no encouraging; claret was already an important part of the victuals of that kingdom.) For a single year, they allowed the High Country wines free movement, but soon realized that if Bordeaux was to be kept loyal to France, the old oppressive restrictions had to stay.

Twenty years later, with finances pinching, the port was thrown open again to English and Gascon shipping. There were nervous moments in Bordeaux when as many as 7,000 Englishmen congregated there in the shipping season. But trade did not recover its old impetus. The vineyard area contracted, and shipments to England were down to 10,000 tons a year from the thirteenth-century peak of more than 80,000. Part of the reason was jealousy of continued Gascon privileges in England which the English shippers did not like. France was also to become embroiled in its bitter wars of religion, with Bordeaux a stronghold of Protestant dissent. Another, and the most important, reason was the growing number of attractive alternative wines being offered by friendlier countries.

CHAPTER 14

MERCHANTS OF VENICE

It is a fine November day in the Bay of Biscay – too fine for the wine fleet, almost 200 ships spread out from horizon to horizon. Their great square sails, gaudy with dragons and crosses and leopards, are hanging flaccid and useless. The master of the *Margery Cross*, a heavy cog or round ship from the port of Boston on the east coast of England, is looking out from the high sterncastle for any flurry on the oily swell that could mean a breeze.

He has 160 tuns of claret before and aft of his great chunky mast. It has taken two weeks from Bordeaux to get this far; the weather is unseasonably warm; at this rate he could still be at sea come Christmas, the market past and the wine turning sour. A dozen of the crew are throwing leather buckets over the sides and hauling them up to the yard to soak the sail, with the only effect that the *Margery Cross* wallows slightly more ponderously as each unhelpful roller lifts her port quarter and trundles on towards England. There is nothing else for his forty mariners to do – and not much for them to eat either. He has his passport for Port St-Mathieu where there should be bread and meat, but until then the rations are bread and claret – and not very much bread.

His eyes follow a gull to the horizon astern. What is that? Three, no four, strange broad ships, very low in the water, their masts bare of any sail, but definitely coming clearer into view, closing the gap at an impossible speed. Once or twice a flash like a mirror in the sun breaks from the water low beside one of them. Oars! He has heard of the galleys that keep an uncanny, an impossible schedule between Genoa or Venice and Southampton. The merchants of Southampton had craftily persuaded the king to give them a monopoly on importing Mediterranean wines, which did not endear them to the wine merchants of other English ports.

Now the crew have seen them too, and are crowding to the stern with their foul language and their fouler breath. The Winchelsea cog groaning as she rolls three chains off to starboard has suddenly come alive, with half her crew in the rigging, shaking their fists at the galleys, now clear to see, four in formation, with what seems like a thousand oars beating the water; four brown and gleaming birds flapping their wings. Within the morning they have passed through the becalmed fleet, all agog at their mechanical propulsion. On each side were three banks of oars, twenty blades to each. The great lateen sails furled on the booms of the two masts pulled hard for most of the journey, but when the wind died the oarsmen, each one a small private trader with his bag beneath his bench, bent their backs to beat their famous schedule. The record passage had been made by a Venetian galley, from Otranto on the heel of Italy to Southampton on the Solent, in thirty-one days.

As the galleys creamed through the fleet the archers on their decks raised a cheer, then lifted their crossbows and sent a broadside of bolts high through the air, puncturing the impotent heraldry of the sails, and here and there thudding with a shock into a mast. The arrogance of the Venetians was not to be borne.

Genoa, then Venice, had become the powers of the Mediterranean. They were the link between the riches of the East and the mere money of northern Europe. What had woken the Italian cities from their long slumber had been the

Crusades. The monarchs of the North and all their retinues had needed transport, and victualling, and to borrow huge sums of money. The first coastal city to awake was Amalfi, across the Sorrento peninsula from the Bay of Naples, which Greeks and Romans had so profitably occupied before the barbarians came. Amalfi was the outpost of Byzantium in a Saracen lake – the whole Mediterranean – until the lake almost swallowed it in a tidal wave.

Pisa in Tuscany was active too, and soon joined by Genoa in expeditions that were as much like piracy on the Saracen shipping as legitimate trading expeditions. They were beginning to perform the role of trading links, buying silks and spices in the East, and carrying eastwards such mundane things as grain, timber, salt, and of course woollen cloth in return. There was an extraordinary emphasis on wool. So important was it to the growing wealth of Florence (and hence of Pisa) that the house of Frescobaldi, operating as papal tax-gatherers in England to finance the Crusades, were eager to be paid in bales of wool rather than cash.

Among these adolescent rival cities, Venice had several great natural advantages. It was (like Amalfi) historically part of the Eastern Roman Empire of Constantinople. It had in the Adriatic what almost amounted to a private sea. Strongholds on strategic islands were effective against pirates. Ragusa (now Dubrovnik) was such a rich ally that to this day the term "argosy", meaning a ship of Ragusa, is a synonym for bounty. Above all Venice was on the highway to the Holy Land, and uniquely able to act as travel agent, and as banker, and to provide any other service that Crusaders or pilgrims needed.

High on the list of the travellers' needs was wine. They found it all along whichever route they took – for they were travelling through the lands of the Romans and the Greeks: rediscovering, in fact, the qualities of sweetness and strength that the ancients had so much appreciated, but that were now unknown in the North.

Falernian and the other *grands crus* of Rome were long since dead, but Greece and its islands, the Empire of Byzantium, had never entirely abandoned their traditions. The eastern Mediterranean was largely under Muslim control, but this had not stopped the making and selling of wine by Christians and Jews. The whole of the Levant – Syria, Lebanon, Palestine – had wines to sell. Where Byblos had been a byword for excellence in ancient times, Tyre was now the name to conjure with. After the success of the first Crusade in establishing Christian kingdoms from Egypt to Armenia, the monastic orders moved in and planted vineyards with the same single-mindedness as they were doing so at the same time in Burgundy and Germany. In the tenth century Byzantium had won back the islands of Cyprus and Candia, as Crete was then called, from the Saracens; both were excellent sources of wine, whose importance grew and grew throughout the Middle Ages.

At first there was not a great deal of discrimination between wines from these different sources. The term most generally used was malmsey or Malvasia. The word is a corruption of Monemvasia, a Byzantine fortress town on the southwestern corner of the Peloponnese. It may have been a small producer;

LEFT The Aegean island of Santorini had a thriving wine industry under Turkish rule and later became the principal supplier of Mass wine to Turkey's arch-enemy, Russia.

it was certainly a large supplier, giving its name to wines grown on the mainland, but mainly on Candia, and no doubt on such islands as Santorini in between.

Monemvasia also gave its name to the grape variety that produced them. The Malvasia, with many synonyms (in French it is Malvoisie) is alone with the Muscat (and all its synonyms) in having maintained its name and identity clearly throughout the centuries. With its big leaves and its slightly blushing fruit, giving dense and impressive wine, it is a character that stands out – and indeed one of the most venerable varieties we have. What is odd is that it should have picked up the name of a medieval port that made it famous, rather than carrying some reminder of its even remoter past.

In the Ionian Sea, Corfu, Zante, and Cephalonia, all islands under Venetian dominance, made sweet wines of lesser quality that were sold as Romania, which was anglicized as Romaney or Rumney. Most highly prized were the Muscadels (as well as the malmseys) of Candia. Muscadel, with its fresh grape flavour, was so sought after that plantations of Muscat vines were made in Roussillon in the south of France, in Spain, and in Italy. Tuscany's lightweight version of Moscadello remained in favour throughout the Renaissance and greatly took the fancy of those followers in the path of the Crusades, English milords on the Grand Tour.

Tuscany also specialized in Vernaccia, which has been justly described as Italy's native Malvasia, its wine having the same soft texture and potential strength, although it was generally made less sweet. To the English, Vernaccia was known as Vernage. French historians have confused it with Garnache (alias Garnacha or Grenache), one of Spain's most important varieties. The name of Garnache seems to have fallen out of use in 1500, at the same time as Alicante and Málaga, two ports on the Spanish coast not far from Granada, first appeared as the names of wines. (The Grenache grape is also called the Alicante, which seems to make that connection pretty clear.)

What all these wines had in common was more important than what distinguished them. In the Mediterranean sun their grapes reached a very high sugar content, which was encouraged by late harvesting, and often boosted by half-drying the bunches before they were trodden. Winemakers (if they could read) used the old textbooks; no doubt they practised both twisting the stems and piling the grapes on mats in the sun. The Cypriot method was described by Estienne de Lusignan in 1572. The grapes, he said, were ripe at the end of July, but were not picked until September: "When they have been gathered, they are put on the roofs of the houses, which are all flat, and remain there in the sun the space of three days, so that its ardour may consume whatever water may remain in them." The wine, in other words, was made from raisins.

Natural fermentation, especially if it was kept under control by burying the wine jars in the classical manner, could achieve as much as seventeen degrees of alcohol from such sugar-rich must

Venice in the fifteenth and sixteenth centuries was the first great Mediterranean wine emporium since the Ostia of the Ancient Romans. Apart from importing malmseys and other sweet wines from Candia, Greece and Cyprus for re-export, its merchants filled their waterside *maggazini* with wines from both shores of the Adriatic and Venice's own hinterland, made as strong as possible after the Greek model.

The traditions of winemaking in Dalmatia, Istria, and their islands are probably a Venetian revival of ancient practice. Such wines as the Grk of Korčula, Vugava of Vis, Dingač and Postup of the Pelješac peninsula, and the notoriously heady Prošek all involve sun-dried grapes.

Greek malmsey vines were planted in Istria around Fiume (today Rijeka) beside the local Teran, which on the stark karst limestone of this coast gives powerful wines. Prošek – unrelated to the Prosecco that provides Venice's light dry sparkling wine, the *ombra* or "little shade" of Venetian cafés – is made of a grape called Marastina, which on the island of Hvar makes the excellent strong Čara-Smokviča .

The blockade by the Turks of their eastern supplies stimulated the Venetians to develop the vineyards around Verona and on the volcanic Eugenean hills south of Padua, even nearer to home. Bardolino, Valpolicella, and Soave are three regions that were encouraged to make high-alcohol wines by half-drying their grapes. The tradition persists in the powerful Recioto Amarone of Valpolicella and Soave.

– almost twice the strength of the thin northern wines. There would often be unfermented sugar even at this strength. This combination of sweetness and a warm glow as it went down was strong drink indeed: the strongest anyone had tasted until the introduction of distilled spirits. And it had a yet more important quality. It would keep, and travel long distances, without turning sour. Its alcohol content preserved it, and even, under the right conditions, made it capable of maturing. There is no question that it was considered a luxury, and would have been drunk exclusively by the rich; in the fourteenth century only three taverns out of nearly 400 in London were licensed to sell it retail. Wholesale, it was at least twice the price of claret. The most expensive price recorded was for a tun of Vernage: £10. In terms of prestige, sweet wines came first; Rhine wine or "Rhenish" second. Claret was the everyday drink.

The Dominican friar Geoffrey of Waterford was one of the earliest correspondents to bring back critical notes, in 1300. What he said, in a nutshell, was that the farther east you went, the stronger the wines became. This was the wine the Genoese and Venetian galleys carried so profitably to England and Flanders.

In 1204 the hooligan element in the fourth Crusade had sacked Constantinople, and Venice, helping itself to the pickings of the broken Byzantine Empire, appropriated Candia. Opportunism was a Venetian speciality. Its power steadily grew through the strict and brilliant organization of its trade. At first Genoa had the upper hand; it was Genoa that pioneered long-distance, bulk-carrying "carracks" of 1,000 tons or more. Venice then built even larger galleys. There were pitched galley battles with Genoa and Pisa (which can be seen in lurid detail on the walls of the Doge's palace). Venice came off best.

By land it took advantage, like other Italian cities, of the great Champagne cloth fairs of the thirteenth century, not just to trade but also to set up a banking empire. When the fairs lost their momentum its ruling Signoria pioneered the eastern Alpine passes, the Brenner and the Saint Gotthard, giving her direct access overland to the Danube, and via the Rhine to the string of trading cities that culminated in Cologne, Bruges, and London. By sea, its galleys and round ships steadily gained a monopoly of the route through the Strait of Gibraltar, stopping at Lisbon, then forging on to England and Flanders.

In the fifteenth century Venice extended its colonial dominion to Cyprus. After the fall of Acre, Cyprus had become the headquarters of two of the military orders of monks founded in the Holy Land: the Knights Templars, and the Knights of St John, or Hospitallers (who had run the great 1,000-bed hospital at Acre). The Templars had departed, their great wealth appropriated by jealous princes – especially Philippe IV of France. The Hospitallers also moved on, to Rhodes, which they held for 200 years, but kept a Commandery, a sort of embattled priory, in Cyprus, where they continued to make the island's best wine: the intensely sweet Commandaria. The Commandaria vineyards are in the region of Pitsilia, reaching up above Limassol onto the Troodos mountains. Today the villages of Kalokhorio and Zoopiyi grow respectively the white Xynisteri and the red Mavron: stunted vines in ashy and sandy soil that must have looked very much the same when the Venetians arrived.

Venice, of course, was the archetypal exploiting colonist. It planted so many cash crops, mainly sugar, cotton, and vines, that the inhabitants had nowhere to grow their food, and the population dwindled. Sugar cane in particular is a terrible robber of the soil, making it difficult to restore fields to a healthy system of rotation. When eventually the Ottoman Turks captured the island in 1572 the people rejoiced; at last they were allowed to grow what they wanted rather than what the Venetians wanted to sell.

The tough commercial system of Venice did not allow direct carrying, even by its own ships, from foreign port to foreign port. Everything had to come to Venice on the way. Specialist merchantmen, the largest for the longest voyages, went back and forth to Alexandria, Tripoli, the Black Sea, Cyprus, Flanders, and Aigues-Mortes in the south of France. Venice was the entrepôt for it all, a unique mart that tied together East and West and North. It was a serious blow when in 1488 the Portuguese discovered the Cape of Good Hope. A direct sea route to the Indies meant that Venice's quasi-monopoly of Oriental luxuries was over.

When Shakespeare wrote *The Merchant of Venice* the subject was a familiar, if not a topical, one. England and Venice had conducted a long trade war about the shipping of malmsey. The Venetians had seen an opportunity when England lost Bordeaux (it was the same year as the Turks took Constantinople) and without delay had sent the English king eight butts of the their finest wine. England took the bait. Malmsey became the rage. In 1472 a Venetian galley with more than 400 butts of sweet wine for England was taken by French pirates in the Channel. In 1480 an English royal Duke, George

TO
CANARY ISLANDS

COG AND
GALLEY ROUTES

of Clarence, invited to choose the method of his execution for treason, chose, according to the Flemish contemporary historian Philippe de Commines, to be drowned in a butt of malmsey.

For twenty-five years the Venetians charged fifty shillings for a butt of 130 gallons, and were prepared to be paid two-fifths of the value in cloth. Having created a strong demand, they then began to reduce the supply, sending fewer and smaller barrels, down to 108 gallons, charging more than three times as much, and refusing cloth as part payment. The English reacted by sending their own ships into the Mediterranean: gingerly at first – not many English cogs had been that far since King Richard I's crusading fleet. One of the first recorded voyages was that of the *Anne of Bristol*, whose master, Robert Sturmy, reached the Holy Land with her in 1446. Her fate was not encouraging; she was wrecked on Chios, where she had gone for wine on the way home.

By the end of the century there were many more merchant venturers willing to try – especially as Florence, seeing the chance to steal a march on Venice, opened its port of Pisa to

foreign vessels. Pisa had Vernage to sell. The noble houses of Antinori and Frescobaldi, bankers and general traders in the Florentine style, drifted into the wine business by such means, the Antinoris as early as the 1380s.

Venice became anxious and imposed a tax on malmsey bought in Candia by foreigners. England's King Henry VII retaliated by taxing malmsey arriving in England in Venetian ships. But there was fresh competition now for Venice and its sweet wines: new malmsey-style wines being made in Spain and Portugal. Well might Antonio, in *The Merchant of Venice*, be "sad to think upon his merchandise". He had, said Shylock, rubbing his hands, "an argosy bound to Tripolis, another to the Indies… a third for Mexico, a fourth for England". Venice and its competitors stood on the threshold of the New World.

NEXT PAGE This mural in the Church of San Martino dei Buonomini in Florence shows works of mercy: giving food to the hungry, and wine to the thirsty. Wine is apparently being distributed directly from the fermenting vat.

CHAPTER 15

CASTILIAN CONQUEST

"The day is damp with dew and the cheek of the earth is covered with a down of grass. Thy friend invites thee to partake of the enjoyment of the two pots now cooking on the hearth, which give forth an excellent aroma, and of a jug of wine in this most beautiful place. More could he offer should he so desire, but it is not seemly that too much pomp should be displayed to a friend."

This invitation, charming in its mock modesty, was written by an Andalusian Arab of the Middle Ages. It invokes the spirit of Al-Andalus, the most civilized corner of Europe in the years of the Carolingian Emperors and the invasions of the Norsemen – and for many years after that. At a time when Paris was still a cluster of buildings on an island in the Seine, Córdoba, with 100,000 inhabitants, was the greatest city in western Europe – and not just in scale, but also in cultivation and learning.

Córdoba was the pearl of the Arab world, which after its triumphant century of conquest had divided into three caliphates: Baghdad and Cairo in the East, Córdoba in the West. The climate of Al-Andalus, seductive enough today, must have been paradise to the desert dwellers, with its rivers and fertile soils, its matchless grazing, its snow-capped *cordilleras,* and its palm-fringed coast. Andalus probably means "end of light" – the western land where the sun sets. Its inhabitants lived a life of unfanatical ease, as our host's gentle letter shows. Omar Khayyam would have been happy in his company.

The first thrust of the Arab invasion had taken it right through Spain and into France, where it was turned back at Poitiers by Charles Martel. Christian Spain in the ninth century, the inheritance of the Visigoths from the Romans, was cornered in the northern seacoast kingdom of the Asturias, as different from Andalusia as Normandy is from Provence. The two Spains, indeed, are complementary. The South needs the dour products of the North just as the North desires the products of the South. But while northern and southern Europe found each other in the Middle Ages through their developing commerce, the two Spains had to meet through the bloody wars of the *Reconquista.*

The Christian-Moorish frontier moved fitfully south from the ninth century on. The Moors had never occupied the North; there were never enough of them. Nor were there enough Christians to occupy whatever territory they won. By the time of the first Crusade to the Holy Land the frontier ran almost across the middle of Spain. Portugal was Christian as far south as the river Tagus; Toledo became Christian in 1085; on the east coast the boundary was near Alicante. Still there was another century of intermittent conflict and colonization, with adventurers and settlers coexisting in uneasy partnership as they do on any frontier, before the monarchs of the North started a concerted invasion. By the time Cádiz fell in 1262, Moorish Spain was reduced on the map to the Kingdom of Granada – which was to remain Moorish for another two centuries.

The Moors had never been short of wine. Vineyards were plentiful in the South; it was a matter of conscience whether you took your refreshment in liquid or pill form. As the *Reconquista* gradually settled the rest of Spain, the planting of vines was a top priority. Wine was considered an absolute essential, a fundamental daily provision for all.

From the tenth century the Ebro valley, the plains of the Duero, and the green hollows of Galicia were equally planted, and as the Christians controlled more land farther south, and monasteries, many of them Cistercian with Burgundian connections, followed the *reconquistadores*, viticulture became inseparable from any settlement. A vineyard belt gave a green and welcoming look to the surroundings of every town and castle. To plant vines was to make a claim of permanence in holding the land; it would also certainly give pleasure, and had been known to bring solid profit. Moreover, in many areas it was legally enjoined.

By the thirteenth century, all the inhabited parts of Spain grew wine except the mountainous extreme North, which therefore became a target for all wine-growers within reasonable range – which was surprisingly far. Rioja, Navarre, León, the Duero, and the vineyards of Galicia all competed for this market. The Duero probably made the best wine, because its main consumers were the citizens of the important cities of Castile: Burgos, Salamanca, and above all the capital, Valladolid. But fashions changed. In the thirteenth century it was Toro (and to a lesser extent Zamora) that had the great name – for its powerful dark red. Toro continued to be the drink of the dons of the great university of Salamanca for centuries; one draught was enough to make them forget their lectures. A little later it was the district of Rueda, south of Valladolid, that was in vogue.

Burgos drew most of its supplies from the Ribera del Duero, the region of Aranda and Peñafiel, whose wine was dark red, not particularly strong and not a good keeper – which will surprise anyone who knows the resounding reds of the region today. They include the legendary Vega Sicilia, a Gargantua of a wine, and such wines as Pesquera and Protos, which are seemingly ambitious for similar legends of their own.

These were not the wines that the world outside Spain ever met – or very rarely. Some Rioja wine was exported via Bilbão or Santander. It was known as "Ryvere" (presumably from the river Ebro) and appreciated for its "sweetnesse". The first requirement for an export wine is a port, and those nearest busy sea-lanes were first in the running. Shipping between northern Europe and the Mediterranean put into northwestern harbours in Galicia, occasionally into the Portuguese Minho, into the estuary of the Tagus, and into the Bay of Cádiz, or the estuary of the Guadalquivir, the river of Seville. The crusaders were occasional customers at the ports of Galicia and northern Portugal; these were the last places they could stop and load wine before sailing down the long Moorish coast of the peninsula, where they could hardly have expected a friendly reception.

As the *Reconquista* opened up the west coast farther south to Christian wine drinkers, references to Andalusian wines begin. In the fourteenth century the English poet Chaucer described the wine of Lepe (a village near Huelva, between Jerez and the Algarve), "of which there riseth such fumositee" that after three draughts the drinker doesn't know whether he is at La Rochelle, Bordeaux, Lepe, or home in bed. In fact he was talking about a remote ancestor of sherry.

Any remaining idea that fourteenth-century Englishmen had hard heads should be dispelled by Chaucer's French contemporary Froissart. He recounts how the archers sent by England's "king-maker", John of Gaunt, on their way to help King John I of Portugal against the Castilians, landed in Galicia. The best of the local wine there, Ribadavia, is not very different from the Vinho Verde of northern Portugal: light and acidic. Nonetheless, says Froissart, the Englishmen found it so "ardent" that they could scarcely drink it, and when they did, they were helpless for two days afterwards.

They evidently came back for more, because Ribadavia became one of the most exported Spanish wines. Closeness to Compostella must have helped; at the height of its popularity the pilgrimage to the shrine of Santiago, or St James, counted up to two million foot-sloggers a year, each in his long cape and broad-brimmed hat with scallop shells. By the sixteenth century the restrictions on what might or might not be sold as Ribadavia at the port of La Coruña were so strict as almost to amount to an *appellation contrôlée*. English merchants, it is said, helped with their knowledge of shipping, and introduced the use of sulphur. Then, as so often with medieval, and particularly Spanish, wines, a change in the political tide made the customers move on. In this case it was the cooling of Anglo-Spanish, and warming of Anglo-Portuguese, relations in Queen Elizabeth I's reign that made merchants sail farther south, to the Minho, and buy their (not very different) wine at Viana do Castelo.

LEFT The castle at Jerez de la Frontera was built by the Moors, and for a century marked the frontier between Christian and Moorish Spain. Its mosque has recently been restored.

south of the tagus Portugal has such ideal conditions for wine-growing, and the northern part of the country is so thickly planted with vines, that it seems an anomaly that the southern one-third of the country, the Alentejo, or land beyond the river Tagus, has almost no wine-growing tradition.

Both in ancient times and during the Moorish occupation this was wine country, but the wars of the *Reconquista* were particularly fierce in the Alentejo, and the constant capture and recapture of the land over a long period left it destitute and depopulated. The first King of Portugal, Alfonso Henriques, gave every encouragement to the Cistercians to bring their agricultural skills, and in 1153 granted them an enormous estate at Alcobaça, north of Lisbon, which eventually became the largest of Cistercian monasteries, controlling an area of 932 square kilometres (360 square miles). The austerity of St Bernard was soon forgotten in the magnificence of an establishment with up to 900 monks, and with a refectory and kitchen described (in 1774) as "the most distinguished temple of gluttony in Europe". It was the very success of the North that starved the South of resources, particularly after the Black Death decimated the population, and again when the Age of Discoveries emptied the countryside of farmers.

Royal grants of land in the Alentejo were on a huge scale, and made to fighting men who were more inclined to cattle-ranching and hunting than laborious viticulture. Large areas were left as wild forest (with valuable cork oaks) for hunting. Grain was the crop that Portugal needed most, so the Alentejo was left vineless. Where vines have been planted since, the wines have shown as much potential for quality as any in the country.

The *Santa Trinidad*, part of Spain's treasure fleet. The fleet sailed annually from Cádiz to Panama, to rendezvous with the Pacific fleet, which brought a cargo of silver from Peru. With fair winds the journey took seventy days.

Another newcomer, also from Portugal, was *Bastardo* or Bastard. Since there is still a Bastardo grape grown in Portugal (and used in making port) it is just possible that we are talking about a "varietal" wine. That was not the opinion of earlier writers, who said that it was a "mungrell" made of wine and honey as a cheaper substitute for Muscadel. As it was sold either white or brown, this seems more likely than the varietal theory. That it was a downmarket drink is pretty certain. When Shakespeare's Prince Hal said "Your brown Bastard is your only drink", I am sure he put on a cockney accent.

I n many centuries of friendship between Portugal and England no single relationship has had such lasting repercussions as the marriage of John of Gaunt's daughter, Philippa of Lancaster, and King John I in 1387. Their fifth son, Prince Henry, nicknamed the Navigator, was the visionary whose dreams discovered the New World for Portugal.

During his lifetime he was responsible for Portugal's discovery of Madeira and the Azores, and for voyages down the coast of Africa. After his death a succession of Portuguese sailors – Dias, Da Gama, Cabral – took their three-masted caravels, the most advanced ships of the time and the first to be able to tack to windward, round the Cape of Good Hope (1488), to India (1498), to the Persian Gulf, Siam, and China (1540), and to Brazil.

In their discoveries they were in competition with the Spaniards, who had discovered the Canary Islands and were also looking for a passage to the Indies. The Genoese Christopher Columbus found his backing from King Ferdinand and Queen Isabella of Castile, and sailed from Seville. In 1494, two years after his discovery of America, the Portuguese and Spanish divided the world by treaty into Portuguese East and Spanish West. The line they drew gave all America to Spain – except Brazil. Had the Portuguese already discovered it, and kept it secret? But in its determination to have the East for its own, the Portuguese nation was exhausting itself. Its countryside was depopulated as farmers went to the coast, to sea, and to the new colonies. In half a century the population halved from two million to one million.

It seems extraordinary that no sooner had the *Reconquista* given the Spanish and Portuguese more land at home than they could use, their frontier spirit drew them overseas to perilous lands from which most of them never returned.

W ith hindsight, Spain's greatest age, the sixteenth century, seems suicidal. It started with the Spaniards' discovery of America and the final conquest of Granada from the Moors. In the same year the Holy Inquisition expelled all Jews from Spain: brains and manpower that could well have been invaluable and that certainly helped its enemies. Moors and Protestants were persecuted. Pure, proud, Catholic Castilians were to rule the world. But there were simply not enough of them. Armies and navies (and priests) were needed to exploit Mexico and Peru.

The Americas, apparently such priceless assets, were at first nothing of the kind. All the bullion of Mexico and Peru made up only about one-sixth of the royal revenue – scarcely enough to pay the interest on the loans the king negotiated with (usually

Genoese) bankers. What subsidized this Castilian octopus was the poor Castilians themselves, paying higher and higher taxes. No wonder they planted Castile almost solid with vineyards; they needed every *maravedi* they could earn to keep troops (and, of course, priests) in The Netherlands, Sicily, Peru… and at the same time to face a continuing onslaught from the East, the advancing crescent of the Ottoman Turks.

Towards the end of Philip II's reign the bullion supply looked up. New mines at Potosi in Peru and Zacatecas in Mexico came into spectacular production. The treasure galleons of the 1580s and 1590s carried four times as much as when he came to the throne. But Philip's ambitions were never limited by his resources. In 1580 he swallowed Portugal and its empire (and another deluge of paperwork). Portugal was to remain under Spanish rule for sixty years, bringing with it more problems.

The New World proved disappointing from another point of view. An acquiescent colony is supposed to deliver cheap raw materials and provide a market for manufactured goods. At first this is what happened. Ships laden with wheat and wine sailed to Vera Cruz in Mexico and to the miserable, feverish harbours on the isthmus of Panama that supplied Peru. There was also Manila in the Philippines. Prices rose sharply as treasure came back. In Andalusia (which had most direct dealings with America), in the forty years after the conquest of Mexico the price

of wheat doubled, and the price of wine rose eight times.

But it soon became clear that the wine and oil the colonies were supposed to be buying could not survive the voyage. Seventy-five days in the tropics (the length of a good passage to Mexico) turned oil rancid and wine to vinegar. From the start the *conquistadores* had taken vines with them. Cortés had commanded every landholder in Mexico to plant vines. By the mid-sixteenth century, although Mexico was no great vineyard, the high southern coastal valleys of Peru, Trujillo, Pisco, Ica, and Nazca were supplying not only Lima and Potosi but also the new colony of Chile, as well as Colombia, Venezuela, Central America, and Mexico. Intercolonial trade cut out the mother country, which protested but could do little. There was even a trade in Chinese goods for silver and wine between Manila and Mexico and Peru.

Santiago in Chile was founded by Pedro de Valdivia in 1541, less than ten years after the conquest of Peru. Wine-growing could not have better conditions than the beautifully cultivated and irrigated fields of the dispossessed Indians. If it was slower to catch on than in Peru it was because food, not wine, was needed for export to the slave-labour force in the Peruvian mines. Nonetheless, our first sighting of "the pirate Drake" is in December 1578, when he seized a ship bound from Chile to Lima containing 1,770 bulging wine skins: a retail rehearsal for his wholesale looting in Andalusia nine years later.

CHAPTER 16

"GOOD STORE OF FERTILE SHERRIS"

Sanlúcar de Barrameda is a fishing village and part-time resort, justly renowned for the delectable prawns that its beach-front cafés grill and serve right on the sandy foreshore. The tawny water before you is the Guadalquivir, where its estuary broadens to the sea. Looking half-left you have the open Atlantic in full view. Farther left, out of sight down the coast, is the fortress-port of Cádiz. To your right, seventy winding miles upstream, is the city of Seville, a busy port despite its distance from the ocean and the shifting shoals in its approach; it is beyond the reach of the worst southwesterly gales – and of pirates.

Up behind you, overlooking the little town from a low hill, is the long white *palacio* of the Dukes of Medina Sidonia, the feudal owners of Sanlúcar. And just in front, where the small boys are pushing bright-sailed dinghies through the surf, is where Columbus left to discover America, followed from the same spot thirty years later by Magellan's five small ships, the first ever to sail around the world.

Sanlúcar was the Cape Canaveral of the sixteenth century. The great voyages were planned and discussed at Sagres, in Genoa, in Lisbon and Madrid. The caravels were built and fitted out in Seville and Cádiz. But the final push of the mariner's bare foot on his homeland was on Sanlúcar beach.

Nothing you have ever tasted is as savoury as these prawns with this narrow tulip of pale amber wine. You are drinking manzanilla, the dry sherry of the surrounding vineyards, matured in the old stone bodegas that cluster close to the beach. It is the exact contemporary, in its inception, of the great voyages of discovery. It was even born to put to sea, for the name it was known by was sack, or *saca*: export goods.

At the close of the fifteenth century the Venetian monopoly of the sweet-wine trade in the eastern Mediterranean was in trouble. Constantinople had fallen to the Turks in the same year as England had lost Bordeaux to the French (and Gutenberg had set up the first printing press). It signalled the final snuffing out of the "Roman" Empire of the eastern Mediterranean and turned people's thoughts towards the West, where the open Atlantic beckoned.

The Spanish seized the opportunity with both hands. Venice could no longer guarantee its trade with the Orient. The sweet-wine supply for all of Europe was in the balance. Seville, Cádiz, Sanlúcar, and Jerez, just inland, could become the world's great source of luxury wine, strong enough for long-distance travel. The Spanish even called their wine Romania or Rumney: a frank admission that it was Greek wine they were imitating and whose market they wanted.

The Duke of Medina Sidonia took the initiative. In 1491 he abolished taxes on the export of wine from Sanlúcar in both Spanish and foreign ships. In 1517 he gave English merchants preferential status: eight houses in the town, the right to bear arms by day or night, and even the site for their own church (which still stands, dedicated to St George). He also took steps to distinguish clearly between Bastards, which were second-rate wines, and Rumneys and Sacks, which had to be individually gauged, and kept in stores with two locks. Although the English name sack does not appear in any

document before 1530, its Spanish root, *saca*, was common. An English version simply means that it was becoming a familiar name in England.

This was the honeymoon period. Henry VIII of England married the daughter of Spain's Catholic monarchs, Catherine of Aragón. England joined the "Holy League" with Spain against France (partly in the hope of regaining Bordeaux). But life for everybody in Spain was being made tense by the severity of the Inquisition.

English merchants soon heard from this fearsome body. Many merchants managed to keep a low profile or be protected by their Spanish trading partners (in 1541, sixty English ships arrived as a fleet to load wine in Andalusia), but in some other parts of Spain they were actually burned.

Trade with Spain began to seize up. Many merchants, even those who had been in Spain for a generation, turned privateer or, less politely, pirate.

It is remarkable how much wine got through despite these inconveniences – and how hard the poor Dukes of Medina Sidonia kept trying to sweeten their best customers and worst

A probably imaginary view of sixteenth-century Sanlúcar, from the memoirs of Jerome Coler of Nuremberg, who sailed from Sanlúcar on his way to Venezuela in 1533.

enemies. In 1566 the Duke again extended special privileges to the English at Sanlúcar. In this period, no less than 40,000 of the 60,000 butts of wine made annually in the region were reaching England and The Netherlands, along with up to 2,000 beautiful foals from some of the best bloodstock in Europe, one of the Arabs' many bequests to Spain.

Nor was the Jerez area the only source of what was now generally known as sack. The Spanish, having exterminated the Guanches, the aboriginal inhabitants of the Canary Islands (who may have been a race left over from the Cro-Magnon age), in the 1490s, planted the island's volcanic soil with vines from Crete. "Canary sack" was almost as popular in London and Antwerp as "sherry" or "sheris" sack ("sherry" being the English attempt at "Jerez"). Málaga, in the former kingdom of Granada, took to using the name sack (also sometimes "mountain") for what it once sold as Garnache. Raisins, another Moorish inheritance, were its other speciality. And from 1537 malmsey

The complete costings of Ferdinand Magellan's fleet for his expedition around the world in 1519-21 have been preserved, and reveal some striking aspects of his priorities. He took five ships, the largest, the *San Antonio*, of 120 tons, the smallest, the *Santiago*, of seventy-five.

The *San Antonio* cost 330,000 *maravedis*, the old Spanish unit of currency, and all five ships together cost 1.3 million. The wages of the 237 crewmen for four months were calculated at 1.154 million (an average of 1,217 *maravedis* per man per month). Cannon, shot, powder, armour, muskets, swords, and all armaments for the fleet came to a total of 566,684 *maravedis*. *Vino de Jerez* for the fleet, including the cost of hiring one Juan Nicolas to travel from Seville to Jerez to choose the wine and arrange for its transport, came to 594,790 *maravedis*.

Thus Magellan spent more on sherry than on armaments. The expedition was the first to successfully circumnavigate the globe, although Magellan himself died on the way. He discovered the Strait of Magellan as a route around South America almost a century before an expedition rounded Cape Horn, and was the first to reveal the Pacific as the greatest ocean. But of the five ships only one returned, and of the 237 men only eighteen saw Sanlúcar beach again.

vines (but much more sugar cane) had been successfully planted on the new Portuguese colony of Madeira. When Cyprus fell to the Turks in 1571, its wine was scarcely missed.

B y the 1580s, though, the temper of the Spanish bull, constantly baited by the English bulldog, was not to be soothed by mere commerce. Philip II gave orders for an invasion of England. Cádiz now had the world's greatest naval dockyard, and it was there in 1587 that a large part of the Armada for England was being prepared when Sir Francis Drake paid his most famous visit.

Already he was so well known on the coast of Spain that mothers would say to their children: "*Mira que viene el Draque*" – "Look out, Drake is coming". This time he came with a fleet twenty-four strong, scattered the squadron of galleys that guarded the entrance to Cádiz, and sailed straight in.

The outer and inner harbours were crammed with shipping in various degrees of helplessness: without sails, without ammunition, or without crews. In Drake's own terse words: "… among the rest, thirty-two ships of exceeding great burden, laden, or to be laden, with provision and prepared to furnish the King's navy, intended with all speed against England; the which, when we had boarded and thereout furnished our ships with such provision as we thought sufficient, we burned." The work took two days and nights. Many small ships fled through the shoals to nearby Puerto de Santa Maria, but among the galleons destroyed was the 1,400-ton flagship of the Admiral of the Armada, the Marques de Santa Cruz, who shortly after died, it is said, of a broken heart. Philip replaced him as commander with the unfortunate, seasick, anglophile Duke of Medina Sidonia. Had Spain no other noblemen?

Among the extensive loot that Drake's fleet took away, having found time to load four prize ships as packhorses, was his most celebrated trophy – or at least the one with which his exploit was most celebrated when he brought it home. Two thousand nine hundred butts of sack had been waiting on the shore for loading. There can hardly have been a tavern in England that year and for years afterwards whose sack was not advertised as "authentic Cádiz".

W e have the perfect way of tasting the flavour of the time. In 1597 Sir John Falstaff first heaved himself onto the stage; the preposterous parasite, the chuckling cutpurse, the arrant knave, coward, and liar, and the most lovable character Shakespeare ever created.

Sack is Falstaff's constant drinking (although on Good Friday "he sold himself to the Devil for a cup of madeira and a cold capon's leg", and Doll Tearsheet, a close acquaintance, declares that "there's a whole merchant's venture of Bordeaux stuff in him"). His supper bill, found in his pocket (but never, you can be sure, paid) itemizes his consumption: a capon; sauce; sack, two gallons; anchovies and sack after supper; bread. Cost of sack (and anchovies) eight shillings and twopence; cost of supper, two shillings and sixpence halfpenny.

Sack is sometimes sweetened with sugar, served with a piece of toast in it, or (to Falstaff's disgust) whipped up with eggs: "I'll have no pullet-sperm in my brewage". All this, though, is but a preamble to the fat knight's considered opinion, delivered not at The Boar's Head but upon a Yorkshire battlefield:

"A good sherris-sack hath a two-fold operation in it. It ascends me into the brain, dries me there all the foolish and crudy vapours which environ it, makes it apprehensive, quick, forgetive, full of nimble, fiery, and delectable shapes, which delivered o'er the voice, the tongue, which is the birth, becomes excellent wit. The second property of your excellent sherris is the warming of the blood, which before (cold and settled) left the liver white and pale, which is the badge of pusillanimity and cowardice, but the sherris warms it and makes it course from the inwards to the parts extreme. It illumineth the face, which as a beacon gives warning to all the rest of this little kingdom, man, to arm. And then the vital commoners, and inland petty spirits, muster me all to their captain, the heart; who, great and puffed up with this retinue, doth any deed of courage; and this valour comes of sherris. So that skill in the weapon is nothing without sack (for that sets it a-work), and learning a mere hoard of gold kept by a devil, till sack commences it and sets it in act and use… If I had a thousand sons, the first humane principle I would teach them should be, to forswear thin potations, and to addict themselves to sack."

By thin potations he meant, of course, all the light wines of the North, whether Gascon or Rhenish. He expressed, in fact, the taste for strong wines that is supposed to be peculiarly English. Not that his sack was strong by modern standards. It was not a fortified wine. If vintage port had existed in Falstaff's day, he would probably have relegated the sack he knew to the category of "thin potations".

At a maximum natural alcoholic strength of sixteen degrees or so, Elizabethan sack would have had something of the character and weight of a present-day montilla – Córdoba's local variant on the theme, which is still locally drunk at its natural strength (although fortified a little for export).

A nineteenth-century view of Falstaff by the American painter George Whiting Flagg, "unbuttoned after supper", as Prince Hal, the future Henry V, puts it.

The conditions for producing good sherry were all present in the sixteenth century. What grapes they grew is not certain, but the best modern grape for dry sherry, Listan or Palomino, was probably present in a minority in the vineyard, and Pedro Ximénez, the grape used for dark, sweet wine, was certainly there. They also grew Malvasia (malmsey), maybe Muscat, and such varieties as Torrontes which are still used elsewhere in Spain.

The best sherry today comes from a belt of chalk soil west of (and close to) Jerez. The earliest vineyards were on sandy soil nearer the coast, whose wine is not so fine – except in the immediate neighbourhood of Sanlúcar. But ageing sack was not part of the plan, so differences that are obvious today were unimportant: the goal was freshness and strength. Probably the wine started to grow *flor*, the peculiar floating white yeast that gives modern fino its essential character. But *flor* needs time and encouragement, so it can have had little effect. Sack was what is classed today as an oloroso – the word means pungent – which by definition means that it needed years to develop great character; years that it never got. It was also normally and naturally dry – hence the addition of sugar at The Boar's Head. Perhaps ancient Roman techniques of boiling down the must were sometimes used to sweeten it – but it was usually Canary sack that was qualified by the word sweet.

The development of high-quality sherry, carefully matured, started soon after, and not in Jerez but in Bristol. By 1634 the wine that was sold as "Bristol Milk" must surely have been softened, if not by time, at least by the vintner's art.

CHAPTER 17

THE BEVERAGE REVOLUTION

The age of Shakespeare is a good time to pause and scan the horizon. In the story of wine (and much else) it is one of history's hinges. In wine it saw the last of the age of innocence (innocence of knowledge, that is, not of malpractice).

Wine up to this time has been an essential part of diet, with only beer as an alternative. From this time on it begins to be discretionary, the choice gets wider, and wine has to justify itself by being more than just readily available. The French philosopher Michel de Montaigne seems to sum up for the age of innocence in his essay "On Drunkenness": "If you make your pleasure depend on drinking good wine, you condemn yourself to the pain of sometimes drinking bad wine. We must have a less exacting and freer taste. To be a good drinker, one must not have so delicate a palate."

In 1613 Shakespeare, having written his last play, *The Tempest*, retired to a new house outside London at Battersea. In the same year at the opposite side of London in Islington, a village on a hill overlooking the City, a revolutionary project was completed. The New River, an aqueduct thirty-eight miles long, the project of a Welshman called Hugh Myddelton, brought fresh water in abundant supply into London for the first time.

Fresh water helped to remove the most basic of reasons for drinking wine – simply to quench thirst safely. Now suddenly there was a host of reasons not to. In the course of the seventeenth century we move from a Europe that was almost perpetually under the sedation of alcohol to one that had a whole range of both sedatives and stimulants to choose from. The politics and religious convictions of the time did not exactly encourage wine drinking, nor did they encourage winemakers to improve their quality or enlarge their repertoire. The troubles of the first half of the seventeenth century included the cataclysmic Thirty Years War, which almost closed down Germany altogether, religious wars in France, the growth of the Puritan movement (the *Mayflower* sailed in 1620), persistent new taxation, and new laws restricting the freedom of shipping. Wine also met a succession of formidable new rivals that each in turn stole the limelight as the social drink of the day.

Of these the first in time was *aqua vitae*, or distilled spirits. The invention has been credited to the Chinese, the Persians and the Arabs – whose words "alcohol" and "alembic" certainly seem to implicate them. The Medical School of Salerno seems to have understood distillation in the twelfth century, and Arnaldus de Villanova, the sage of Montpellier (whose education was in Moorish Spain), cited *aqua vitae* – among many other things – as a panacea. By 1485 an illustration (from Salerno) of distilling apparatus shows it well advanced and on an almost industrial scale. But the acceptance of spirits as a drink in their own right, or as a useful addition to wine, was slow in coming – presumably because, the principle being imperfectly understood, some noxious forms of *vinum ardens*, or "burning wine", were produced. Germany seems to have been the first place in Europe where *aqua vitae* caught on. Fernand Braudel quotes a Nuremberg doctor of the 1490s who wrote: "In view of the fact that everyone at present has got into the habit of drinking *aqua vitae* it is necessary to remember the quantity that one can permit oneself to drink if one wishes to behave like a gentleman."

The sixteenth century saw the very slow advance of distillation, with the Germans still apparently unusual in considering spirits a drink rather than a medicine. Alsace was soon involved in "burning" its excess wine (the word "brandy" comes from *gebrandt* [burnt] *wein*). But the real industrialization and commercialization of spirits had to wait for the ingenious Dutch in the seventeenth century. It was the ever-increasing Dutch fleet from the end of the sixteenth century that found the first great outlet for distilled wine or fermented grain – whichever was cheaper. It was ideal for long voyages, took up little space, kept perfectly, and worked wonders on the natives at the far end.

Tobacco, in being narcotic and sedative, cannot be left out of the equation. By Shakespeare's time its use was widespread. It was either smoked, chewed, or (rather later) sniffed as snuff. In its effects it could be seen as a rival to wine and beer; in practice it was more often a complement.

Beer itself had become more of a challenge to wine in Shakespeare's lifetime, again thanks to the Dutch. Ale, as drunk in most northern countries, was a very mild-flavoured drink. The Dutch added the aroma and bitterness of hops, as Andrew Boorde reported in 1542: "Beer is made of malt, and hops, and water; it is a natural drink for a Dutchman. And now of late days it is much used in England to the detriment of many Englishmen." Not all, though, by any means. The controversy between ale and beer was still going strong a century later. John Taylor, the eccentric "water poet", a Gloucestershire countryman turned Thames bargeman who diverted all London with his antics and rhymes (he invented a very sinkable brown-paper boat) was still, in 1651, of the view that: "Beer is a Dutch boorish liquor, a thing not known in England, till of late

days an Alien to our Nation, till such times as Hops and Heresies came amongst us, it is a sawcy intruder in this Land."

By Taylor's time the saucy intruders were coming thick and fast. Chocolate had been brought to Spain as long ago as 1504 from its home in Mexico. Cortés had found that the Aztecs valued the cocoa bean so highly that they used it as currency. The alarmingly stimulating drink of Montezuma's banquets was brewed from cocoa, vanilla, maize, herbs, and spices (including chillis), and fermented, so that it combined the effects of caffeine and alcohol, not to mention red-hot peppers, in one potation – which even Falstaff could hardly have described as "thin".

The secret of *xocoatl* was guarded by the Spanish, who added sugar and concocted a recipe we would recognize as chocolate. Not until the 1600s did cakes of chocolate paste made in Madrid reach Italy and Flanders. Cocoa beans were so little understood that in the 1640s when "English and Hollanders" took a good prize at sea, a (Spanish) ship laden with cocoa, "in anger and wrath we have hurled overboard this good commodity, not regarding the worth of it". Chocolate became the fashion in France in 1660 when Louis XIV married the Spanish princess Maria Theresa. It was regarded as something between a drink and a medicine, and inspired one of Madame de Sevigné's most delicious stories: "The Marquise de Coëtlogon took so much chocolate, being pregnant last year, that she was brought to bed of a little boy as black as the devil". London first met it in June 1657, "In Bishopsgate Street, in Queen's Head Alley, at a Frenchman's house" [where] "is an excellent West Indian drink called

A London coffee house, 1668. The word "tip" is said to have been coined here, from the initials TIP (To Insure Promptness) on a collecting box on the counter.

Coffee received a fortuitous boost in publicity, especially in France, from the outcome of the 1683 Siege of Vienna by the Turks – their final attempt at adding Austria to their Empire, that then included Hungary. Louis XIV notoriously did nothing to help his Christian fellow-monarch, the Emperor Leopold I, ward off the Muslim invasion. But with the help of the Polish hero Jan Sobieski, the Austrians and their allies routed the Turks, capturing their baggage and a small mountain of coffee.

Distributed around the capitals of Europe, Vienna's Turkish coffee had something of the effect of Drake's sack from Cádiz.

chocolate to be sold, where you may have it at any time, and also unmade at reasonable rates".

By this time London was just getting used to coffee houses. While chocolate came from the New World, coffee came from the very old, the East, which still provided the most luxurious articles of commerce. Its origins are in Ethiopia, but it was first traded at Mocha near Aden in the Red Sea, in the fifteenth century, and from there spread quickly through the Arab world – a cause of profound Islamic debate, because its effects, although the opposite of those of wine, were obviously distinctly mind-altering. Some rulers declared that the Koran prohibited it: that it was, in fact, a sort of wine. Others claimed that Mohammed himself had been given it to keep him awake during his long sessions with the angel Gabriel.

European travellers started to meet coffee in the East in the sixteenth century. Turkish Constantinople had scores of coffee houses. A Greek at Oxford introduced it to the diarist John Evelyn in 1637, and it was in Oxford that one Jacob opened England's first coffee house in 1650. Within a few years Londoners had taken to the idea like bees to lavender. The old taverns must have left something to be desired for their clientele to change their habits with such alacrity. Coffee was cheap: coffee houses were nicknamed "penny universities" because a penny was all it cost to drink a cup and stay as long as you liked, reading the newspaper provided and debating its contents. The novelty of drinks that were not alcoholic was a powerful attraction; and so no doubt was the effect of the coffee.

A catalogue of coffee houses, and the groups who gathered in them, would show almost every shade of political sentiment, of literary taste, and even of commercial activity in London in the later years of the seventeenth century. Will's in Bow Street, Covent Garden, was the smartest literary resort, where the great poet Dryden held court; Man's at Charing Cross was for fashionable beaux; Child's, near St Paul's Cathedral, was full of clergymen; the St James's was the meeting place of the Whig Party; and White's in St James's Street was chock-full of aristocrats. Jonathan's in the City was where stockbrokers met; and Lloyd's, first in Tower Street, then Lombard Street, the most famous of all, was from 1688 the place where ship owners and ship masters met.

Edward Lloyd, the owner, took the imaginative step of publishing his own paper, *Lloyd's News*, whose first issue appeared in 1696. It established his coffee house as the centre of marine mercantile life. When goods from prize ships were to be auctioned, we read in the *London Gazette* that Lloyd's became the auction room. (Its first sale, in 1703, was of "a parcel of Turkey coffee".) Up to 1804, when the insurance business of Lloyd's involved whole convoys of ships, it retained the pretence of being a coffee house and referred to its employees as "waiters".

Lloyd's was exceptional in evolving from casual meeting place to world-famous business enterprise. The coffee houses of the fashionable parish of St James's had very different progeny. From them emerged that most characteristic London upper-class institution, the gentlemen's club. Of the clubs still extant, White's, Brooks's and Boodles, all in St James's Street, are the direct or indirect descendants of coffee houses. Of course, wine soon made up its lost ground, and much more port and claret than coffee was being drunk in clubs in the eighteenth century.

Coffee was introduced to fashionable Paris by a Turkish ambassador in 1669. Parisians delighted in the oriental chic of the new drink and bought their first cups from the brass trays of turbanned Armenians who brewed it on little stoves in the streets. One of them opened a stall in the market of St Germain des Prés in 1672, without success; he moved to London. But a Sicilian who had worked for him, Procopio Coltelli, tried again with more determination. The lavish coffee house he opened in 1686, under the name Procope, had mirrored walls, and chandeliers and carpets, and served not only coffee but food and wine; it was, in fact, the prototype of the Paris café. Procope is still in business, in the rue des Fossés St Germain, making the not untenable claim that it is the oldest restaurant in Paris.

In France the coffee house still survives; the café as a national institution has scarcely altered since it caught on in the eighteenth century (Paris soon had 600 or more). England, its fashionable clubs apart, turned back to something much closer to its traditional taverns. The severely named "public house", dealing mostly in beer, was the revenge of the powerful brewers on their apostate customers – who in any case were much more taken by the latest of the exotic stimulants to make its mark: tea.

Again we have the Dutch to thank. In the early years of the seventeenth century they made a successful grab for Indonesia and the trade with the Spice Islands. The Portuguese and English who stood in their way were summarily dealt with. In Bantam, their first trading post at the western end of Java, they learned the Chinese habit of drinking tea, and were soon importing not just the leaves but the necessary paraphernalia, pots and cups, to Amsterdam. Unlike coffee, tea first appeared as an expensive luxury. The diarist Samuel Pepys had his first cup, in a coffee house, in September 1660. The price came down when the rival Dutch and English East India Companies began carrying tea in quantity around the turn of the eighteenth century, but by then the craze was for The Netherland's latest contribution to the range of new beverages thronging the market: gin.

In England the evils of gin, and its eventual conquest by tea, were matters of deep concern in the eighteenth century. Meanwhile, in the seventeenth, the vintners had plenty to worry about. It was time to devise new wines that could compete with such novel patterns of consumption.

CHAPTER 18

WAGGONERS OF THE SEA

If Shakespeare had written his plays half a century later, they might well have included *The Merchant of Amsterdam* and *The Two Gentlemen of Haarlem*, and Romeo and Juliet might have found their ecstasy on a balcony in Leyden or Delft. Such was the extent to which The Netherlands seized the initiative in Europe in the first half of the seventeenth century. It was the Dutch, rather than the Italians, the Spanish or the French, who taught Europe the meaning of commercial power and translated it into cultural conquest.

The story is astonishing, because for more than a century the Dutch had been mere vassals of the Spanish, an unimportant, resourceless peasant outpost of Spain's great Empire whose few flat fields could not support its population, but which relied on its fishermen for food. Under the leadership of William the Silent, Prince of Orange in Provence and Nassau in Germany, and his sons Maurice and Frederick-Henry, the seven northern provinces of what is now The Netherlands united against Spain and the Inquisition and harried them out of the country.

By 1650 the Dutch had the greatest merchant fleet the world had ever seen, with some 10,000 ships, despite the fact that up to 1648 they had been at war with Spain for eighty years with only one twelve-year truce. Not only were they "the waggoners of the seas", they also peopled their ships with corsairs able to teach the Barbary pirates lessons in ferocity. If there was lucrative smuggling to be done the Dutch were there, too.

With ruthless vigour the United Provinces established colonies in the East and West Indies, in North America, in Ceylon, and at the Cape of Good Hope, discovered Tasmania and New Zealand, fought in the Thirty Years' War in Germany, and twice against England, and repelled an invasion by Louis XIV, all within the space of one lifetime.

Dutch commercial enterprise introduced so many new stimulants and narcotics to Europe, in the form of brandy, beer – so much stronger than the mild-flavoured ale drunk in most northern countries – tea, and coffee, that wine almost fell by the wayside. But as the dominant trading nation, with far more ships than any other, the Dutch also called the tune in the growing and distribution of wine.

The Netherlands, like Venice, made its fortune importing and exporting the same goods. Transit trade was the livelihood of Amsterdam, which grew rich by linking the Baltic with the Mediterranean and the Indies (despite such formidable obstacles as a harbour approach so shallow that big freighters had to be piggybacked over the shoals by pumped-out lighters lashed alongside). The British ambassador, Sir William Temple, observed: "Never any country traded so much, and consumed so little… They are the great masters of Indian spices, and Persian silks; but wear plain woollen, and feed upon their own fish and roots." Of all these wares, only one remained behind in goodly quantities in the stomachs of the merchants: wine, for which Rotterdam was the chief port. Rhine wine was the most convenient – Rotterdam lies at the mouth of that river. White wine, preferably sweet, was also very much to the Dutch taste. But the Rhineland was so devastated by the Thirty Years' War in the first half of the seventeenth century, and the Palatinate by Louis XIV in the second half, that Germany had little wine (and perhaps

Hard drinking was endemic in seventeenth-century Holland. This *Merry Company* by D. Ryckaert, 1650, looks less set on total inebriation than many of its genre.

none of quality) to export. It was in the seventeenth century that wine as Germany's national drink was largely replaced by beer.

The Dutch bought from every source, even from Spain, although they were at war. Their tasters were sighted sniffing around the old kingdom of Aragón, just over the Pyrenees from France. The overland route to Spain was as familiar as the sea-lanes. In Venice's old monopoly, the eastern Mediterranean, they were able to make arrangements with the Turks for supplies of Greek wine (as they did for supplies of tulip bulbs, another Turkish speciality and Dutch passion). The Turks, recently beaten by the Spanish and Venetians at the sea battle of Lepanto, were delighted with this chance to insult both enemies at once.

For the bulk supplies they needed to furnish all their northern clients and top up their taverns, the Dutch turned to the great well of wine represented by the west coast of France and its hinterland, from Nantes at the mouth of the Loire south

to Bordeaux and Bayonne. The old annual wine-fleet idea was out of date; they wanted a constant flow. As far as they were concerned, all the elaborate traditions and privileges, the pecking order of ports, the *police des vins* at Bordeaux, were worse than out of date. Where they could get away with it they ignored them (they did not apply to distilled wine). In several cases they married into local families to qualify for privileges. But principally they concentrated on such areas as the Dordogne where there were no rules to get in the way.

They were welcomed at first at Bordeaux, both as buyers of wine on a bigger scale than the English had been for centuries and also as skilled drainage engineers, with the experience of their *polders*, who could drain the marshy land along the rivers. But whereas the English only looked for traditional, light red claret, the Dutch wanted things done differently. They bought huge quantities of white wine, the sweeter the better, and even huger quantities of ordinary wine suitable for distilling into brandy. Brandy was routinely added to the drinking water on board ship to make it both safer and more palatable. As for red wine, the Dutch liked it dark and strong. Cahors in the High Country was their ideal. By planting the *palus*, the newly drained alluvial land along Bordeaux's rivers, they achieved (at least in the better vintages) what they were looking for, a wine that was the antithesis of claret.

Their preferences and buying power soon persuaded farmers to switch from red grapes to white, not only in Bergerac up the Dordogne but even in Bordeaux's own backyard, in Sauternes. The Dutch brought with them (presumably from the Rhineland) a trick that would stabilize sweet wines and prevent them from finishing their fermentation on the way to the customer. It was the sulphur (alias "brimstone") candle, or wick dipped in sulphur and burned in the barrel before it was filled. Formerly it had been possible to stabilize sweet wines up to a point, but only very laboriously by repeated racking from one barrel to another, and by shipping in cold weather. The Dutch were not so finicky, and were prepared to add sugar and indeed spirits before they re-exported the wine onwards from Rotterdam.

The French were not slow to adopt the sulphur technique, at first calling the candles *allumettes hollandaises*; later *mèches soufrées*. It is doubtful, judging by the report of a Scottish traveller in France in 1665–7, whether, having learned the trick, they observed much restraint in using it. Sir John Lauder, Lord Fountainhall, wrote: "There comes no wine out of France to foreign country, save that which they brimstone a little, otherwise it could not keep on the sea, but it would spoil. It's true the wine works much of it out again, yet this makes that wine much more unwholesome and heady than that we drink in the country where it grows at hand. We [in Scotland] have very strict laws against the adulterating of wines, and I have heard the English confess that they wished they had the like…"

The Dutch soon began to identify the areas that could produce fairly sweet wines by delaying the harvest until the grapes were as ripe as possible, and others where exceptional conditions of soil and climate could give them really sweet *vins liquoreux*, the equivalent of modern Sauternes. There is no specific mention of waiting for the grapes to rot under the influence of *Botrytis cinerea*, the so-called "noble mould", until much later: the late eighteenth century (the period when its effects were also "discovered" in the Rheingau). But it is hard to believe that the sweet wines of Bergerac and Sauternes, and also of Anjou, which the Dutch bought at a premium, were not at least partially achieved through the action of botrytis.

Ordinary wine supplies for distilling were no problem, but for economy and efficiency the Dutch looked for areas where the second necessary element was also plentiful: timber to fuel their stills and build their barrels. Armagnac was a forest region with no proud wine tradition. True, it was not on a convenient river, but distilling reduced the volume to be transported to a mere one-sixth or one-eighth. Furthermore, in these backwoods there was no bourgeoisie to haggle over the price. Armagnac's *brandewijn* was taken by waggon to the nearest little rivers, the Adour and the Midouze, which took it to the sea at the port of Bayonne.

The country of the Charente, north of Bordeaux, also had everything the Dutch wanted. For centuries the coastline south of La Rochelle had been one of Europe's chief suppliers of salt, and rich in grain. Vines here took second place. But the hinterland, between Saintes and Angoulême, was also familiar to the Dutch. Angoulême had streams where in the sixteenth century Flemings had established papermills to make "Holland paper".

The chalky "Champagne" slopes south and east of Cognac were available for huge harvests of distilling wine, with no shortage of firewood for the stills. Perhaps their wine could have been good for drinking, but that was not what the Dutch wanted. They were making fortunes in distilling, whether of undrinkable beer at Schiedam near Rotterdam, or of scarcely drinkable wine up and down the French coast. They were also doing well selling Swedish copper to the French to build stills, then buying back their brandy. It was a matter of sheer chance that the light wines of the Charente produced a brandy with relatively little of the unpleasant taste of crude spirits that normally needed disguising, as Dutch gin was with juniper berries.

Another great source of wine that the Dutch did not neglect was along the river Loire. Angers and Tours were surrounded with vineyards growing the ancient and excellent Pineau de la Loire, usually known today as the Chenin Blanc, whose wine has great keeping qualities, and in sunny autumns can also become distinctly sweet. The Dutch were too canny to involve themselves in the stately traditions of commerce in privileged cities such as Angers. They went instead to a district nearby which could be persuaded to produce cut-price Anjou wine; the valley of the little river Layon. Here, it must be said, they left behind them a goodly inheritance.

High-quality sweet wines were the only ones it was worth shipping down the Loire from Touraine and Anjou, because at the border of Brittany, at the little port of Ingrandes, there were high duties to be paid. Dutch commercial logic therefore identified the vineyards below Ingrandes as the place for cheap wine. So here it was the Muscadet and the Gros Plant, low-grade, bulk-producing vines, that they encouraged. It seems their purses of guilders could persuade the poor French farmers to jump through hoops. The biggest source of cheap wine and cheap brandy of all, however, they failed to tap to much effect. They had watched (and helped) with mounting interest as the extraordinary project of the Canal des Deux Mers arrived at completion. This Herculean feat of engineering, a winding waterway linking the Mediterranean at Sète with the Garonne and thence with Bordeaux, and climbing hills in ladders of locks

disciplined excess Never let it be thought that the Dutch led coldly efficient lives on their quarterdecks and in their counting houses. On their capacity for drink, the baffled English ambassador, Sir William Temple, hazarded: "The qualities in their air may incline them to drinking. For though the use or excess of drinking may destroy men's abilities who live in better climates, yet on the other side, it may improve men's parts and abilities in dull air, and may be necessary to thaw and move the frozen or unactive spirits of the brain." A most ingenious excuse.

Seventeenth-century Bordeaux had its trade dominated by the Dutch, who owned three-quarters of all the ships in Europe. Their chief interest was cheap white wine.

in the process, was completed in 1681. One can imagine the excitement in the Languedoc as the growers thought the Atlantic was about to be opened to them. They had reckoned without Bordeaux and its *police des vins*. Throughout the eighteenth century, only five per cent of Languedoc's wines and spirits was exported through the new canal. Even the Dutch had to sail around Spain and through the Straits of Gibraltar to fetch them direct from Sète.

The worm began to turn in the 1650s. First the English, then the French, became increasingly jealous. In 1651 the Commonwealth Government of Oliver Cromwell, reigning between the unfortunate King Charles I and his son Charles II, passed a Navigation Act, which was intended to prohibit the use of third-country (*i.e.* Dutch) ships between English and foreign ports. (Of every six ships leaving English ports, it was said, five were Dutch.) In 1652 Cromwell declared war on The Netherlands, a war in which the English captured some 1,500 Dutch ships, enough to double the size of their own comparatively puny merchant fleet. In 1664 Charles II started a second Dutch war with much less success. The Great Plague and the Great Fire of London paralysed him. The Dutch fleet, emulating Drake, sailed into Chatham harbour and burnt the

English fleet. The score may be said to have been evened, though, by the English acquisition of New Amsterdam, which they renamed New York.

Meanwhile, Louis XIV's Minister of Finance, Colbert, resolved that France should have a navy worthy of its power. The merchants of Nantes and Bordeaux were among many who were telling him that the Dutch shipping monopoly was insufferable and their methods of business less than respectful. Colbert found that France had indeed miserably few ships. His estimate (in 1669) was that Europe's total merchant fleet consisted of some 20,000 vessels, of which 15,000–16,000 were Dutch, 3,000–4,000 were English, and 500–600 French. With wonderful deliberateness and foresight he ordered the planting of oak forests in the Limousin and Tronçais to build French ships far into the future – oaks whose timber now flavours some of the finest wines. A few of Colbert's original trees still stand as memorials to his faith in wooden walls. From oaks of older planting, he built a fleet, and by 1672 was ready for a Dutch war.

The Dutch, of course, took their custom elsewhere, at least for the duration, and went prospecting anew in Spain and Portugal. It was a day of rejoicing for Jerez and Málaga, Alicante and the Canary Islands, Lisbon, and even (once more) the isles of Greece. By 1675 they had opened yet another chapter in the history of wine: they bought a small quantity of potent red from the hills of the Douro in Portugal at its port, Oporto.

CHAPTER 19

JUG AND BOTTLE

Up to the advent of the adulterating Dutch with their *aqua vitae* and their sulphur matches, the chief concern of every wine merchant was to get the goods off his hands as quickly as possible. It was like playing pass-the-parcel. A barrel of wine was perishable, with a sell-by date approaching perilously fast.

With such rare exceptions as the merchants of Venice, who dealt in strong wines, and the abbots or prince-bishops of the Rhine, who possessed cold cellars and enormous casks, the first axiom of everyone making or dealing in wine was to ship it quickly. There is more mention of ships than of cellars in the foregoing chapters. What the French call the *élevage* of wine – its "upbringing" in cellars where it is carefully aged and sometimes blended – scarcely existed. If the product did not keep, there was no call for complicated commercial organization. In the Middle Ages, vinegar merchants in France were more organized than wine merchants; their product could be stored, blended, and distributed on demand.

Why did wine so rapidly turn to vinegar? Because several of the bacteria it contains, but in particular one called *Acetobacter aceti*, only need a supply of oxygen to multiply catastrophically. Acetic acid, or vinegar, is the result. As with all biochemical reactions, the lower the temperature, the slower the process: hence the virtue of cold Rhineland cellars. The virtue of giant barrels was simply that a greater volume of liquid has a smaller proportionate surface area, therefore there is less contact between the *Acetobacter* and its food supply.

A high alcohol content is also protective; the bacteria are less nimbly reproductive under its influence. Sulphur dioxide equally inhibits their sex life. These scientific facts were unknown, but their empirical results were what the Dutch so profitably exploited when they burnt their sulphur matches and added their *brandewijn*. Still, however, they were handling wine in bulk, selling it by the barrel, unwittingly giving it every opportunity for contact with air. The Germans in their cellars, again empirically, knew better; they took whatever steps were necessary to keep their storage tanks (barrels is scarcely the word for such monsters) full to the brim. When they drew wine off, they topped them up from smaller barrels of similar wine. If there was nothing suitable at hand, they even dropped stones into the bunghole to displace the air and keep the *Fuder* full.

Revolution came with the bottle, and a secure means of sealing it. This was the great contribution of the seventeenth century to the story of wine: bottles and corks. Without them the quality of wine could advance – but its capacity to age could not. Nobody knew, or had known since the Romans, what transformations can take place when good wine is sealed away from the air for long periods of time. We are talking not just of a pleasanter or smoother taste, but a different dimension of taste altogether. A little science is needed to explain this felicitous phenomenon.

Wine in bottle, securely corked, has no access to the air, nor the air to it. The bottle contains a small amount of oxygen, as it does of carbon dioxide. Both these gases are soluble, are present when the wine is bottled, and thus find their way into the bottle with the wine. But at that point their amount is fixed. The wine

A quintessentially Dutch meal, painted by Pieter Claesz in 1641. The wine would have been from the Rhineland, drunk from a glass known as a Roemer.

may be swarming with microbes and bacteria. But if they need oxygen to reproduce (as they do), the amount of reproduction they are capable of is limited by the tiny amount of oxygen in the bottle. All the life processes of the organisms that make up the flavour and aroma of wine are slowed down to a crawl in a sealed bottle: slower still if the bottle is kept in a cool place.

There are other biochemical reactions going on, too, which are also competing for oxygen as their fuel. Pigments, tannins, acids, hundreds of natural organic compounds are inherently unstable. They will combine and recombine to form new compounds. Some reactions can take place anaerobically – without, that is, any supply of air. Most need the presence of oxygen to rearrange their chemical structure. So the wine in the bottle is in what is called a "reductive" state: any change reduces the possibility of further change by using up the oxygen supply.

Very fine tuning indeed is what happens under these circumstances. It takes a wine with good inherent qualities: good balance, for example, between its components of acidity, tannins, and sugar (closer to 500 than 400 different natural components have been identified in wine). Given this inbuilt structure, though, the fine tuning can merit the happy description of a "chemical symphony".

All this was not even a gleam in the eye of the bottle-makers of the sixteenth century. Bottles were only made for the convenience of bringing wine to table from its barrel. They varied widely in strength and elegance – from leather "jacks" to stoneware jugs to very beautiful flagons of clear glass. Glass was one of the more expensive materials, and also the most fragile. For those who could not afford glass, the most popular substitute was a form of salt-glazed stoneware originally made in the Rhineland. It was glazed by throwing handfuls of common salt into the kiln during firing. The salt reacted with minerals in the clay to produce a glassy, mottled, usually greyish or brownish surface.

The fragility of glass bottles made in the Italian fashion (when most glass technology came from Italy) was overcome by jacketing them in straw or wicker or leather. The still-familiar Tuscan *fiasco* dates from the fourteenth or fifteenth century. Workaday bottles were made of pewter, tin, even wood – meaning that you could never see if they were thoroughly clean. But while all glass was blown thin it was bound to remain a luxury, and indeed no separate bottle works existed; bottles were made at the same glass houses as drinking glasses and window glass.

Nevertheless, demand rose so much in the early seventeenth century that the Crown became concerned about the destruction of woodlands to fire the innumerable furnaces. The result was a proclamation from King James I "to provide that matters of superfluity do not devour matters of necessity and defence; understanding that of late years the waste of wood and timber hath been exceeding great and intolerable by the glass houses…. Therefore we do straightly ordain, that… no person… shall melt, make or cause to be melted or made, any… Glasses whatsoever with timber or wood, within this our Kingdom…"

So it was to be stoneware jugs and windows made of little pieces of glass in lead "lattices" unless the glassworks changed their fuel. In those days the king offered monopolies in manufacture – naturally for a very substantial fee. The monopolist who bought all the rights to make glass in coal furnaces was Sir Robert Mansell, who in the 1620s made his headquarters near England's best-known coalmines, at Newcastle-upon-Tyne in the northeast. He was allowed to sublet his monopoly to others, and thus coal-fired glass houses sprang up in many parts of the country. It was found that the higher temperatures of coal fires made stronger glass, if not so white as the Venetian style.

At this stage the history of bottle-making, as everything else in England, becomes confused by the troubles of the royal house of Stuart, culminating in the civil war of 1642–9. All the evidence, though, points to an extraordinary courtier, author, alchemist, and even part-time pirate called Sir Kenelm Digby as the inventor of the successor to Mansell's still relatively frail bottles. Some time in the 1630s, and possibly at Newnham-on-Severn in Gloucestershire, near the collieries of the Forest of Dean, Digby started making bottles that were thicker, heavier, stronger, and darker – and cheaper – than any known before.

They were globular in shape, a simple bubble, with a high tapering neck ending in a "collar" or "string-rim" for tying down a stopper. They held about a quart, or quarter of a gallon (which, confusingly, is almost the measure the French at that time called a *pinte*). The bottom had a deep "kick-up" or "punt" where the blowpipe had been attached, which made the bottles very stable standing up. Digby had apparently found a way of making his coal furnace even hotter, using a wind tunnel, to melt a glass mixture with more sand and less potash and lime. The "metal" was darkened to brown or dark olive-green or almost black by the coal fumes, but this was seen as a sign of strength (and was to have the unforeseen advantage of protecting the contents from the light). Digby was shortly afterwards imprisoned as a Royalist and Roman Catholic, and others claimed to have invented his process. But in 1662 Parliament decided it was indeed his invention. He was the

father of the modern wine bottle. His technique was not used in The Netherlands until about 1670, and in France not until 1709 (when the bottles were described as "in the English fashion"). It now remained to equip them with the perfect stopper.

How to plug bottles of whatever sort was a very old problem. The Romans had used corks, but their use had been forgotten. Looking at medieval paintings one sees twists of cloth being used, or cloth being tied over the top. Leather was also used, and sometimes covered with sealing wax. Corks begin to be mentioned in the middle of the sixteenth century.

It has often been suggested, and may well be true, that cork became known to the thousands of pilgrims who tramped across northern Spain to Santiago de Compostella.

It seems that the marriage of cork and bottle, at least in England, took place by degrees over the first half of the seventeenth century; stoppers of ground glass made to fit the bottle neck snugly held their own for a remarkably long time. It is clear from John Worlidge's *Treatise of Cider*, published in 1676, that great care was needed in choosing good corks, "much liquor being absolutely spoiled through the only defect of the cork. Therefore are glass stoppels to be preferred…" – at the cost of no small trouble, since each one had to be ground to fit a particular

A Bellarmine stoneware jug, made in the Rhineland in the seventeenth century. The mask was supposed to be that of Cardinal Bellarmine, a hated opponent of the reformed churches. These jugs were made over a long period, and widely exported.

Cork bark stacked to dry after harvesting. Cork is cut from mature trees every nine or ten years, and corks are cut as plugs from the thickness of the bark. The longest and most even corks are the most expensive, and used for the best wine.

cork Cork is the thick outer bark of the cork oak, *Quercus suber*, a slow-growing, evergreen tree which has evolved this spongy substance for protection and insulation, particularly against fire. The world supply of cork is concentrated in the western Mediterranean and the neighbouring Atlantic coasts. Portugal, above all, furnishes half of the total, and almost all of the top-grade cork for use in wine bottles.

What makes cork so ideal for sealing wine? Its lightness, its cleanness, and the fact that it is available in vast quantities are all important. It is almost impermeable. It is smooth, yet it stays put in the neck of the bottle. It is unaffected by temperature. It rarely rots. Most important of all, it is uniquely elastic. Corking machines are based on this simple principle: you can squeeze a cork enough to slip it easily into the bottle and it will immediately spring out to fill the neck without a cranny to spare. As for its life span, it very slowly goes brittle and crumbly, over a period of between twenty and fifty years. Immaculately run cellars (some of the great Bordeaux châteaux, for example) recork their stocks of old wines every twenty-five years or so, and one or two even send experts to recork their old wines in customers' cellars. But many corks continue to do their job for half a century.

bottle, using emery powder and oil. The "stoppel" was then tied to the bottle by a piece of packthread around a "button" on top, because of course it would fit only the bottle it was ground for. As late as 1825, the ultimate luxury bottle stopper was still, at least in some eyes, a ground-glass one. Beautiful handmade bottles, *bouchée a l'émeri* (that is, with glass stoppers ground with emery), were used for some of the wine of Château Lafite in 1820 and 1825. It was (wrongly) believed that cork allowed air to reach the wine and spoil it; in reality the problem was probably just poor-quality cork giving the wine a "corky" taste. Eventually, glass stoppers were abandoned because they were usually impossible to extract without breaking the bottle.

Cider, beer, and homemade wines were what the seventeenth-century householder chiefly bottled. Bottling by wine merchants only began at the very end of the century. In 1609, Sir Hugh Plat's *Delights for Ladies* advised keeping beer in the barrel ten or twelve days before bottling it (presumably in stoneware bottles), "making your corks very fit for the bottles, and stop them close." By 1676, when Worlidge wrote his *Treatise of Cider*, all the elements were in place for modern-style bottling. Having chosen good corks, says Worlidge, steep them in scalding water and "they will comply better with the mouth of the bottle, than if forc'd in dry; also the moisture of the cork doth advantage it in detaining the spirits".

"Therefore", he goes on, "is laying the bottle sideways to be commended, not only for preserving the corks moist, but for that the air that remains in the bottle is on the side of the bottle from which it can neither expire" (i.e. escape) "nor can new be admitted, the liquor being against the cork. Some place their bottles on a frame with their noses downward for that end" – not a good idea, says Worlidge, because (as any visitor to a Champagne house knows) any sediment then rests on the cork, and "you are sure to have it in the first glass". His ideal cellar is one with a "cool refrigerating spring" which will keep cider "until it be come to the strength even of Canary itself." Seventeenth-century cellars still exist equipped with shelves with holes to take the "noses" of upside-down bottles. Others used a bed of sand for the same purpose. What is clear is that by this time the principle of "binning" liquors in corked bottles to age them was well understood.

Only two facilities remained to be invented: a corkscrew so that the cork could be driven right in, not left half-out like a stopper, and a cylindrical bottle that could be binned on its side, not ostrich-fashion. The second evolved over the first half of the eighteenth century. The first remains a teasing mystery.

The first mention of a corkscrew in print is rather later than you might expect: 1681. It was described (by one N. Grew) as "a steel worm used for the drawing of corks out of bottles". "Steel worms" had been in use for at least half a century for drawing bullets and wadding from firearms that had (rather unnervingly) failed to fire. When did imagination, provoked by thirst, make the connection with bottles? No one knows. But the word corkscrew was not coined until 1720. The original of the essential implement was called a "bottlescrew".

CHAPTER 20

BORDEAUX REBORN

There have been few times in European history when the rivalries of nations were more blatantly, petulantly, one could almost say childishly displayed than the closing years of the seventeenth century. Whatever irked a monarch was a pretext to go to war. Underlying the major themes of dynastic successions, rival religions, and the Divine Right of Kings ran a dialogue of bickering and jealousy about trade, and tariffs, and whose ships should carry what that kept international relations in ferment at every level. The three nations most involved were France, The Netherlands, and England, in a web of intrigue and treachery that reflects little credit on anyone.

We have seen repeatedly throughout our story how politics shape trade, and trade fashions the wine it wants from wherever it is forced to buy. At this juncture, politics pushed trade about until it grew almost dizzy. But at the same time trade had found a new impetus: the wine trade in particular was supplying new classes of customer that encouraged it to diversify.

On April 10, 1663 (a full three weeks since his last renewal of his fervent vow to abstain from wine entirely), Samuel Pepys, then aged thirty, spent an evening drinking at the Royall Oak Tavern in Lombard Street in the City of London. Next day in his peculiar coded diary Pepys wrote the most momentous tasting note in the history of Bordeaux. "Drank", he wrote, "a sort of French wine, called Ho Bryan, that hath a good and most particular taste that I ever met with." Pepys, no great connoisseur but a man who liked to be up with the fashion, was the first to record a completely new kind of wine, and that within a few years of its invention. What is

more, he characterized it perfectly in that one word, "particular". What he had tasted was Haut-Brion, the first wine from Bordeaux ever to be sold under the name of the estate where it was made; the prototype of every château wine from that day to this.

For sixteen centuries England had been buying the majority of its wine from Bordeaux. But it had always been a simple bulk commodity, better or less good according to its freshness, the season, and the competence and honesty of the traders involved. Suddenly, faced with competing new drinks and the impudent thrift of the Dutch, Bordeaux's most dynamic citizen, the first president of the regional parliament, had taken the initiative. In 1660 he started marketing (the modern term seems quite appropriate) the wine of his estate as a distinct brand (another term as yet uncoined) at a substantial premium. And he directed his campaign not at the Dutch, the biggest buyers of the time, but deliberately at Bordeaux's most loyal and oldest market: London.

The Pontac family had been in the ascendant for well over a century. They were landowners and lawyers, self-confident members of the rising class of merchants, descended from artisans and heading for titles of nobility. Already in 1505 an Arnaud de Pontac had risen by the classic formula of exporting wine and importing cloth to become mayor of Bordeaux.

The Pontac pattern was to be followed time and again in the following centuries. Trade bought land; land brought power – but the acquisitive instinct did not fade in the new proprietors as it had in the old aristocracy they were eventually to replace.

In 1660 the Pontac in power was another Arnaud. His

Arnaud de Pontac staked his family name on his Bordeaux; it was the first wine to be known by a brand name, and was sold in London at the sign of Pontack's Head.

ancestral country house was an hour's ride to the south: the stone-built château of Haut-Brion, sited by his great-grandfather on the meanest patch of gravel in the region that took its name from its parched and stony soil – the Graves.

Experience had shown that the arid, gritty soil was as good for vines as it was poor for anything else. The Archbishop's estate close by had been admired in centuries past. Not until the second Arnaud, though, did anyone see fit to capitalize on that.

As though to underline the novelty of his move, in 1647 a committee had sat to establish prices for the different wines of Bordeaux: a sort of distant foreshadowing of the celebrated classification of 1855. The scale of prices is a direct reflection of the formidable new Dutch influence. In 1635 the Dutch had become allies of the French, and by 1647 they were calling the tune in the affairs of Bordeaux: hence a price scale that put their favourite white Sauternes at the top. Dark *palus* wines, made from Petit Verdot grapes, often on the Bec d'Ambès, the drained marshes at the confluence of the Dordogne and Garonne, came close. But the scale made no distinction of the best sources of claret. It trailed the coarse *palus* wines in price. And not a single estate is mentioned by name. This was the situation that inspired

Arnaud de Pontac to carve out a new sort of market.

What was new about the "Ho Bryan" that Pepys found "most particular" – apart from its name? We can only suppose that Pontac's standards of winemaking were as elevated as his social position. He could afford to be a perfectionist. He could charge for his name; he could limit his crop to gain more flavour and strength; he could reject mouldy grapes, and less successful barrels. He presumably possessed a press, and may possibly have judged it a good idea to use a little press-wine to stiffen his claret and give it more colour and character. Extra time in the vat is a probability – Pontac is described in several references as deep in colour. Pontac could use new barrels for all his wines if he chose, and see to it that the barrels were kept topped right up to the bung. All these practices became standard in the eighteenth century on prosperous estates setting out to make their reputations. Up to Pontac's time they were rare or non-existent.

There is no evidence that he was concerned about specific grape varieties, nor that he was aware that older vines make tastier wine. Although it was certainly unusual to have a large block of specialized vineyard, the best conclusion seems to be that his real innovation was marketing. He made Haut-Brion his "first-growth"; then, like that other prince of the vine three centuries later, Philippe de Rothschild, he lent his family name to the wine of his other properties, of which, unexpectedly, the principal was the estate of de Pez, in St-Estèphe, far to the North in the then largely undeveloped Médoc, reachable only by river. His Médoc wine (some also came from Le Taillan, just north of the city) he sold simply as "Pontac". With the two brands he attacked the London market – with perfect timing.

In 1660 the English had restored a monarch to their throne and ended a decade of Puritan Commonwealth rule. Five years later Pontac sent his son François-Auguste to open a tavern more luxurious than any seen before in England (or possibly even in France), under the sign of Pontack's Head. It was a roaring success. It stood just behind the Old Bailey, and seems to have remained in business for more than a century, until it was demolished in 1780. Pontack's Head has been called London's first restaurant. Its prices were extremely high: dinner could cost two guineas. Haut-Brion sold for seven shillings a bottle (when two shillings was a normal price for good wine). Pontac and Haut-Brion were also sold retail, to a clientele of London's aristocracy and fashionable men of letters.

Pontac's initiative had been dazzling. It almost proved premature nonetheless. In 1679 a tariff squabble led the English government to ban French wines. Colbert took advantage of the distress in Bordeaux to try to abolish its *police des vins*. In 1682 Arnaud de Pontac died, leaving a messy succession involving lawsuits and resulting in divided ownership – so often the curse of French estates. The English market reopened to a flood of claret in 1685 (in 1687 more barrels were shipped than in any year between the fourteenth and twentieth centuries) – only to be slammed shut again three years later by the Glorious Revolution and the arrival of William III, whose thrust was anti-French.

To make matters worse, the years 1692–5 saw four catastrophic vintages in a row. Bordeaux was even (for one year) forced to admit Languedoc wine via the Canal des Deux Mers to fulfil its depleted order book and supply Paris (where, too, the harvest had failed) and the naval arsenals at La Rochelle and Brest, where the French navy, bottled up by the British blockade, was presumably consoling itself at table. The accounts of Haut-Brion for these years show such wine as there was being sold to the navy or to the hostelries of Bordeaux. There was a similar tale of woe at Château Latour, just emerging from the anonymity of the Médoc. Its owner, the Marquis Daulède, sold no wine at all in the four years up to 1693.

There was immense relief on both sides in 1697 when William III and Louis XIV signed a treaty – considerably tempered by the fact that the English government then charged duty on French wines at more than double the rate charged on Spanish and Portuguese. After a decade of doing without claret, with an ever-greater range of alternatives being offered at lower prices (and not just wines, but spirits, coffee, tea, and the rest), it is a wonder that the English persisted in their old affection at all. Most, of course, did not. The great change, foreseen by Arnaud de Pontac, was that claret in England had become a luxury wine, and a status symbol for a new breed of political potentate.

The shipping figures for the port of Bordeaux in the year 1699–1700 tell the story. Of 86,000 *tonneaux* loaded in the port, less than 2,000 were (officially) destined for England, a similar number for Ireland (where Dublin was already a considerable city, and the population of the country almost half that of England), and 1,000 for Scotland. Of the rest, more than half (but mainly white wine) was loaded for The Netherlands, the Baltic and northern Germany, especially Hamburg, and not much less (mainly red) for Brittany and French north-coast ports. How much of this was destined for smuggling to England there is no knowing, although a certain suspicion must rest on the tiny Ile d'Yeu off the French coast, which supplied a very large number of small boats, and whose inhabitants (if they drank what they imported) were getting through something like 200 litres of claret a head a year.

Up to this point, the Médoc has only had a passing mention. By its very nature it is cut off: a long tongue of forested and marshy land running north from Bordeaux between the Gironde estuary and the ocean, with dunes of sand (the world's highest) on the ocean side, and not dissimilar "dunes" of gravel deposited over many millennia along its river shore. Where it narrows at its northern end (the "Bas-Médoc") it was so marshy that the northernmost Roman settlement was an island (to them Noviomagus; today "Brion") three miles west of St-Estèphe, where they cultivated oysters. Not until the Dutch *dessiccateurs* were given drainage concessions there in the early seventeenth century did fertile fields begin to emerge from the swamps.

"*Sauvage et solitaire*" ("wild and lonely") was the description given to the whole of the Médoc in the sixteenth century.

Château Haut-Brion, the "Ho Bryan" of Pepys' diary, and the finest quality wine that Arnaud de Pontac had to sell. His lesser wine he sold simply as "Pontac".

Fortresses going back to the Hundred Years War dotted the length of the Gironde, but there was no road: communication was by boat between the little harbours and jetties of Macau, Margaux, St-Julien, Pauillac, St-Estèphe, and points between. Only the villages nearest Bordeaux, Blanquefort and Le Taillan, had some direct commercial activity, selling wine in taverns in the town. Most landowners were absentees, deriving scant rents from scattered hamlets in the forest. Where there were vines, they were part of a mixed subsistence agriculture. In 1572 the domaine of Lafite was divided among some sixty tenants, who mainly grew wheat.

Nonetheless, it was only a few years after the Pontacs started work on their Graves estate that a handful of Bordeaux lawyers and *parlementaires* had a similar idea about the Médoc. The old aristocracy was not unwilling to sell its rights over such marginal fragments. The name of the game was consolidation. What is immediately striking is that the first estates to be consolidated remain the "first-growths" to this day. It must have been very clear to these ambitious investors that the best vineyard land was, like Haut-Brion, the most unpromising-looking gravel, which, particularly in the Médoc, is found on the highest of the low swellings of the land (they scarcely merit the name of hills) designated by the names "Lafite", "Lamotte" – and also "Brion".

In the 1570s, one Pierre de Lestonnac began assembling small parcels of land around "Lamothe-Margaux", the future Château Margaux. In the same years the Pontacs were acquiring properties in St-Estèphe, Le Taillan, and the Bas-Médoc. Best documented of all is the enterprise of Arnaud de Mullet, who by 1595 had become proprietor of the estate of Latour de St-Mambert – known to future generations simply as Latour. His son Denis was to absorb all the micro-properties of tenants, buy more adjoining land, and by the 1650s complete the transformation from a feudal patchwork to an estate in the modern sense, run by a salaried manager or *regisseur*. At the same time he planted vines where wheat had grown before, taking advantage of his right as a privileged citizen of Bordeaux to send his wine upriver to the city by *gabare* (the shallow-draft Bordeaux barge) to be sold on the Bordeaux market.

There is no doubt that agriculturally the new nobility of Bordeaux had profited from the example of the Dutch (as well as their engineering). When the Dutch put in their new vineyards in the dark earth of the *palus* beside the river it was in the tidy *polder* style: the vines all of one kind, in straight rows so that oxen could pull a plough between them. Old Bordeaux vineyards had been planted *en foule* – the French for higgledy-piggledy – propagated by layering, and workable only laboriously with a spade.

When Denis died the Latour estate was inherited by the family of Daulède de Lestonnac, already proprietors of Château Margaux and in due course to succeed to a share of Haut-Brion. To an extraordinary extent it was one family, or rather one close-knit and interrelated group of local politicians, which founded and developed the whole concept of the Bordeaux château – and the "first-growth" one at that.

A map by Amsterdam cartographer Jocondus Hondius, showing the route up the river Gironde to Bordeaux from the sea, in about 1629. The Médoc is in the foreground.

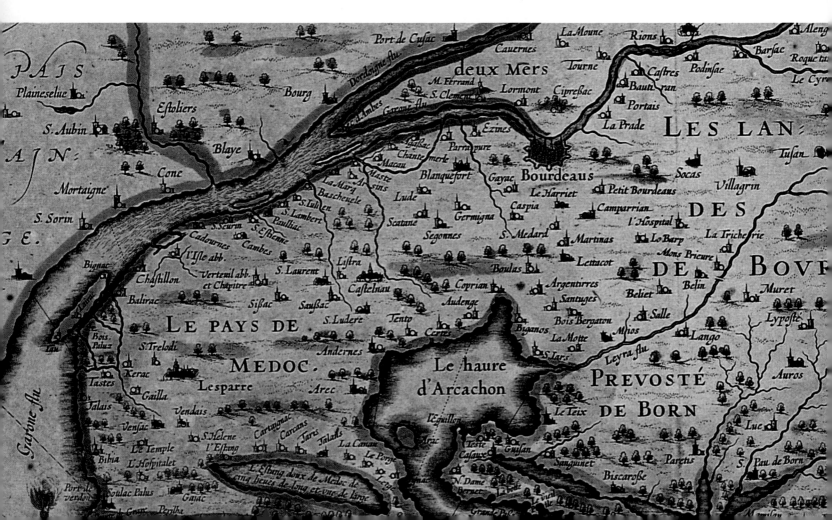

The breathing space between the Treaty of 1697 and the outbreak of the next and more widespread war was too brief to allow a serious new initiative by the "first-growths" in England. London was being provisioned by Spain and Portugal – and also by Tuscany, whose "florence", bottled in flasks and packed in wicker hampers, was a fashionable alternative to an all-Iberian diet. The principal change when war started again was the exclusion of the (now enemy) Spanish wines – to the glee of the Portuguese.

The English were to grow more and more accustomed to drinking white wine from Lisbon and red wine from Oporto, not to mention madeira and even "Fayall" from the Azores: every Portuguese flavour, in fact. A little relief came down the Rhine in the form of rhenish, or via the merchants of Amsterdam, who managed, even at the height of the war, between 1705 and 1709, to negotiate passports for their ships into Bordeaux. But for top-quality claret and other French wines, the only recourse was the harvest from privateers operating under all colours in the western approaches and the English Channel. The record of sales of "prize wines" – wines captured at sea by privateers, to be sold by auction in the coffee houses of London, Bristol or Plymouth – gives a fascinating insight into the progress of the "first-growths", their recognition by the British public, and the prices they fetched. It also poses a question with no apparent answer: what were these precious goods doing at all in the narrow waters infested with sea robbers that separated France from England?

In 1703, the year war broke out, one of the first prizes to be brought in was the good ship *Prophet Daniel*, laden with white wines from Bordeaux and the High Country, and also with claret, unspecified. The white wines fetched £8 a tun; the claret £25. The *Golden Pearl of Stettin* (evidently a Baltic ship) carried a similar cargo, but with claret of widely different qualities that fetched between £8 and £60 a tun. Other ships captured were carrying Spanish wines.

By 1705 prizes had been brought into port with cargoes of Loire wines and brandies as well as the usual barrels from Bordeaux, the High Country, and divers parts of Spain. But in May 1705 a sequence of substantial auctions of "first-growth" claret began. In the first auction there were 200 barrels of Haut-Brion and Pontac (sold two barrels at a time), a month later 230 barrels of Haut-Brion and "Margose" (Château Margaux now had the same proprietor as Haut-Brion), and only two weeks after that the cargo of the *St-Jean-Baptiste*: 288 barrels of Pontac, Margaux and Haut-Brion. The prices fetched were about £60 a tun.

It is very hard not to smell a rat in this sudden apparition, on the high seas, of a quantity of one proprietor's wines that must have represented his entire production. Not many years earlier the harvest at Haut-Brion filled fifty-odd barrels. Even with the production of de Pez and his other properties, 718 barrels is a remarkable amount. What prudent proprietor would have loaded it all in three ships at the same time? Where were they going? And who had bought the wine? Was it a mad merchant of Amsterdam taking the risk?

"pure white sand, mixed with a little gravel" The English philosopher John Locke, during his five-year stay in France, was intrigued enough to pay a visit to see the apparently unique vineyard that could produce such a "particular" taste. When he arrived at Haut-Brion, on May 14, 1677, he inspected the vineyard and found it on a little hillock facing west, whose soil "is nothing but pure white sand, mixed with a little gravel. One would imagine it scarce fit to bear anything". As for the price of the wine, he blamed his fellow-countrymen: "A tun of the best wine at Bordeaux, which is that of Médoc or Pontac, is worth... eighty or 100 crowns. For t his the English may thank their own folly, for, whereas some years since the same wine was sold for fifty or sixty crowns per tun, the fashionable sending over orders to have the best wine sent to them at any rate, they have, by striving who should get it, brought it to that price."

Locke's mention of the Médoc is surprising, since his pilgrimage was to Haut-Brion in the Graves, on the opposite side of town. Vines in the Médoc then were few and scattered. Some, however, did belong to the Pontacs. This is the earliest evidence that the district name (as opposed to the family name) carried any weight.

Various suspicions cross my mind. First, it seems probable, if not obvious, that the Pontacs and Daulèdes were making a calculated assault once more on the London market: their only serious market, war or no war. Second, since the privateer received a large proportion of the price (the government getting the rest, with a fee to the coffee-house owner), is it just possible that the privateer was under charter to the châteaux owners? Nobody could afford to lose his entire crop to the enemy year after year (which is more or less what happened). The simplest explanation is that a private arrangement brought the auction price, less some fairly hefty commissions, back to Bordeaux.

However the system worked, it encouraged the owners of Bordeaux's two other "first-growths" to follow suit. In May 1707, "an entire parcel of New French Clarets" was offered at Brewer's Key, near the Tower of London, "being of the growths of Lafite, Margaux and Latour". They were the new season's wines, shipped without racking on their "gross lees". In the same week the cargo of the *Liberté* was auctioned: 200 barrels of Haut-Brion. Who can doubt that it was all a cosy arrangement? If the only way to your market was to steal your own goods, what harm was done?

By the later stages of the war, it must have become clear to proprietors in the Médoc that the peace would bring them a fortune. At last the Dutch star was falling in Bordeaux. After 1709 no passports were issued to Dutch ships, and the price of their favourite white and *palus* wines fell, while the English appetite for "new French claret" from the Médoc promised a golden future. Tasting notes described with relish these splendid clarets, better than anything known before, not just as "particular", Pepys-fashion, but as "bright, deep, fresh and neat".

When in 1709 a terrible winter froze northern Europe, killing large numbers of the Bordeaux vines, the need to replant to be ready for the end of the war seized the Médoc and started what contemporaries described as "a fury of planting". In the next twenty years the Médoc we know today was born.

CHAPTER 21

THE FIRST
PERFECTIONIST

O f all the world's great wines, only one is popularly credited with an inventor. The wine is Champagne, and the man held responsible a Benedictine monk, Dom Pierre Pérignon, the treasurer of the Abbey of Hautvillers, which has overlooked the river Marne from its vine-covered slope since the time of the ascetic St Columbanus.

Many different claims have been made about good Father Pérignon. The easiest to dismiss is that Champagne suddenly became sparkling in his cellars. Many legends about him, such as the idea that he was blind, that he was the first to use corks, that he said "I am drinking stars", or that he could unfailingly name a precise vineyard by tasting a single grape of its production, seem to have been inspired by the fantasies of the last treasurer of the Abbey, Dom Grossard, who was obliged to leave when the Revolution closed it down. It may be argued that Grossard had had access to the lost archives (although nobody before him had told these stories), but it seems more likely that he simply liked to embroider the already lofty reputation of his predecessor. For Pérignon seems to have become almost the patron saint of Champagne within his own lifetime. It is intriguing that we can only surmize the reason why.

I n a sense Champagne was only recovering lost ground. It had been acknowledged in Paris in the fifteenth century that the wines of Aÿ (originally considered among the *vins de France*, rather than coming from a distinct region) were of

exceptional quality. In the early sixteenth century, King François I was glad to call himself "*Roi d'Aÿ et de Gonesse*" – Gonesse was the place reputed to produce the finest flour for white bread in the north of France. The name of Aÿ came to be used as shorthand for the whole district, just as "Beaune" was used for Burgundy. The same wines were alternatively known as "*vins de la rivière*": wines, that is, from the north bank of the Marne opposite Epernay. The vineyards here slope steeply up to the "mountain" that separates the Marne valley from the district of Reims. "Mountain" is a slight exaggeration for this substantial flat-topped hill, crowned with a forest of beech, but "*vins de la montagne*" was the term for the less highly esteemed production of the vineyards on its gentle northern slope.

T he abbey that appointed Dom Pérignon as its treasurer in 1668 had already set its sights on developing its wine business. In 1661 the Abbot had commissioned a great new vaulted cellar. Hautvillers possessed a modest ten hectares/ twenty-five acres of vineyards of its own, but was paid tithes of grapes from villages around, most notably Aÿ and Avenay. The payment of these tithes was a matter for endless wrangling that raises the most fundamental question about the wine of the region at the time. We know that it was not sparkling. We know they were growing black grapes, the Pinot Noir among them. But was the wine red or white, or something in between?

The debate arose over tithes because they were collected in kind, in the vineyards, during the vintage. Small barrels called *trentins* were distributed, and had to be filled with grapes packed tight by treading. In the case of Aÿ, the Abbey had the

right to one barrel in eleven. The citizens objected that if they trod their grapes into the *trentins* the juice would be stained red by the skins. It ruined their chance of making their best wine, which was white. They would prefer to pay in wine (or cash) when the wine was made.

The question of red or white was crucial because the region had set out to compete with Burgundy as far back as the days of the Valois Dukes. It was probably then, in the fifteenth century, that Pinot Noir was planted. And red was what was wanted. Reims was on the road used by Flemish wine merchants travelling to Beaune; they were glad to be offered a cheaper alternative with a similar flavour and after a shorter journey. The wines did not quite achieve the *moëlleux*, the richness, of burgundy, but their colour could be (and was) deepened with elderberries.

Why then did the people of Aÿ want to make white? Because experience showed that if their red could never be truly first class, their best attempts at white wine could. White wine made from white grapes had nothing like the same flavour and, they found, quickly turned yellow. What they actually made was a very pale wine, varying with the vintage from claret colour to *gris* (grey), a slightly darkened white, but more often *oeil de perdrix* (partridge eye), a shade of delicate pink caused by the white juice having brief contact with the red skins. Hence the fuss about the *trentins* for the tithes. And hence, it seems probable, the first success of Dom Pérignon. He organized the harvesting so as to achieve truly white wine, and at the same time studied the best vineyards, the best timing, the best techniques, and the best way of preserving the wine to make it as aromatic as possible, silky in texture and long in flavour.

The golden rules of winemaking that were established in Dom Pérignon's time, presumably by him, were set out in 1718, three years after his death, by the very precise Canon Godinot. First, use only Pinot Noir. The vineyards of the region also contained Pinot Meunier, Pinot Gris (or Fromenteau), Pinot Blanc (or Morillon), Chasselas, and perhaps Chardonnay. Dom Pérignon did not approve of white grapes partly because they increased a latent tendency in the wine to referment.

Second, prune the vines hard so that they grow no higher than three feet and produce a small crop.

Third, harvest so that the grapes are kept intact, on their stalks, and as cool as possible. Work early in the morning. In hot weather choose showery days. And reject any grapes that are broken or even bruised. Small grapes are better than big ones. Lay out wicker trays in the vineyard, and pick over the crop for rotten grapes, leaves, or anything undesirable. Even lay a damp cloth over the grapes in the sun. They must be kept fresh. If possible have the press house nearby so that you can carry the harvest in by hand, but if animals are essential, choose mules – they are less excitable than horses – or failing mules, donkeys.

Fourth, on no account tread the grapes or allow any maceration of the skins in the juice. An efficient and fast-working press is essential (peasants, therefore, stood no chance of making this kind of wine). The press must be used repeatedly and briefly, and the juice from each pressing kept apart. The first, the *vin de goutte*, runs with the mere weight of the wooden beams being laid on the grapes. Its wine alone is too delicate; it lacks body. The next two pressings, the first and second *tailles*, or cuts (because the cake of grapes must be cut up and replaced in the press), are of good quality. The fourth, the *vin de taille*, is rarely acceptable, and any further cuts are *vins de pressoir*, but this time distinctly coloured and of no use to the perfectionist cellarmaster. The press-house workers were completely exhausted by the quick-fire work, day after day for three weeks or more. That was part of the price for extraordinarily fine wine.

The blending of wines was a regular practice, but Pérignon, it is said, blended the grapes from different vineyards before they even went into the press. He had three press houses at his disposal, and grapes from many different plots. It was his discovery that carefully judged proportions of grapes from a number of different vineyards, according to their ripeness and the distinctive flavours derived from their soils, made a better and more consistent wine than lots pressed individually. It is the exact opposite of the philosophy of Cîteaux, whose monks strove to distinguish and differentiate, letting the soil show through the Pinot Noir. At its simplest it could be explained as an attempt to guarantee quality and consistency, which makes it sound almost suspiciously like the public-relations patter of a modern Champagne house.

The more one learns about Dom Pérignon, the harder it is to decide exactly what he did to make his Abbey's wines as valuable as their invoices show that they were. In 1700 the "most excellent" wines of the region sold for 500 *livres* a cask, but those of Hautvillers (and also of another Abbey, St-Pierre-aux-Monts at Pierry, whose treasurer, Dom Oudart, was a friend and colleague of Dom Pérignon's) sold for 800 to 900 *livres*. So famous was Pérignon by this time that Parisians took him to be a village like Aÿ, or an abbey like Hautvillers, and looked for his name on the map. But the most impressive evidence of the advance of Champagne in his lifetime is the fact that in 1706 it was reported that "a recent traveller had drunk Champagne in Siam and Surinam". Such travels would have been impossible without the mastery of bottling.

His region's wine presented one great problem to Pérignon. It had an inherent instability: a tendency to stop fermenting as the cold weather closed in in autumn, then start again with rising temperatures in spring. This did no harm while the wine was still in cask in the cellar, but Pérignon was not enamoured of the cask. He found it "tired" his wines, and they lost all their famous aroma unless they were bottled as soon as possible. Pérignon used intensive cellar-work to prepare them. The abbé Pluche, who seems to have known his methods, wrote in 1744, "Lees and air are the two plagues of wine". To rid the wine of all lees needed repeated rackings into clean barrels, with the attendant risk of exposing the wine to too much air. The answer was laborious: as many as twelve successive rackings by the method that allowed the least splashing and contact with air, by forcing the wine from one cask to another with a bellows providing pressure from the top.

The lighter and greener the wine, the more subject it was to fizzing in the spring. White-grape wine was fizziest: one of the reasons why Pérignon used only black grapes. But black-grape wine, made with his precautions, also lasted and matured for far longer. "Formerly the wine of Aÿ lasted hardly a year", wrote the abbé Pluche, "but since white grapes have not been used in the wines of Champagne, those of the mountain of Reims keep for eight to ten years, and those of the Marne easily go five or six."

In England, cellar work was not so meticulous. A treatise under the title *The Mysterie of Vintners* was presented to the newly formed Royal Society in 1662. Its subtitle tells all: "A Brief Discourse concerning the various sicknesses of wines, and their respective remedies, at this day commonly used." Among the remedies were beetroot for colouring pale claret, elderflowers, lavender, cinnamon, cloves, ginger… To preserve Rhenish must, the author tells us, the Dutch "rub the insides of the vessel with cheese". More alarmingly, "country vintners feed their fretting wine with raw beef", and most off-putting, "herrings roes preserve any *stum* [that is, muted or stopped] wine". These are the practices of honest vintners. "Many other ways there are of adulterating wines, daily practised in this our (otherwise well-governed) City."

Many wines are mentioned by name; Champagne is not among them. But one sentence is momentous in our story: "Our wine-coopers of later times use vast quantities of Sugar and molasses to all sorts of wines, to make them drink brisk and sparkling." In the very next year, 1663, the satirist Samuel

Dom Pérignon in the vineyards, from a stained-glass window at Epernay. In spite of the legends about him, he was more interested in making still wine than sparkling.

Butler, in his poem *Hudibras*, makes the first English mention of "brisk Champagne". Champagne was not a normal part of the repertoire of the English wine trade, but it was already known in London, and coming into fashion, three years after Charles II took the throne (and five years before Dom Pérignon moved to Hautvillers). And there is an implication (although less than evidence) that it was rather fizzy. By 1676 it was specifically described, on stage, as "sparkling".

Paris was already in love with the lively white wine whose "perfume so embalms the senses that it could raise one from the dead". In 1674 Champagne was "so frantically fashionable that all other wines scarcely passed, in smart circles, as more than *vinasse*" – or as we might say, plonk. Louis XIV had simply never drunk anything else. He was a great conservative. He never tried coffee, or chocolate, or tea, or spirits, until in 1695 his all-powerful physician Fagon put him onto a mixture of old (*usé*) burgundy and water. The Burgundians were no doubt delighted, but by this time Champagne was established.

Louis XIV gave the signal for the start of regular commerce in Champagne in 1691. He created the office of *courtier-commissionnaire*, giving (for a hefty price) the right to set prices, arrange purchases, and take commissions, although not actually to buy and sell. This essential activity was still done by personal contact or at an open market: buying to hold stock

These *crayères*, or Roman chalk quarries, are underneath Reims. In the nineteenth century they became used as cellars; in World War I they became shelters from the guns.

was not unknown, but it was illegal. It was also illegal to sell or transport Champagne in anything but barrels. A trade in sparkling Champagne was therefore strictly speaking impossible. Admittedly wine was delivered in bottles by, among others, Dom Pérignon. He wrote in 1694: "I gave [he does not say sold] twenty-six bottles of wine, the best in the world." It was also impossible for another reason: France did not have bottles

strong enough to take any pressure. Its glassworks were still wood-fired. There were experiments with different shapes, from globes to pears, and English glass-blowers went to work at Ste-Menehould, the nearest glasshouse. But the problem remained: if Champagne became really *mousseux*, the bottle would probably burst.

The precise Canon Godinot gives us the best indication of when the fashion changed. In 1718 he wrote: "For more than twenty years French taste has preferred *vin mousseux*." To reconcile the state of taste and the lack of bottles is a problem.

The solution, perhaps, is that *mousseux* is a relative term. Given only the natural tendency to referment, wine bottled in March (the full moon was preferred, when high atmospheric pressure helps to keep the wine "tranquil" and clear) would be variably fizzy, but probably most often in the condition known until recently as *crémant* with just enough gas to pop the cork.

By the time Dom Pérignon was sixty, fashion was demanding more and more of the sparkling wine he had spent his career trying to avoid. Nobody knew more about it than he – his experience of cellar work would have been invaluable whether you wanted bubbles or not. He certainly knew, for example, that the cooler the vintage, and the lighter and more acidic the wine, the less fully it fermented in autumn; therefore the more potential it had for sparkling the following year. White wines from white grapes were lighter and more prone to referment, so a proportion of them was increasingly added. At first the desire for sparkle led makers into overdoing the under-ripeness. The Epernay landowner, and one of the first Champagne merchants, Bertin de Rocheret, described one Champagne in about 1700 as "green and hard as a dog, dry as the devil". "Montagne" wines were rarely used: the famous Sillery remained "*vin gris*", and utterly tranquil, until the early nineteenth century: the Champagne of old-fashioned, unfrivolous connoisseurs. Increasingly, the best white-grape wines came from certain villages on the hills south of Epernay: Cramant, Avize, Le Mesnil.

A most important factor, increasingly so with sparkling wines, was good cellarage. Deep cellars with unchanging temperatures could make all the difference between bottles bursting or not. The subsoil (and indeed the soil) of Champagne is solid chalk: the ideal material for excavating deep, capacious cellars with little risk of collapse. It is said that Dom Ruinart, another colleague of Dom Pérignon, made the momentous discovery, under the city of Reims itself, of gigantic funnel-shaped chalk quarries dug by the Romans for building stone and long since forgotten. Ruinart's nephew Nicolas founded what is considered the oldest surviving Champagne "house", using these *crayères*, in 1729. In 1716 an even more familiar name had made its appearance: Claude Moët, a grower of Epernay, bought himself the recently created office of a *courtier-commissionnaire*. Now that Champagne-making was becoming so complicated, involving capital to buy and bottle wine, the development of a specialized manufacturing side to the business was inevitable.

Still the fizziness or otherwise of the wine remained a hit-and-miss affair, and the sufficient strength of the bottles extremely uncertain – so much so that once an order was placed the risk of *casse*, of bottles bursting, was borne by the purchaser. Depending largely on the vintage, anything between twenty per cent and ninety per cent of the bottles exploded. It was the height of folly to walk through a Champagne cellar without an iron mask to protect your face from flying glass.

There was also the question of sediment. Any refermentation produces a residue of dead yeast, which is trapped in the bottle

We know who was responsible for the prompt modishness of Champagne in London at a time when it was still a rarefied taste in Paris. It was the Marquis de St-Evremond, a soldier, courtier and irrepressible satirist. In Paris, St-Evremond and his friends were known as Epicureans, or laughingly as the *Ordre des Coteaux* because they would drink nothing but Coteaux d'Aÿ, Coteaux d'Hautvillers or Coteaux d'Avenay.

In London St-Evremond made himself the unofficial agent of Champagne. In 1664 the Earl of Bedford ordered three *tonneaux* of Sillery for his palace at Woburn. All the grandees of the day took to the new taste. With it they ordered bottles and corks: the new strong bottle invented by Sir Kenelm Digby. Unlike the vintners, they probably did not "use vast quantities of Sugar and molasses". But they did find their Champagne, bottled on arrival, was perceptibly fizzy, if not downright frothing, when they opened it months, perhaps even years, later. What is more, to the disgust of St-Evremond, they were delighted with the fizz. The old epicure was as repelled by bubbles in his favourite wine as we would be by bubbles in our claret.

and will look unsightly in the glass. Modern Champagne-making, which involves adding both sugar and yeast to achieve a high degree of sparkle, produces so much sediment that removing it is an essential part of the process. But when there was only a little yeast left naturally in the wine the sediment was usually tolerable. Early eighteenth-century Champagne glasses, elegant conical "flutes", were often made with a dimpled surface to hide any slight sediment in the wine. In years when the sediment was substantial there was nothing for it but the uncertain and wasteful process of *dépotage*, or decanting the wine into another bottle, losing a great deal of the precious gas en route. The modern system of *remuage*, indeed the whole process understood by the term *méthode champenoise*, was not to begin for almost another hundred years. Throughout the eighteenth century the majority of Champagne remained still wine (and much of it red). It was only a minority of light-minded customers (and rich ones, too) who became addicted to the *saute-bouchon*.

Just how light-minded is made remarkably clear in the memoirs of the Regency that followed the death of Louis XIV in 1715. The later years of the Sun King's reign had been less than brilliant. Although Paris was enjoying an economic boom, life at Versailles was austere. The Regent, Philippe d'Orléans, held a very different court at the Palais Royal.

The nightly *petits soupers* there deserved all the scandalized gossip that surrounded them. The Duc de Richelieu laid all the blame on the fashionable wine: "The orgies never started until everyone was in that state of joy that Champagne brings." The games were led by the Regent himself, who liked to see his mistresses (including the Duchesse de Berry, his own daughter) perform tableaux as Greek goddesses, although less modestly dressed. The candles were taken away to give free rein to the emotions provoked by Champagne.

No other wine, no other drink, had ever created a mood that almost amounted to a way of life. The perfectionism of the Abbey treasurer had given the world a model that all wines with pretensions to excellence would have to emulate.

CHAPTER 22

ANYTHING BUT PORT

If Champagne, and the "new French clarets" of the Bordeaux parlementaires, were wines created specifically for a growing class of rich and more or less discriminating customers, port, which shares their birth date almost precisely, was just as precisely the opposite. It was a makeshift, wished on the English by their politicians. Two elements entered their calculations: an embargo on imports from enemy France, and the brazen intention of taking advantage of an old ally. There were few scruples in the way England imposed itself upon the luckless Portuguese. The port-wine trade is a happy ending to a story with a fairly discreditable start.

Portugal in the fifteenth and sixteenth centuries had flung itself recklessly into overseas exploration and expansion. The feats of its navigators had gone to the nation's head. This tiny nation had fanned out across the world from Greenland to Goa, from China to Brazil, but in doing so they almost shut up shop at home. In 1580 the cold-blooded Philip II of Spain annexed his neighbour's realms. The "captivity" of Portugal by Spain lasted for sixty years. By 1644, when Portugal achieved independence from Spain, its relations with England had become distinctly one-sided and rather too close for comfort. Portugal was at risk of becoming an English colony. The English were so well established in Portugal, with so many privileges, that when they quarrelled with France it is no wonder they came to Portugal for wine. It was already almost as though they were buying it from themselves.

In the 1660s there were three established English trading headquarters in Portugal: the *feitorias*, or factories, at Lisbon, Oporto, and Viana in the Minho, the northernmost province. Viana began to lose its importance to Oporto as trade with the bigger city grew, and as Viana's harbour started to silt up. The sandbar at the mouth of the Douro was also a problem, but more traffic and a narrower entrance here made it easier to keep open. The wine country was still considered to be the Minho, north of Oporto up the coast, with a preference for the wines of Monção on the border with Spanish Galicia. Monção grows a better grape variety, the white Alvarinho (some said it was introduced by the English from Greece). It is trained low, not up trees, and makes a stronger, more stable wine than the usual Minho lightweight.

The Minho is intensely fertile, densely populated, and highly cultivated country where the vine has to take its chance with every sort of agriculture, and is consequently grown overhead, out of the way, up tall trees in the ancient Roman fashion. (More recently vines were grown on high pergolas; now many are trained on wires.) Today the quality of its wine – freshness, not to say sharpness – is appreciated and taken advantage of as "Vinho Verde". The familiar white exported version, though, is a mere polite parody of the original. In the seventeenth century Minho wine was considered a just passable alternative to claret. Then, as now, the great majority of the region's produce was full-coloured red, light in body but with an alarmingly acidic "bite" and considerable astringency. At an old

LEFT The steep landscape of the upper Douro had to be rebuilt with terraces to make cultivation of the vine possible. This is the immaculately kept Quinta do Noval.

barcos rabelos Today the Douro is a sequence of lagoons between hydroelectric dams, placid except for the water-skiing families of the port shippers. But up until the 1960s much of the journey down-river could still be made by *barco*. With thirty or forty pipes of port piled high on board, the unwieldy ship cruised quietly enough along calm stretches of water, then became agitated as soon as one f the many rapids approached. In the mounting clamour of river over rocks, with high stone banks closing in to form a gorge, the oarsmen took a deep swig from a big wooden bottle, then almost delicately directed the accelerating vessel towards the main channel, while the helmsman, perched high on a rickety bridge astern to look out for rocks ahead, shouted directions. With a sense of huge weight effortlessly propelled, the boat plunged down the white water sluice, sheets of spume flying from the bow, then settled calmly among the whirling eddies, while the helmsman set the prow straight for the next *cachão*.

the Upper Douro today, an entirely man-made landscape, where terrace upon terrace reaches from horizon to horizon, it is almost impossible to believe that in 1700 it was nothing but stark, scrubby schist. Infinite pains built the fortress-like walls that hold the soil in place on the mountainsides; infinite

The city of Oporto in the early eighteenth century, seen from Vila Nova de Gaia. The heart of the city looks much the same today, but the river has much less shipping.

pains are still needed to cultivate them, and to lug out the entire vintage in baskets shoulder-high where not even a mule can go.

The British at last had a source of the strong wine they had always hankered after, almost entirely under their control. Their methods of control were none too delicate: a farmer's daughter, it was said, was often the price he had to pay for striking a reasonable bargain. The shippers built warehouses, or "lodges", to handle the huge quantities of wine at Vila Nova de Gaia, on the south bank of the Douro near its mouth, facing the steep bluff on which Oporto stands from a gentler and more manageable slope. In 1727 the British shippers formed themselves into an association, largely to be able to browbeat the growers and keep down their prices. But Portugal was, for once, thriving. Gold and diamonds pouring in from Brazil made the government feel able to cope with even the domineering British.

It soon occurred to the less scrupulous vintners that it was altogether too much trouble to go mountaineering up the Douro, and that something they could pass off as port to a gullible public could be concocted out of almost any wine, so long as the result was thick and fiery. The vintner's trade had rarely had a conscience about adulteration. Brandy was not the only thing that began to be added. Deep colour was provided by

elderberries; the fiery flavour the English began to crave by adding dried pimentos. The merchants' greed eventually had the inevitable result. The fashionable drink was denounced by envious brewers and distillers – and by honest vintners, too. In the 1730s the price of port began to falter; in the 1750s it began seriously to slide.

Self-righteously the British shippers in Oporto wrote a letter blaming their woes entirely on their suppliers, whom they accused of growing inferior wine in the wrong places, not treading it long enough, adding too much brandy of inferior quality too soon, and using elderberries for colour. The growers' commissioners threw back similar accusations in the face of the British. There was a degree of right on both sides; both seem to have had an idea of an ideal port wine which scarcely, at that time, existed.

Neither had made the discovery that for brandy really to stabilize the wine and make it sweet, as well as strong, it must be added halfway through fermentation, and in substantial quantities. Adding small amounts merely postponed the end of fermentation, and virtually guaranteed murky and unstable wine. The shippers were right in thinking the vineyards could have been better, too. Vines had not yet been planted around the highest reaches of the river, where the wine was eventually to be the very richest, and most high-flavoured of all. But in the 1750s river traffic stopped at the Valeira gorge, a fall too rapid even for the *barcos rabelos*. Above the gorge (which was later to play a tragic part in our story) the schistous mountains stretched moonlike, still waiting for the vine.

T he argument might have dragged on interminably, had not Portugal been struck, in 1755, by a devastating calamity. Lisbon in all its prosperity was almost totally destroyed by an earthquake that killed 40,000 people. Perhaps for the first time in history the international community reacted with sympathy, and sent relief supplies. The hero of the hour was the King's chief minister, Sebastião de Carvalho – who was later created Marquês de Pombal. This intelligent and dedicated patriot soon acquired almost dictatorial powers. To finance the rebuilding of the capital, he conceived of a series of monopolistic trading companies. The following year he established the General Company of Agriculture of the Wines of the Upper Douro, and seized effective control of the port trade.

T he Douro Wine Company, as it was soon called for short, had sweeping powers. Its charter obliged it to control all exports of port, to reserve 10,000 pipes a year for export to Brazil (to be sold for gold), and to demarcate the vineyards in which port could be grown in two quality zones: *ramo* for domestic and Brazilian consumption, and *feitoria* for the better wines to go to Britain and northern Europe. It controlled the quantities produced, fixed maximum and minimum prices, and arbitrated in all disputes. In 1761 it also acquired the monopoly of the sale of brandy for fortifying the wines. Whether this improved the quality of the brandy is hard to say, but it must have inclined the Company to

encourage its use. The only exception to its export monopoly was that British firms could ship wines, once they had been passed by the Company's tasters as being of *feitoria* quality, to Britain. Foreigners could become shareholders in (but not officers of) the Company.

The British, of course, were furious. From virtual monopolists themselves they were now reduced to mere middlemen who were told what they could buy and at what price, and where they could sell it. An accommodation had to be found, though, because buyer and seller still depended on each other. Indeed, in 1762 Portugal had to cope with another Spanish invasion – which it could only repel with the help of British arms. It soon became known whom, and how much, to bribe; but bribes added to the cost of the wine.

There is no doubt that Pombal intended to improve quality as well as to break the British stranglehold. He ordered and enforced the uprooting of all elderberry trees in northern Portugal. He also strictly limited the use of manure in *feitoria* vineyards. But it was in delimiting the best wine-growing areas that he was positively visionary. By choosing only the schistous soil (and avoiding the granite outcrops in the area) he foreshadowed the whole notion of controlled appellations. Port-growers today bear out his judgment. If you are buying a vineyard, they say, go to see it by moonlight. The quartz in granite soil glints under the moon; true schist is unreflecting black. You will be able to taste the difference in the wine.

Pombal's stated reason was that vines should not grow where corn could be planted: an argument that increased the quantity of food, and the quality of wine, at a stroke. The destiny of the high wilderness of the Douro was to be wine. In acting as he did he made Oporto the specialist wine port and obliged Lisbon to diversify. As for his own splendid estate, just west of Lisbon at Carcavelos, it was said to grow some of the best red wine in Portugal, so it could do no harm to sell it, if the price was right, as port.

Port was not yet by any means a wine of refinement. In 1763 James Boswell, Dr Johnson's biographer, wrote: "A bottle of thick English port is a very heavy and very inflammatory dose. I felt it last time that I drank it for several days, and this morning it was boiling in my veins." But the best must already have had the potential to mature into an excellent drink. Strength cannot have been its only commendation to Englishmen who could afford to drink any wine they wanted. As the eighteenth century progressed so did the Englishman's cellar, full of bottles quietly metamorphosing into plenitude.

table matters Today we can be objective about the table wine of the Douro, which was what the first port wine in England was. Since the 1980s there has been an accelerating move among port shippers and independent growers to sell the wine they have always enjoyed themselves as a daily mealtime drink, and it is delicious: intensely fruity, and varying in style from soft and light to structured and dense. Indeed the Douro is establishing itself as one of Portugal's leading table wine regions, and has overtaken traditional regions like Dão and Bairrada in quality.

CHAPTER 23

TOKAJI ESSENCE

The same war that forced the British to accept Portuguese wines as their destiny was responsible for the promotion of another wine, scarcely less novel and not at all less noble, at the extreme other end of Europe. In 1703, the year of the Methuen Treaty, Ferenc Rákóczi, the Prince of Transylvania and a Protestant, took up arms against the (Catholic) Austrian occupation of his native Hungary. Louis XIV saw his intervention as a useful distraction. His enemy the Emperor of Austria would be obliged to keep a guard on his back door as well as his front. The Sun King was also extremely impressed by the present of wine that arrived from Rákóczi's estates: a wine that already had a reputation in eastern Europe, but had never before reached Paris. Its name (slightly simplified from the Hungarian) was Tokaji.

Eastern Europe has been absent from our story for many centuries, but the long silence has not meant that wine-growing fell into disuse. It is doubtful whether at any time since the Greeks introduced it via the Black Sea (if that is what happened) the valley of the Danube has been without wine.

Neither Attila and his Huns, nor the Avars who succeeded them (to be crushed in due course by Charlemagne), nor the Magyars who founded the Hungarian nation had any motive to destroy the amenity of vineyards. The Church played its usual role in the Middle Ages in propagating and stabilizing wine-growing, encouraged by such enlightened monarchs as Bela IV, who imported Italians and Flemings skilled in wine, and the famous wine-lover King Matthias Corvinus, whose realm stretched (briefly) from Bohemia to the Carpathians.

Like their contemporaries in the wine villages of the Rhineland, serfs who worked conscientiously with their vines acquired privileges. Hill vineyards were distinguished from flat ones, for sound empirical reasons, and the communities that established them became remarkably democratic, with rights of inheritance, and privileged access to the market, matched by duties of loyalty, service, and attendance at assemblies to check the quality of their wine. Vineyards were surrounded by hedges that defined privileged areas. These were surprisingly early moves in the direction of controlled quality. The results were that such communities as Sopron, Somló, Eger, and Debrö built reputations that went far beyond Hungary, to its natural market in northern lands with no wine of their own. Poland, Russia, Sweden, and the Baltic countries all looked to Hungary for more potent and flavoursome wine than (for example) the north of France could provide. Summers are hot in Hungary. Its continental climate is tempered by the influence of the Mediterranean. The Hungarian hill regions could provide wine halfway between the light wines of the North and the expensive malmseys of the old Greek world. This promising scenario was disastrously interrupted in 1526 by the Ottoman Turks under Suleiman I, who destroyed the Hungarian knights at the Battle of Mohács on the Danube. For 160 years the Turks were to occupy the greater part of Hungary. Wine-growing was not entirely suppressed (the Turks were content to collect taxes, and not exactly allergic to wine themselves), but its high morale was

LEFT The castle at Sárospatak, in Tokaj, came into the ownership of the Rákószi family in 1617. They used control of the wines of Tokaj as a diplomatic weapon.

at an end in most of the country. The exceptions were along the northern borders, where Eger's famous resistance to a siege by Ali Pasha earned its wine the name of Bull's Blood, and where the hills of Tokaj-Hegyalja, rising from the banks of the Tisza and the Bodrog, presented the invaders with no obviously desirable prize. The worst threat here was Turkish slave raids – Hungarians fetched good prices in the market at Istanbul.

The very early history of this singular region is little known. What is reported is that King Bela invited Italians here in the thirteenth century, and that they brought with them their favourite vine, the Furmint, which, together with the more succulently flavoured Hárslevelü and a little Muscat, composes the modern wine of Tokaji. As early as 1502 a deed of sale, to the noble family of Garay, mentions two individual vineyards, Hetszoló and Mezes Mály. Both are still in existence. Many of the unique small-bore cellars tunnelled in the tufa are much older still. Whatever wine they made in such a naturally favoured site was surely above average, but it had no international importance until the Turkish invasion, when it became one of the few potential sources of revenue for the beleaguered Hungarians.

The Rákóczi family makes its appearance in the story in 1617, when it acquired the estate of Sárospatak and started a long campaign to monopolize the wines of the region, by this time regarded as Hungary's best. Thirty years later the Rákóczis acquired the old castle of Tokaj itself. It was surely not coincidence that only three years after that their overseer delayed the vintage, on the pretext of an expected Turkish attack. So legend explains the discovery of the noble mould,

Botrytis cinerea, which shrivelled the grapes, and led to the most luscious wine anyone had ever tasted. This account antedates the similar story of its discovery in Germany by 120 years. More likely, though, late-harvesting was already ancient practice.

The Turks did attack in 1678, and pillaged the region. It was their last fling; five years later they were routed at Vienna, with enthusiastic help from the King of Poland, and in 1686 lost Budapest. The Hapsburg Empire had them on the run.

Ferenc Rákóczi used Tokaji as his diplomatic weapon in trying to save Hungary, now free of Turks, from being similarly overrun by Austrians. Louis XIV loved the wine. He described it as "*le roi des vins et le vin des rois*" (and France promptly flattered it with imitation). But he did nothing to help Hungary. Austria and its allies (England included) won the war, and the Hapsburgs began their rule of the long-suffering Hungarians. But already in 1700 Rákóczi had established a classification of the quality of the Tokaj vineyards in three ranks, according to their soils and situations – the first such classification in Europe. It was rapidly, in 1723, ratified by the new Hapsburg government.

Tokaji was much the finest wine of the Hapsburg Empire, which stretched from Dalmatia to Poland, so the Emperors appropriated its best vineyards, and used it, as the Dukes of Burgundy had used their Beaune, for impressing and ingratiating themselves with foreign monarchs. Peter the Great of Russia and Frederick I of Prussia both rapidly became addicts. The Tsars established a Commission for Hungarian Wines at St Petersburg to ensure regular supplies, leased vineyards (but banned foreigners from buying them), and took vines to the Crimea to try making their own. What did not go to Vienna, Moscow, St Petersburg, Warsaw, Berlin, or Prague was snapped up by the grandees of Britain, The Netherlands and France. The world had no wine to

The Polish knights who helped to end the siege of Vienna in 1683, defeating the Ottoman invader Kara Mustafa, took home a keen interest in the wines of Tokaj.

compare with it for sweetness – except perhaps an exceptional cask in some prince-bishop's cellar of the Rhine. Port was still "blackstrap" while Tokaji was a wonderfully perfumed syrup.

The precise method of making Tokaji, and the way in which its sweetness and intensity are determined and measured, are still unique in the world of wine. They seem to relate more closely to Pliny's way of describing different degrees of concentrated sweetness in a Falernian than any current wine-making techniques. The most fabled liquor of all is (or was) Tokaji Eszencia or essence. *Eszencia* is made only of the syrupy drops squeezed from a tub of grapes – if "grapes" is the word for the perished mass, half raisin, half fungus – by their own weight.

These first drops have a sugar content so high that they preserve themselves against fermentation. In cool conditions they remain simply grape juice of incredibly sticky sweetness and overwhelming flavour, pouring as slowly as treacle and by no means transparently clear. They are a blending ingredient, rather than a drink. Their very scarcity, though, as well as their searing sweetness, makes them a legendary luxury. Tsars and archdukes were pleased to believe that failing powers of almost any kind could be restored by this elixir. There are countless stories of inert noblemen and enormously senior men of religion springing from their beds – or alternatively into them – as a drop touched their lips, and of octogenarians becoming fathers of large families. To make more of a drink of such a sticky fluid, the merchants often added brandy. It helped to discourage any effort of the *eszencia* at fermentation, and gave the patient (drinker is scarcely the word) more of an impression of fortifying power.

The Tokaji that was traded as wine, rather than an imperial elixir, was what is known in Hungarian as *aszú*, and in German as *Ausbruch*. The original procedure was to wait until the Essence had oozed from the shrivelled grapes, then pour the juice of the remaining grapes over this "*aszú* dough" and tread them together. The must of this first treading fermented to produce *aszú*. A second treading of the same "dough" with more juice of normally ripe grapes gave the second-quality wine, known as *maslas*, and a third, *forditas*. Wine made of all the grapes harvested together without distinction is *szamarodni*, a Polish word meaning "as it comes". The Tokaji known as Imperial and drunk by the Emperors in Vienna was the *aszú* blended with a measure of the *eszencia*.

Today the richness of Tokaji is precisely defined. Nominally it consists of a stated number of measures (tubs called *puttonyos*) of the must of the shrivelled *aszú* grapes displacing the contents of a barrel of normal juice. The modern reality is more humdrum: richness is measured in grams of sugar per litre. The maximum number of virtual *puttonyos* is six, resulting in an intensely sweet wine with almost limitless ageing potential. A very little of the Imperial-style wine is still sold, as *aszú eszencia*. And an infinitesimal amount of *eszencia*.

What gives Tokaji its singular flavour is harder to define: the grapes; the soils; the continental climate; the native yeasts; its long slow fermentation in small barrels in damp cold cellars,

The tunnel-like cellars of Tokaj have some of the most dramatic cellar mould to be seen anywhere in the world. It is pleasingly soft and dry to the touch. The wines are still aged here in half-size casks, a process vital to their unique character.

lined with a mould as particular in its way as the penicillin of the Roquefort caves. The finest wines, though, have this in common: vivid scents and flavours of dried fruits, among them apples, pears, quinces, and oranges, maturing over many years (fifty, even 100 may not be too many) to something between butterscotch and marmalade. Its power lies in its concentration; like a sweet German wine, its alcohol content is modest. But like madeira, a wine with a similar lifespan, its acidity is awesome. The result: a mouth-coating tang that can last an hour.

The meaning of Tokaji in the story of wine is simple. Another and better kind of wine could invent itself, given a very peculiar set of natural conditions – and the help of a princely patron. A wine so striking would have political consequences. And the world, or the worldly, would beat a path to its door.

pole position The centre of Tokaji connoisseurship throughout the eighteenth century was Warsaw. The famous merchant house of Fukier there maintained a cellar of every vintage since 1606 (of which vintage the Nazis stole 328 bottles in 1939). The bottles were always kept standing up, their corks renewed every six years. Tokaji was always in demand, despite the jealousy of the Hapsburgs, who decreed that for every barrel of noble Hungarian wine exported, a barrel of their relatively pedestrian Austrian wine must be sold as well.

CHAPTER 24

GROOT CONSTANTIA

In 1816, an apparently omniscient Frenchman named André Jullien published a work of breathtaking breadth and boldness, leaving far behind every book that had ever attempted to catalogue the wines of the world. He called it *Topographie de Tous les Vignobles Connus* – "the topography [it should really be translated as "whereabouts"] of all known vineyards". He might well have added "and unknown" to his title: his researches discovered pockets of wine-growing in corners of Asia, Africa, America, and eastern Europe, on islands in the ocean, and in passes, of the Hindu Kush, where nobody would expect any such thing.

Most remarkable of all Jullien's undertakings, perhaps, is his bold-as-brass classification of almost every wine in the world into one of five categories of quality. Few, it is true, were likely to take issue with him on whether the Cossack productions of Ekaterinoslav or those of General Bekelof in the outskirts of Astrakhan rightly belonged in class four or five. He was more exposed, though, when he described the wine of Constantia at the Cape of Good Hope as "among the finest liqueur wines of the world, ranking immediately after that of Tokay". This was the generally accepted view of his time, reflected in the alarming prices Constantia fetched in Europe.

Stranger still is the fact that Constantia and Tokaji rose to eminence at almost exactly the same time; that the first wine of the New World to be acknowledged great is yet another product of the era that gave us sparkling Champagne, first-growth claret, Tokaji, and the first fumblings of port. Perhaps Constantia was only a first fumbling in the seventeenth century, but Constantia is the more remarkable in demonstrating how even in a savage,

and backward environment, infinite pains can procure excellence – also how when the pains stop, so does the quality.

The Portuguese navigators who discovered the Cape of Good Hope found nothing to interest them in this empty land, sparsely inhabited by savages. They were looking for cities rich in spices, and sailed on for India. In 1652 Johan van Riebeeck set up the first permanent victualling station for his masters in the Dutch East India Company, a fort and a farm. He wrote to the seventeen directors for vine cuttings, which they sent in 1654. The Company had taken the trouble to fetch cuttings from the Rhineland and sew them up in damp little packets of sailcloth. Too damp, in all probability; they did not take root.

The next year's batch, assembled from Germany, France, Spain, and Bohemia, was more successful. The first vintage was pressed in the Cape in 1659: fifteen litres from French Muscadel grapes. The "Hanepoot Spanish" were "not yet ripe". Hanepoot, or sometimes Hanepop, is a Cape Dutch word for the most ancient of Muscat grapes, the Muscat of Alexandria, brought from the eastern Mediterranean as the mainstay of Málaga, and also planted in the Canary Islands. The latter may have been a staging post for some of the vines that eventually found their way to South Africa and later Australia.

But the development of a wine industry was no part of the Company's plans for its possession at the Cape. Rice to feed the slaves was more important. The Company has been

LEFT The Constantia estate was founded by the first governer of the Cape, Simon van der Stel; it was the size of Amsterdam and was divided into three parts after his death.

described as "that most profitable blend of unblushing piracy and commercialized Protestantism". It only allowed a few chosen, and hopefully sober, ex-servants, released from service to become Free Burghers and farm on their own behalf, to make and sell wine locally. Anyone else who hoped to earn from wine-growing had to send his produce all the way to Batavia. Gradually the Dutch factors in the Indies realized that their best hope of drinkable wine was to encourage the Cape to make it, and arranged for a winemaker from Alsace, a press, and a cooper to make barrels on the Company's farm of Rustenburg. Twenty-

five years after van Riebeeck's settlement there were still only 189 European settlers (including 117 children) and 191 slaves.

The man who brought prosperity and civilized life (at least for himself) to the Cape was the Company's new Commander, Simon van der Stel. He was forty when he was sent to the Cape in 1679. Among his recruits he took with him a French winegrower. He founded the new settlement of Stellenbosch in a lovely wooded valley a few miles inland, and in 1685 contrived to be granted (against the law and custom of the Company) an estate at the back of Table Mountain: a big estate, exactly the size of the

whole of Amsterdam at the time, and about fifteen times as much as a normal land grant. He named it Constantia, perhaps after one of the Company's ships, or possibly in honour of a quality he admired. The legend that it was named after his wife is false. She was called Johanna, and stayed behind in Amsterdam, never to see her husband or children again.

Van der Stel developed Constantia with extraordinary speed into an almost princely estate. He planted avenues of European oaks to break the force of the destructive southeast gales, leading through the glittering clusters of the native silver-

the great and the small Today Groot Constantia is a national monument, its vineyards a state wine farm whose wine, although good, does not attempt to reproduce the famous dessert wine of the eighteenth century. That challenge has been taken up by its neighbour, Klein Constantia, which since 1986 has produced an excellent sweet Muscat under the name Vin de Constance. So what was the original like? In 1970 I was privileged to drink a glass of the 1830 vintage from the London cellar of the publisher George Rainbird. The wine was in an English pint bottle of the period, sealed with wax over the cork. It was in beautiful condition: extremely soft, pale amber in colour, with odours of balsam, and I thought, a trace of orange, it was still sweet, mouth-filling, and exceptionally harmonious, with a flavour that seemed to combine a tang of citrus and a smoky richness. The only wine I have tasted that it resembled was a Málaga of about the same period from the Duke of Wellington's estate of Molino del Rey, which shared these smoky-orange aromas and soft richness. Neither had any trace of the very recognizable Muscat flavour – which is not to say they never did.

trees to a substantial mansion. In his extravagant gardens he planted every sort of fruit tree, but lavished most care on his vineyards. The first tasting note came back from Batavia in 1692: "The wine from Constantia is of a much higher quality than any sent out so far, but obviously only available in small quantities". By 1705 (when Count Rákóczi was sending his Tokaji to Louis XIV), F. Valentijn, in his *Description of the Cape of Good Hope*, could write: "The lovely red Constantia wine… need not yield place in strength and charm to the best Persian wine or to the Italian Lacryma Christi, and in addition this estate has also an exceptionally good, in fact the best, Steenwyn and Krystalwyn, so divine and enchanting in taste, that only a truly fine palate could distinguish it from the best Tosca…"

The comparison with Persian wine is teasing. Other references imply that Persian vines were taken to the Cape. Were they from Shiraz? The Steen grape is the Chenin Blanc, imported from the Loire valley, but what "Krystalwyn" was is a matter for conjecture, as indeed is the "best Tosca".

There are just enough glimpses of Constantia in those early days to show what perfectionism went into its winemaking. A visitor in 1710 reported, "I saw the wine-pressing house with all the casks… their woodwork and all equipment is scrubbed white and clean". Van der Stel planted many varieties of vine, often under confusing names. "White French" was the Spanish variety Palomino, used for making sherry, "Green Grape" was Sémillon, and nobody knows what "Pontac" was – although one may imagine it came from Bordeaux. It seems that he also planted Steen. But his fame was to come from Muscat varieties.

Such was the first flowering of Constantia – and it was brief. The Governor, as he was to become in 1691, retired in 1699, and his seemingly loathesome son Willem Adriaan inherited the post. He was recalled to The Netherlands in disgrace, and when Simon died in 1712 his empire was divided. Two of the three parts had vineyards: Groot and Klein (Great and Little) Constantia. It was Klein Constantia, under Johannes Colijn, that

An aerial view of Constantia. The Cape has an ideal climate for making fine wine, and some of the most beautiful and dramatic landscapes of any wine country.

took up the challenge of making the Cape's outstanding wine.

Colijn was evidently a good businessman. He sold his wine to the Company regularly to make sure that the Dutch market was made aware of it. He charged twice as much for the red wine as for the white, and seems to have been able to stretch his supplies by buying wine from his neighbours. In 1733 Groot Constantia once more came on the market, and he was able to unite the properties. When he died in 1743 the ownership became complicated, but the two Constantias were perceived as being one wine estate again, and remained so, although with a somewhat dimmer reputation, for his widow's lifetime.

In the 1770s Groot Constantia was sold again, in a very run-down condition, to a rich middle-aged landowner, Hendrik Cloete of Stellenbosch, who "possessed about one hundred slaves, and enjoyed every comfort obtainable in the country". Cloete replanted the vineyards and in 1790 built the new cellar which is the best example of the Cape Dutch architecture of its day. The farmers of the Cape had developed a homely style of building of enormous charm, characterized by a gable in the middle of a long wall of the building over the door. The purpose of this gable was to protect the doorway from burning thatch if the house caught fire. Long hooked poles were used to pull the thatch off, so the exit had to be kept clear. At Groot Constantia, the gable was the frame for a masterpiece of Bacchic baroque sculpture in the dazzling white of every Cape farmhouse.

Hendrik Cloete used his 100 slaves to extraordinary purpose. In his pursuit of perfection he stationed them among the vines so that if an insect dared to land on one of his grapes it was instantly removed. His wine was acknowledged magnificent, but his business sense was less so. In 1793 he made the fatal mistake of signing a perpetual contract with the Company to sell it sixty casks of his best wine every year at a fixed price – with no allowance for inflation. He did not live to reap the whirlwind. It was his son Hendrik, who took over the management in 1794, who had to face the problem – compounded with another and more immediate one: the invading British.

I n 1795 the British landed at the Cape and rapidly overwhelmed the slight Dutch forces at the Battle of Muizenberg, almost within sight of Constantia. Hendrik Cloete commanded the Stellenbosch Burgher Cavalry. But there was scarcely a fight. Under the British there was no interference with the peaceful farming life of the Cape settlers, just a new set of bureaucrats to deal with – and a much-augmented stream of sightseers. The languid tones of the British upper class can be heard loud and clear in their memoirs. Robert Percival was, I fear, typical: he did not even trouble to find out Hendrik Cloete's name: "The farm which produces this richly flavoured wine belongs to a Dutchman, Mynheer Pluter, and has long been in his family…" Not entirely surprisingly, Percival did not find "Pluter" in a good humour. He and his friends simply tipped the Constantia slaves and were shown all over the estate – including a wine tasting.

At least Percival appreciated the wine. "Its exquisite flavour", he wrote, "is chiefly to be attributed to the great care taken in the rearing, dressing and encouragement of the vines…

and not suffering the leaves, stalks and unripe fruit to be mixed in the press as done by the other Dutch farmers." He added: "A couple of glasses are quite as much as one would wish to drink at a time."

British possession of the Cape was confirmed in 1814. At first the only wine the British were interested in was the famous Constantia. Having promised the inhabitants freedom from "the monopolies and oppressions which have been hitherto exercised by the East India Company… Everyone may buy from whom he will, sell to whom he will", the British commander, Sir Henry Craig, discovered to his glee the agreement Cloete's father had made with the Company, and promptly forgot all fine sentiments about oppression. Disregarding Cloete's protests, he left the new Governor, Lord Macartney, to enforce the letter of the unfortunate contract, keeping enough barrels of each vintage, bought at a knockdown price, to give the British high officials at the Cape a wonderful perquisite to which they had not a shadow of right, and sending the bulk to England "to be at his Majesty's disposal".

Under the impossible circumstances, with the virtual confiscation of a large part of his production, it is a great tribute to Cloete that he kept up his standards as long as he did. It is true that Constantia was now world famous. Napoleon, exiled on St Helena, was known to have enjoyed it. King Louis-Philippe of France in due course joined the appreciation society. But the British government not only starved the goose that laid the golden eggs; it also removed the workforce that made such luxury possible. In 1799 Macartney's secretary, John Barrow, was writing memoranda about trading wine for slaves with America, "a trade that seems susceptible of very considerable augmentation". Thirty-five years later slavery was proscribed in all British dominions and the Royal Navy used to blockade slave-trade ports. A British army captain at the Cape made a very pertinent observation, even if Constantia was the exception that proved the rule: "Among the terrible reactions produced by the slave trade, none is perhaps more merited or more evident than the dissoluteness of morals and ferocity of disposition which it creates among people who are concerned with it." The standard of wine farming at the Cape was generally lamentable. "The defects in the Cape wine proceed from the avarice of the planter on the one hand and his extreme indolence on the other," wrote Barrow.

A hasty step by the British government was to make it worse. Suddenly alive to the fact that a British possession could supply cheap wine, it reduced the duty on its import to one-third of that on Portuguese wines. By creating a virtually open market for any sort of rubbish, it pre-empted any move by South Africa to capitalize on Constantia's reputation. Constantia alone held its standards for as long as it could, under the dogged Cloete. Having encouraged cheap winemaking, the British then changed their minds and (in 1841) raised the tariffs, so that South Africa's cut-price wines were uncompetitive in Britain.

The end of the story of Constantia was sad but inevitable. In 1859 the fatal vine mildew oidium appeared at the Cape. In 1861 Britain removed its tariff barrier against French wines. In 1866 phylloxera struck.

CHAPTER 25

ISLAND OF THE IMMORTALS

Great wines are made by their markets; that is an axiom you can apply at any stage of history. Of course they are not made without good grapes and a tolerable climate, still less without investment and diligence. Only one wine, though, has gained its place in history by the brutal way it has been treated. The masochist is madeira. If it had remained in its beautiful island home, or merely been shipped the few hundred miles to Europe, its unique qualities would never have emerged. But its fate was to suffer the tropics, and conditions that destroyed its competitors. Madeira became what it is (or rather has been) – the longest-living, most pungent and luxurious, yet most vigorous and energizing of wines – because its market lay across oceans, even across the Equator – and by some miracle it had the constitution to survive.

Madeira is the largest of a group of islands 400 miles into the Atlantic off the coast of Morocco: the nearest of the Atlantic archipelagos that had been dimly known to the ancients as the Isles of the Blest, and perhaps given rise to the legend of Atlantis.

The Canary Islands were the first to be rediscovered in the fourteenth-century Age of Exploration, probably by the inquisitive Genoese following the coast of Africa southwards. None seem to have returned, though, from a course due westwards straight out into the Atlantic, until in about 1345 a cog from Bristol was blown off its course for the Mediterranean, and after thirteen days of tempest made a landfall on an unknown island. The story is full of pathos. The cog belonged to a Bristol merchant-venturer, Robert à Machin, who was eloping with the daughter of a nobleman above his station. Both died on

the island and were buried on the beach where a village now stands bearing a Portuguese version of his name, Machico.

When the crew set sail again eastward they were captured by Moorish pirates and the cog, *La Welyfare*, was taken into Tangier. There, in the prison, they met a captive Spanish pilot, Juan de Morales of Seville, and told him their story. Morales was ransomed, but on his way home was captured once more, this time by a Portuguese captain trained by Henry the Navigator, Juan Gonçalves, known as Zarco, the one-eyed.

Two years later, in 1418, Zarco, together with the Genoese pilot Perestrello, in turn found himself blown off course en route for West Africa, and landed on an island that they supposed to be Machin's discovery. From it, on the southwest horizon, they watched a dark cloud like "vapours rising from the mouth of hell". The experienced Genoese knew it must be a considerable island, and stayed with his ship while Zarco returned to Portugal to report to Prince Henry. The Prince gave him men and stores. In July 1420 they landed on an island of mountains that Perestrello named in Italian Lolegname, the Island of Woods, and the Portuguese just "Wood": Madeira.

Madeira had no inhabitants. From the shoreline to the top of its 1.8-kilometre (6,000-foot) crags it was one dense forest. Under its characteristic cloud its climate was quite different from that of the Saharan coast only 644 kilometres (400 miles) away: almost equally warm but never short of rainfall and immensely fertile. Prince Henry gave command of the island to Zarco, and ordered it to be planted with sugar cane and vines from Crete. For revenue, no crop could be expected to

equal the luxurious produce of the eastern Mediterranean, then falling more and more under Turkish control. To clear the land for planting the settlers started bushfires, which tradition says burned for seven years, laying waste the rich indigenous forest but leaving an enriching covering of wood ash. Sugar cane was the great success. The previous sources of sugar for Europe had been Sicily, the eastern Mediterranean, North Africa, and a little in Andalusia and the Algarve, but everywhere it was a luxury. It grew so well on Madeira that between 1470 and 1500 the European price of sugar halved. At the start of the sixteenth century, Madeira was the world's greatest sugar producer. As early as 1456 records also show that madeira wine was imported into England.

Of all the Atlantic islands, the first whose wine found a ready market and made a name were the Canaries. Canary sack, modelled by the Spanish on sherry sack and Málaga, was well-established in England by the middle of the sixteenth century. Shakespeare's most vivid tasting note concerns Canary: "A marvellous searching wine; and it perfumes the blood ere one can say 'what's this?'" It seems to have been, in general, sweeter than sherry sack and more like Málaga, mostly of the Malmsey grape, although that known as Vidonia, from Tenerife, was a relatively dry and high-acid wine that aged well – Vidonia is another name for the Verdelho grape of Madeira. Canary remained popular in northern Europe throughout the seventeenth century and most of the eighteenth, reaching its peak in England in the 1660s.

Madeira owed its rise to fame partly to its peculiar natural constitution, the result of the island's soil and climate, but more particularly to its position on the Atlantic shipping lanes. In several ways it has been the Americas that have shaped Madeira's fortune. The first was that sugar plantations in Brazil produced better (and, with slave labour, cheaper) sugar. In the 1570s the island found that wine was a more profitable crop. But Madeira's style of wine, even from the best Malmsey grapes, was light and acid (especially by sack lovers' standards). Falstaff washed down his cold capon's leg with it; he did not compose an ode to it.

The second was the development of plantations by the English in North America and the West Indies. The colonization of Virginia was begun in 1607, of Massachusetts Bay in 1629, of Maryland in 1632. The Leeward Islands and Barbados became British in the 1630s. Oliver Cromwell took Jamaica from Spain in 1655. South Carolina was settled in 1663. By the reign of Charles II there was a widespread demand for wine along the North American seaboard and south into the West Indies. King Charles confirmed Cromwell's Navigation Act, designed to give the monopoly of shipping goods from Europe to the colonies to English ships alone. Colonial ships therefore had to go to England for everything they needed.

But Charles made one exception: Madeira. Some say it was out of respect for his Portuguese queen, others that Madeira is more truly Africa than Europe. It could hardly have been an oversight. Almost every westbound ship for the Americas stopped there in any case, if only to fill its water casks. It was a question of winds. The prevailing winds make the westerly passage a penance in the north Atlantic. The natural sea-lane lies south down the coast of Portugal to meet the northeasterly trade winds at about the thirtieth degree of latitude, between Madeira and the Canaries. A direct run westwards then takes you to Bermuda and Charleston or Savannah, but the prevailing winds on the North American coast are southerly, making the run up to more northern ports a simple matter. Thus almost every ship, whether British or American, put in to the open harbour, the "roads" at Funchal, the capital of Madeira, and loaded wine for the crossing.

At this stage most madeira was still an ordinary beverage wine, made in September, racked in December or January and shipped out as soon as possible to be drunk within the year. A distinction was made between the regular beverage wines and malmseys, which were grown only in the best sites and probably represented about four per cent of the total. The Malmsey grape was in a class apart for rich wines. For dry, the Sercial emerged as much the finest. Legend had it – quite wrongly – that it was the same grape as the Riesling. André Jullien made the comparison between Sercial and Rhine wines, on the grounds that they were the two longest-lived white wines in the world. Between the best sweet and the best dry came the Bual or Bagoual grape, good for medium-rich wines, and the Verdelho (alias Vidonia) for medium and milder ones. Very good wines were also made from Muscat and a grape called Terrantez (now a rarity). Ordinary wines were made from the Tinta. They were astringent and were recommended for treating dysentery – which gave them a steady market in the tropics.

It was originally Malmseys that the Funchal merchants began to store and age on the island, to sell at higher prices. They had no cool cellarage, so kept their pipes in the open air, or in the lofts of their "lodges", where, although the wine oxidized (the French say *maderisé* or maderized) and turned brown, the high temperatures seemed to do the flavour nothing but good. Arriving at their destination the pipes were commonly syphoned off into great glass demijohns or carboys, protected with wicker casing, where they lay in high summer temperatures with no protection from oxygen. All this maltreatment did was to make them smoother and more pungent. The parallel with Falernian is remarkable; one feels that Pliny would shrug his shoulders and say "of course".

Madeira in the seventeenth century was chronically short of food, especially after 1640 when Portugal was once more at war with Spain (and hence with the granary of the Canaries). The Azores had plenty of grain, but the Lisbon government directed it to its latter-day Crusaders, its garrison in Morocco, leaving Madeira to fend for itself – which it did by making foreign ships, calling for wine, turn aside for a wearisome voyage to the Azores and back (often returning empty-handed). As soon as the North American plantations had

An eighteenth-century tiled panel from Portugal, showing Bacchus with grapes. The Portuguese planted Madeira with vines and sugar; at first sugar was the more successful.

grain to spare, therefore, Madeira welcomed a two-way trade that was profitable for both. New England in particular sent grain and maize. "In return, Madeira had little to offer but wines, wines, and more wines" – wines that, it is said, "softened the rigidities" of Puritanism, and made the inhabitants of New England seaport towns altogether more human.

Old England, meanwhile, despite its sworn brotherhood with Portugal, for a long time remained faithful to Canary. What awakened London's interest in madeira was the information of how good it had become in America. The great botanist Sir Joseph Banks, sailing with Captain Cook on HMS *Endeavour* to Australia, left a graphic but not exactly flattering picture of Madeira in 1768:

"When first approached from seaward the island has a very beautiful appearance, the sides of the hills being entirely covered with vineyards almost as high as the eye can distinguish. The people here in general seem to be as idle, or rather uninformed, a set, as I ever yet saw; all their instruments, even those with which their wine, the only genuine article of trade in the island, is made, are perfectly simple and unimproved. In making the wine the grapes are put into a square wooden vessel… into which the servants get (having taken off their stockings and jackets), and with their feet and elbows squeeze out as much of the juice as they can; the stalks, etc, are then collected, tied together with a rope, and put under a square piece of wood which is pressed down by a lever, to the other end of which is fastened a stone that may be raised up at pleasure by a screw. By this means and this only they make their wine, and by this probably Noah made his when he had newly planted his first vineyard after the general destruction of mankind and their arts, although it is not impossible he might

the cellars of savannah Nowhere were the idiosyncrasies of Madeira more lovingly studied than in East Coast America. Savannah, Georgia, which happens to be on exactly the same latitude as Funchal, was famous in the first half of the nineteenth century for its madeira cellars, and particularly for the wines of a merchant named William Neyle Habersham. The Habersham mansion in the handsome seaport town contained, over the ballroom, a solarium, accessible only through his dressing-room, where he apparently aged and blended the wines he sold for fabulous prices. One Habersham speciality was "Rainwater", a pale blend of Verdelho wine whose name is the subject of various legends – some of them obvious. Whether because of the appeal of its name, or of a singular softness in the mouth, "Rainwater" became a firm American favourite.

The first name that was usually given to a madeira when it was decanted into carboys in a Savannah cellar was that of the ship that carried it; the most famous being not a merchantman at all, but the US Navy frigate *Constitution*, built as an escort to shepherd American ships through waters infested with Algerian pirates. The wine she brought home in 1802 was considered a great treasure. Something about the marriage of a wine and a ship had enormous romantic appeal. Lovingly handwritten labels recall the *Juno, Comet, Hurricane, Catherine Banks, Southern Cross*, the famous clipper *Red Jacket*, and even the ship that took madeira all the way to Japan and back with Commodore Perry in 1852, the *Susquehanna*.

Often the ship's name was followed by that of the buyer of the wine, then even of succeeding generations who in due course inherited the heirloom, so that its label became almost like the flyleaf of a family Bible. Sometimes the style of wine – "Malmsey", "Rainwater" – was mentioned; sometimes not. One jeroboam in the cellars of the Owens-Thomas house in Savannah bears the simple legend "Miss Wright's Delight".

RIGHT Madeira is the perfect wine to serve from a decanter. It might have thrown a deposit in the bottle, but practical reasons apart, the colour is too glorious to hide.

have used a better, if he remembered the methods he had seen before the flood."

Cook bought more than 3,000 gallons of wine on the island for the ninety-four crewmen and scientists on the *Endeavour*. Brandy was added to this wine to help preserve it for a voyage that lasted two and a half years.

From about this time the ledgers of the merchant houses of Madeira (increasingly in English ownership) begin to record another excellent market for their wine: the new British possessions in India. (Portugal's Indian *feitorias* had undoubtedly used a steady supply since they were founded in the fifteenth century.) The island was equally as en route for an East Indiaman as it was for a ship plying to America. By the start of the nineteenth century almost half the island's shipments were crossing the equator, rounding the Cape, crossing the equator again, and having the same refreshing effect in the East Indies as the West. The records of Cossart, Gordon and Co., one of the oldest firms on the island, record exactly which wine went to each of the many British regimental messes in such Imperial bastions as Meerut, Bangalore, Secunderabad, Rawal Pindee, and Lucknow.

Madeira's young wines before their adventures begin are surprisingly light and unimpressive, except for their noticeable edge of acidity. For these long voyages the wines were undoubtedly fortified with spirits; "two bucketfuls of brandy a pipe" sounds very much like the practice with mid-eighteenth-century port. The dessert qualities, made of Malmsey, Bual or sometimes Verdelho grapes, were also often sweetened with *vinho de surdo*, a mixture of unfermented must and brandy. The extra strength helped their already uncanny stability; the extra sweetness simply made them taste even more luxurious on the verandah at the end of the voyage.

If one voyage across the Atlantic (or the Equator) was good for the wine, two, it was argued, must be better. It certainly turned out so. By the second half of the eighteenth century, orders were arriving from London for pipes to be loaded on ships outward-bound for the West (or even the East) Indies, to be treated as ballast, and to return with the ship to Europe.

Barrels of extra size and strength were built to be stowed in the bilges of an East Indiaman, whose voyage from Funchal to Bombay and back to London would take at least half a year. Why these wines, constantly in motion in stifling heat, the barrels often submerged in foetid bilgewater, did not turn out undrinkable is a mystery. On the contrary, they developed softness and depth of flavour, while never losing their piquant liveliness that made people think of them almost as eccentric but much-loved old friends. Even more eccentric was the method of ageing them in bottles buried in a pit of horse manure for six months, which Jullien reports. What quality this was expected to add is hard to imagine. With any other author one would suspect a hoax.

The trouble and expense of shipping barrels back and forth across the oceans inevitably led in the end to an industrial shortcut. If long periods at high temperatures were what was required, they could be provided more simply than by travelling halfway around the world. In 1794 Funchal saw its first *estufa*, a lodge equipped with a huge stove that circulated hot water to provide tropical heat. The pipes of wine are stacked high and left in this stifling atmosphere for months on end. There is no nautical motion, no smelly bilgewater.

Originally, *estufa* wines were thought to be inferior to ones that had travelled the oceans. In 1832 Jullien wrote that "wines aged in a stove never rise to the heights of a *vinho da roda*. When one of these is thirty or forty years old it has formed a thick crust inside its bottle; it is white and clear as water; its perfume is so powerful when the bottle is opened that persons with delicate nerves can be quite alarmed by it." But such glorious wines have been made by the stove method over the last two centuries that even nostalgia can find nothing to complain about. *Estufa* Malmseys over a century old are as full of vigour and sumptuous flavour as ever, and seem only to improve however long they are kept. No drink, no foodstuff, one might almost say no living thing, shares the apparent immortality of old vintage madeira.

The practice of *vinhos da roda* did not entirely die out until World War I. But long before that time, the island had suffered from the vine diseases that threatened all the world's vineyards in the nineteenth century, and from which they have not entirely recovered to this day.

CHAPTER 26

LE GRAND THEATRE

Bordeaux began the eighteenth century as a town still surrounded by its medieval walls. By the time of the Revolution in 1789, it was the most handsome modern city in France, and the country's greatest port. It had added to its ancient wine trade in quantity, and revolutionized it in quality. More dramatically, perhaps, it had become the country's principal point of contact with its colonies: half of all colonial trade, above all West Indian trade, passed through Bordeaux's famous crescent-moon-shaped harbour. To celebrate its worldly success, in the 1780s its citizens built Le Grand Théâtre, symbolically upstaging the Gothic cathedral, the heart of the old town, with something more in keeping with the spirit of the times; the most magnificent theatre built in Europe since the Romans.

What had produced this flowering? Civic pride, diligence, and a strong itch for gold. The Parlement where Pontac had presided continued to produce a race of lawyers, the *noblesse de robe*, whose wits and ambitions made short work of the old *noblesse d'epée*, families whose inheritance ran back to deeds of knightly valour, but who liked to hunt their land, rather than farm it. Alongside and overlapping with the *parlementaires* were the risk-taking merchants, the *négociants* who freighted ships for the booming West Indies: with luck a much more profitable pastime even than waiting for Dutchmen to come and haggle over the latest vintage.

Ten years into the eighteenth century, losing the War of the Spanish Succession made Frenchmen look forwards rather than back to the fading glories of the Sun King. The vineyards of all of France had been devastated by a winter in which temperatures plunged to -17.5°C (0.5°F) in Marseilles. It was time to get going, on the farm, and on the ocean that the French, inimitably, call *le grand large*. In the seventeenth century "America", for France, had meant Newfoundland and the (very profitable) cod fisheries. But already during the war, wafts of spicy breezes had been coming in from France's new plantations in the Antilles. During the war, two ships a month had been arriving with sugar and spices. Bordeaux did well by re-exporting them to northern ports on the Dutch ships that had negotiated passports to come to the city to buy wine.

The 1770s saw the fastest growth of colonial trade in Bordeaux, with ships from the Indies (East and West) arriving at the rate of five a week, and turning round, as one observer put it, "without careening or anything". Bordeaux was in a unique position among French ports to profit fully by all this shipping: its own produce was wanted everywhere. Wine was the main export, but the hinterland – which Bordeaux's citizens, mindful of their taxes, liked to describe to the government as "*maigre et infertil*" ("meagre and infertile") – provided bountiful grain, *eaux-de-vie*, the plums of the Agenais, hemp for cordage, sailcloth (another speciality of Agen), and such necessaries for the colonies as stoves and mills (and also stills). Every part of inland France crowded to the great March fair in the city to find exporters for its produce.

RIGHT The splendid interior of Le Grand Théâtre, built in Bordeaux in the 1780s, was a potent symbol of the town's prosperity as the leading port in France.

In 1685 Louis XIV had caused a diaspora of French commercial talent by removing the people's freedom of religion. The Protestant Huguenots fled, mainly to The Netherlands, Germany and England. More and more, Bordeaux looked to Germany, and beyond to the Baltic, for a two-way trade that was both profitable and essential. Ships that left Bordeaux with wine returned with barrel staves of Baltic oak, the best wood in the world for the casks that were needed for high-quality wine. Polish, Pomeranian, and East Prussian oak forests produced close-grained timber that gave a less obvious flavour to the wine than French-grown oak, while still providing enough tannin. The fussy English, paying whatever it cost to buy their "first-growths", their Latour, Lafite, Margaux, and Haut-Brion, specified Stettin oak as best of all. Hamburg merchants provided timber of all grades – including much that went into the floors and the delicate *boiseries* (panelling) of Bordeaux's new mansions – and gratifyingly took a massive amount of coffee, as well as claret, on the homeward voyage.

I n point of time, the famous "fury of planting" struck Bordeaux before the "colonial fever". The lead had been so daringly and successfully given by the "first-growths" at the end of the seventeenth century that they were to prove uncatchable. The owners of the "first-growths" had, quite simply, secured the best sites in the Médoc, buying up and planting the three places where the gravel soil was coarsest, best drained, and warmest, and it was to the Médoc that *parlementaires* and merchants rushed to emulate them. One of the first was an ambitious merchant called Pierre de Rauzan, who acted as manager of the Latour estate between 1679 and 1693, and profited by its example and his position to buy up as much of the neighbouring land as he could on his own behalf. By 1690 he had assembled some twenty hectares (fifty acres) of good vineyard land (not yet all planted), which passed by the marriage of his daughter Thérèse to Jacques François de Pichon, seigneur de Longueville, becoming the basis of the great Pichon-Longueville estate.

Professor Pijassou of the University of Bordeaux points out, in his great work on the Médoc, that "the vineyard of Pichon is a little less well situated than the first-growth [Latour]; the pebbles there are a little smaller, the proportion of sand greater, the pattern of slopes more gentle". These factors meant that, in the firmly held belief of Bordeaux's experts from that day to this, the wine could never be quite as good. Rauzan was then operating in the other part of the Médoc that was acknowledged supreme, as close as he could get to Château Margaux. He was able to bequeath to Thérèse's three brothers about twenty-four hectares (sixty acres) of vines "around the house called Gassies". This one man laid the foundations for what today are four "second-growths": Châteaux Pichon-Longueville, Pichon-Lalande, Rauzan-Gassies, and Rauzan-Ségla.

A t a very early stage, in 1638, another merchant, Monsieur Moytié, had started a similar process of assembling little parcels of land on the hillock just south of Latour, across the stream that divides the parish of St-Julien from Pauillac. He named his gravel "dune" Mont-Moytié. A

century later it was bought by another President of the Parlement, Monsieur Léoville. At this stage it was possibly the largest vineyard in the Médoc. Today it is three, all "second-growths", distinguished by the names of subsequent owners: Châteaux Léoville-Las-Cases, Léoville-Barton, and Léoville-Poyferre.

Among the other estates whose owners and approximate extents are recorded from the first half of the eighteenth century are those of the *parlementaire* the Marquis de Brazier, who owned the medieval fortress of Lamarque and in 1757 built Château Beychevelle by the river at St-Julien: certainly the most monumental and architecturally sophisticated of all Médoc wine properties. He also owned the "Poujaux" estate at Moulis, with a total of sixty hectares (150 acres) of vines.

The Avocat de Gorsse was another lawyer whose name lives on in various versions in smaller properties north of Margaux, but whose original Château de Gorce (he spelt as badly as Shakespeare) is now the "second-growth" Brane-Cantenac. Others were Counsellor Malescot, who had twenty-four hectares (sixty acres) in Margaux; and Counsellor de Castelnau, who owned the beautiful medieval moated Château d'Issan with twenty acres of vines. In 1723 Issan became one of the first properties besides the first-growths to be sold by name in London.

T hese relatively small areas do not in themselves sound exactly like a "fury of planting", but we must remember that they were being repeated all over what had never been dedicated vine-growing land before, and that similar things were happening in all the other country districts around Bordeaux. In 1744 the Intendant's subdelegate estimated that "half of his jurisdiction" was planted as vineyard, nine-tenths of it belonging to the wealthy bourgeois and nobility of Bordeaux. By this time the government had been concerned for nearly fifty years (since the 1690s) that more vines would mean less corn. The phrase "*fureur de planter*" was coined by *Intendant* Boucher as early as 1724. "For ten leagues around Bordeaux", he said, "you see nothing but vines. The same mania has taken hold on the rest of the province." His solution, though, showed that a great deal of the planting was on *palus* and former corn lands, and that he was aware of the value of the new estates on gravel sites: "All the vines planted since 1709 [the year of the great frost] must be ripped out, in all the high country and in the Bordeaux district, except those in the graves of the Médoc, Graves of Bordeaux [the modern Graves], and the Côtes" – in other words, the traditional vineyard land plus the best sites of the Médoc.

O ther evidence makes it clear that Paris saw too many vines as a national problem. In the 1720s France seemed to be going wine-mad; prices fell, the common people spent all their time in bars (*cabarets*) drinking wine from tankards. In 1725, Boucher's ban became legally enforceable in Bordeaux. In 1731 it was royally decreed that no more vines should be planted anywhere in France without the King's express permission. For an objective point of view on the ban

it is interesting to read Adam Smith, the Scottish philosopher and economist, who wrote, in *The Wealth of Nations*: "The pretence of this order was the scarcity of corn and pasture, and the superabundance of wine", while the real cause was "the anxiety of the proprietors of the old vineyards to prevent the planting of new ones".

Those who objected to the ban, in Bordeaux at least, had an eloquent spokesman. Charles de Secondat, Baron de Montesquieu, the inheritor of the magnificent moated castle of La Brède just south of Bordeaux, had just written his first book expressing his liberal political views in the form of letters from an imaginary Persian visitor to France. Montesquieu's name was known throughout the country. He challenged Boucher in a forthright manifesto for market forces and free trade. He could, he said, buy 9.7 hecatres (twenty-four acres) of waste land (admittedly near Haut-Brion) for sixty *livres*, turn them into vineyard and sell them for 400,000. (He already owned about 1,417 hectares or 3,500 acres.) Why interrupt the new planting which is bringing in so much good foreign business? Why send the business away to the profit of the Portuguese? In the event, it seems that Boucher was not even supported by his own deputies: Pontet, for example, who built the beautiful château in St-Julien

The merchants' houses on the Quai des Chartrons have long *chais* at their backs for cellaring wine in barrel. The name comes from an old Carthusian monastery.

which is now called Langoa-Barton. Venal officials sold planting permissions. By the 1760s the government had given way.

Winemaking methods, at least in the new estates, had begun to stabilize by the 1760s. At last it is clear just how the wine was made as well as how it was bought and sold. The Scots family Johnston had settled in Bordeaux in 1734 and prospered as *négociants* (later they became château owners; today, still prospering, they are wine brokers). A notebook dated 1765 records the Johnston technique for judging vintages and properties, and buying and shipping at the best moments. It is interesting that Mr Johnston did not turn up his nose at peasants' wines, so long as he could rescue them from the peasants' keeping before they had ruined them. This attitude explains the vociferous opposition of the big landowners to a road being built up the Médoc from Bordeaux; an argument that raged from 1730 to 1750. They did not want *négociants* discovering small growers' wines for themselves, when they were in all likelihood buying them cheap for topping up their own barrels. The bourgeois had access to the

Nicolas-Alexandre, Marquis de Ségur, was known as the "Prince des Vignes" and famed for his extensive wealth. Importantly, he also defined the Lafite and Mouton estates.

On the other hand we have the merchants, who bought and sold their wine, making potent brews with it that must have changed its nature altogether. Johnston's recipe involved strong Spanish reds, Alicante or Benicarlo, sometimes Rivesaltes from the Midi, often dark *palus* wine from over the river, and occasionally Cahors or Hermitage, not just mixed with Lafite or Latour, but actually made to referment with it. To start the fermentation they used a bucket of *stum* (juice whose fermentation has never been allowed to start, by dint of adding sulphur and/or *eau-de-vie*). So what was sold at very high prices as "first-growth" claret in the mid-eighteenth century was often a brew-up, with as much as one-third of the total coming from outside the region (or even from outside France).

As witness to the fact that the growers were doing their utmost, they regularly sacrificed a substantial amount of their potential income by down-grading large parts of their crop to "second wine". It was a regular practice with the "first-growths" from the start – and for good reason: vintages were extremely irregular in quality and quantity, there were no means of countering rotting grapes except by sorting them out and throwing them away, and perhaps most of all because they had a muddle of vine varieties, including many white ones. Even "new French claret", improved though it was, was still in some senses "claret" in the old meaning of the word, with white grapes in it, picked early (almost always in September), and given a short fermentation, a week at the most, which would rarely have made deep-coloured or full-bodied wine. Château Lafite regularly had nine or ten degrees of alcohol, instead of the twelve or thirteen we expect today. These are reasons why the merchants of the Chartrons intervened: to give their customers, the English especially, something more full-blooded, something closer to their favourite Portuguese wine, while still keeping the flavour of Bordeaux.

It was not until about the time of the Revolution and the Napoleonic wars that such celebrated *régisseurs*, or managers, as Domenger, who saw Lafite and Latour through the Revolution, and his successors at Lafite (Goudal) and Latour (Poitevin and Lamothe) became absolute masters of their vineyards and their wines. Lamothe was an ex-ship's captain who had seen every ocean before he settled, aged fifty-three, in Bordeaux, and threw all his energies into running Latour. His predecessors had been weeding out the white vines bit by bit. Lamothe went much further. He found out how to cut the tops off white vines and graft on red ones, and he is the first on record in the Médoc to have named Cabernet Sauvignon as the best grape of all, and planted it massively. "All the Cabernet", he wrote to his employer, "which is the best variety, has gone into the *Grand Vin*." He also observed (although he was probably not the first) that older vines produced better wine.

It seems very late in the day to be talking about vine varieties in Bordeaux for the first time. The fact is that up to now they had been given little thought. The old-established parts of the region had a mixture of dozens. At Cadillac, up the

gabares that plied the river, carrying wine from their jetties up to the merchants on the Quai des Chartrons. A visit from a broker or merchant on horseback was welcome, but not a waggon going from *chai* to *chai*.

Johnston's notes on tasting show what he was looking for: body, flavour, good colour, cleanness in taste, no taste of rot or greenness. His instructions are most precise about sniffing at the bunghole of each cask to detect any taint of rot; about the use of the "Dutch [sulphur] match" to disinfect casks – he was the first to describe this – and about avoiding contact with air while racking. He also describes what became known as the *travail à l'Anglaise*: the blending or "cutting" of pure light wines with darker, more full-bodied, or harsher ones to suit the customers' taste.

There is a strange contradiction here which has never found a clear explanation. On the one hand we have every indication that the proprietors of the "first-growths" and their imitators were doing everything in their power to make the best possible wines, modifying their techniques as they learned, and pouring back money into the land. Their expertise (or that of their managers) grew steadily. Towards the end of the century the managers of Lafite, Latour, and Margaux were well known and highly respected in their own right. They were acutely aware of their better and less good patches of soil, and of the problem of drainage – even stony slopes needed help from artificial drains. They believed in renewing the vigour of the soil, and dug up common lands wholesale to cart in fresh topsoil, to the extreme chagrin of the locals. Nothing was too much trouble.

Garonne, in 1796 a priest of great intelligence, the abbé Bellet, had listed eighteen black varieties and twenty white. The Dutch had been very selective in choosing only the Verdot for their *palus* plantings. Because the Médoc was a new vineyard its repertoire was relatively limited: about four black varieties and four white. These included Petit Vidure, alias Cabernet Sauvignon (Vidure means "*vigne dure*": the Cabernet has very hard wood). Lafite was largely planted with Malbec (alias Noir de Pressac) and Petit Verdot, but had a minority of vines from Hermitage on the Rhône, which were presumably Petite Sirah. Latour was largely Malbec and Cabernet Sauvignon. There is no mention of any Merlot, by a recognizable name, in the Médoc, and only a little Cabernet Franc, or Bouchet.

I t is also time to cross the river. The town of Libourne, east of Bordeaux across two rivers, the Garonne and the Dordogne – a thirty-two kilometre/twenty-mile (and two ferries) ride through the area that takes its name from them, Entre-Deux-Mers – was an important target of the Dutch commercial invasion of the seventeenth century. Libourne itself had *palus* wines that the Dutch bought, but acted mainly as the exit port for their huge purchases of white wines up the Dordogne at Bergerac. St-Emilion, Pomerol, and Fronsac, the three regions of potentially high quality grouped around Libourne, the Dutch more or less ignored.

There were a number of reasons why little happened here until the mid-eighteenth century. One was the presence of the Church and religious institutions as landowners (which they were not in the Médoc). The Cathedral Chapter of Bordeaux had a strong hold over St-Emilion, and much of Pomerol belonged to the (formerly Crusader) Knights Hospitallers. Instead of feudal micro-properties, the land-holding was in the less vulnerable (to developers) form of share-cropping. In the case of Fronsac, which largely belonged to the Ducs de Richelieu, their feudal tenants were not encouraged to grow vines.

From the shipping point of view, Libourne had a major disadvantage. Until 1728 it had no port registrar who was authorized to clear cargos for export, so any ship loading there had to make a great detour back up the Garonne to Bordeaux for clearance. The War of the Spanish Succession was a help here. Navy supply officers buying wine for the fleet simply ignored the regulations and commissioned the merchants of Libourne who sold them salt to find them wine as well. The 1730s saw the arrival of Amsterdam and Rotterdam freighters of 100 tons and more. Then in 1740 the winter was cold enough to kill many vines. Like the winter of 1709 in the Médoc it stimulated replanting, which usually meant better planting, and even a certain selectivity over varieties. The Libourne region seems to have been ahead of its time in concentrating on the best grapes. The 1740s were the starting point, when Libourne merchants took the initiative and began looking for markets, less in The Netherlands than in Brittany, along the north coast of France, and in Flanders. The English aristocracy with their Médoc fixation were beyond them. To an extraordinary extent the pattern of trade that was set up in those early years continues to

the prince des vignes Of all the grandees of the Bordeaux *parlement*, none can be compared with the President Nicolas-Alexandre, Marquis de Ségur (1697–1755), who in the first half of the eighteenth century owned the two "first-growths" of Lafite and Latour, plus Mouton (today "first-growth"), the great estate of Calon-Ségur in St-Estèphe and other properties in the Médoc and Graves. Louis XV dubbed him the Prince des Vignes, after being told that the (apparently diamond) buttons of his coat were the precious stones of his vineyard, cut and polished. Ségur's income from Lafite and Latour alone was estated at 100,000 *livres* a year, of which sixty per cent was profit. He complained to *Intendant* de Tourny that 1744 was a bad vintage and that his taxes should be reduced. The official reckoning was an income of 272,000 *livres*, with expenses of 34,000.

While most talk of this exceptionally prosperous man concentrates on his income, it should be remembered that it was he who drew the definite boundaries between the land of Lafite and the neighbouring Mouton, thus creating two profoundly different styles of wine, and gave their reputations the solid foundation that has never foundered. Latour belonged to his descendants until 1963.

this day. St-Emilion and Pomerol are better known and loved in the North of France and Belgium than they are in England.

L ibourne became a little less remote from Bordeaux when Intendant de Tourny built a road across Entre-Deux-Mers. From the 1760s we have detailed reports of everything going on in the region. It is clear that the top of the St-Emilion Côtes, the hill around the old town, was already taking the strange form that we see today, with deep stone quarries cut into the hill just below the surface, leaving pillars of the limestone rock to support vineyards hanging as it were in mid-air above them. The vineyards (many of them walled) of Châteaux Belair, Canon, Berliquet, Clos Fourtet, Magdelaine and Ausone date from about this time. In 1750, what is now Château Tropchaud (then Trochau) in Pomerol was inherited in a decrepit state by the remarkable Monsieur Fontemoing. He wrote that he proposed to dig drains, pull up the old vines, and plant "Bouchet, Noir de Pressac" (Cabernet Franc and Malbec) "and Cabernet". He was also doing away with the white varieties, notwithstanding that Pomerol had a reputation for good white wines where the soil is clay. (In Burgundy, too, Chardonnay is planted where there is most clay.)

Elsewhere in Pomerol, within the next two decades, the little estates of Trotanoy, La Conseillante (so the charismatic Madame Conseillan called her property), Nenin, Beauregard, Gazin, Vieux Château Certan, and the Arnaud family at Pétrus make their appearance under direct ownership as opposed to share-cropping – presumably with similar planting plans to those of Trochau.

Between Pomerol and St-Emilion on the plateau stood the one really big estate in the area: Figeac, with a history going back to the Romans and an enterprising owner, Vital de Carle. Over the period between about 1730 and the end of the century, Vital, followed by his son Elie, took the whole estate in hand, cleared woodland and planted at least thirty hectares (seventy-five acres) of vineyard. The imposing château was rebuilt by Elie's nephew Jacques, a soldier who commanded the garrisons at Dunkerque and Boulogne – coincidentally the very heart of the main market for St-Emilion wines.

The wines of Fronsac were held in equal esteem with the best of St-Emilion. Indeed, the whole of the 1783 harvest of the eminent Monsieur Boyer's Château Canon at St-Michel de Fronsac was reserved for the court of the Dauphin at Versailles.

The region of Bordeaux whose eighteenth-century history is still least clearly understood is Sauternes and its neighbouring communes, the gentle green and yellow hills lying back from the west bank of the Garonne about forty kilometres (twenty-five miles) before the river reaches the clutter of shipping and clamour of the town. Sauternes is a relatively modern term for a region that used to be known by the names of

Noble rot, or *pourriture noble*, on a bunch of Sauternes grapes. It is not clear from the records when Sauternes started using such grapes deliberately to make sweet wines.

its different centres: Langon, Barsac, Sauternes, Preignac, Bommes. There is no mystery about the fact that they sold a good deal of more or less sweet wine to the Dutch in the seventeenth century. But it has been the convention in the past to regard the great characteristic of Sauternes, the fact that it is best when made from rotten grapes, as a development of the mid-nineteenth century. It is difficult to understand this when Tokaji had been famous for this very fact since the end of the seventeenth century.

Much has been made of the fact that in the 1830s the proprietor of an estate close to the great Château Yquem, Château La Tour Blanche, was a Monsieur Focke from the Rhineland, who supposedly introduced the technique of waiting for *Botrytis cinerea* to shrivel the grapes to make, in effect, a Bordeaux Auslese. Yet there is plenty of detailed evidence that a century before Focke's time the white grapes of the region (which also grew red) were sometimes harvested as late as the end of November. The abbé Bellet, whom we have met counting grape varieties in Cadillac, over the Garonne from Sauternes, kept an account of every vintage in Cadillac between 1717 and 1736. He confirms that the Sémillon was an important grape in the vineyards. By October, in the conditions of the Garonne valley (but particularly in Sauternes), the Sémillon is almost always attacked to a great or less extent by the botrytis mould.

What is hard to discern, at least in reading the abbé's vintage notes, is whether the mould was viewed as noble or the opposite. He speaks of going around the vineyard several times selecting either the rotten or the ripe but not rotten grapes. But he is silent on whether the mouldy ones were used or rejected. The general inference is the latter. He even mentions that in "Italy and Provence" grapes for sweet wine are over-ripened by twisting their stems and leaving them on the vine, which suggests that sun-dried, raisin-like grapes were the most highly prized.

There is no question that sweetness was the goal. It may have been achieved partly by the Dutch trick of adding *stum*. One vintage had so much sugar, the abbé records, that they used no less than twelve sulphur matches in a barrel but still could not prevent the fermentation (in order to make *stum*). Nine were usually enough.

One theory that has its advocates is that nobody wanted to admit that they made their wine from rotten grapes. This might have been true of the priesthood, for sweet wine was the holy wine of the Sacrament. There is a strong hint in the first printed description of Sauternes, by another priest, the abbé Baurein, in 1786, that the place has a secret, and that "if the silence, into which they retreat, does damage to our project [which is to describe the parish] it is of greater benefit to… those who are determined to keep it." If this oracular remark does not mean that Sauternes has something to hide, it is hard to make head or tail of it.

The acknowledged "first-growth" of the Sauternes region is Château Yquem. It has stood as a fortress at the highest point in the parish since the twelfth century, when it was an English stronghold. In the sixteenth century it became the property of the family of Sauvage d'Yquem, whose eventual sole inheritor, Françoise-Josephine, married the young Comte Louis-Amédée de Lur Saluces in 1785. Poor Louis-Amédée, a colonel, fell off his horse on manoeuvres only three years later and died, but the Lur Saluces family still presides at Yquem. We should be able to discover the secret from them. Tantalizingly, the archives of the château, possibly the most complete of any in Bordeaux, have never yet been thoroughly investigated. So we must be content with an educated guess.

Alexandre, the present Comte de Lur Saluces, has pointed out that all white wines in the eighteenth century and before were made as sweet as nature allowed. The modern notion of a "crisp" dry wine would have been regarded as a very thin potation. The same applied in the Graves (which was largely planted with white varieties), in Entre-Deux-Mers, in Cadillac, and in Sauternes and its district. All picked their grapes as late and as ripe as possible. The difference was in the natural conditions. Where autumn mists were prevalent, botrytis was a regular occurrence. There can be no doubt about the sweetness of rotten grapes: you have only to lick your fingers. In Sauternes more than anywhere, a golden autumn day is followed by a rising river mist. Its wine was always likely to be sweeter than that of Graves.

The real question is when did the market make it worthwhile to make Tokaji-style wine only from the rotten grapes? To pick in repeated *tries*, selecting, waiting, and selecting again, is a very long and costly undertaking. Tokaji had been developed as a princely promotion and found a market in Imperial courts. But the customers for such an exotic and expensive style of wine only appeared in Bordeaux (and apparently in Paris) in the years leading up to the Revolution.

The most famous customer was Thomas Jefferson. In 1784, at the age of forty-one, he was dispatched (as a Commissioner, then Minister) by the new government of the United States to France – not without considerable distaste. "I would go to hell for my country" was his reaction; and his journals in France make clear that he found its government diabolical. He was a laconic, not to say terse, journalist. You meet almost nobody and see few sights in his daily chronicle; just statistics, details of the land and its produce, a panorama of more or less starving peasantry, and damning reflections on the regime that was about to pass away.

Among the few moments of (moderate) enthusiasm are when, in his two excursions through France and Italy in 1787 and 1788, he reaches a wine region. Jefferson was eager to learn about wine-growing; first in order to introduce it to America, but also to supply himself with the best wines he could buy.

In Bordeaux he quickly informed himself about the red "first-growths". He also listed a dozen "second-" and "third-growths". "Of white wines", he recorded, "those made in the canton of Grave are most esteemed at Bordeaux." He listed as best Pontac (a former Pontac property), St-Brise (then a Pontac property) and the Benedictine abbey De Carbonius (now Château Carbonnieux).

"Those made in the 3 parishes next above Grave and more

the chartrons Foreign merchants in Bordeaux were obliged to stay outside the old city and develop a northern suburb of their own, just downstream from the menacing Château Trompette. The Quai des Chartrons took its name from the Carthusian monastery there, and its merchant class soon became a distinct and influential body, referred to as the Chartronnais.

They were viewed with mixed feelings by the Bordeaux bourgeoisie. Wine growers accustomed to selling via brokers to visiting merchants could see snags in a new class of substantial traders holding stocks on their doorstep.

Foreigners operated as both brokers and *négociants*; the brokers travelling from property to property, the *négociants* commuting from Bordeaux to their native ports. Most started as general merchants. The oldest firm is that of Beyerman, founded from Rotterdam in 1620. Several of the most famous were Irish, including the celebrated broker Abraham Lawton from Cork, who in the 1740s had 2,500 accounts, and the exceptionally successful Tom Barton, whose family is still Franco-Irish after nearly 300 years in Bordeaux. Barton, still referred to by his descendants as "French Tom", set up in Bordeaux with perfect timing in 1715, when "first-growths" had become the height of English and Irish fashion, and peace had a last broken out. He became much the biggest buyer of "first-growths", buying a great estate in Tipperary and marrying his daughters to English noblemen. In 1821 his descendants bought the magnificent Château Langoa, in which they still live.

A list of Chartronnais names gives an idea of their origins. Nathaniel Johnston came from Ulster; Lynch was another highly successful Irishman. Such names as Sandilands, Jernon, Knox and Cope, Power, Chalmers, Fennwick, Bonfield, Sullivan, Ferguson, Horish, Bethmann, Schroder and Schÿler, MacCarthy, Halford, Sichel, Thomson, O'Brien, Coppinger and Kressman represents a spread over northern Europe, with a strong stress on Britain and Ireland. One German family, Cruse, became the epitome of everything Chartronnais. But even the French elements, of which Luze, Dolor, and Eschenauer (from Alsace), and Calvet (from the Rhône) are examples, acquired an almost Anglo-Saxon air. Their intermarriages produced a closed society which lasted untill the 1970s.

esteemed at Paris", he continued, "are 1. Sauterne. The best crop belongs to M. Diquem at Bordeaux, or to M. de Salus his son-in-law." He then listed "2. Prignac" and "3. Barsac". "Sauterne is the pleasantest… and all [are] stronger than Grave" – surely if he had tasted the wines "sweeter" is the word he would have used. When he did taste the Yquem he had bought, back in Paris, and later at home in America, he was moved to write: "This [Yquem] proves a most excellent wine, and seems to have hit the palate of the Americans more than any wine I have ever seen in France." To Louis-Amedée (Jefferson did not know he had been killed) he wrote from Philadelphia: "The white wine of Sauterne, of your growth… was so well received by the Americans who tasted it that I do not doubt it will conform generally to the taste of my compatriots. Now that I am established here I have persuaded our President, General Washington, to try a sample. He asks for thirty dozen [bottles], sir, and I ask you for ten dozen for myself…"

Jefferson visited Bordeaux at the culmination of its eighteenth-century expansion – and on the eve of the Revolution. All was bustle. England was buying wine in greater quantities than for many years. There were no starving peasants here, and not even the tension of class conflict that was evident on the streets of Paris. On its thronging quays nobody would have believed that the hour of the guillotine was at hand. The Grand Théâtre was finished. But so was the play.

CHAPTER 27

MAPPING
THE COTE

If your hot-air balloon were to land you on the hill of Corton, or in the vineyards of Volnay or Chambertin, on a spring day 250 years ago, you would know exactly where you were – supposing, that is, that those hillsides are familiar to you now. You would rub your eyes at the strange dense tangle of vines without wires putting out green shoots around you. (The villagers would rub their eyes, too: the Montgolfier brothers, inventors of the "Aerostat", had not yet produced their first model.) You would be surprised to see the panorama of vines broken up with so many hedges and walls. But fundamentally, from the church spire in the cleft of the hills at Volnay to the beret of woodland on the brow of Corton, you would be looking at the same vineyards as today. And when you found your way to a cellar you would be offered, in your silver tastevin, a not very different wine. The rising mint-fresh scent of the Pinot Noir would tell you that this was indeed the Côte d'Or. The scent above all is the clue. In the words of Claude Arnoux, the priest who wrote *La Situation de la Bourgogne* in 1728, the wines of Burgundy have "sweet vapours". They are drunk "in two ways, through the nose and through the mouth, either at the same time or separately".

Burgundy had no experience like the boomtime of eighteenth-century Bordeaux. No new wines were invented, no new districts planted. The Bordeaux picture is all expansion and creation; the Burgundy one of evolving tastes and techniques, of new market forces, and overall of slowly progressing definition: a more precise notion of the character, style and value of the wine from each corner of the Côte .

Burgundy, of course, is not just the Côte d'Or, and a balloon trip over the northern and southern, extremes of the sprawling region would be much more confusing. In the north, in "Lower Burgundy", where Chablis is now the only substantial vineyard area, your eye would travel over miles and miles of rolling vine and orchard country, interspersed with woods: perhaps 40,500 hecatres of vines in the region of Auxerre and Tonnerre (Chablis included) whose produce, red and white, was destined for the daily drinking of Paris.

Drifting south, following what is now the Autoroute du Soleil, the same concentration of vines continued, with breaks, all the way down to Dijon. Châtillon-sur-Seine and Pouilly-en-Auxois were wine centres; Avallon had a wine-press set up permanently in the town square for the use of small growers who had no access to any other. At Dijon, where the distinctive ridge of the Côte d'Or begins, the vineyards crowded round the town, then followed the ridge south, spreading out a mile or more into the plain at Gevrey, failing to reach the sprawling abbeys of Cîteaux and Mezières, hugging the hill at Beaune, invading the little valleys behind the ridge at Auxey near Meursault, and continuing over the natural gap at Chagny into more mixed cultivation through Mercurey, Rully, and the villages down to Chalon-sur-Saône.

Finally, before leaving Burgundy and sailing over the grey-gold city of Lyons, clustered round the confluence of the Saône and the Rhône, we pass the softly contoured mountains of the Beaujolais. The slopes are more densely planted with vines; the tall plants of Gamay surround every village on the

lower ground and reach up in patches here and there into the chestnut woods above. This and the hills of Mâcon are the newest parts of the Burgundy vineyard: a creation, largely, of the seventeenth century. From end to end of Burgundy, from the borders of Champagne to the gates of Lyons, the vine has rarely been out of sight for long.

R eading the writings of the time of our balloon trip, the feeling of familiarity is just as striking. The vocabulary is different – simpler, less metaphorical than today's, but this helps to emphasize the unchanging basics. The eighteenth-century commentators (most of them priests; if anyone doubts the continuing influence of the Church on wine-making, these oenological abbots clinch the point) were the first to find words for the distinguishing styles of wines from each parish, and for the most highly-regarded individual vineyards. But there is a strong sense, in reading them, that they were simply writing down what had long been known and passed on by tradition. The difference between Volnay and Pommard, or Chambertin

A True Portrait of the Town of Beaune, *made in 1575. The moat still exists, though it is now dry, and the château (in the centre at the top) is now mostly demolished.*

and Nuits, was not a discovery of the eighteenth century; it went back to the Valois dukes of the fifteenth century, and before them to the pioneering monasteries and churches. An ancient practice is slowly being revealed in all its depth of experience, and all the variety of local customs that have been built up over 500 years of doing the same things in the same place. "Terroir" is the almost mystical Burgundian word for the unchanging unity made up of the soil, the situation, and every facet of the vine's environment. It is terroir that interprets Pinot Noir, or Pinot Noir that interprets terroir: either way, intimately linked, the two together are the key to the variety of the Côte d'Or.

T he sixteenth and seventeenth centuries had not been without changes. One was the introduction of good white wines; another the increased demand for common wines, which means that Gamay had invaded the Côte d'Or over the dead body of Duke Philippe, and the vineyard had strayed down from the Côte to invade the plain. The old domaine of the Dukes themselves had declined. And in the seventeenth century the Church started selling lands to the bourgeoisie of Dijon.

Dijon, like Bordeaux, had its Parlement, and at about the same time, the early 1600s, its lawyers began to look lustfully at the prestigious vineyards on their doorstep. Unlike the Bordeaux *parlementaires*, they could not start by assembling the scrappy tenancies on unexploited land. Instead, they offered the abbots and the Cathedral chapters what sounded like generous terms for their vineyards: money upfront, and a proportion of the wine till kingdom come. The Abbey of St-Vivant sold La Romanée at Vosne in 1631, the Cathedral at Langres sold the Clos de Bèze in 1651, and the Cistercians of Cîteaux sold their land in Corton in 1660, and their Clos de la Perrière at Fixin near Dijon in 1662. In 1660 the Chapter of Saulieu sold its famous legacy from the great emperor, the Corton vineyard of Charlemagne.

Partly, perhaps, because of the investment of Dijon's money,

for most of the seventeenth century the *vins de Dijon*, those, that is, from the northern end of the Côte de Nuits, were the most fashionable. Chambertin and the Clos de Bèze, which lie side by side only an hour's ride from the city, were considered the best. Their wines were uncompromisingly red. Later in the century Volnay in the Côte de Beaune became highly fashionable, but for a very different sort of wine, very pale in colour, almost the *oeil de perdrix* of Champagne, known as *vin paille* (*paille* means straw) because the grapes were pressed between layers of straw to help the juice drain out quickly. They were *vins non-cuvés*; they went straight to the press, it seems without any treading, and without spending any time fermenting in the *cuve*, or vat, with their skins. "You only leave, you only can leave the grapes of this terroir a short time in the vat," said Arnoux. "If they are left there a moment longer than necessary, the wine will lose its delicacy and smell of the bunch or the stem to which the grapes are attached." Volnay of the time was also made with a high proportion of Fromenteau, or Pinot Gris: a grape with very little red pigment in its skin.

During this period, then, while Champagne was rising in reputation, having started by imitating burgundy with wines as red as possible, Burgundy (or at least Volnay) was returning the compliment by producing something not dissimilar from the

Michel Bouchard started off as a travelling textile merchant, but in the 1730s he set up as a wine merchant in Beaune. His wine list is in the back of this textile sample book. Holding stocks of wine to mature and blend was a departure from tradition.

vins gris of the mountain of Reims. Volnay was a *primeur* wine, *premier potable* – or the first to be drunk after the vintage. "This slope produces the finest, the liveliest, and the most delicate wine of Burgundy… The finest comes from a part of the vineyard called Champan." This is a note from Arnoux in 1728; Volnay had not changed its style. Still as late as 1775 Volnay was being described as "the finest, the lightest, the first to drink".

M uch was written about the rivalry between burgundy and Champagne. When Louis XIV was advised by his physician Fagon to drink mature "Nuys", or Nuits-St-Georges, it was considered a great propaganda coup for Burgundy. That the wine was recommended on medical grounds is completely consistent with convictions that go back to the Middle Ages, when Savigny (next door to Beaune) was described as "*nourissant, théologique, morbifuge*" – a hard phrase to translate, but literally meaning "nourishing, theological, and apt to chase out illness". "Easy to digest" was a compliment paid by Erasmus to the wine of Beaune. How much, though, should we read into the fact that Fagon did not specify the light *primeur* wines of Volnay and the Côte de Beaune, those closest in style to Champagne, but Nuits, whose wine seems always to have been considered (and still is) a *vin de garde*, a wine to keep (even in those days for three or four years, rather than the customary one)?

Burgundy in the eighteenth century, it seems, was in several different states of transition at once. The two parts of the Côte, the Côte de Nuits running from Dijon to Nuits-St-Georges, and the Côte de Beaune, from Corton south to Santenay, had quite different traditions. The Côte de Beaune was in several ways less advanced. It had fewer specific *crus*: substantial plots with one owner. The name "Clos" occurs much less often here than in the Côte de Nuits.

Vineyards in the Côte de Beaune were still overcrowded with a jumble of plants increased haphazardly by *provignage*, or layering. When vines are layered they are constantly making new roots near the surface, and their wine therefore tends to have more of the quality of young vines than old; it is lighter, less deep and forceful in flavour. Since the wine was traditionally intended for drinking early, no great trouble was made to select the best grapes, or keep apart the grapes from the best plots.

The exceptions to this were the vineyards in Meursault and Puligny (and some in Volnay and Chassagne) that had begun to specialize in fine white wines. Their emergence had been one of the principal changes of the seventeenth century. Montrachet, the most celebrated white wine vineyard of Burgundy, was first mentioned by name about 1600. By the early eighteenth century Montrachet, and to a lesser degree Meursault, were recognized as white wines at least on a par with the long-established Chablis of Lower Burgundy. "Mulsault" (sic) was "as fine and clear as spring-water", but "Morachet" (sic), which was in the noble ownership of the family of Clermont-Montoison, "possesses a vein of soil that makes its terroir unique of its kind. It produces the most original and the most delicious white wine of France". No Côte-Rôtie, says Arnoux, no Muscat of Frontignan equals it. Montrachet must be ordered a year in advance because there is so little and it is so sought after: "This wine has qualities of which neither the Latin tongue nor the French can express the sweetness; I have drunk it at six and seven years old. Words fail me to express its delicacy and excellence."

Ironically Montrachet and Meursault, Puligny, and part of Chassagne next door had been forced into their speciality against their inclination by the combination of hard limestone and heavy clay in their soil. Good as their white wines were, they were a long time catching up with the prices of their neighbours' reds, and the people of these villages lived in relative poverty in the eighteenth century. Jefferson's note runs:

"At Pommard and Voulenay [sic] I observed them eating good wheat bread; at Meursault, rye. I asked the reason for the difference. They told me that the white wines fail in quality much oftener than the red, and remain on hand. The farmer therefore cannot afford to feed his labourers so well. At Meursault only white wines are made, because there is too much stone for the red. On such slight circumstances depends the condition of man!"

I n the Côte de Nuits the notion of the *cru* was further advanced. Its red wines were, and are, generally more full-bodied and less easy to drink *en primeur*. How much of this is due to the influence of the monks, bishops, and noblemen who had traditionally concentrated their efforts here is hard to judge, but it seems that selectivity was more part of the local tradition than in the Côte de Beaune. The vineyards were generally less

the fragmentation of burgundy Since 1889 the Clos de Vougeot has been sold off in so many little lots that there are now about eighty growers who can claim to own parts of the Clos de Vougeot. It is a true homogeneous *grand cru* no longer.

To talk of such fragmentation, while vitally relevant today, is to look well beyond the eighteenth century. It is a process that started with the French Revolution, when the lands of the Church and the aristocracy were confiscated and sold by auction as *Biens Nationaux*. The fate of the Clos de Vougeot was typical of the chaos of the time, and of the big business machinations that soon took over. It was auctioned in 1791 as national property, but the highest bidder never paid. There was no alternative but to ask the abbey's last cellarer, a popular monk called Dom Lambert Goblet, to continue his good work in the name of the nation – which he did so conscientiously that he was voted a special reward. Two Paris bankers – so much for *Egalité* – then each bought half the Clos. (One of them was soon in jail.) In 1818 its was reunited, nominally in the hand of another banker, Victor Ouvrard, who promptly gave it to his nineteen-year-old cousin Julien-Jules.

The young Ouvrard was a worthy proprietor. He came to live nearby and became not only Mayor, but manager of several other great *crus* – including La Romanée-Conti, whose wine was made, under him, at the Clos de Vougeot. When he died in 1861 the Clos de Vougeot was divided among his sister Betsy's four children (all titled aristocrats), who put it up for sale in lots. This time Baron Thénard saved it (the great fear was that the British would buy it), only to sell it back to the Ouvrard descendants. They put it on the market again in 1887. Again the sale was a flop; it was held in the hunting season and the likeliest buyer, M. de Vilaine, was too busy hunting to turn up. At last, in 1889, a century after the Revolution (and with phylloxera beginning seriously to damage the vines) it was bought by fifteen *négociants* of Beaune, Dijon, and Nuits, and its progressive fragmentation began.

overcrowded, and by now were planted with cuttings rather than layers, hence more deep-rooting. Increasingly, in the eighteenth century, owners of the most prestigious *crus* selected their best grapes to make separate *cuvées*, the best vat being called the *tête de cuvée*. The object was to make the most of its distinctive character, which led to more treading and longer fermentation with the skins before pressing, which in turn made the wine darker and more tannic, needing longer ageing.

By the 1780s the abbé Rozier, the most influential of the textbook writers, was advocating, where necessary, adding honey to the juice to raise the sugar, and hence the alcohol content. In 1763 the abbé Teinturier (whose name, coincidentally, means a grape with red juice as well as a red skin) accused "foreigners" – Flemings, Germans, and northern Frenchmen – of wanting their burgundy as dark and heavy as possible. They were on the road to perdition. When Jean-Antoine Chaptal, Napoleon's Minister of the Interior, recommended adding sugar to beef up the wine, the modern misconception of burgundy as a high-alcohol, dense, dark-coloured wine was conceived – to be born in due time, and to subvert the whole character and reputation of the region.

Meanwhile the curious situation had arisen that the Côte de Nuits deliberately kept a proportion of white grapes in its vineyards to soften the increasing tendency of its wine to deep colour and initial hardness of flavour, while the Côte de Beaune did precisely the opposite. As the eighteenth century progressed it cut down on the light grapes to make its red wine more positively red – although Volnay seems to have been the exception. Up to the mid-nineteenth century the Côte de Nuits still made white wines, from vineyards scattered about among the red. There was, for example, white Chambertin (there is still white Musigny). But no parish or *cru* dedicated itself to white wine because none had to, and in the end virtually all the land was turned over to Pinot Noir.

Bit by bit the practice of the Côte de Nuits, of deliberately selecting *têtes de cuvée* within their *clos*, gave its best wines the edge, in both individuality and their ability to age for long periods. Long maturing revealed yet more qualities: from the lovely but relatively simple aroma of Pinot Noir, piercing and fresh, one of the most mouthwatering of smells, the mature wine conjured bouquets of unimagined sublety and depth. The process fed on itself. The more care you took, the more arrestingly individual the wine would be, and the longer it would live to cover itself with glory.

I am speaking of course of the most ambitious *crus*, usually those with noble or priestly owners, but increasingly also the properties of Dijon *parlementaires* and merchants, where no trouble was too much. The most famous *clos* of all was the Romanée *clos* of the Prince de Conti. Everyone had to renew their soil on the slopes when it was washed away or when it lost its fertility. Manuring was done very gingerly, lest it affect the flavour. The best way was to bring in new soil altogether as top-dressing. In 1749 La Romanée-Conti was "refreshed" with hundreds of waggon-loads of chopped-up turf from the hills

behind, the Arrières-Côtes. The Church, seeing how much improved were some of the vineyards it had sold a century before, made vain attempts to buy them back. The new owner of the Clos de Bèze, Monsieur Jobart, was accused of not sending good enough wine to the Chapter at Langres. Probably the wine was much better than a century previously; what pained the Church was the rise in value of the land it had sold.

The first official classification of the Côte d'Or was not undertaken until 1861, by Dr Jules Lavalle for the Comité d'Agriculture de Beaune, for the Paris Exposition Universelle the next year – stimulated no doubt by the success of Bordeaux's classification for a similar event in 1855. It revealed how far ahead the ambitions of the Côte de Nuits had taken it. The *têtes de cuvée* were far more numerous in the Côte de Nuits than in the Côte de Beaune – and even then the owners of the Côte de Nuits felt hard done by. Eventually *têtes de cuvée* became exalted to the status of *grands crus* by the new laws of *Appellation d'Origine Contrôlée* in the 1930s. The process of perfecting the wine-making had become, as it were, part of the official geography. There were twenty-odd *grands crus* among the red wines of the Côte de Nuits, and only one, Corton, in the Côte de Beaune. The Côte de Beaune on the other hand had the only *grand cru* white wines.

There will always be an argument over whether the soil (in all its variety) is inherently superior for Pinot Noir in the Côte de Nuits; whether with the same traditions and motivation the Côte de Beaune could have selected *têtes de cuvée* that would match the *grand crus*. It will never be answered because the pattern is set. The historical moment when considerable parcels of vineyard could be acquired and experimented with, is past. The different *crus* of Burgundy have existed since the end of the eighteenth century not just as physical facts (now enshrined in law) but also as metaphysical facts in the consumer's mind. If they did not correspond to reality and fulfil expectations they would crumble away. One need look no further than the Clos de Vougeot, the first, biggest, and most famous of all *crus*, for proof.

Its Cistercian creators gradually assembled their great *clos* and eventually farmed it as a single unit, all 120 acres of it. They made their *tête de cuvée* selections according to the vintage. Generally the wine from highest on the hill was best; in certain vintages the wine from the middle had either better or complementary qualities; sometimes the wine from the bottom by the road rose above the middling, and was judged to have something to offer to the *cuvée*. The philosophy was expressed by the famous abbé Teinturier: "We need [grapes that are] cooked, roasted, and green; even this last is necessary; it improves in the *cuve* by fermenting with the others; it is this that brings liveliness to the wine."

As for who drank burgundy in the eighteenth century, and how they got it, there was, if not a revolution, at least a considerable augmentation of the clientele in the middle of the century. Beaune always suffered from transport problems. It is the one great wine centre not well served by a river. Its wines had to be valuable to be worth the enormously high cost (and risk) of ox-cart transport over abysmal roads for weeks on end.

In 1700 the clientele was what it had always been: Dijon; south by the Saône from Chalon to Lyons and the Rhône; north overland to Flanders, faithful to the memory of the Dukes; and in small quantity, and with much effort, up to Auxerre by road to join the barge-fleet of the Yonne to Paris.

Several developments in mid-century greatly altered the picture. One was a long-overdue road-improving effort, led by the reforming Minister Turgot, that made the way to Auxerre much quicker, and reduced the journey-time to Flanders to two weeks. The cost of freight dropped from about twice the value of the wine to (for fine wine) one-fifth. In 1776 Turgot also abolished a whole cat's cradle of legal limitations on the free movement of wine around France.

Another trend was connected. It was the branching out of the long-established cloth trade of eastern France with Flanders. Among the first to combine cloth trading with dealing in burgundy was Michel Bouchard, a merchant from the Dauphiné in south-east France, who regularly passed through Beaune to buy textiles in Liège, or Antwerp, or Bruges. In the 1730s he invested in wine at Beaune on the way north and made good profits, and did the same with his textiles back in Beaune. The house of Bouchard Père et Fils that he founded still has the evidence: a vellum book full of cloth samples at the front, and a wine-list (the other way up) at the back. The houses of Champy, Poulet, and Chanson are three other *négociants* in Beaune with similar dates of foundation that still survive.

The ancient way of buying and selling wine through officials called *courtiers-gourmets* was strictly controlled by the municipality. There were very strict limits to what they could do – which was, fundamentally, to check the quality of each barrel, and introduce a prospective buyer to its owner. They acted only for sellers, but were not allowed to solicit buyers or buy for themselves. In the seventeenth century the function of broker on the buyer's behalf became important, and the role of *commissionaire* slowly supplanted the old *courtiers-gourmets*. By the eighteenth century the *commissionaires* were becoming merchants – and even holding stocks. There was great benefit (as well as obvious risk) for growers and customers in having stock-holding merchants at hand. By investing in young wines and taking them into their own cellars they could give them the after-care that good wine needs: new barrels, racking, and maturing until it is ready to drink. In response, growers were more ready to take pains to make vigorous wines to repay keeping. By the 1780s mature burgundy was for sale in bottles, ready to travel in wicker hampers to the lucky few who could afford it all over Europe.

An eighteenth-century wine-press in Burgundy, painted by Etienne Jeaurat. This was a time of transition in Burgundy, as the current system of *crus* emerged.

CHAPTER 28

PARIS
CABARET

If the great fortress of the Bastille, stormed and sacked on July 14, 1789, will always stand as the symbolic start of the French Revolution, a much less spectacular, indeed a fairly squalid, little event that took place three nights before has at least an equal claim to be considered the first shot in the battle.

Late in the evening of July 11, two prosperous reprobates named Monnier and Darbon led a party that set fire to a barrier, la Barrière Blanche, that blocked the street called the Chaussée d'Antin just before the corner of the Rue St-Lazare. The following day a larger crowd did the same to similar gates across the roads leading into Paris from the villages of Montmartre, Monceaux, and Clichy, to the northwest, and the day after, July 13, to the barriers of the Faubourg St-Martin and Faubourg St-Antoine to the north and east.

All these barriers were key points in a customs wall that entirely surrounded Paris, the city's primitive and ill-conceived means of taxing the consumption of goods being brought within its limits: above all, wine. A tax called the *droit d'entrée*, dating back more than 400 years and frequently increased, had led to the situation in which the most basic wine cost three times as much inside Paris as immediately outside it – to the common people. The nobility and the bourgeoisie were privileged to bring in whatever they pleased. The most obvious consequence was that the city was surrounded, just outside the customs zone, with drinking places known as *guinguettes* – "pleasure-gardens" is a pretty euphemism. But all the villages of the suburbs lived almost by this trade alone: as resorts where Parisians flocked daily to get drunk on cheap wine, and as bases for smugglers

who did a roaring trade avoiding the barriers by various ingenious devices. The village of Passy, it was said, had no other commerce "but that of the mouth".

Monnier, the hero of the Barrière Blanche, was such a smuggler. In fact it is rather puzzling that he led the destruction of the customs posts that indirectly provided his income. It seems that he was set on making a quick killing. At three in the morning of July 12 he was seen in the driving seat of a waggon piled with barrels heading through the barrier for his warehouse in town. The next day it was two groaning carts into the seedy area known as La Petite Pologne (Little Poland) just below the hill of Montmartre. Before destroying each barrier it seems he did a deal with the nearest wine merchant and had his waggons ready.

His steady income before these events had come from more ingenious (if scarcely subtle) smuggling activities. In the rue de la Pepinière, which ran along the city boundary, he had set up a "machine" for throwing bulging wineskins over the wall. He sold the wine at bargain rates (by city standards) in his two bars (*cabarets*) in town. It is not known whether he was party to the remarkable underground pipeline of "*taffeta gommé*" – some sort of waterproofed linen – that ran for "over 400 fathoms", or 732 kilometres (800 yards), from near the village of Monceaux into the city. A hot-air balloon, or "Montgolfier", was also occasionally used.

Monnier and his kind (there were scores, if not hundreds, of similar smugglers) made their fortunes. Opinions were divided on their credentials as revolutionaries. After the fall of the Bastille their "brigandage" was described as "an insult to the Revolution". It was a hollow triumph that brought an immediate crisis to the city; most of its revenue came from the *droit d'entrée*; without it there was no money to run the hospitals and what few public services there were (or to pay the innumerable bureaucrats). The King (who was still, however uncertainly, in charge) recruited 600 new guards for the customs posts. The smugglers were the first to volunteer. In 1791 the *droit* was abolished, and Paris went bankrupt. In 1798 a similar system was introduced under another name. But meanwhile in the full fervour of revolution, an official memoir of 1795 made the claim that: "It is by the destruction of these barriers that the dawn of liberty first shone on the people of Paris. It was from this moment that they first felt themselves freed of the shackles which had weighed upon them. The overthrow of the barriers and that of the Bastille are two facts linked together in the annals of the Revolution; they will be inseparable."

What Paris drank was naturally of interest not just to the Parisians but also to aspiring vineyard areas over a large part of France. From the Middle Ages there had been a clear distinction between the bourgeoisie and the common people, and the predictable contrast that Goethe had summed up: "The rich want good wine; the poor a lot of wine".

The result was a steady growth in wine-growing by and for the common people as near to town as possible. The bourgeoisie did not like it; such coarse wines spoiled the good name of the area. But the process was inexorable.

border province Alsace was utterly devastated in the first half of the seventeenth century by the Thirty Years War – in 1650 it was almost an empty land, open to resettlement from the Alps, Lorraine, and the North. Now in French hands, its wines were cut off from their traditional export route down the Rhine through Germany. Switzerland, and its own cities of Strasbourg and Colmar, were to be its principal markets for a century. Its monastic vineyards continued, however, and it is striking how many of the family firms in business there today were founded in the terrible seventeenth century: Hugel, Humbrecht, Kuehn, Dopff, Trimbach.

Under more settled conditions in the eighteenth century the Riesling grape was introduced, perhaps from the Rheingau. Alsace began to revive, and to become, during Napoleon's wars, a scene of bustle and prosperity for the first time in nearly 200 years.

It seems an extraordinary contradiction that at the same time laws were passed that forbade the entry into Paris, for sale in taverns and *cabarets*, of any wine from within twenty leagues (eighty-nine kilometres or fifty-five miles) of the walls – except, of course, that grown by the bourgeoisie. Two developments that flowed from this were the suburban ring of *guinguettes*, where the populace flocked to refresh themselves, and a twenty-league cordon in which there was no commercial incentive to make good wine.

The long-term result of this bizarre exercise in tax gathering was the downfall of three great vineyard areas

Wine was taxed at the city limits of Paris at customs barriers like this. This contemporary print shows rejoicing at its destruction: the first stirrings of the Revolution.

whose wines used to be well made from good grape varieties. Orléans was the first to go. Admittedly it was pushed. In the sixteenth century Orléans wine was high in royal favour; indeed reckoned the equal of Beaune, and enjoyed a wide market through Paris to the north – even to England. It had one of the best highways in France for access to Paris, since 1577 paved along its whole length. Henry IV, however, who is supposed to have said "Paris is worth a Mass" and turned Catholic to gain the capital, did not hesitate to switch to Parisian wines (or *vins de France* as they were still called).

In 1606 the royal doctor Du Chesne absolutely banned Orléans wine from the royal table. The effect was almost as though the Department of Health declared that all wine from Calais (let me not libel a real wine region) was carcinogenic.

Auxerre and the huge vineyards of Lower Burgundy were the next to suffer in reputation and decline in value as their fatal privilege took hold. Being the first recourse of the capital for

cheap wine inevitably ruined their name. The twenty-league rule sent them the wholesalers or the tavern keepers whose only interest was price.

Paris was the last to go. The killing winter of 1709 is blamed for much of the decline in quality, here and elsewhere. The total replanting that was needed was done not with the high-quality grapes that some, at least, of the suburban vineyards grew (Chardonnay, Pinot Noir, and Fromenteau, or Pinot Gris, among them). Growers seized the chance to plant the "disloyal" bulk-producing Gamay. Paris had several important wine villages on its outskirts – all to the west, along the windings of the Seine from the Bois de Boulogne to the royal palace of St-Germain-en-Laye. The biggest was Argenteuil, which in 1788 provided more than 5,000 barrels for the capital. What the wine tasted like is better left unimagined.

Paris grew mightily in the eighteenth century. Its population rose by almost a quarter between 1720 and 1789 and its demand for wine with it. It was always the magnet for inland wine regions with any practicable means of access to it – even those as far away as Beaujolais. Beaujolais is one of the success stories of the period. Its serious development started in the seventeenth century, growing Gamay on the outskirts of Lyons, the second city of France. Lower Beaujolais, nearest to Lyons, was a land of peasants living relatively well on tiny plots. But Upper Beaujolais looked more ambitiously northwards to Paris. Its wine was of the fair-medium quality that the bourgeoisie were glad to buy. And surprisingly, it was only a matter of around fory-eight kilometres (thirty-odd miles) to the west over good stony roads to the little port of Pouilly-sous-Charlieu on the Loire. The Loire flows northwards from there all the way to the new Canal de Briare, and so Beaujolais was only two or three days by waggon from a water route all the way to Paris – a cheaper and easier route, although longer in miles, than from either Mâcon or the Côte d'Or. The development of the *crus* of Upper Beaujolais was done in a business-like manner with finance from Lyons. Being well outside the twenty-league band was exactly the right stimulus. Quality could be made to pay.

The same conditions stimulated, although in much smaller quantities, and at a higher price, the wines of the ancient vineyards of the northern Rhône: the extremely fine wines of Côte-Rôtie and Condrieu from their cliff-hanging vineyards near Vienne. The road to the Loire is a little longer and steeper here, winding up to the north of St-Etienne. But these were high-value wines, whether for aristocratic tables or for *coupage*, blending with baser matter to give an unusually tasty drink. Hermitage had to come even further, but for the power and character of these southern wines merchants were quite willing to pay the price. In Paris's wine repertoire of the eighteenth century, Hermitage and Côte-Rôtie, Beaune and Champagne were the best wines that arrived, by devious ways, down the Seine. Very little came up the river. Paris was not a sea-port, and the flavours of Bordeaux were only familiar in the circles that were curious to try the best of everything.

the deep south France's oldest, and now by far its largest, wine region seems to have had little part to play in this sad act of the national story. On the contrary, the Languedoc never ceased to increase its acreage from the reign of Louis XIV on, when the far-seeing Colbert planned for it the new port of Sète, which was opened in 1670, and the Canal des Deux Mers, which linked Sète with Toulouse and Bordeaux a dozen years later. We have seen how the citizens of Bordeaux did not exactly encourage wines even from their own hinterland, still less from the distant Midi, to issue via their jealously guarded port. But Sète found other channels of distribution: the Rhône valley to Lyons and Switzerland; the considerable market patronized especially by the English at Livorno (or Leghorn) in Tuscany; Genoa for Piedmont; even Germany and Russia.

The Languedoc had few quality products to distribute, the most notable being being the sweet Muscats of Frontignan, Mireval, and Lunel, although Montpellier, a city of ancient culture, was proud of the red wine of a village in the hills just to the north, St-Georges-d'Orques, and the fizzy Blanquette de Limoux, from the hills to the west near Carcassonne, made itself an early reputation that even reached Paris. But here, too, the fury of planting took hold after the winter of 1709, and every peasant set about improving his lot by invading marginal lands. Instead of banning more planting here, as in the 1730s they did in Bordeaux and most of France, the *Intendants* declared it was the only way the people could pay their taxes.

The great business of the Languedoc was brandy. (It is interesting that it was at Montpellier that Arnaldus da Villanova had perhaps introduced the still into France.) Brandy had the great advantage of relatively small bulk to transport, and found a ready market with the quartermasters of armies and navies. It was much used by northern European merchants for strengthening and disguising low-grade wine. A second distillation, it was discovered, made a better spirit at higher strength and lower volume which became known as *trois-six* (three-six).

The vast majority of Languedoc wines were white, from such neutral grapes as the Clairette and the Picpoul. But their very success inevitably led to them invading the corn lands. "Vines grow marvellously there," said the *Intendant* in 1776. "They give huge crops; but it is easy to tell that the wines are coarse, inferior in quality and rapidly spoil." At this stage they were still in polyculture with fruit, vegetables, and grain. It was, ironically, the huge demand for brandy caused by Napoleon's wars that encouraged the bourgeoisie to move in and industrialize the production. As we shall see, the ever-growing, low-quality vineyard was eventually to suffer utter disaster.

CHAPTER 29

CABINET WINE

Perhaps the oldest bottle of wine that anyone has ever drunk (and enjoyed) was opened in London in 1961 when it was 421 years old. It was a Steinwein: wine, that is, from the steep vineyard called Stein that looks down on Würzburg on the river Main, the baroque capital city of Franconia. Its provenance was impeccable. 1540 (twenty-four years before the birth of Shakespeare) was a freak vintage, a legend. The summer was so hot that the Rhine dried up and you could walk across; wine was cheaper than water, and according to some slightly confused accounts there were two distinct grape harvests. Certainly some extraordinarily sweet wine was made from overripe grapes.

The cask from which the Steinwein came still lies in the cellars of the Residenz of the Prince-Bishops of Würzburg – cellars almost as lofty and dramatic as the salons of the stupendous palace above. Its contents are thought to have been bottled in the late seventeenth century, in other words as soon as bottles and corks became available. The last remaining bottles were kept in the cellar of King Ludwig II of Bavaria (Franconia is the northern part of Bavaria) in the nineteenth century. Eventually they were auctioned, and the London wine-merchant Ehrmann bought them.

What was it like, this pre-Shakespearean wine? The expectations of our little group of tasters were not high. Its opening was preceded by two much younger bottles from the same cellar: a Rüdesheimer 1857, and a Schloss Johannisberger 1820. Both had completely perished: they actually smelled of corruption. But the Steinwein of 1540 was still alive. Nothing has ever demonstrated to me so clearly that wine is indeed a living organism, and that this brown, madeira-like fluid still held the active principles of the life that had been conceived in it by the sun of that distant summer. It even hinted, though it is hard to say how, of its German origins. For perhaps two mouthfuls we sipped a substance that had lived for over four centuries, before the exposure to air killed it. It gave up the ghost and became vinegar in our glasses.

It was a moving event in any case to drink history like this. What made it all the more moving was to have experienced a physical link with the golden age of German wine. The early tenth century was the climax of Germany's success as the producer of the most, and the best, wine of northern Europe. In England Rhenish (the English term for Rhine, and hence all German, wine) was a luxury almost as great as malmsey, when claret was an everyday drink.

There is some evidence that the late fifteenth and early sixteenth centuries witnessed a period of exceptionally warm weather that made wine-growing possible and profitable in parts of Germany where it has since become impossible or marginal. The stories that come down from that age of huge harvests make clear that they were guzzled with almost incredible gusto. In the fifteenth century Germans were drinking over 120 litres of wine a head a year. The allowance for a patient in hospital (also for a doctor) was seven litres a day. It is said that teetotalism ruled out any chance of preferment in the priesthood. The Bishop of Strasbourg in the 1590s, Johann von Manersheid, founded a drinking club for religious nobles called *Vom Horn*. The horn which its members had to drink at a single draught contained four litres. Perhaps it is not surprising that the Bishop joined the angels at the age of thirty-three. But quantity was not the only god; this is also the period in which the first unequivocal references are found to the Riesling, the grape that was eventually to ennoble German wine.

In 1577 the first German edition of the Latin treatise of Hieronymus Bock said: "Riesling grows on the Mosel, the Rhine and in the region of Worms".

All this bustle and gulping began to slow down about the middle of the sixteenth century. Various reasons have

RIGHT The Tiepolo ceiling of the Residenz at Würzburg is one of the sights of Europe. The cellars of the palace, just as imposing in their way, are full of wine from the State Domain.

contains lead

Chronic lead-poisoning has often been cited as one of the causes of the decline of ancient Rome. Lead cisterns and water-pipes are usually blamed. Still scarcely acknowledged, though, is the effect of the Roman practice of concentrating grape-juice into a syrup (called *sapa*, or *defrutum*) by boiling it over a slow fire. In Pliny's words, "leaden and not bronze vessels should be used". Columella agreed.

Where the Greeks used resin to preserve their wines from spoiling, the Romans discovered that lead also gave them a sweet taste and succulent texture. It preserved them because lead ions have a drastically inhibitory effect on enzyme growth, and hence on all living organisms. Lead ointment, for example, was widely and sometimes effectively used before antibiotics were discovered for the treatment of wounds: no bacteria could survive it. (Occasional external use may be beneficial, but regular face-painting with white lead as a cosmetic in the eighteenth century undoubtedly killed many.)

Early in the seventeenth century a French physician accurately described the acute symptoms of lead-poisoning under the name of *Colica Pictonum*, or the colic of Poitou, where it was endemic: all wine-drinkers suffered from it, because all Poitou wine was then treated with what was known as *litharge*, a lead oxide, to sweeten it and mask its acidity, making it more like the expensive Loire wines.

A description of the symptoms is almost too much to read. They include unbearable gripes, fever, complete constipation, jaundice, the loss of control of extremities ("hand and foot drop"), loss of speech, blindness, insanity, paralysis – and, mercifully, death. It was noted that epidemics were commonest after cold years and bad vintages (when most lead was used for sweetening), yet nobody connected the two.

Dr Gockel's discovery took place in Ulm, one of Germany's greatest wine-trading cities, at the time when bad vintage had followed bad vintage all over Europe, and the wines of the Neckar, Ulm's stock-in-trade, were undrinkably sour without the addition of *litharge*. Gockel gave credit to Samuel Stockhausen, who in 1656 published his findings on mortality among workers in lead-mines and described very similar symptoms. He proved his theory on himself, however, by sampling the wine that was poisoning his monastic patients and experiencing some of the pains. Yet despite his work, its acceptance by the Duke of Württemberg, and a ducal edict of severe penalties for using lead in wine, the embarrassing truth was successfully suppressed by wine-merchants for many years. It was not until the mid-eighteenth century that most states passed laws prohibiting it. In France as late as 1884 lead musket-balls were reportedly used for sweetening wine.

been suggested. One is that the wine-trade overreached itself, overpricing good wine and doctoring bad, another that countless towns on the rivers asserting their rights and increasing their tolls on barge-traffic made many wines uncompetitive. Growers also had to contend with deteriorating weather.

Starting in the second quarter of the seventeenth century, and continuing until about 1715, the behaviour of the sun went through a cycle known to science as the "Maunder Minimum". There were no sunspots, and the consequent changes in the Earth's upper atmosphere resulted in the coldest weather recorded in the past 1,000 years. The miserable harvests of the 1690s in France and the famous freeze of 1709 were all part of the pattern.

Cumulative these causes may have been, but the Thirty Years War dwarfed them all. From 1618 to 1648 Germany was the vortex of a pitiless struggle that drew in the forces of all its neighbours. Spaniards, Swedes, Poles, French, Danes, Swiss, Austrians, Bohemians, Bavarians, Hungarians, Dutch, and even Russians, all behaved in the usual manner of soldiery, so that by 1648 many German cities, and most property, had been destroyed or badly damaged. Vineyards, press-houses, cellars, and boats – all the capital equipment of the wine industry – were gone; and so were great numbers of the people.

The country, now divided into a series of more or less despotic states and starving cities, tried to raise revenue from a wine trade that scarcely existed – except in the hands of the Dutch and French. From this catastrophic position the Church, aided by the nobility, with a zeal that reminds one of the thirteenth century, began to reconstruct the wine industry of a broken Germany.

When a massive replanting of vineyards is needed, history repeatedly shows us that the easiest and most prolific vines are planted first, however poor their produce. Any sort of wine will sell, and there is no money in the bank to allow for the inevitably slow build-up to quality. There was another disincentive to the common man to plant the best grapes, which without exception give smaller crops than coarser sorts: he had to pay taxes in kind, which meant a proportion of his crop, either as tithes to the church or the equivalent to a landlord.

Against this background the abbeys went into battle for the Riesling. Its exact origin is unknown, its early history obscure, but the quality of this grape was never in doubt. It is hardy against all weathers; it ripens late (very late for the traditionally early harvest of a northern country), but in ripening it does something no other grape quite manages: it achieves exceptional sweetness while maintaining a high degree of (extremely tasty) acidity. Both sweetness and acidity preserve it. When they are concentrated in a small crop the wine maintains its balance of intense and yet transparent flavours for improbable periods of time. When Thomas Jefferson (he went to Germany too) stayed at the Great Red House Hotel in Frankfurt the list of the wines offered – not just by the bottle, but from the barrel – went back from 1783 to 1726.

No one, surely, would have pretended that the casks contained these vintages unmixed. The custom was clearly to operate a sort of *solera* system by topping up. It cannot have been at random, though, if they were to charge (as they did) three and a half times as much for the oldest wines as the youngest.

Once the qualities of the Riesling were known the devout mind could scarcely trifle with alternatives. In 1672 the abbot of St Clara in Mainz, with vineyards in the Rheingau, gave instructions that his vines (then mainly red) vines should be replaced with "Rissling-holz", and the same year the Bishop of Speyer specified Riesling for his vineyards at Deidesheim in the Palatinate. The great Benedictine abbey of St Maximin at Trier, which in the Middle Ages had owned vineyards in seventy-four different places along the Mosel and its tributaries the Saar and the Ruwer, started a programme of clearing forests around Trier to compensate for the more distant vineyards that it had lost. In 1695 its Abbot Wittman planted over 100,000 new vines which will certainly have been principally Riesling. The superlative Ruwer vineyard of

Maximin Grünhaus, today one of the best in Germany, is witness to the extinct abbey and its perfectionist standards.

Most famously, in 1716 the Prince-Abbot Constantin of the Imperial abbey of Fulda, Charlemagne's creation in the northern part of Hesse, bought what was left of the old Benedictine monastery of Johannisberg in the Rheingau, ruined in the "Great War", rebuilt it more or less as the mansion you see today, and completely replanted its splendid southern slopes to the Rhine exclusively with Riesling vines, at the rate of over 200,000 plants a year over five years. Interestingly, many of the plants came from Flörsheim, just across the river Main from Rüsselsheim, the home of the counts Katzenelnbogen. Their fifteenth-century records include the first mention of the Riesling in literature.

Kloster Eberbach was the headquarters of the Swedish king Gustavus Adolphus in the war. Its cellars had been drunk dry by Swedish and Hessian troops, but its buildings survived, and so, apparently, did its famous vineyard, the Steinberg. The Cistercians, like the Benedictines, planted Riesling, and in the 1760s built the high protective wall that gives the vineyard a superficial resemblance to its Burgundian cousin, the Clos de Vougeot.

Of all the great religious authorities, the only ones not to

Schloss Johannisberg in the Rheingau. This was not only the first vineyard to be planted entirely with Riesling, but also the site of the first official Spätlese vintage.

insist on more and more Riesling were the Prince-Bishops of Würzburg and their Franconian peers. Riesling is not the right grape for Franconia. The heavy, often limey, soil and the more extreme climate further east were better suited to the earlier-ripening Sylvaner, originally from Austria, the source of wines of a presence and potency that seem perfectly to fit their almost stiflingly baroque environment.

Toward the end of the eighteenth century the potentate of the Mosel, the Prince Elector (and Archbishop) Clemenz Wenceslaus of Trier, became perfectly categorical. You have seven years, he told his flock, to replace all your vines with Riesling. They were almost the last seven years of the *ancien régime* in Germany.

The records of the eighteenth century not only show the recognition that in most parts of Germany, on good vineyard soils, Riesling has no peer. But they also reveal the gradual discovery of its greatest qualities and the techniques for achieving them. The recovering economy and population had several beneficial effects on the country's wine. One was the increased demand for food, which filled the fertile lands with corn and put the vines back where they belonged; on the steep and stony hillsides. Another was the growing sense of prosperity and security that allowed Germany's cold damp cellars to fill up and work their slow-motion metamorphosis on wines that cannot be hurried.

It almost goes without saying that the most looked-for characteristic of all German wine was sweetness – or if not sweetness, strength. A good vintage was one that provided this naturally. Failing ripe grapes, the ways of artfully assisting nature had hardly changed since Roman times. Boiling the must to reduce its volume and increase the ratio of sugar was one. Drying the grapes in the sun to make what the French call a *vin de paille* was another. The use of sulphur, the "Dutch match", was routine by this period to prevent the wines from fermenting completely dry; it also partly accounted for the very long time wines were kept in cask – until its obvious smell and taste had worn off. One should not underestimate the importance of Germany's very cold cellars, either, in preventing the fermentation from ever finally consuming all the wine's natural sugar.

Better weather in the eighteenth century coincided with the spread of the Riesling. Its grapes showed their qualities in continuing to ripen into sunny October days to make mouthwatering, naturally sweet wines. This was the context for the inception of the so-called Cabinet cellar: a cabinet in the sense of a receptacle for precious objects, or a cellar for the use of the dignitaries who formed a cabinet in the political sense. The precise semantics of the term have been debated ad nauseam by adherents to one view or the other. Who used it first, and precisely what they meant by it, are matters we can safely leave to discussion by the supporters of Schloss Johannisberg on the one hand and those of Kloster Eberbach on the other: the Benedictines versus the Cistercians.

What is significant is the increasingly selective approach of their cellar-masters at vintage time. They kept the best grapes for the cabinet wine. They can hardly have been unaware of the incidence of the noble rot – the German term is *Edelfaule*. A famous vintage was made from rotten grapes in the low-lying Burgenland in Austria as far back as 1526. Tokaji owed its great reputation entirely to the late-harvesting of rotten grapes. We can even pin it to the Rheingau: in 1687 a Dutch scientist, van Leeuwenhoek, one of the inventors of the microscope, drew the fungus *Botrytis cinerea* which he saw on Rheingau grapes, and claimed that he himself had found it in no other vineyards.

There are records of single casks of outstanding quality at intervals through the eighteenth century. In 1753 in the Steinberg one was made entirely from rotten grapes; in 1760 fifteen were made from rotten and very ripe grapes together, and pronounced of "delicate" quality. The Rheingau poses a similar question to Sauternes: was there a real reluctance to use rotten grapes to make sweet wine, or was it just something nobody liked to admit?

In Germany, history is made characteristically tidy. 1775 was the first official Spätlese, or late-gathered, vintage. Schloss Johannisberg was the place. The manager was Herr J.M. Engert from Dittingheim on the Tauber. And his age was forty-seven. Yet the account of this famous harvest makes it all sound like a miraculous mistake. Permission to pick was always given by the owner – in this case the abbot of Fulda. Directions were sent by courier. Judging his time (Fulda was seven days' ride), Engert sent word to the abbot that the grapes were ripe, and, considering the weather, in danger of rot. For a reason never explained, the courier took so long on the road that by the time he came back with the order to pick, all the neighbouring properties had finished, and Johannisberg had a vineyard full of rotten grapes.

The next scene is the cellar, the following February. Johann Engert, a puzzled man, is tasting. "The new wine", he reports, "is mostly still cloudy and has stopped fermenting with a spicy sweetness. We are hoping for something extraordinary!" Scene three, same place, April 10: "This 1775 wine is so extraordinary that from the eight tasters no word was heard other than – I have never had such a wine in my mouth before!"

Stage-managed or not, the Spätlese had been born. Not Spätlese in the modern sense, which means normally ripe grapes with a good concentration of sugar, but Spätlese as a concept: the harvest delayed until, rot or no rot, the wine could be expected to be naturally sweet. With remarkable alacrity the government at Mainz took it up. In 1788 it enjoined each community to choose its own harvest date, but to bear in mind that only fully ripe or nobly rotten grapes could make the finest wines. Thus in almost their last year of office the father abbots of the Rhine relinquished the secrets of their cabinets (if that is what they were) and set the pattern for a great Rhenish flowering in the nineteenth century, when Auslesen and Beerenauslesen, Trockenbeeren- and Edelbeerenauslesen were to bloom. In the 1790s the Rhineland was occupied by the Revolutionary French, and Eberbach and Fulda, like Cîteaux and Cluny, were taken from their monks for ever.

CHAPTER 30

THREE-
BOTTLE MEN

If the principal glory of wine, and what distinguishes it from all other drinks and foods, is the endless variety of its qualities and flavours, then that variety was first appreciated and celebrated, albeit by a small minority of plutocrats, in the England of the first King George. What happened in the stately mansions of the great, serene in their deer parks, may not seem very relevant to the wider population. But it certainly made its impact in the vineyards of the world, which vied for the patronage of this unique class of discriminating, unbiased, and infinitely wealthy connoisseurs.

Great Britain had emerged from the War of the Spanish Succession as the most powerful nation in Europe, militarily supreme on land and sea, hungry for empire and anxious to be cultured. At home, the English developed, in the course of the eighteenth century, an aesthetic of such suave elegance, so understated, so harmonious and trim, that to this day it remains the most admired product of English taste. A *jardin anglais* is one that apes, however misguidedly, the classic 1750s line of "Capability" Brown. The rough edges of this society were all too obvious, but the gloss it put on its vigour, on the vitality and inventiveness that produced the Industrial Revolution, set the continuing standard for sophisticated wealth right round the world.

A catholic taste in wine was one of the hallmarks of this new English breeding. It was always a prerogative of the wealthy (the government saw to that in high taxation), but to some degree it permeated at least through the gentry and professional classes. Even at very earthy levels English taverns

liked to pretend they kept a range of Portuguese, Spanish, Italian, and French wines, even if, as a French visitor, Monsieur Grosley, reported in 1765, they were often really home-made.

The red wine in one tavern, he claimed, was made of blackberries and aloes with turnip juice; "port" was turnip juice fermented with "wild fruit beer" and a small (one hopes) addition of lead oxide. As for the white wine, he adds (exaggerating, to be sure) that it was mostly made in England by such enthusiasts as Mr Hamilton of Cobham, who actually grew grapes. Six weeks in England was perhaps not enough to give Grosley the total picture. The best bottle he drank, he said, was one of Mâcon that a surgeon had brought back with him from France and that they shared on the Dover coach. To be even-handed he did add that he would have fared no better in France, outside of wine country.

The normal English wine list, up to the end of the seventeenth century at least, was still extremely limited. For political reasons French wines were usually unobtainable or very expensive. Claret was something to hanker after (except in Scotland, where it was almost, it seems, something to bath in, so liberally did the Scottish treat themselves). As far south as Yorkshire in England arrangements could be made to be supplied with claret from Edinburgh's port, Leith on the Firth of Forth.

Rhenish, England's other ancient favourite, was in its time of troubles. Imports to England never dried up completely, but the wine was expensive and probably not very good. Even the fact of German kings on the English throne only made "Hock" and "Moselle" (Rhenish was becoming an archaic term) a necessity at court: not in a tavern or in a gentleman's cellar.

The Brilliants was a London club whose only rule was the minimum number of bottles every member had to drink. Rowlandson made this print of a session in 1798.

Italian wines, unless imported privately, and with extravagant care, had the reputation of arriving in poor condition or not keeping. Overwhelmingly it was from Spain and Portugal that England drew its regular supplies – and as travellers found, the wines shipped to England were made for the purpose. They were not the wines the inhabitants drank at home.

Others would disagree about Portugal, particularly about Lisbon, but we only have to examine Samuel Pepys's cellar to see that little had changed: "I have two *tierces* [a third of a pipe; rather more than a barrel] of Claret, two quarter casks of Canary, and a smaller vessel of sack; a vessel of Tent, another of Malaga, and another of white wine, all in my wine cellar together." It was a lavish cellar indeed (for which he thanked God) – especially for a man who had solemnly forsworn wine. But take away the claret (England and France were not often at peace) and all the other wines, barring perhaps the white, were Spanish. As between Canary, sack, Tent, and Málaga one could hardly imagine a less interesting variety. Pepys himself must have found it so: he tried blending and didn't like that either.

Even at a lordly level things were scarcely more thrilling. Hatfield House, the red-brick Jacobean palace of the Cecil family, Earls (now Marquesses) of Salisbury, a short ride north of London, has in its archives the wine-bills of every age since Queen Elizabeth's. Those of the 1660s are startlingly simple. Lord Salisbury and his guests (including the king) apparently drank either Canary or white wine, some from Langon (close to Sauternes) and some from "my lord Bristol", logged in as "Paries wine"; in all probability something that John Hervey, the first Earl of Bristol, had tasted and approved in Paris, rather than something grown there. Could it have been Chablis? The Duke of Bedford in 1661 recorded buying "Shably" – the first mention of this oldest of white burgundies by name in England.

"High Countrie wine" appears in an earlier account, and in 1670 Lord Salisbury bought a hogshead of burgundy for £17 (the Langon white had cost him £6). Rhenish, "Muscadine" and sack are mentioned; then in 1677 "six gallons of Haut Brion wine", and a very expensive hogshead of "Tournane alias Hermitage wine" for £20. Tournon is the town on the Rhône where Hermitage is grown; whether the wine was white or red is not mentioned, but white Hermitage for a long time held a reputation as one of France's two or three greatest white wines, with a greater capacity for ageing than any. The duties on such French wines (even the best) were commonly double the value of the wine. When the Duke of Bedford bought some Haut-Brion in 1671, two hogsheads cost him £4 in Bordeaux: the customs and other charges brought the total bill to over £15.

Leafing through the old bills it is clear to see how the

aristocratic taste-buds were aroused in the last years of the seventeenth century. The fourth Earl of Salisbury, who was politically naïve to say the least, had spent several years in the Tower of London; his wine bills show extra charges for delivery to his cell. The fifth Earl ran up enormous bills with Thwaites, his wine merchant. To analyse his consumption would be a labour of love: in essence his bills simply show that fashion required (or at least suggested) a vastly wider range of wines as the eighteenth century approached. Canary was the most expensive, port about half as much – and the same price as Pontack.

In 1692 the Earl, for the first time, bought a considerable quantity of Champagne – though it was not called that. All wine accounts of the time show that it was the common practice in noble households (when buying direct from abroad, rather than through an English merchant) to share shipments with friends; in this case he bought half a consignment of six barrels of wine under the names of their respective "river" and "mountain" vineyards: Hautvillers, Sillery (spelt "Cellary") and "Espernay". The wine travelled north from Champagne via Brussels (where customs dues had to be paid) and on into Holland (the ship sailed from The Hague). With the barrels the Earl bought 150 new bottles (which cost £1 for fifty) and sufficient corks, so he clearly had some of the wine bottled on arrival at Hatfield.

John Hervey, later the first Earl of Bristol, cast his net wider than Lord Salisbury. The accounts of his cellar at Ickworth Lodge, his "seat" in Suffolk, from about 1690 to 1740, start with the usual emphasis on Spain. He was fond of Lucena – today's montilla – and Galicia. There was also a suspicious number of purchases of "Navarre" during wars with France. (Navarra is the Spanish province closest to the French border and Bordeaux.)

As though with a premonition of the war that started in 1703, Hervey laid in no less than four hogsheads of Haut-Brion the previous year. (When he bought Margaux in the middle of the war it cost him twice the price.) He had wine sent in bottles, packed in chests, from Florence (this was the standard way with Tuscan wine) and, unusually, from Avignon: this is a very early bottling of Châteauneuf-du-Pape. Not until 1710, seven years after the Methuen Treaty, did he record his first purchase of "Portugal wine". "Red-port" he called it in 1714, and in 1716 "Port-wine" – although as late as 1730 there is an entry in the ledger for "Methuen-wine": the Treaty must still have been firmly in people's minds.

When peace was made with France Lord Bristol bought "burgundy for dear wife" and experimented with white Condrieu from the Rhône. In 1719 he bought Meursault for the first time, spelling its name "Muljo"; then La Tour claret, La Fitte claret, and several times "Côte Rôty". There was a growing fashion for Rhône wines, despite the difficulty of bringing these from the very heart of France. The significant thing is that they were good enough, and different enough, to send for by whatever laborious means.

Grandest of the grandees, and most discriminating in his taste for wine, was James Brydges, who held the supremely lucrative post of Paymaster-General to the Forces in the Duke of Marlborough's wars. A percentage of every private's

pay and every naval rating's meagre stipend stuck to the Paymaster's fingers, and went to embellish "the most magnificent house in England", Defoe's description of Canons, his long-since demolished palace at Edgware, north of London. If Brydges is remembered for anything today, it is for his employment of Handel as the *Kapellmeister* of his private choir. Handel's Chandos anthems were written when his employer was created Duke of Chandos in 1719.

Like Lord Bristol, Brydges was an enthusiast for Hermitage, and in 1711 bought white as well as red for the first time. One French wine that was drunk at Canons but was evidently rare was "Capbreton". It was a claret-like wine from sandy seaside vineyards in the Landes in southwest France, just north of the port of Bayonne (which saw a great deal of Dutch trade as the harbour for Armagnac, and was a busy entrepôt at times when it was politic to disguise French wines as Spanish). Brydges thought highly of his *rancio* of Navarra, which was also shipped from Bayonne – along with, for some unfathomable reason, Rhenish. *Rancio* is a taste much appreciated in Spain and the French provinces near the Pyrenees: the nutty tang of deliberate oxidation over several years. In 1736 Brydges described it as "a noble strong-bodied wine. I have had some 20 years in the cellar and it is grown to be a strong racy wine, the sweetness all gone." (We have the advantage of Brydges' own tasting notes.) Tokaji from Breslau in the south of Poland he shipped via Holland.

After the war the number of hogsheads of French wine arriving at Canons suggest non-stop entertaining on the most lavish scale. In 1716 Brydges bought no less than fifty hogsheads of Hermitage at £60 each: a stupendous amount of a top growth for any cellar. But Brydges' taste was becoming more and more demanding and catholic at the same time. His Canary had to be the finest "Palme", from Tenerife, a light yellow wine with a scent of pineapple; his French repertoire extended to Montrachet, Pommard, "Bone" and Nuits, as well as the "first-growth" clarets, the best Rhône wines and even something called "Kill-priest" from the Dauphiné: "… tho' light in the mouth, the strongest French wine I have ever tasted".

Less conventionally, Brydges was a connoisseur of Italian wines, which he bought mainly through the British consul at Livorno, or Leghorn. Tuscany and Sicily were his chief sources. He bought Tuscan red Montepulciano and white Verdea and the inevitable "chests of Florence", but principally the Moscadellos or Muscatines that were a speciality of Montalcino in Tuscany, Montefiasconi near Rome, Calabria, and Syracuse in Sicily. From Sicily he also bought "red dry Syracuse, strong-bodied and fine-flavoured, not sweet or luscious, but very rich…"

Like the merchants of ancient Pompeii, his friends in Leghorn dealt in Greek wine as well. There is a very antique ring about the Zante and Cephalonia, not to mention the Chios (once spelt "Chaos") that joined the more modish barrels rolling into the Canons cellars. Not until 1722 did the Duke buy any port or madeira. He considered Champagne (both "green" and red) "a very ticklish purchase". Yet in 1736 he paid a high price for red Constantia from the Cape of Good Hope, and had his merchant in Southampton on the look-out for madeira that had been to the West Indies and back. Nor did he turn his back on Rhenish, but in the 1730s bought such old vintages as 1666, 1684, and 1696.

The cellar of Canons was a prodigy for its time, the hobby of a multi-millionaire. It shows better than any the resources available in the early eighteenth century – and the level of connoisseurship of the time. England's most famous contemporary cellar, though, was more conventional. Sir Robert Walpole was the son of a Norfolk squire who rose by ruthlessness and charm to become the most powerful man of his age: in fact, if not precisely in title, Britain's first Prime Minister. Norfolk's port of King's Lynn was second only to London as the principal wine port of England in 1700. Its hinterland was where England's political power-base lay: the rich agricultural counties of East Anglia and the East Midlands, counties such as Norfolk and Northampton which have more massive mansions than the Loire has châteaux, hunting country where hard riding and hard drinking were the accepted way of life. Lynn even had its own recognizable style of port, lighter than "the heavy London cut".

Claret was Walpole's favourite wine. Walpole, one feels, was the model Englishman whom the proprietors of the Bordeaux "first-growths" had in mind. He bought his Château Margaux four hogsheads at a time, regularly every three months a hogshead of Lafite, and always had some Pontac in his cellar – not to be kept for long; he evidently drank his claret brisk and young, unlike "old burgundy" which be bought in chests of bottles, at a considerably higher price.

There was port, of course, in the cellars of Houghton Hall, his Palladian palace, but it was definitely second choice to claret. Sir Robert seems to have preferred the more expensive white Lisbon, which he bought in massive quantities. He did not trouble with sack or sherry, and canary was going out of fashion. He bought Champagne and Rhenish (six dozen "Hoghmer of the year 1706" is a very specific reference, both to vintage and to vineyard: Hoghmer is Norfolk spelling for Hochheimer). By no means to be forgotten was the Houghton Hall strong beer, which

A façon de Venise drinking glass, painted by Jan van der Velde in the seventeenth century. Façon de Venise was thin, delicate Venetian-style glass made outside Venice.

canary In order of price and quality, in Pepys's time and for another forty years, Canary probably led Málaga, and Málaga led (sherry) sack. The Canary Islands having the warmest climate, their wine was naturally the richest and strongest. All southern Spain tried to copy it for export; Málaga, less hidebound by tradition than Jerez and Sanlúcar, did the best job.

The Pedro Ximénez was the favourite Andalusian grape. It makes the strong brown wine of Málaga, the strong but lighter wine of Montilla and Lucena, inland near Córdoba, and sherry in the sack style (i.e. strong and brown, but not fragrant or fine).

Andalusians did not drink sherry sack: they preferred pale young wine approaching what is now called *fino*, and drank it with water or ice. Canary lost its supremacy not only because it was successfully imitated, but also because its thinly-populated islands were a poor market for exports. Not needing cloth, they had to be paid in cash. Mainland Spain, in contrast, could even buy merchants' goods with silver bullion. Overtaken in Europe by Málaga, Canary tried the American market. But preferential treatment of Madeira by the British government applied in America too. About 1720 the Boston customs would "usually pass consignments of Canary up to fifty or sixty tuns provided they were declared as Madeira". The Islands, however, did not give up, and the Napoleonic wars saw (at least a brief) revival of their wine trade. The twenty-first century is seeing another.

was brought up to the dining room by pipes from the cellar with taps on the front of the marble serving tables.

Walpole's attitude to the laws of the land was typical enough of his time, but still alarming to find in the highest of public servants. During the War of the Spanish Succession he plotted with his friend Josiah Burchett, who was secretary to the Admiralty (Walpole was then on the Admiralty Council), to smuggle a large quantity of claret, burgundy, and Champagne from The Netherlands – actually using an official Admiralty launch under the customs officers' noses. In Lynn his smuggling was less successful: one shipment was impounded. On another occasion an employee "with the help of brandy secured all the officers" while the casks were sent out to Houghton by waggon. Such peccadillos as declaring French wine as Portuguese in order to pay the lower duty were standard practice.

Wine and port were almost synonymous to most of the population throughout the eighteenth century. Portuguese wines accounted for about three-quarters of the total imports of Great Britain. With one voice the people complained, with another they called for more. Certainly their consumption, of a wine frequently described as "fiery", as "blackstrap", as "boiling in the blood", was heroic. "Athletes of liquor" is how one historian has described the squires, the parsons, the officers, and the university dons who were to be found, night after night, drinking themselves under the table. So common was the term "three-bottle man", meaning one who regularly drank three bottles of port at a sitting (or perhaps during the course of the day) that to provoke comment greater efforts were needed.

Part of the explanation lies in the size of the bottles. Wine was normally bottled in either pints or quarts. The pint (just over half of a modern bottle) was presumably the standard measure of consumption, which reduces a three-bottle man to (a mere) one-and-two-thirds man. There may also have been considerable lees which would be left in the bottle. As to the strength of the wine, it began the eighteenth century as high-strength table wine, but was dosed with more and more brandy as the years went on. Yet far from deterring its drinkers, extra strength coincided with still higher consumption.

The explanation probably lies in the maturing state of the wine. It was during the third quarter of the eighteenth century that the wine bottle was redesigned to lie snugly horizontal on a shelf. Its shape had been evolving for over a century from an onion to a mallet; now quite suddenly it became a cylinder with a relatively short neck; close to the ideal shape for stacking.

Before the eighteenth century the cellar of a house (if it had one) was identical in function to the cellar of an inn. Barrels (in England they would generally be of cider and beer) stayed in them until they were emptied, by daily drawing off. Mansions at first, then rapidly smaller town-houses, manors, and farms, adapted their cellars for storing the new bottles. The standard arrangement was open shelving of brick, stone or slate, often vaulted, in "bins" that held twenty-five dozen bottles: the contents of a hogshead. To buy a pipe of port (enough to fill two bins) became almost a convention among country gentlemen with plenty of room in their cellars. Usually the merchant would send two men to bottle the wine in the customer's cellar and lay it down in the bins.

Even the three-bottle man, at this rate, would soon find himself drinking port that had been in its bottle for a year or two, and notice how it "crusted" the side of its bottle with a dark, clinging film, while the wine itself changed colour from almost black to glowing ruby, and its fieriness gave place to a lingering glow.

Democratization of the wine-cellar in England – that is from the aristocracy to the middle classes – may be said to date from the 1760s, when for the first time a London book-seller thought it worthwhile to issue a cellar-record book. (It went into at least three editions.) The bookseller was Robert Dodsley, of Pall Mall, who had been responsible for Samuel Johnson's great *Dictionary*. *The Cellar-Book, or Butler's Assistant, in keeping a Regular Account of his Liquors*, is prefaced by remarks on its "usefulness… to any gentleman, who has a stock of liquors in his cellar, and is willing to know how it is expended… and the method proposed is so easy, that any common servant may keep the account".

Most telling, and the surest evidence we can have of the wines to be expected in a gentleman's cellar a century after Pepys, is the printed specimen page in the book suggesting its probable contents. These are the numbers of bottles: "Ale 235; Cyder sixty; Port 400; Claret forty-eight; White-wine eighty-five; Sack four; Madeira twenty-nine; Champagne nineteen; Burgundy forty-eight; Brandy four; Rum eighteen; and Arrack [the spirit much used for punch] thirty-four". Almost twice as much port, in other words, as all the other wines combined.

CHAPTER 31

REVOLUTION
AND AFTER

The glinting wedge-shaped dead-weight of the guillotine in its fatal drop is such a powerful symbol of the end of the old regime, not just in France but in all of continental Europe, that it is tempting to think of a new world in new hands at the start of the nineteenth century. The wars that followed, as Napoleon came close to turning Europe into a French Empire, and the Mediterranean into a French lake, obscure with battle-smoke the petty affairs of the next twenty years. When the smoke clears, it is a surprise to see so much that is familiar still in place: incredible that one-and-a-half million Frenchmen have been led off to more or less glorious deaths and France continues to function; vintage after vintage picked, trodden, and consumed.

In the Peninsula the chaos of war raged around the two principal wine-exporting centres, Oporto and Jerez, and to a lesser extent Málaga. Both Oporto and Cádiz were besieged, and yet their trade continued. The fighting spared their vineyards. The war in Portugal, where the Duke of Wellington and the best part of the British Army were deeply engaged for three years, was to make a whole generation of British officers proudly familiar with every shade of Portuguese wine – as well as the port they knew so well already. Their entertainment in Oporto alone was enough to addict them to its liquor for life.

Wartime produces byzantine patterns of intrigue between partners in trade who depend on each other – whatever the policies of their governments. Bonaparte attempted to impose a "Continental System" of blockading trade between Britain and all European ports. It failed, because such trade was as essential to the French as it was to their newly-conquered vassals. He was

forced to issue licences of exemption to merchants, but they were widely abused and circumvented. The French army was even said to be dressed in Yorkshire broadcloth. The Emperor tried to avoid buying manufactured goods from the enemy, but was glad of the market for each wine harvest. His only preference was that as much as possible was smuggled past the British customs to deprive his enemy's government of useful income.

The British government, for its part, was glad to have French brandy, as it saved the corn supply for making bread rather than gin. There was also a thriving re-export business. Of nearly 5,000 tuns of brandy imported into Britain from France in 1808, over half was sold on to Sweden and the Baltic countries, which were under French blockade. That year and the next British docks were said to be choked with thousands of tuns of French and Spanish wines en route for third countries. There was a tacit agreement even at the height of hostilities that France would manage Europe's internal trade, while Britain would be the waggoner of the sea.

War serves to forge or reinforce personal ties. Foreign merchants forced to evacuate a town had no option but to trust a native rival with their business. Mr Barton of Bordeaux, for example, placed his entire business in the hands of Monsieur Guestier (and did so again, 150 years later, in World War II). Seldom were any such trusts betrayed.

The single greatest change that the Revolution in France, and Napoleon elsewhere, made to the *ancien régime* of wine was to dispossess the monasteries and the Church of their enormous holdings. New aristocrats (or at least new money) soon filled the shoes of the unfortunates who lost their heads, but the divorce of Church and land was a radical and permanent change. We have seen how it affected Burgundy. Bordeaux was never very clerical country. Germany was the place where it most directly affected the most famous estates.

The Mosel was the first German district to fall to France: to a *sans-culotte* army of revolutionaries who must have appeared to the citizens of Trier as savage, and as formidable, as the Franks of 1,400 years before. From 1795 for eighteen years, the Mosel, as well as Alsace, the Palatinate, and all the west bank of the Rhine, was in French hands. Unlike their Frankish forebears, though, the revolutionaries brought with them a legal system, an administrative machine, and a very different method of taxation from the old feudal dues. Princes and Electors, the despots of each German mini-state, were stripped of power and place.

On the Mosel, the most church-dominated of the German regions, France thus seized a quarter of all the vineyards, and very much more than a quarter of the best. As *Biens Nationaux* they were sold (or sometimes leased) to those who could afford them. It was high time, according to some, for business motives to replace the privileges of the past. Was there such a clear advantage in the dispossession of the Cistercians from Kloster Eberbach to

A "dipping bottle" for serving half a gallon of marsala at a time from an open barrel. It is painted with Lord Nelson's portrait and his great victory at Trafalgar.

make room for the Duke of Nassau? In practical terms, no. On the contrary, to dismiss such an elite of experienced technicians and connoisseurs was the height of folly, but in philosophical terms it had been a foregone conclusion for half a century. Napoleon was the agent, merely, of the Enlightenment, answering the call of rationalists already in their graves. Montesquieu would have nodded, Rousseau shrugged his shoulders, Voltaire smiled his benevolent and enigmatic smile.

I n the field of practical science, as opposed to philosophy, one figure dominates the world that Napoleon fashioned: his Minister of the Interior, Jean-Antoine Chaptal. Today his name is known to the world of wine for one thing only. Chaptalization means adding sugar to the juice to increase the alcoholic content of the wine. But Chaptal deserves a place among the immortal names in wine's long history. His *Traité sur la Culture de la Vigne* (he wrote Book II himself – the rest is a compilation under his direction) went far beyond the efforts of previous writers. It is the first treatise which we can properly call modern – in the sense of not looking back to the classics for justification, but starting with the evidence of recent (that is eighteenth-century) science.

What he had to deal with was a present crisis – of falling standards, overproduction, fabrication, and plain incompetence – in France's greatest industry of all. "How is it then", he wrote, "that a great number of French wines, famous in former times, are fallen into discredit? Why is their quality so mediocre, while those from other districts acquire or maintain a well-deserved reputation? Only a little thought is needed to see that it is not the situation, the climate or the soil that is to blame: the fault lies with careless cultivation, with the repetition of unthinking routine, with ignorance or forgetfulness." Above all, "with the preference for the grapes that give the maximum of vulgar juice over those that produce the best quality."

Not that Chaptal was the first to identify the problems. On the one hand there were such archaic laws as the twenty-league rule, and systems of taxation that encouraged bad wine. On the other, a great increase in population had made the Gamay mentality endemic outside the most commercially privileged regions. Worst of all, though not exactly freely admitted so soon after the Revolution, was the total anarchy in the planting of new vineyards on any farmland anywhere in France. That was the meaning to most peasants of the great word *Liberté*.

One of Balzac's characters, barely a generation after Chaptal, enunciated all too clearly the cynic's view: "The bourgeois – I mean monsieur le marquis, monsieur le comte, monsieur this that and the other, claim that I make junk instead of wine. What use is education? You figure out what it means. Listen: these gentlemen harvest seven, sometimes eight barrels to the acre, and sell them at sixty francs apiece, which makes at the most 400 francs an acre in a good year. Me, I harvest twenty barrels and sell them at thirty francs, total 600 francs. So who's the ninny? Quality, quality! What use is quality to me? They can keep their quality, the marquises and all. For me, quality is cash."

C haptal was not a farmer, but he was a scientist with a most practical bent. A discovery was of interest only if it could be put to immediate use. In several fields of manufacture he freed France from dependence on its neighbours. He organised mass production of gunpowder. He will always be associated with sugar because he developed its extraction from beet.

After the scientist, there followed the encyclopedist: André Jullien, whom we have already met classifying Constantia, and collating statistics about every wine region under the sun. There seems to be a quantum leap here: from the tentative investigation, the humility of a scientist, to confident pronouncements that smack more of the journalist – or at least the professional deeply engaged in the wine trade. Only fifteen years separate them: Chaptal's *Traité* in 1801, Jullien's *Topographie* in 1816 – yet in comparison Chaptal sounds like the summing up of the eighteenth century, Jullien like the nineteenth century already in full unblushing cry.

Topographie de Tous les Vignobles Connus is the foundation of modern writing about wine. Its introduction is modest: "We possess several good books on the culture of the vine and on the best procedures to follow in winemaking; but none, to my knowledge, deals with the characteristics which distinguish between them the wines of different vineyards, and still less with the nuance of quality which is often noticed in the produce of adjacent *crus*, which, being so close together, it would seem ought to resemble each other exactly. I have tried to fill this gap and to gather together… all the details likely to interest the owners of vineyards, as well as persons anxious to keep a good cellar."

The author's methodical approach, his definition of his terms, his deliberate categorizing of each wine in relation to its neighbours all have a familiar ring: they have been imitated so many times. Jullien was a wholesale wine merchant in Paris who, according to the great bibliophile André Simon, was born in 1766 and travelled widely and regularly around the wine regions of France. "He made it a practice to write down everything that interested him" – like Jefferson. "Later on in life he undertook to visit most of the vine-growing districts of Europe, and even passed into Asia." His *Topographie*, says Simon, "is of the highest interest, because most of the information it contains is completely original" – and also because his practised palate had a worthy partner in his analytic and descriptive powers.

There were five editions of *Topographie* over no less than fifty years, the last two "corrected and augmented by C.E. Jullien", who was probably the son of the industrious wine merchant. There has never been such an ambitious and original undertaking in its field. Each edition covers more ground, with constant updating of details, of prices, of quantities, even of rates of duty in importing countries – all of which meant correspondence from Paris to every part of the world. In this, above all, lies the originality and enduring influence of Jullien's work – perhaps more outside France than within it. He puts France firmly first, naturally enough, but, unlike many later French writers, takes the whole world into account. "What distinguishes the wines of France from those of other countries is their astonishing variety," he writes. Nobody could deny that this still holds true. Beyond that, however, and the loving care with which he enumerates them, he ranges around the world making comparisons, without the slightest chauvinism, in a way that few French have ever done.

Writing about wine from the consumer's point of view had been almost a branch of medicine, sometimes practised with great wit and skill even when specific information was lacking. Andrew Boorde's sixteenth-century contemporary, the Italian physician Andrea Bacci, was also much quoted, in a more poetic vein. Such writing was to become the speciality of the English, for the simple reason that English wealth, at the top of the social ladder, had accumulated the most varied cellars of top-quality wines on earth. Despite a preponderance of Portuguese and Spanish wines in taverns, English minds were open – which even Jullien admitted was never the case in France. "The Bordelais", he wrote (in his one other book, the *Manuel du Sommelier*), "find the wines of Burgundy too heady… the Burgundian accuses Bordeaux wine of being tart and cold; both scorn Rhine wines because of their sharp taste, and those of Spain and other southern countries because they are sweet."

The first Englishman to offer a more ambitious survey was, indeed, a doctor: Sir Edward Barry, who in 1775 published *Observations, Historical, Critical and Medical, on the Wines of the Ancients and the Analogy between them and Modern Wines*. The book is a magnificent production, but is awkwardly stuck in the mould of classical education, believing that ancient wine, like ancient architecture, was of a quality that could only be humbly imitated. "Modern" wines form a mere appendix to the information on the ancients. More awkwardly still, Sir Edward contrives a lengthy commercial for the curative powers of the waters of Bath Spa, in which he was no doubt professionally interested.

marsala When the smoke of battle cleared, a single new recruit had joined the international wine list: marsala from Sicily. Its manufacture was a pre-war idea, the venture of an Englishman named John Woodhouse. It had occurred to him in the 1770s that Sicily, poverty-stricken, and misruled by the notorious Naples branch of the Bourbon family, had once been the source of famous Greek wines and could be so again. He went to Málaga to learn how "Mountain" was made, then organized his own version in the vineyards of western Sicily, with Marsala as his headquarters.

Fame came through his contacts with Nelson's Mediterranean fleet. Before his victory at the Battle of the Nile in 1798 Nelson had stocked his battleships with Woodhouse's strong brown wine in place of rum. After it, in the most disreputable episode in his career, he helped the King of Naples escape from the French. His reward from the King was the Dukedom of Bronte, a village on Mount Etna. Emma Hamilton, the wife of the British ambassador in Naples, also famously rewarded him.

During this time Sicily effectively became a British colony. The presence of 17,000 British soldiers and investment from London brought great prosperity. The marsala shippers were at the forefront of this mini-boom. Nelson ordered 500 pipes of some 50,000 gallons of Woodhouse's marsala "to be delivered to our ships at Malta". On this foundation was built one of the great wine fortunes of the nineteenth century, as the related Ingham and Whitaker families overtook John Woodhouse as the lords of this curious English colony in Mafia country. The secret of Ingham's eventual milions was the American market: he reinvested his American profits in the new-fangled railroads. In 1860 he owned forty per cent of the New York Central Railroad stock and vast amounts of real estate in New York City.

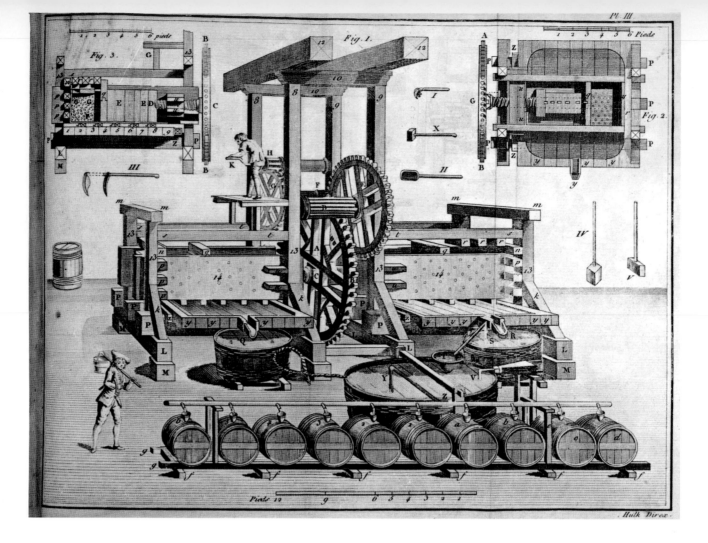

Chaptal's *Traité Théorique et Pratique sur la Culture de la Vigne* is the forerunner of today's wine primers, with its diagram of a "highly efficient mechanized press".

V ery much more to the point, and indeed almost the English equivalent of Jullien (though with a chapter borrowed, without acknowledgement, straight from Chaptal) is the *History and Description of Modern Wines* by Cyrus Redding. Redding, a journalist born in Cornwall who lived for some years in Paris, can truly be called the first of many hundreds in English to catalogue and compare the wines of the modern world. His *History* was published in 1833. In André Simon's words: "No other book written in English on the subject of wines has ever been more popular nor so copiously copied from by later writers." To compare his book with Jullien's in point of style is hardly fair. The Frenchman is a wine merchant with a genius for analysis, organization, and measured judgement, working to a formula, while Redding is a writer whose curiosity and enthusiasm lead him up byways of anecdote, and onto mountain-tops of speculation, as well as through crowded lanes of local practice, and down avenues of statistics.

Being a journalist he is angry, and quite specific, about abuse and adulteration. "The clumsy attempts at wine brewing made a century ago", he says, "would be scorned by a modern adept". But, he observes, it is the fault of the British themselves if they are fooled, because they will drink port and fiery wines which are easily imitated – and because they import them already so dosed with brandy that if they met a genuine example they would not recognize it. Redding laments that even "the delicious sherries of Spain" must be strengthened for British consumption: "For England no wine will do without brandy. An attempt to fabricate Romanée-Conti would never answer, because the fineness, delicacy and perfume of the wine are not to be copied."

Above all, Redding is a genuine companion whose honest opinions and sympathies shine through his book. He recalls in his introduction the disastrous cold and rainy vintage of 1816 (the year that Jullien was first published). Redding – an English traveller to the marrow – "was shooting in vineyards, where even in November the fruit hung neglected… I witnessed the disappointment of the laborious vine cultivator… The vintage is immemorially an ancient jubilee, of which, when, as is rarely the case, there is no joyous celebration, the toil of the labourer becomes doubly onerous, the bosoms generally cheerful are oppressed, and the gripe of poverty clutches its toil-worn victims with redoubled violence." Despite the passage of more than 150 years, *Modern Wine* remains a volume to carry with you to the vineyards.

B ut even before Redding was published a new breed of writer was on the prowl: the investigator from the New World. What Thomas Jefferson had been in the almost dilettante spirit of the eighteenth century, James Busby, visiting Europe from Australia in 1825, was in the practical and pragmatic spirit of a colonial; determined to bootstrap his extremely raw young country into the proper appreciation of nature's great gift.

CHAPTER 32

BODEGAS AND LODGES

The retreat of Napoleon's army from Spain left one wine-merchant devastated. Juan Carlos Haurie, the leading sherry-shipper of his day, was in trouble. Although he was born in Andalusia, his family was French, and he had supported the French invasion of Spain by collaborating fully with the occupying forces of Marshal Soult in Jerez. He had considered it an honour to provision the troops, which meant commandeering the food and wine supplies of his neighbours, and even exacting taxes from the Jerezanos to pay for their enemies' keep.

Jerez was occupied from 1810 to 1812, while the British supported the Spanish in holding nearby Cádiz. Cádiz prospered while Jerez starved. In 1812, harried by Wellington in Spain, and stretched by their invasion of Russia, the French withdrew, leaving poor Haurie unpaid, ruined, his entire fortune lost in paying compensation. The Haurie story, though, neither begins nor ends with this incident. The firm he inherited was probably the first to encompass the whole business of growing, making, ageing, and shipping sherry in the modern sense, and went on, after his bankruptcy, and under a new name, to become one of the greatest in the world of wine.

After its well-publicized launch in Tudor times, sherry sack had become a staple wine for northern Europe. Throughout the seventeenth century it flowed freely, not earning the extravagant praise that Falstaff had heaped upon it, perhaps, but an indispensable part of any cellar. Its principal rival was Canary sack, which was generally considered sweeter and better. The Canary Islands, though, were less profitable to trade with than mainland Spain. In Spain a merchant bringing "rags" (even then the cloth-trade was known by this disrespectful term) could take his pick between wine and silver bullion (not to mention horses) in exchange. Sanlúcar, Cádiz, and the growing Puerto de Santa Maria, serving Jerez, were much visited ports – especially by the ubiquitous Dutch.

Then came the War of the Spanish Succession at the start of the eighteenth century. The Methuen Treaty diverted English traders to Portugal and Madeira. Dutch trade fell away. There was little business in sherry country. Newly fashionable orangeries of northern Europe made orange trees a more profitable crop.

In Jerez apathy was compounded by protectionist regulations. One factor not to be ignored was the Church. The Carthusian monks and Dominican friars in Jerez were the only holders of large stocks of wine (no doubt some of it both old and excellent). And as a consumer of new wines the Church must have been the biggest single customer. Seville cathedral alone had twenty-four altars celebrating 400 Masses each day – for which it needed an annual total of 2,500 tuns of wine.

The church was naturally well represented on the *Gremio*, the guild of wine growers that controlled the trade. Growers might stock their wine, but merchants were severely limited in the amount they could buy and hold. It was precisely the opposite arrangement to the way the port trade operated, where the growers were isolated inland, far up the perilous Douro, and stock-holding merchants were essential at Oporto. Here the growers were all around the town, with as much access to the market as the merchants. It was the *Gremio's* policy to keep the merchants in their place.

Sample bottles in the tasting room of Don Manuel Maria Gonzales, founder of Gonzales Byass, who died in 1887. His room has been preserved as he left it ever since.

Not entirely discouraged by the lack of trade, or seeing it perhaps as an opportunity (or just liking the climate of Andalusia), a trickle of foreign merchants continued to set up shop beside the very few Spanish houses. (J.M. Rivero, founded in 1650, is the oldest firm, and its mark C.Z. perhaps the oldest brand-name of any wine.) As in Bordeaux at the same time, the Irish were particularly active – some of them Catholic refugees from the British persecution of the seventeenth century, some from the Irish weather. Patrick Murphy was quite possibly in the second category; he arrived about the same time, a farmer who became a grape-grower, but was hampered by poor health. It was Murphy who induced his French-born merchant neighbour, Jean Haurie, into the sherry business – and it was Haurie who challenged the *Gremio* for the right not only to grow his wine, but to stock it until it was mature, and ship it to his customers himself.

In 1772 he won a crucial court case: the Haurie bodega (Murphy had died and left him the business) became the first to control its wine at every stage of its production. It was probably from this time that sherry began to gain what today is called market-share. The years between this and Napoleon's invasion – despite yet another war with England – saw several new bodegas founded, mostly by Scots, English, or Irishmen. Sir James Duff was a Scot. He bought his first wine from Haurie, and was British consul in Cádiz throughout the Peninsular War. James Gordon was another Scotsman; William Garvey came from Waterford in Ireland; Thomas Osborne from Devonshire. At the same time the companies of Averys and Harveys were founded in Bristol, the most famous remaining names in a tradition that was already old: of holding the stocks which the *Gremio* disallowed, and doing the blending at the consuming end. Meanwhile Jean Haurie died, and five nephews inherited his business, the biggest in Jerez. One was the unfortunate Don Juan Carlos. Another was Don Pedro Domecq.

The structure of the sherry industry was now in place. How did the wine it sold differ from the sack of previous centuries?

The first difference may simply have been its age. After half a century of a flat market, those wines with the quality and structure to age (which were those from the chalk soils, called *albarizas*, mainly towards the north and west of Jerez and towards Sanlúcar) will have become concentrated, nutty-flavoured: capable of giving a smack of mature quality even to young wines blended with them. It is the nature of sherry to oxidize gracefully (and also peacefully, in a silent stately chamber, without the frantic tourism that Madeira demanded). Yet with time and gradual evaporation it can achieve Madeira-like potency, both of flavour and of alcohol.

The characteristic system for ageing sherry, in what is now known as a *solera*, probably started as a result of sluggish sales. "Fractional blending" is the modern term. Whatever you draw off from a barrel you replace with a similar but younger wine. It was not an invention of Jerez, but a development of the system of topping-up that we have seen in the Rhineland, and might occur naturally in any cellar where the wines keep well, and customers like to a buy a consistent wine, without fluctuations from year to year.

But the regular use of the *solera* revealed to the Jerezanos aspects of their wine that they had scarcely known about. Far from all having the simple character of sack, in ageing it became several different sorts of wine. The nose, it came to be said, told all. Some of the young wines, of better quality and not too strong, were apt to develop a floating white scum in the barrel which gave them extra fragrance. It was a yeast (this they did not know) which they christened *flor*, or flower.

The preference of the export market was for a strong sweet style, which could easily be made by simply leaving standard wines, liberally dosed with brandy, for not very long in their great boat-shaped "butts". No *flor* grew; there was too much alcohol. Here the *solera* was used simply for consistency of flavour. The name coined for the best of this kind of sherry was oloroso, or pungent. But ninety per cent of it was second-grade wine, known as *raya*, which had been given the Jerezano version of the *travail à l'anglaise*.

The locals, of course, knew which was best. The Andalusian taste was for pale young wine with a lively tang, at its best from the Listan, or Palomino, grape, even picked slightly underripe. Unaged, this was the *vin de pays* of the district, "preferred to all other wines by people of all ranks". To produce this racy drink consistently the *solera* had to be refreshed with new wines much more often – which provoked, it was discovered, a much more abundant growth of the fragrant *flor*. By keeping barrels only perhaps seven-eighths full, with plenty of "head-space", it was found that the crust of *flor* on the best quality wines would grow several inches thick – protecting the wines from oxidization as effectively as a cork in a bottle. What the frequent refreshment did was to provide the nutrients, the proteins that the *flor* needed to flourish. Fino was the name given to this delicate style. In its lightest and most extreme form, made from grapes shaded from the sun, it was even compared with the freshness of an apple: *manzana*. Manzanilla or "little apple wine" – there are various theories about how this name came about – is the speciality of Sanlúcar, of bodegas air-conditioned by the breezes off the sea. Fino was sold dry (while export wine was always sweetened with cooked must).

There were other possibilities too. In the good old days (as some must have thought) before the *Gremio* was formed to protect the growers of Jerez, wine from the inland regions of Montilla and Lucena was brought down to Jerez, either for blending or for passing off as sherry.

The style of that wine was soft and nutty, the produce of the Pedro Ximénez grape, ripened in the hottest grape-growing area of Spain. With age it oxidizes into a different scale of fragrances and flavours – and gains perceptibly in alcoholic strength. The effect could be achieved, they found, by taking wine with fino inclinations, but refreshing its *solera* less frequently, so that the growth of *flor* was less abundant, and over a period of years a gradual oxidization and concentration took over, making it something between fino and oloroso. "Amontillado" was the term they coined for it: sherry in the style of well-aged Montilla. At its natural best it could be sublime. But again, what was exported as amontillado was usually a blend of cheap *rayas*, smothered with brandy and sugar.

These were the developments, or some of them, that sprang from the liberation of the shippers to hold stocks for as long as they liked – whether of their own wines or wines they had bought. Their art was to fashion them in the ways that customers in different countries wanted. Up to that time any such fashioning had had to be done in the customer's own cellars abroad. (Bristol Milk was the first famous example: a sweetened oloroso aged to singular smoothness in the cool cellars of Bristol. Perhaps its name derived from the local practice of fining the wine with milk.) After the Napoleonic wars the tastes of their foreign markets were well understood by the shippers in Jerez, both Spanish and, above all British, who built enormous warehouses to hold their ever more varied stocks, improving at the same time with ingenuity and age. No building built to house wine can be compared with the great church-like barns that began to fill Jerez: nave upon nave of white-washed arches soaring over the grave geometry of countless grey oak butts. By the end of the century there were to be almost a thousand such bodegas in the district.

The unfortunate Haurie had backed the wrong horse. The best hope a Spanish wine would ever have in France would be to be blended (even sherry was sometimes used for the *travail à l'anglaise*). Two hundred years later the French still remain in ignorance of one of the world's great apéritifs, preferring, of all things, sweet port before a meal. The wars over, though, all obstacles to trade with Britain were out of the way – and Haurie's cousin Pedro had been to school in England. Did it need a Franco-Spaniard to make the running, with so many British merchants in Jerez? It needed a man who could move in the right circles, and this was almost the definition of Don Pedro Domecq Lembeye.

The Australian James Busby visited Don Pedro in 1831. He found him on the best of Haurie's old estates at Macharnudo, a chalk hill of blinding whiteness four miles north of Jerez. "Mr Dumeque", Busby wrote, "is a gentleman of French extraction and speaks English fluently. We found him under the verandah of his wine cellar, and having mentioned the object of our visit, he undertook, with great readiness, to give us all the information we should ask. He… explained his proceedings in the manner of a man who was thoroughly acquainted with his subject, and had not been accustomed to follow blindly the practices he had found established." Nor were there any flies on Domecq's partners, John James Ruskin and Henry Telford, who rapidly and dramatically increased the company's English sales. Mr Ruskin confirmed James Busby's opinion: although Don Pedro "lived chiefly in Paris, rarely visiting his Spanish estate", he had "perfect knowledge of the proper process of its cultivation, and authority over his labourers almost like a chiefs over his clan".

The story of Jerez in the nineteenth century is very much a matter of clans. Those who could envisage and organize manufacture on a very big scale grew prodigiously, married their children to those of their business associates or rivals, and grew more prodigiously still. The name Gonzales (with Domecq, the greatest name of all) first appeared in the annals of Jerez in 1795, when a dashing young member of the Royal Bodyguard (who dashed, rumour had it, just a whisker too close to a Royal body) was made Administrator of the King's extremely profitable salt monopoly at Sanlúcar – so profitable that bandits made regular visits. The combination of soldier and courtier was Don José Antonio Gonzales y Rodriguez, who married before long the most eligible of the beauties of the region, a Doña Angel. It was his youngest son, Manuel Maria, who in 1835 started the firm now called Gonzales Byass.

Soleras in a bodega built by Domecq in Moorish style. Founded by a Franco-Spaniard, Domecq became the most famous name in sherry, and its most powerful family.

the factory house The living symbol of the historical British presence in Oporto is the stately stone building of 1790 known officially as the British Association, but universally referred to as the Factory House. It is a masterpiece of eighteenth-century English understatement in architecture, in the busiest part of Oporto.

Inside, its pillared entrance hall, monumental staircase, ballroom, drawing room, library and map room have the same understated opulence, and seem designed more for comfortable private life than for commerce; indeed, it feels as though the most urgent business transacted there was the regular luncheon and dinners. They had a unique feature: the drawing room and the dessert room, placed end to end, are equipped so that the guests can move onto an identical table in another room to drink their port undistracted by the smell of food.

The original function of a "factory", or *feitoria*, for foreign merchants was abandoned shortly after the building was finished. In 1814 it became simply a private club rather after the manner of those in London, but jealously guarded by the established port-shippers against incursions by parvenues, fish-merchants, and others. At the frequent formal balls of the nineteenth century it was decreed: "No Portuguese officer under the rank of Field Officer can be invited."

Today members, still all of them port-shippers and most of them British, meet weekly for Wednesday lunch, except during the vintage. The time-honoured ritual of passing the decanter to the left is observed. A glass of tawny port is followed by a vintage wine whose identity only the chairman knows – and a modest wager (the oldest English custom of all) is placed on which vintage, and from which shipper, it turns out to be.

By the 1830s Jerez was a boom town, by some accounts the richest city in Spain, a city of discreetly palatial houses around Moorish-style courtyards and cathedral-like bodegas, many of them built with South American fortunes. At that moment (with first Argentina, then Chile, then Mexico declaring independence from Spain) they could hardly have invested more shrewdly than in this remote, still outwardly backward provincial town, their vineyards within view from the walls, their wines stacked visibly and pungently around them, and with a direct line to the richest wine-importing country in the world. In 1827 the export route almost became Spain's first railway line: George Stephenson, the pioneer of the railway, accepted an invitation to come and lay out a track to Puerto de Santa Maria. It was not built until 1854 – but even then it was only the third railway in Spain.

The export figures speak for themselves. In 1810 Jerez exported some 10,000 butts; by 1840 more than double that amount; by the 1860s, double again, and in 1873, the record year, over 68,000 butts. Over ninety per cent of the sherry exported went to Britain (some, it is true, to be re-exported from the cellars of Bristol). In 1864, at the height of the British craze for sherry, it accounted for no less than forty-three per cent of the nation's total wine imports. From this moment, as we shall see, the Free Trade movement started to allow French wines to catch up again.

What, in the meanwhile, had happened to port? Were the British adding this tide of sherry to their already formidable national intake of strong wines from Portugal? At the end of the Napoleonic wars port (and all Portuguese wines) surged back into fashion with the returning heroes. The ratio of Portuguese wine to Spanish was in the order of three to one. But as the nineteenth century adopted manners less robust than the eighteenth, wine-drinking figures lagged rapidly behind the increasing population.

And this was the age of chapel building: a Puritan religious revival that for the first time promoted the idea of Temperance. Port, in particular, carried with it associations with three-bottle men that sherry, the newcomer, was innocent of. There was a significant moment in the 1820s when the pages of the Royal household, up to then issued with a bottle of port a day, found it replaced by sherry. In 1837 the Victorian age began. The 1840s saw sherry draw level with port; in 1859 sherry overtook.

Port had started the century holding all the cards. Perhaps one of the reasons why it was so successfully challenged was that it was still, well over a century after Pombal had tried to define it, perpetually in a crisis of identity. Even in 1877, on a visit to the port country, the English journalist Henry Vizetelly complained: "There are almost as many styles of port wine as shades of ribbon in a haberdasher's shop".

Before the Peninsular War this was perhaps partly accounted for by the poor communications between the shippers and the distant growers, and the fact that the Douro Wine Company was an unwanted intermediary in every transaction. But in the nineteenth century the shippers began to buy *quintas*, or farms, up the

Douro, and become makers of some of their wine themselves. More fundamentally, it was because the climate of the Upper Douro is almost as wayward as that of, say, Bordeaux. Unlike the Andalusian seaside, where every season is not unlike the last, different vintages in different valleys high above the river Corgo sent down wines varying from mulberry-coloured monsters to quite pale insipid fluids.

The effect of adding brandy to the first was to make what we now think of as a vintage port; a wine of huge but rugged character that needs many years to mature in bottle. The same amount of brandy added to the second produced nothing but the inflammatory sort of dose James Boswell so bitterly condemned: all fire and no flavour.

The *solera* system had almost by chance presented Jerez with various but consistent personalities for its different wines. Customers could pick and choose from a known range of samples – and indeed blend their own brands, which is what they increasingly came to do. Port was just finding its way, and ageing its wines more in wood before selling them, when a single, superlative vintage pushed it towards a conclusion. 1820 was the year: a magnificent summer and ports of such natural "generosity", so rich, sweet and fruity, that they could not be improved. Unfortunately it created a demand that could not be satisfied. The only way in succeeding years to try to match the

Baron Forrester campaigned for better quality port, made without the addition of elderberry juice – and without brandy, which he considered ruined it. He also railed against the idea that the darker a wine was, the better it was.

1820 was by increasing the contentious dosage of brandy.

Portugal meanwhile was thrown into a series of revolutions and civil wars. In 1852 the Upper Douro was seized by the "Miguelites", the followers of the would-be dictator Dom Miguel. Oporto was held by his brother and rival Dom Pedro, the former Emperor of Brazil. In due course Dom Miguel laid siege to the town and occupied the wine lodges across the river. There followed eighteen months of extreme discomfort, in which the exploits of a motley mercenary army, largely from Glasgow, loom large in local folklore. There was more than alarm when the Miguelites blew up the stores of the Douro Wine Company, the great brandy depot: the flames threatened everybody's port. Happily a British warship, stationed in the river, as Britain's prime minister Palmerston said, to "see fair play", landed a fire-fighting force that prevented a general conflagration, but had to watch as 27,000 pipes "of boiling port" – approximately one year's exports to England – made their muddy way down to the Douro .

The final throes of port's struggle for identity were still to come. They were precipitated by a young man who arrived from England, at the age of twenty-two, just in time to become one of the minor heroes of the siege, crossing the river by night to stand guard in the lodges of his family's firm, Offley Forrester & Co.

Joseph James Forrester was a polymath and a dreamer, a good farmer, a tolerable businessman, a talented artist and portraitist, and a scientist and cartographer of genius. He rapidly made himself fluent in Portuguese and known to all classes, from the aristocracy of Oporto to the peasantry of the Upper Douro, where he spent months on foot, in the wildest country, surveying for his masterpiece: his maps.

One of these maps charts the whole river from the Spanish border to the sea; another, whose detailed draughtsmanship makes it a work of art, covers the wine country, which he grew to know better than any man. In the 1850s, when the deadly vine fungus oidium reached the Douro, Forrester's study of its nature and possible cure was well in advance of his time.

The Portuguese title of Baron was just one of many honours showered on Joseph Forrester by governments all over Europe.

Ten years, or a little more, of watching port grown, fermented, and prepared for shipping convinced Forrester that the accepted methods were destroying its potential. He, more than anyone, should have known what he was talking about. He owned the Quinta Boa Vista, high up the river, and signed himself "Douro Farmer and British Merchant". In 1844 he published a pamphlet whose title, *A Word or Two about Port Wine,* is a masterpiece of understatement. In essence, he repeated the accusations that had been tossed back and forth a century before: that brandy and elderberry juice were ruining port, which should be, and always had been (this is certainly not true), a "natural" wine, without fortification.

If no brandy was used, what was the Douro Wine Company for? Its monopoly of brandy was its trump card – and may have been, to do the Miguelites justice, the reason why they blew up

The Battle of Oporto in 1809 left the city in the hands of the British. Wellington's forces, having liberated the Factory House from the French, dined there often until the war took them into Spain in 1812.

its stores. As to the quality of its brandy, that was another matter. Redding (writing before Forrester) described it as "execrable… distilled from figs and raisins of which no other use can be made. They even once tried to make it from locust pods…"

As to the potential of the Douro to make excellent natural wine he was right: there is no longer any doubt. That there was general use of elderberries again was also true (though not, perhaps, of very great importance).

Forrester was wrong about English taste – which was, when all is said and done, the sole arbiter of what is or is not good port. He was so disingenuous as to believe that "My countrymen do not desire… wine full of brandy; they prefer wines the most pure, and the least inebriative possible." Would that it were so.

Forrester fought a passionate campaign, but lost it with good grace. He did not alter the nature of port; probably he reduced its adulteration. He lived in the heyday of the industry, when it was not too difficult to forgive: demand was steady, and a series of excellent vintages, maturing in bottle to ever more delicate fragrance, was proving that blackstrap was not the only outcome of adding brandy to the wine. By the 1840s something akin to the pattern of port today was being developed. Charles Dickens, in 1844, made the first reference in literature to

"tawny": port wine made lighter, faded in colour, and with its fruity taste transmuted by ageing for a decade or more in barrel. Even the shippers' names, or most of them, are familiar to us now, and the *quintas* that they built, higher and higher in the canyons of the Douro, became the setting for a social life that a contemporary tea-planter would have recognized.

This is where Forrester, fittingly, met his end. Famous and respected, in the prime of middle age, he set out with two of the aristocrats of the Upper Douro, owners of many farms and terraced hills, from the Fladgates' Quinta de Vargellas to sail down-river to Pinhão. He had decorated his map with the beauty spots of the river. One of them was the Cachão de Valeira: the deep gorge that up to the eighteenth century was the limit of navigation. Even today, with the Douro dammed and placid, it is a haunting spot, between smooth granite walls that rise sheer from the water. In May 1862 the river was in spate; the pinnace hit a rock. Donna Antonia Ferreira and Baroness Fladgate floated to safety on their crinolines. Forrester's body was never found.

CHAPTER 33

METHODE CHAMPENOISE

The sun rising over Champagne on September 10, 1815, found something more stirring to illuminate than the usual placid dewy vines, their leaves yellowing, and their grapes turning gold for the approaching vintage.

On the plain south of Epernay, where the first light had touched the little hill of Mont Aimé among the eastern slopes by the village of Vertus, a seemingly endless army was assembling from bivouacs in all the villages around. The light of dawn flashed on the cuirasses of hussars and glowed on the bearskins of great-coated grenadiers. It gleamed on the flanks of Cossack ponies and gilded the long barrels of muskets and field artillery. Marching files of infantry half a mile long broke to make way for cavalry squadrons at the trot, kicking up the chalk, their harness slapping and jingling, their officers standing in their stirrups, straining to find their place in what seemed the biggest battle-plan Europe had ever seen.

At seven o'clock, the muster was in order. Seven Russian army corps, almost 300,000 fighting men, formed phalanx after phalanx as far as the eye could see. At eight, a mounted procession climbed Mont Aimé, whose top had been levelled for the occasion. Alexander I, the Tsar of Russia, was flanked by the Emperor of Austria and the King of Prussia, the Prince Royal of Bavaria, the Prince of Wrede, and the Duke of Wellington. They had been invited to inspect the contemporary equivalent of Russia's strategic ballistic missiles – and in the heart of France.

This extraordinary piece of power-play stemmed from the Tsar's discomfort at seeing his two great military neighbours, Prussia and Austria, set on dismembering a defeated France. Russia's interest lay in keeping France as a power to be reckoned with at the far end of Europe, to give the Austrians and Prussians a second front to worry about. Thus the Tsar and the newly-restored King of France, Louis XVIII (Louis XVII was lost and never found), had common cause. The show of strength on the fields of Champagne took place with French consent. It was a strange outcome to Napoleon's invasion of Russia three years earlier. And politics apart, it was the greatest public relations event that any wine region would ever see.

But the story is more complex, and might be started anywhere back in the eighteenth century, where such pioneers as Moët, Ruinart, Roederer, and Heidsieck were wooing crowned heads, building on the brilliant debut of Champagne at the courts of London and Paris.

Since its launch over a century before, Champagne had pursued three different careers at least: as one of France's most celebrated still white wines (largely in the form of Sillery) for the conservative gourmand; as an honourable red alternative to one of the lighter sorts of burgundy; and in its sparkling form as the wine of the sinfully rich and richly sinful. But the region really made its bread and butter from oceans of cheap red wine. At the start of the nineteenth century red wine was ninety per cent of its production; by 1850 it had only been reduced to two-thirds.

While the reputation of sparkling Champagne had grown, and the demand now reached several hundred thousand bottles a year, its technology had not. A large part of the fun (thought those frivolous times) was in cutting the string that held down the cork, and sprinkling the *filles de joie* with the expensive mousse. Ageing courtiers in particular found irresistible symbolism in the explosion of froth. They were still often disappointed by bottles with very little gas, or with a few big bubbles that were horribly described as *yeux de crapauds* – "toads' eyes" – or by various ailments of unstable wine that produced the effect of a slimy worm in the bottle, or just a thick and murky fluid. Meanwhile a depressingly large proportion of the bottles continued to explode in the cellars.

There was no shortage of potential customers, for anyone who had drunk a good bottle, as Monsieur Moët and his colleagues found, was hooked for life. The only catch was that they had to be very rich; the laborious and uncertain manufacture was extremely expensive. If sparkling Champagne was ever to become a universal wine that could be packed off abroad with confidence, and in industrial quantities, many technical problems still needed to be solved.

In all of history only one woman is known as "the widow", without qualification. If it is true that the perfectionism of Dom Pérignon earned for Champagne a unique place as the wine of princes and palaces throughout Europe, it is no less true that Nicole-Barbe Clicquot-Ponsardin, widowed with a baby daughter in 1805 at the age of twenty-seven, found the way to make it the celebratory wine of the entire world.

The Russians, with their unerring taste for the most effective liquor, were her improbable allies in her enterprise – not her

the technique spreads Once the technology of making sparkling wine was mastered, Germany and Burgundy were quick to adopt it. By 1830 it was in use for white burgundy, mainly of Buxy near Mercurey, which fizzed well enough to break plenty of bottles, but did not keep its mousse for years like Champagne. Wine made from red grapes did better, and soon red burgundy was being put through the *méthode champenoise*. Nuits-St-Georges became the centre of the industry, which enjoyed a vogue among Paris dandies, and which at one point went so far as to make a sparkling Romanée-Conti (but spoilt it, it was said, by blending in some Chablis).

countrymen (though many were her rivals), nor the British, whose bilious national taste for brandied wine only gave way to Champagne later in the century. In Russia she conquered a wider market for her sparkling wine than Champagne had ever known. In order to supply it she was obliged to industrialize its manufacture. The firm her husband started was a little country practice; as a widow she transformed its yellow label into the most widely recognized on earth.

The Revolution had been a distressing interlude for an industry that catered for the very heads the guillotine removed. One merchant of Champagne, it is said, saved several heads, including his own, by deleting the titles of each of his

An early production line in Champagne: disgorging, liqueuring, corking, stringing, and wiring are being done efficiently and by hand. Champagne was "industrialized" early.

customers and writing the word Citizen instead. Napoleon's wars caused the removal of all ready cash from the scene in France, before it was exacted for the Imperial levies. To export was the answer, but elaborate blockading and counter-blockading had made trade between European ports uncertain, to say the least. Representatives of the Champagne houses followed the armies, vulture-like, to quench the victors' thirsts while the bodies were counted. But there was a limit to the amount of expansion that could be based on celebrating the Imperial victories, and after 1811 their number started steeply to decline.

The Widow Clicquot was fortunate in having a salesman of genius, a Mr Bohne. He first tried England, without much success, then took his wares to Russia, Prussia, and Austria. One of his letters, written from St Petersburg in 1806, epitomizes the rivalries involved: "The Tsarina is with child. If it is a Prince, gallons of Champagne will be drunk all over this vast country. Do not mention it, or all our rivals will be here at once."

Napoleon's invasion of Russia in 1811 was the turning-point. Many had misgivings about the distance and difficulty of the Emperor's most ambitious enterprise. In 1812 at Borodino, just outside Moscow, the pessimists were proved right. The Russians and their deadly allies, Generals Janvier and Février, turned what had appeared to be the relentless tide. The retreat from Moscow was an ice-bound shambles that left the Emperor with no alternative but to hurry home and raise the new forces he now needed to defend France.

Napoleon's last defensive battles before his abdication were fought in the spring of 1814 in and around Champagne. Reims and Epernay fell to the Russians and the Prussians. The day before Epernay fell, taking his leave of his loyal friend Jean-Rémy Moët, the Emperor pinned on his breast his own cross of the Légion d'Honneur, then left for Paris and his abdication.

T he Russians undoubtedly had the best of the occupation, and if the legends are true, requisitions did not need to be extracted. They were carried up willingly from, amongst others, the cellars of the far-sighted Widow Clicquot. "Today they drink," were her tight-lipped words, "tomorrow they will pay."

Nor did she hesitate for a moment before putting her maxim into effect. She ignored the fact that the borders of Russia were still officially closed to French goods. The occupying forces left in May 1814. By the beginning of June, scarcely giving them time to reach home, she had a ship chartered, a 75-ton Dutch *flute*, the *Sweers Gebroeders*, loaded with Mr Bohne and as much Champagne as it could carry (and that the Russians had left undrunk), and sailing for the Baltic. 1811, the year of Halley's comet, had been a wonderful vintage. She sent as much as she had. The ship reached Köenigsberg (today's Kaliningrad) on July 3, to find that French goods were no longer excluded. Bohne had the field to himself. There was not another *voyageur* from Champagne within 500 miles.

"It is with infinite satisfaction", wrote Mr Bohne, "that I have examined the samples. Spring water is infinitely less limpid than they are. Everyone is agog at the idea of tasting them." The Tsar had arrived back in Köenigsberg; even the Imperial door

was not closed to Mr Bohne. "You see", he wrote again to the Widow in Reims, "what authority one has when one has good merchandize to provide. I had only to let drop the number of my hotel room, and a queue formed outside my door."

O ne of the reasons why the Russians so doted on what they called "Klikofskoe" was that the Widow made it extremely sweet. Before dispatching her bottles she removed the sediment – an essential operation – and filled its place (even as much as a third of the bottle) with a syrupy mixture of wine, sugar and brandy. As to the limpidity that gave Mr Bohne so much satisfaction, there is little doubt that the art of clearing the wine of sediment was the great Clicquot contribution to the technology of Champagne – arrived at, so the legend goes, by the nightly vigils of the Widow, lantern in hand: the Florence Nightingale of the cellar.

I n the first years of the nineteenth century sediment was an increasing problem. The more sparkling the wine was required to be, the more sugar was added to produce more fermentation in the bottle and – provided that the bottle withstood the pressure – the more dead yeast cells would result.

To remove this sediment it had to be collected. The standard way was by periodically picking the bottle up, giving it either a sharp tap or a rousing shake, and then putting it back in its pile. The intention was to concentrate the sediment in as narrow a compass as possible along the lower side of the bottle, so that at the next stage, *dépotage*, or decanting into another bottle, the maximum of clear wine could be poured out before the sediment started to move and cloud it. Every bottle, in other words, required as delicate a decanting operation as an old bottle of burgundy. It goes without saying that at least half the pressure of gas was lost in the process. It was not the Widow herself, but one of her employees, Antoine de Muller, who devised a better method. If the bottle was kept with the cork downwards the *marc* could be persuaded to collect, not along the side of the bottle, but on the cork. Then when the cork was removed the sediment would fly out first, and there would be no need to decant the rest of the wine and lose half its fizz. It could simply be topped up with *liqueur* and equipped with a new cork. Folklore joins in here, suggesting that the Clicquot kitchen table was taken down to the cellar and pierced with holes to take the necks of the bottles; at first vertically, then, with the refinement of practice, at an oblique angle.

Certainly it was on some such table that the first modern-style *remuage* took place. The new technique was to wait until the *marc* had come to rest on the side of the bottle, then put it in a hole in the table, and at frequent intervals lift it half out of the hole, give it a sharp shake, and drop it back in. The jerk against the table gave the sediment another impulsion towards the cork. Up to 1821 the firm of Clicquot was the only one practising this technique and had managed to keep it a secret.

C hampagne became an industry once the secret of *remuage* was known. It could be organized on a production-line scale in a way that decanting never could. In the 1820s alone four famous houses began to trade: Irroy, Joseph

Perrier, Mumm, and Bollinger. In the same year the first sparkling-wine house opened in Burgundy – to make, of all unlikely things, sparkling red Nuits-St-Georges. Before the middle of the century Pommery & Greno, Deutz & Geldermann, Krug, and Pol Roger had all founded houses in Reims or Epernay. Five out of these ten familiar names came from Germany.

From a total sales figure for sparkling Champagne at the end of the eighteenth century of something like 300,000 bottles, by 1853 the total had reached twenty million. As in the sherry business, which was growing at almost the same rate at the same time (both Reims and Jerez, by coincidence, acquired a railway link the same year: 1854), there seemed to be no limit to the money to be made. Sherry and Champagne shared a new concept in the wine industry: the elaboration of wines by manufacturing methods that require time and capital tied up in stocks which are beyond the reach of almost any farmer. In Champagne particularly the industrialist found it easy to dominate his supplier; he could refuse to buy grapes until they were in danger of becoming worthless and the farmer grew desperate. Nor were there any workable regulations to prevent him from buying grapes outside the region, which was not then defined in any meaningful way by law. There were many cowboys in the trade, and much appalling wine sold as Champagne to a gullible newly-prosperous public. It was easily masked behind a heavy dosage of sweet *liqueur*: the concept of dry Champagne had yet to be invented.

Meanwhile, from the maker's point of view, by far the most serious problem remained the dreaded explosions below ground as the unpredictable pressure shattered the unreliable bottles. 1828 was a disastrous year: eighty per cent of the bottles burst. The unanswered question was how to estimate the sugar needed for the second fermentation to produce the right

These cups, from the dairy at Rambouillet, were made for Marie-Antoinette. They are certainly more convincing than the Champagne *coupes* popularly thought to have been modelled on the queen's breasts.

amount of gas, other than simply by tasting. Another unknown was not even suspected: how much yeast the wine contained. No one yet knew that yeasts were involved in fermentation.

1836 saw the first of the problems partly solved. A chemist named François from Châlons-sur-Marne invented the *sucre-oenométre*: an instrument for measuring the sugar content. With its help the number of breakages was reduced until, in 1866, André Jullien could report that the average was only fifteen or

industrial champagne

Henry Vizetelly was England's most thorough, and most entertaining, chronicler of Champagne. *A History of Champagne,* published in 1882, brings home the fact that Champagne is a product of the Industrial Revolution: "What with the incessant thud of the corking machines, the continual rolling of iron-wheeled trucks over the concrete floor, the rattling and creaking of the machinery working the lifts, the occasional sharp report of a bursting bottle, and the loudly-shouted orders of the foremen, who display the national partiality for making a noise to perfection, the din becomes at times all but unbearable. The number of bottles filled in the course of the day naturally varies, still Messrs Moët & Chandon reckon that during the month of June a daily average of 100,000 are taken in the morning from the stacks in the *salle de rinçage*, washed, dried, filled, corked, wired, lowered into the cellars, and carefully arranged in symmetrical order. This represents a total of two and a half million bottles during that month alone."

It was the proceeds of the Industrial Revolution, supporting the affluence of a middle class unknown before in history, that allowed the once exclusive luxury of the aristocracy to break out at balls, picnics, and parties all over the world. As early as 1828 the English had adopted Champagne as the drink of the turf: the first Champagne Stakes were run that year.

Parisian eating habits changed during the Siege of Paris. The contents of the zoo could be bought at the butchers, if one was lucky; or one could find one's own dinner.

partly accounts for its sweetness. The *coupe* glass with its wide and shallow bowl was invented in about 1840 (although the PR machine has long since attributed its shape to the bosom of Marie-Antoinette). The wine served in it was *frappé* – best translated, perhaps, as "knocked cold": it was almost as much a sorbet as a drink. It was also often tinted with euphemistically titled *vin de fismes*: our old friend elderberry juice.

The credit for thinking dry goes to a London wine merchant named Burnes, who in 1848 tasted the excellent Perrier-Jouët vintage of 1846 in its natural, unsweetened state. His reasoning was that the English were already only too well supplied with sticky drinks for dessert; that Champagne would never oust port, but that (its price apart) it would be a wonderful drink to go with dinner if it tasted winey rather than sugary. It was also, to borrow Jullien's marvellous phrase, more "*susceptible d'être bu à haute dose sans incommoder*". Shipped completely without sweetening it caused more shock than pleasure, but from the 1850s on house after house in Champagne started shipping somewhat drier wines to England. 1865 was an excellent vintage: both Ayala and Bollinger scored hits with the Prince of Wales when they shipped it unsweetened – or almost. Even the house of Clicquot sold a "dry" 1857, but waited respectfully until 1869, after the death of the Widow, before shipping a "perfectly dry wine", or Brut. 1874 was the outstandingly fine vintage that made the practice general – at least for the English market; to this day in France the preference is for a medium-dry version.

Having to produce unsweetened wine was salutary for the Champagne industry. Sweetness is a mask for many faults; dry wine put the producers on their mettle. Few were substantial vineyard owners in relation to their demand for grapes, so they were forced to buy a higher proportion of their raw materials from the villages of the "river", "mountain", and the Côte des Blancs that produced the best quality. Dry Champagne, it might be said, was the spur to the proper reward of the growers of the best grapes. Those in such famous villages as Aÿ, Hautvillers, Verzenay, Bouzy, Avize, and Vertus had always made a relatively good living, but competition among the producers now led to a serious classification by quality of the villages of the region.

It is fitting to leave Champagne once more to the tramp of marching feet that has always been the refrain to its story. In 1860 the Widow died at the age of eighty-nine, having lived her later years in a state of superfluous pomp which expressed only too well the self-satisfaction of the Champenois. Her Château de Boursault, overlooking the valley of the Marne, might have been the place Byron had in mind when he wrote "wealth had done wonders; taste not much". In 1869 the Prussians were back, Champagne was a battlefield again, and the ignominy of two years of enemy occupation settled once more over the region.

The winter siege of Paris by the Prussians in 1870 provides a gastronomic footnote. There was no food in the city, but plenty of wine. The Christmas Day menu at the famous restaurant Voisin proposed (I'm leaving it in the decent obscurity of the original tongue) "*chat flanqué de rats, accompagné d'un Bollinger frappé*".

twenty per cent. It was still unwise to go into a Champagne cellar, at least in spring, without a wire mask to protect your face.

The last development that was needed to bring the Champagne of history into its modern context was its drying-out from the Sauternes-like sweetness which made it a dessert wine – at least in the Widow's time – to something that could be drunk with any food, or in the new-fangled role (the word first appeared in 1894) of an apéritif.

In mid-century the degree of syrupy *liqueur* added to the wine varied from country to country of its destination, but all were very sweet. Measured in grams of sugar per litre for France it was about 165; for Germany a little more; for Scandinavia as much as 200; while Russians would drink anything from 250 to 330 – which would have made an actress's slipper very sticky indeed. The United States had a drier taste, from 110 to 165 grams, while England, eccentrically, required only twenty-two to sixty-six grams; that is two to six per cent of *liqueur d'expédition*. For comparison, the figures today for sweet Champagne may rise as high as fifty grams, for "dry" as high as thirty-five; brut has up to fifteen grams, while true or "ultra" brut has no *liqueur* at all.

The manner of drinking Champagne in the 1840s and 1850s

CHAPTER 34

JOHN BULL'S VINEYARD

" **I** **n a climate so favourable, the cultivation of the vine**
may be carried to any degree of perfection, and should no
other article of commerce divert the settlers from this point,
the wines of New South Wales may perhaps hereafter be
sought with avidity and become an indispensable part of
European tables."

These words were written by Captain Arthur Phillip of the
Royal Navy, the first Governor of the new penal colony on the
east coast of Australia, on September 28, 1788, within nine
months of his landing his small force and the 700 convicts they
were to guard on the shores of Sydney Harbour. Suiting his
action to his words, on the banks of what is now Farm Cove he
planted the vine cuttings he had brought with him from home.

Unfortunately, many articles were to divert the settlers.
They were to found fortunes with sheep, and ruin themselves
with rum; to spend twenty years in a sometimes cruelly
disciplined, more often chaotic, and almost perpetually
drunken state before anything resembling civilization was to
take root in the colony. When it did, it was a sad caricature of the
motherland that had disowned her unfortunates. The privileges
of the military guards of the convicts, the New South Wales
Corps, were so cynically exploited that they rapidly became
known as the Rum Corps. By monopolising the supply of the
only liquor available, rum from Bengal, they cornered the
accepted currency, and were able to use convicts as slaves on the
land that was given to them as of right.

Governor Phillip was right about the potential of Australian
wine – but wrong in his timing by almost two hundred years.

The chronicle of those two centuries, and why the process was
so slow, is the story of wine in Australia.

N ot surprisingly it was the paymaster of the Rum Corps
who first procured himself a comfortable, and immensely
profitable, billet. He was John Macarthur, the son of a Plymouth
corset-maker. Macarthur's (and his wife's, for she was a leading
actor in all this) principal part in the making of New South
Wales was their grazing and breeding of the greatest number of
the colony's best sheep.

With the devil's luck, he was sent home to England for court-
martial for wounding an officer in a duel – and arrived at the very
moment when, for two brief years, Napoleon's "Continental
System" was pinching. It was depriving the booming English
textile industry, the first great success of the Industrial Revolution,
of its raw material from Spain and the grazing lands of eastern
Germany. Macarthur arrived with samples of Australian wool in
his pocket, contrived to be acquitted at his court martial, and was
back in New South Wales in 1805 with a gift of several of the King's
own prize Merino sheep, and a special grant of 810 hecatres
(2,000 acres) of the best grazing land in the colony to raise them
on. The land, which he renamed Camden Park after the Treasury
Minister who presented it to him, lies sixty-four kilometres (forty
miles) south of Sydney along the Nepean river.

This was where Macarthur made his home, bred his
sheep, and, more germane to our story, planted his vineyard.
Eventually his mansion, which would look more in place in
Sussex or Hampshire, stood in 24,300 hectares (60,000 acres)
of Macarthur land, including enough vineyard to merit a

substantial (now ruined), stone-built winery with half a dozen capacious vats. In 1815 he took two of his sons to France to visit vineyards and collect cuttings, and did the same at Madeira and the Cape on the way home. Records of his production are scant (although it is known that he kept a nursery and sold vines), but the medals they won are not, and nor, amazingly, were unopened bottles when I visited his descendant in his almost unchanged house in 1988. The undated bottle that we tasted (which might have been of any vintage between 1825 and 1870) was sumptuous; deep oily garnet in colour, of enormous richness, with some of the singular tang of oranges that I had once detected in a Constantia of the same approximate date. It seems likely that this bottle was the work of Macarthur's son, Sir William, who became a respected authority on vines and winemaking, contributed to periodicals (under the pen-name Maro), and whose nursery, as we shall see, supplied plants for new enterprises all over Australia.

The first newspaper published in Australia was the *Sydney Gazette* of March 5, 1803. That there was a public with ideas beyond Bengali rum is proved by the article on the back page, the first of a series on how to plant a vineyard and make wine. It may well be that the editor's motive was to free his readers from the monopoly of the Rum Corps in getting any drink at all beside their lethal spirit. Unfortunately, although the readers undoubtedly made some sort of wine for a while, any dreams they had of Sydney as a new Bordeaux (or even Douro) were short-lived. They did not know what ailed the vines; it was the humid, subtropical climate. Nor, probably, was there anyone among them who could indicate even what kind of wine they should be trying to make. The Britain they had left behind was the land where port reigned supreme; the very idea of light wines was unfamiliar to almost anybody who found himself in Australia. The climate, moreover, if it allowed grape-growing at all, was likely to produce extremely sweet fruit – hence strong wine; the inclination would be to dose it with brandy, both to help it keep, and to make it more port-like.

Tasmania, 500 miles south, has a very much cooler climate than New South Wales. This is the first recorded hint of a theme that has run right through the story of wine in Australia up to the present time: that the cooler the climate, the finer the wine. It found its first clear expression in a booklet, *On Colonial Wines,* published in 1867 by Australia's direct successor to the wine-loving priests who had for so long led the way in Europe.

Father John Bleasdale was a Lisbon-trained Jesuit who settled in Melbourne. "Whatever the wine is, sweet or dry, one thing is certain," he wrote; "that in hot climates you can never produce wine with the perfume peculiar to those of colder regions… If you are to have the perfumed wine of France – Sauterne or fine Chablis for example – you must also have the

other conditions, especially slow, long-continued fermentation at a low temperature." Bleasdale was, of course, begging one question: whether the Australians wanted fine wines or just strong ones. The fact is that from the start they made both more or less haphazardly, but the national taste favoured strength and sweetness above refinement – and so indeed did the popular taste in their export market, Britain: a situation which held back the progress of the industry for 150 years.

Most fundamental, although either ignored or just muddled by most of the early planters, was what variety of vine to plant. Many of the first introductions were from northern Europe and almost certainly doomed to failure, either as vines or as wine, in the New South Wales climate. Probably most of the first successes were from vines collected en route at Madeira or the Cape (where, for instance, the Macarthurs collected "Black Constantia"), or indeed Rio de Janeiro, where the First Fleet had put in for provisions.

The man who turned his mind to this problem, and who has been labelled "the father of Australian wine" as a result, was a young immigrant from Edinburgh, James Busby, who with notable precociousness and foresight, before leaving for Australia with his parents at the age of twenty-three, made a visit to France to find out what he could about wines and vines. He whiled away the months on the voyage out to Australia by writing *A Treatise on the Culture of the Vine and the Art of Making Wine*, largely culled from Chaptal, but also full of such pungently original remarks as, "Constantia has a taste rather than a flavour"; "the flavour of Madeira is nothing but that which we know is given by means of bitter almonds"; "the wretched Lisbon wines acquire what little taste they have from oak chips", and, concerning brandy being added to port, "of which the chief fault is that of being too strong already", the result is "fit for hogs only".

Busby's *Treatise* was addressed to the "higher classes" in New South Wales who he supposed would be interested in wine-growing. Five years later, with experience of the realities of Australia, having managed a curious sort of orphanage which was a farm, and sat at the feet of Macarthur, he published a smaller and extremely practical *Manual of Plain Directions* for "the class of smaller settlers" – a book which had a widespread popular influence, and must have set many stumbling growers on their feet. (His father, meanwhile, had furnished Sydney with its first regular water supply.)

At the same time, with what seems extraordinary foresight, he struck out about 160 kilometres (100 miles) north of Sydney to the Hunter River Valley and started a farm he called Kirkton after his Edinburgh birthplace, left it to his brother-in-law to manage, and in 1830 set sail again for Europe to deepen his knowledge of winemaking, but above all to collect suitable and correctly identified vines.

The Journal of a Tour through some of the Vineyards of France and Spain, published on his return in 1833, is an exact contemporary of Cyrus Redding's great *History*. It dispenses with literary airs and graces, but loses very little as a result. Its

RIGHT Yeringberg, in the Yarra Valley, was founded by the Swiss de Pury family, who were persuaded to come to this cool, European-looking spot by the Swiss governor of Victoria. Their direct descendants are still there.

Vintage time at Chateau Tahbilk in the 1880s. The property dates from 1860 and has hardly changed; indeed, it is a much prized part of Australia's heritage.

observations could not be more pithy or to the point. Meeting with some soldiers from Algeria, for example, he took the opportunity of quizzing them on wine-growing in a country he conceived to be similar to New South Wales. Little seems to have escaped his attention, from prices to table manners. ("Fine wine" in France, he observed, was drunk from a wine glass; "wine" from tumblers with water).

As for his vines, collected and labelled at Montpellier and in Paris (also at Málaga and Jerez), he contrived to have them transported free on the convict ship *Camden* which was on the point of sailing when he arrived in London. No fewer than 570 varieties arrived in Sydney in good condition. He gave a specimen of each to the Botanic Gardens on Sydney Harbour and planted the remainder at Kirkton.

By the age of thirty-five, therefore, this driven Scotsman had told Australians how to make wine, supplied the plants, and discovered and founded, it seems almost by fluke, its first (and still one of its best) wine-growing regions. His motives were a clear-sighted mixture of business sense and philanthropy. He firmly believed that a supply of good wine would put an end to the drunkenness engendered by spirits. He also saw wine as the ideal return-voyage cargo for the convict ships. John Bull had been let down in his earlier attempt at his own vineyard, in South Africa, chiefly, said Busby, by the idleness and bad husbandry of the Boers. There was no reason for Australia to fail – and there was the whole Indian Empire, besides Britain, as a market.

This quixotic young man – his portrait shows a sensitive, saturnine face – did not stay to see his dreams to fruition, to advise Australia, or even to make wine. He departed for New Zealand in 1833 with the appointment of British Resident. But his legacy was vital.

The Hunter Valley turned out to have a curious local climate that mitigated the heat of the New South Wales sun with a regular afternoon haze; often clouds would roll in from the ocean to form as it were a parasol over the baking vines. Port-minded or not, such early settlers as George Wyndham and Adam Roth found themselves making wine they likened to burgundy. One of the early growers, James King, exhibited sparkling wines among others at the Paris Exhibition of 1855 (the same at which the famous classification of Bordeaux was made known), and, no doubt to his astonishment, one of his wines (along with one from Camden Park) was chosen to be served to Napoleon III at the state banquet that closed the exhibition.

The official report of the exhibition judges, quoted by James Halliday in his historical account of "the Hunter", read: "The [Hunter Valley] wines included white wines akin to those of the Rhine; red light wines like those of Burgundy; Mousseux varieties with a bouquet, body and flavour equal to the first Champagnes; Muscats and other sweet wines, rivalling the Montignac of the Cape." "Montignac" seems to have slipped from history, but the verdict is unequivocal. Within twenty-five years of Busby's Hunter Valley enterprise, New South Wales wine had entered European high society. Not surprisingly, a grape-rush filled the valley. In the 1860s and 1870s, its acreage multiplied several times. If it did not last (and things went very quiet later in the century) it was because all Australia's large wine companies, even those such as Lindemans and MacWilliams, which had grown up in the Hunter Valley, found the taste for table wines was a minority one. The money was to be made from ports, sherries or Muscats grown in hotter areas elsewhere.

Formal federation did not come to Australia until 1901. The different regions of the continent were separately explored and developed. Both Adelaide and Melbourne proved excellent vineyard country: cooler and less humid than Sydney, and capable from the first of making extremely good wines.

Perhaps the most auspicious start was made by a Devonshire farmer's son called John Reynell in the "Southern Vales" just south of Adelaide in 1838. He brought cuttings from the Cape and was encouraged by Sir William Macarthur (whose nursery at Camden must have seemed almost as far away). By the time, a dozen years later, that he took on another Devonshire immigrant called Tom Hardy as a labourer he had already built the unique cellar which still squats, a half-submerged barn like an enormous grassy burial mound, beside his verandahed farmhouse. It is typical of Australia's story that Reynella, the most perfectly preserved of the country's original wineries, is now the headquarters of Thomas Hardy and Sons, descendants of the muscular young Tom.

In the 1840s wine-farms (the drab word winery had not been invented) were springing up all around Adelaide, each with its stirring, or touching, or funny story of another hopeful immigrant, for the most part British, prepared to work every daylight hour for the freedom and satisfaction (and even the money) that winemaking brought. In the hills at Magill overlooking Adelaide from the east the young Dr. Christopher Penfold from Sussex started both a general practice and one of Australia's most famous vineyards, with a view out to the distant Saint Vincent Gulf. The practice came first; wine-growing was an afterthought, as he discovered how wonderfully his patients cheered up when he prescribed a glass.

The famous exception to the Anglo-Saxon domination of South Australian wine-growing is the Barossa Valley, forty-eight kilometres (thirty miles) northeast of Adelaide,

Tahbilk has had a coat of paint, but its vineyards by the Goulburn River still grow its traditional Riesling, Cabernet Sauvignon, Marsanne, and Shiraz.

which was colonized in 1841 by a philanthropic Scot, George Angas, as a profitable means of releasing dissenters from religious persecution. It is perhaps fanciful to suggest that there is a direct connection between the valley's German settlers and its affinity with Rhine Riesling. Much the greater part of its production has always been fortified wines and brandy. Nonetheless, soft, strong and baked brown as they may have been, Rieslings have long been a special feature of "the Barossa". The valley floor is categorically too hot to suit such a northern vine, but the stony uplands around are not, and now produce some of the best Rhine Riesling in Australia.

the louse arrives The thriving multiplication of vineyards all over Victoria would probably have resulted in its becoming Australia's most viticultural state, but for the arrival of phylloxera on a shipment of vines to Geelong on Port Phillip Bay in 1877. Slowly but inexorably, helped by the prevailing southwest winds, it found its way to almost all the scattered plantings of vines in the state and wiped them out. A few, such as Chateau Tahbilk, were at least partly protected by having sandy soil; others, such as Great Western, by their remoteness (and position slightly up-wind). It took nearly twenty years for the pest to reach Rutherglen in the north-east of the state – where it stopped: there were hundreds of miles of vineless grazing land in southern New South Wales.

The means to combat phylloxera by grafting were available. Unfortunately Australians had already demonstrated their lack of enthusiasm for the delicate table wines of the southern areas that were worst affected. There was no point in replanting while all the demand was for wines that South Australia could so easily provide. Providentially, the pest was never delivered alive to Adelaide, nor do winds from Victoria blow that way. South Australia therefore remained phylloxera-free, with the Victorian market at its feet.

What was to become the state of Victoria was settled from two directions at once: from the sea at Melbourne on Port Phillip Bay, and overland from New South Wales in 1837 by William Ryrie, who brought with him both sheep and (Macarthur) vine-cuttings. The two could almost be called the armorial attributes of the infant state. Ryrie settled in the beautiful Yarra Valley just north of Melbourne, and it was there, and in Melbourne itself, and at Geelong just along the bay, that the 1840s saw the first successes of Victorian wine.

Of Australia's three first centres of population, southern Victoria came much the closest to the cool conditions John Bleasdale had recommended. It also had the fortuitous advantage of a leading citizen, and from 1851 a first Governor, who was a native of a European wine region.

Charles La Trobe had lived at Neuchâtel in Switzerland, where he had prudently married a very well-connected lady. He was so greatly taken with Melbourne and the country around that he and his wife's family prevailed on two more Swiss families, the de Castellas and the de Purys, along with two winegrowers called Deschamps, to emigrate and settle in the Yarra Valley.

Paul de Castella, a native of Gruyère (which is scarcely the heart of Swiss wine-country), bought the Ryrie property of Yering, and soon caught the wine bug. He was not content with Camden cuttings; he acquired 20,000 three-footers from Château Lafite. Trailing him by some years was his brother Hubert, who modestly called his vineyard St Hubert's; by 1875 it covered eighty-one hectares (200 acres). Baron de Pury's property (where his descendants still live) is called Yeringberg. Together with the more famous Chateau Tahbilk, on the Goulburn River in the heart of Victoria, Yeringberg is a priceless, almost unaltered relic of the highly enjoyable Victorian heyday of a century-and-a-half ago.

The atmosphere of the Yarra Valley is very different from the Hunter or the Barossa. All are beautiful in their low-key, soft-contoured Australian way: Lilydale and Coldstream, the villages of the Yarra, particularly so. The Yarra Valley has never made the sort of wine that in Australia grows big wineries; it is too cool, and it was (and still is) the fixed intention of its settlers to make the finest table wines they could. They sent them to competitions in Europe, and Europe accepted them without question. Medals from Vienna in 1873, Brussels in 1876, and Bordeaux in 1882 tell the story in gold, silver, and bronze.

The human face of Victoria was changed almost overnight by the gold-rush of 1851; by a strange coincidence, only three years after gold-fever had hit California. It brought in the manpower and the money to expand from the little base around Port Phillip Bay all over the state. Immigrants who poured in in the 1850s prospected everywhere; there was no single "mother lode". If they failed to find gold (or when it ran out) they planted vines. The wine-growing map of Victoria can only be explained in these terms: a haphazard scattering of vineyards where the gold was, and some where it wasn't. In the 1870s and 1880s the goldfields of Ballarat, of Bendigo, of Great Western, and up on

the Murray River in the northeast round Rutherglen all turned their energies to winemaking – with considerable success, even if more by luck than judgment.

Untutored and uninhibited, they discovered for themselves the sort of wines their soils and climates dictated – and also what the market would buy. Some turned out to be great originals: no dessert Muscat in the world since Constantia has had the astonishing honeyed-velvet quality of some from northeast Victoria. On the whole, though, it was the cheap, sweet and strong that would sell – also the fizzy. Inland Victoria, warmer and more generous than the Yarra Valley, rapidly overtook it in the market. However fine the cool-climate wines were, the time was not ripe, and vineyards gradually gave way again to grazing.

The oldest wine-farm still in production in Australia is in none of the regions we have visited, but 3,219 kilometres (2,000 miles) nearer "home", as the settlers' ships sailed, on the banks of the Swan River in Western Australia. The vine rooted there in 1829, several years before it was introduced to either South Australia or Victoria. Conditions here are hotter even than in the Barossa Valley: the natural produce is very strong wine indeed. It is typical of Australian resourcefulness that in such an area one of the country's classic originals was born. The "white burgundy", made since the 1920s by Houghton's (founded in 1840, and still in the suburbs of Perth) contrives to be soft yet intense, full of flavour but remarkably refreshing.

The sad part of the story, here as in all of Australia, was that for most of the existence of the industry the overwhelming demand was simply for strong drink, sweet or dry. The remote Coonawarra, adventurously settled in the 1890s as the Penola Fruit Colony but then abandoned, offered South Australia all the possibilities of a cooler climate. The same thing happened at the same time in Western Australia. Two hundred miles south of Perth the Margaret River was discovered to be an excellent source of grapes for good table wine, cooled by the breezes off the Indian Ocean. Both shared the fate of the Yarra Valley: no demand.

Australia is the France of the southern hemisphere; there seems to be no limit to its potential (enormously reinforced by modern technology) for producing ideally-balanced, delicate wine very much in the French style (though with original touches of its own). But potential alone has never been enough. Fine wine has only been made at moments in history when the market has asked for it.

One anecdote, painful as it is to relate, sums up the attitude that held back Australia's potential for a century and a half. The time is the 1930s, the place London. The sales director of a famous South Australian company is visiting the buyer of an important chain of British stores. Having been kept waiting for two hours he is briefly admitted to the buyer's office for a short and very depressing discussion, only about prices. At the end of the interview he offers his samples, carefully cradled over 19,300 kilometres (12,000 miles). "Samples be damned," was the buyer's answer. "If the wine's no good I'll send it back."

CHAPTER 35

EAST COAST, WEST COAST

North America made its first appearance in our story when Leif Ericsson was moved by the great vines clambering and cascading in its forests to call it Vinland. Much the same feature of their new surroundings must have struck the sixteenth-century seamen who made their landfall much further south. Huguenot refugees from the Wars of Religion in France, building their cabins in Florida near where Jacksonville now stands, must have been nonplussed by the peculiar vines that congested the woods, vines whose huge grapes grew not in tight bunches but spaced apart in clusters, and whose tough skins slipped off, leaving the flesh like a slimy marble. Having no others, they tried to make wine of sorts from these grapes, and found it strong, very dry, or harsh, but better than no wine at all. And the pattern was repeated almost everywhere settlers landed along the east coast: there were plenty of grapes, none of them familiar, and nobody much liked their wine.

Looking around among the wonderful woods of this wilderness, coming right down to the shore in many places, countrymen and gardeners among the settlers, wherever they came from in Europe, found themselves half-recognizing many plants. Instead of one kind of oak there were a dozen more or less oak-like trees – none of them the familiar *Quercus robur* that framed their ships. It was the same with vines: the differences in leaf were no greater, perhaps, than between two varieties of *Vitis vinifera*. Not all fruit was as bizarre as the Scuppernong grape of Florida. But its wine was hard to take. Why, therefore, take it? Why not bring cuttings over and plant this fertile virgin soil with the grapes of Burgundy, Bordeaux, and the Rhine?

The seventeenth and eighteenth centuries are a repetitive saga of wasted effort, trying to do what appeared so simple. Wheat, beans, apples – almost everything else from Europe grew. When it failed there was usually some obvious and visible reason in the shape of a caterpillar or a hurricane, a blistering heat or weeks without a thaw. In the end, when Lord Delaware, Governor Winthrop, Lord Baltimore, William Penn (to name only four of hundreds who invested money, time and effort) had lavished care on their imported vines – Penn planted eighty-one hectares (200 acres) – and their vines had all died, the consensus was – quite rightly – that the extremes of climate of the east coast are unfriendly to the European vine, and that a variety of insect pests were ready to finish off the struggling plant.

This was the situation in the 1770s when the most famous, and one of the most determined, of America's amateur scientists, gardeners, and naturalists joined the fray. Thomas Jefferson not only had a taste for wine, which we have seen him cultivating in France; he was also convinced that lack of wine, except of the expensive, imported kind, was driving America to strong drink. He welcomed the legislation which in 1791 put an excise tax on liquor, but exempted American-made wines. "I rejoice," he wrote, "as a moralist, at the prospect of a reduction of the duties on wine by our national legislature. It is an error to view a tax on that liquor as merely a tax on the rich... No nation is drunken where wine is cheap; and none sober, where the dearness of wine substitutes ardent spirits as the common beverage. It is, in truth, the only antidote to the bane of whiskey."

Long before he went to France he experimented on his estate in Virginia, and encouraged friends and neighbours to do likewise. The most ambitious of these projects was the invitation, originally issued by Thomas Adams to a Florentine named Philip Mazzei, to import Tuscan winegrowers and vines from the best vineyards of Europe to give the Virginian wine industry the best possible start.

Mazzei's experiments were frustrated by the events of the War of Independence, and he moved on to Poland and further adventures. One Tuscan, however, Anthony Giannini, stayed on at Monticello and became Jefferson's estate manager, continuing to experiment with vines during Jefferson's three-year absence. The Monticello vineyard has been reconstructed, staked out boldly on the steep slope under the garden wall. How dogged these efforts were is shown by the fact that in 1802, almost thirty years after his first essays with European vines, Jefferson was

still importing cuttings – and still none of them lived for long.

What finally seems to have altered his view, and reconciled him to the fact that America must make the best of its own vines, was the influence of a surveyor in Georgetown, John Adlum, who had served in the war as a major. In October 1809 Jefferson wrote to Adlum: "I think it would be well to push the culture of that grape without losing our time and efforts in

search of foreign vines, which it will take centuries to adapt to our soil and climate…" He went on to ask for cuttings of this vine, the Alexander, a seedling (possibly a chance hybrid between the American *Vitis labrusca* and a plant of *Vitis vinifera*) found by the eponymous gardener to Governor John Penn (William's son) in Philadelphia. "I have drank of the wine," wrote Jefferson. "It resembles the Comartin Burgundy." Could he have meant Chambertin?

From this time on Jefferson became increasingly reconciled to the strange taste and smell, known as "foxy", of American vines, particularly the hardy and prolific *Vitis labrusca*, which Jancis Robinson describes (and who can contradict her?) as "like an artificial strawberry drink". By 1817 he was convinced that the Scuppernong might be used to make fine wine, even if he was a trifle confused as to exactly how. North Carolina's "Scuppernon wine… would be distinguished on the best tables of Europe, for its fine aroma, ["resembling Frontiniac", he says elsewhere] and chrystalline transparence. Unhappily that aroma, in most of the samples I have seen, has been entirely submerged in brandy. This coarse taste and practice is the peculiarity of the Englishmen, and of their apes, Americans. I hope it will be discontinued…" Jefferson, in his seventies, was growing a little tetchy, even perhaps forgetting the taste of French wine.

But Scuppernong wine, it seems, cannot be made without brandy. A 1909 report of the North Carolina Agriculture Experimental Station describes the process. The grapes are squeezed "in a cider press as soon as they are gathered, when it is put in a clean barrel. In every three quarts of grape juice one quart of brandy is added… Some have tried fermentation but it did not answer." It is, in other words, to use the good old Dutch term, a *stum* wine.

Adlum, meanwhile, had had a lucky find of his own, a vine growing beside an inn in Maryland, transplanted there from North Carolina in 1802. He took cuttings, was delighted with the resulting wine, and named the vine Tokay. In 1823 he sent a bottle to the octogenarian Jefferson, who found it "truly a fine wine, of high flavour, and as you assure me there was not a drop of brandy or other spirit in it, I may say it is a wine of a good body of its own". Jefferson thus, three years before he died, tasted the first all-American wine that would make his dreams come true. The "Tokay" was soon after renamed by Adlum the Catawba, after the river in North Carolina.

The Catawba was to be not a stop-gap, but a smash-hit, in the hands of America's first big-time commercial winemaker, the diminutive Nicholas Longworth (he stood five foot one in his socks) from New Jersey.

Allowing for journalistic hyperbole, it seems that not only America but also Europe became enamoured of his strange strawberryish liquor. Leon Adams quotes from *The Illustrated London News* of 1858, which described the still Catawba as "a

The Napa Valley emerged as a Californian wine region in the 1850s propelled by German settlers, many Rhineland wine-growers, and the energies of Charles Krug.

There was a brisk market in San Francisco, Haraszthy discovered, for eating grapes. What he could not supply he bought in Los Angeles – the Mission grape was good to eat. Perhaps buying different varieties from "Don Luis" in Los Angeles he realized the possibilities (and the need) for more varieties in much larger numbers in North California. In any case he rapidly abandoned his foggy property and moved down the San Francisco peninsula about forty kilometres (twenty-five miles) to Crystal Springs, where by 1856 he had managed to acquire some 405 hectares. Cattle, fruit trees, strawberries, grain, grapes: he raised them all. He also went into the gold-assaying business, which was frantically overstretched by the flow of gold from the mines, and in no time was made the US government's smelter and refiner: the head of the San Francisco mint.

No novelist could have invented Haraszthy. There is a surprise around every corner of his life – and how many lives have had so many corners? After two years of supervising the blazing furnaces of the mint, which ran day and night, he was charged with embezzling $151,000 worth of gold. What had happened, as the jury discovered, was that the rooftops of San Francisco were liberally gilded with the specks of gold that had flown up the overheated chimney.

While the mint was too hot, Crystal Springs, Haraszthy found, was too cold. Even down the peninsula he had a fog problem: his grapes were failing to ripen. In his mind's eye he had an earthly paradise north of the Bay where he had called on General Vallejo. Sitting on the general's porch, the legend runs, he had sipped his host's wine and delivered the deathless line, "General, this stuff ain't bad!" In January 1857 he bought 227 hectares (560 acres) almost next door to Vallejo and set his son Attila to planting cuttings from Crystal Springs, while he projected a sort of Pompeian villa to be called Buena Vista.

This is where his contribution to California's wine-growing really began. In contrast to the General and everyone else, he planted dry slopes with no possibility of irrigation. Most of his vines were still the faithful old Mission, but there was no mistaking the difference in quality that dry-farming made. Furthermore, he persuaded a dozen prominent San Franciscans to invest with him in the new experiment. Charles Krug, shortly to become the virtual founder of the Napa Valley wine industry and the deadly rival of Sonoma, was among them.

Meanwhile Haraszthy, at the request of the Californian State Agricultural Society, wrote a *Report on Grapes and Wines in California*: a manual on planting and winemaking, urging experimentation of all kinds, particularly with different vines on different soils, but also a polemic urging the government to spend money on collecting cuttings in Europe, using the consulate service, and distribute them in California. At Buena Vista he propagated vines by the hundred thousand. And he dug deep tunnels in the hillside to store their produce.

H araszthy was still not ready to pause for breath. He urged that more research was needed. In 1861 the state governor commissioned him to visit Europe to learn all he could in the best wine areas. and to bring back vines. His journey from San Francisco via New York to Southampton took six weeks. From late July to October he stormed round Europe, from Paris to the Rhine, to Switzerland, to Piedmont and Genoa, to the Languedoc, to Bordeaux, round Spain, to Montpellier and Burgundy, and back to Liverpool. Within six months he was back in Sonoma, finishing his book on the whole experience, and awaiting the arrival of 100,000 vines of 300 different varieties, which the Wells Fargo Company delivered in January.

Most writers agree that this collection was the Hungarian's most important contribution to Californian viticulture. It (theoretically) made possible all the experiments that were so necessary to match vines with soils and climates. That they were largely frustrated by the legislature, which declined to distribute the cuttings, or even to pay him for them, was perhaps due partly to the Civil War in the distant east (Haraszthy, as you might expect, supported the rebel South), but largely to the stinginess and apathy of civil servants. Nothing (or not greatly) daunted, Haraszthy did his best to distribute them himself.

Just how essential his imports were is shown in the plantings that, even two years later, he and Vallejo had in Sonoma, the most go-ahead district in the state. Both were still planting the Mission massively. Haraszthy had 120,000 Mission vines established, plus 140,000 newly planted, as against 6,000 "foreign" vines established, and 40,000 new-set.

It was only from the mid-1860s that superior vines were available in any numbers in California, with Sonoma enormously in the lead. The next few years saw the apotheosis of Buena Vista, and its collapse. The final act of Haraszthy's frantic story should be told here, before we survey the rest of the awakening state. In 1868, disillusioned with California, he decided the future lay in Nicaragua, rum, and sawmills. In 1869 he fell into a stream where there were alligators.

T he publicity that always surrounded Haraszthy may well exaggerate his importance; it certainly lays too much stress on his uniqueness. He was not the only one importing vines. Tentative efforts were made, for example, in Santa Clara county, south of San Francisco Bay, and almost the mirror-image of Sonoma, one range back from the sea. In 1849 a French nurseryman, Antoine Delmas, settled here, and was enraptured with the growing conditions.

The man who made Santa Clara famous for wine was a Frenchman, too: Charles Lefranc. In 1857 he founded what was to become the hugely successful Almadén vineyards, planting Cabernet Sauvignon, Pinot Noir, Malbec, Sémillon, and many of the varieties that Haraszthy later imported to distribute. The difference was that Haraszthy operated in the glare of publicity. Lefranc simply made good wine – and so, in due course, did his son-in-law from Beaune, Paul Masson.

W ith so much excitement going on over the hills in Sonoma, it is slightly surprising that the Napa Valley, one range further inland from the ocean, but equally accessible by steamer across the Bay from San Francisco, should have lagged

Buena Vista Ranch February 8th 186[...]

To His Excellency, The Governor,

Sir,—

behind by what, at the speed settlers worked, was a fair margin.

George Yount was the first to settle. He had arrived in California to trap seals for fur, and fetched up at General Vallejo's, looking for work. In 1838 he had ridden over the wild Mayacamas mountains to look at the next valley, to find it, the story goes, a sea of golden poppies. Vallejo granted him 486 hectares, on which he dutifully planted some Mission grapes – though, without help, cattle-ranching was about all he could handle. That very year smallpox carried off almost all the Napa Indians.

The Napa Valley remained, insofar as it was settled at all, stock-raising and cattle-farming land for almost a generation after Yount's arrival. By 1868 there were twenty-nine substantial farmers in the valley with vines, led by the plutocratic Mormon Sam Brannen of San Francisco, who owned most of the northern end of the valley and the hot springs of Calistoga. The second biggest grower was Dr Crane, who is credited with building the first redwood tanks and having the first wine-press in the valley. The third was Charles Krug, who later chronicled the early years.

In the 1860s the vast majority of Napa's grapes were Mission, although "foreign" varieties were grown by such enterprising souls as Dr Crane of St Helena and Mr Osborne of Oak Knoll Farm, Napa (who had bought a standard collection,

Haraszthy planted 300,000 vines here at Buena Vista before leaving California; the house and its vineyards were his grandiloquent answer to his neighbour Vallejo's Lachryma Montis. The winery was re-established in 1943; the cellars are now a showplace.

california vs australia   There is a direct comparison to be made here. Australia's first wine regions (the Hunter Valley, southern Victoria, the Adelaide area, and the Swan River, Western Australia) were all initiated in the same decade, the 1830s, as the missions of California were disbanded. If Australia took off more quickly, planting more varied vines in a more enquiring spirit, it was due to two things: the omnipresence of the Mission grape in California as a disincentive to experiment, and the lack of any organizing authority such as Britain was to its colonies. The mother hen, however far away, was constantly bossing and exhorting her chicks (and sending them supplies). California's Spanish start had to be overcome before there could be real progress. Settlers scattered like bird-shot all over the state, and it was to be a long time before Californians came to understand their great empty land – above all, its climate, dominated by the cold Pacific alongside.

In Australia (other things being equal) north means hotter; south means cooler. But in much of California you can almost say that east and west take the relative places of north and south: the further you go from the ocean, the hotter the climate. Above all, what matters most to any developing enterprise is the market, and here, too, there was a big difference between the two. In Australia the gold rush accelerated what was already happening: in California it changed the name, address, and rules of the game.

The pioneer spirit takes to the rails: in 1869 the Atlantic–Pacific railway opened a vast new market to Californian wines, which had previously suffered from a grape surplus.

mainly of table grapes, that was offered by the nurseries of the East). The most enterprising cultivator was Hamilton Crabb from Ohio, who arrived in 1865 and by 1880 had 400 different varieties growing. But to grow exotic grapes was one thing. To make good wine was another.

"In the next thirty years", according to a later famous winemaker, John Daniel of Inglenook, "Charles Krug was the outstanding figure in Napa wines, not only because of his own operations but because of the leadership he provided… and the training which key industry figures, such as Karl Wente, founder of Wente Bros, Charles Wetmore, founder of Cresta Blanca… and Jacob Beringer… all received when working for him." He was an extremely vocal and persuasive man; and an effective spokesman, when necessary for the whole California wine industry.

I t was to a large extent the Germans who set the Napa Valley on its feet. They arrived in large numbers from the 1850s on, many of them Rhineland winegrowers who were disillusioned with a Germany that was turning more and more to beer, and more seriously, being dominated more and more by Prussia. No doubt California's gold rush also helped them make up their minds.

The calibre of these men is shown by the way they adapted their winemaking to a totally strange world. If the methods of the Rhineland were out of place in northern California, they doggedly found ways to match what they knew with what they found. For years the business of the Napa Valley was conducted in German – and of parts of Sonoma too. Fewer of the early settlers of the north-coast counties were Italian. The brothers Simi from Piedmont were well ahead of their time in 1876 when they built their positively stately stone winery in the Russian River Valley, north of Sonoma. Of the early winemen it could be said in general that the Germans brought the brains, the Italians the brawn – taking over, in many cases, from the Chinese as craftsmen, stone-masons, and labourers.

Three things determine the direction of a new wine industry: its natural conditions; the techniques, traditions and intelligence brought to it by its pioneers; but more even than these, it is the market-place that points the way.

Up to the 1870s California had no mass market for wine. Its chronic problem was a surplus of grapes. Europe and the east coast were effectively almost equally far away. Both had their own wine supplies.

From the opening of the rail link between the coasts in 1869 all this was to change. The conditions that so limited wine-growing in the East were unknown in the West. Californians made much of the fact that their wines never needed the help of added sugar. There were bitter battles as East and West accused each other of malpractice: the Californians of using European labels on their own bad wines; the Easterners of putting California labels on bad European wines. In 1872 Arpad Haraszthy, the count's son, wrote: "The reputation of California wines in Eastern States is… undergoing one of the severest trials… that of palming off upon the confiding public spurious, inferior and bare-faced imitations of the same, which never saw the soil of our state, nor resemble wines in any particular. This unscrupulous traffic is carried on openly thoughout the Eastern States…" The situation was made worse by a short but ugly economic slump that hit the nation. Congress tried to protect both East and West from European imports by protective tariffs – which had the usual effect of provoking retaliation.

Had all the wine-growers known how much worse their problems were to become they might have formed a united front. The Temperance terrorists were stalking them; Kansas became the first "dry" state in 1880. And so was phylloxera; it had already reached Sonoma to begin its slow but deadly work in 1873.

For the moment, the creative energy of northern California's growers was being used in the study and nurture of their precious vines. By the 1880s in the Napa Valley, according to Krug himself, "The new plantations were not any more of Mission, the Zinfandel and Malvoisie for clarets, and the Riesling, Chasselas, Burger and Muscatelles for whites. During the last few years the ambitious winemen planted, or rather grafted… Cabernet Sauvignon, Petit Sirah, Miller Burgundy, Crabb Burgundy, Malbec, Mondeuse, which elegant varieties will improve the character of our clarets wonderfully… and added to the Riesling… such as the Sémillon etc, and to produce white wines of the Sauterne character, such varieties as Sauvignon Blanc…" Was this the influence of Haraszthy, taking so long to cross the hills? The answer is that many worked at the same thing at the same time.

It is much more remarkable, this knowledgeable listing of varieties, when you consider that it was only a century since the first methodical study of them was attempted even at Montpellier or Bordeaux. Less than a century separates the recognition of Cabernet Sauvignon as the best grape for Bordeaux and the same recognition in the Napa Valley.

As always, it was comparing notes that led to progress; as early as 1854 the farmers of Napa had formed an Agricultural Society to exchange their experiences. More help was to come from academic sources. In 1868 the University of California was founded at Berkeley with a Professor of Agriculture; in 1874 it had the good fortune to acquire a German-born soil-scientist of genius, Eugene Waldemar Hilgard, who might be said to have taken on Haraszthy's mantle – or one of them. Hilgard had some powerful things to say about growers who sold their wine under foreign labels "after two trips across the Atlantic, or even perhaps only across the Bay". "The growers need to know," he said, "and that quickly, which of the 2,500 varieties they should choose." His thinking was eventually to lead to the formal analysis of the whole of California into its wayward and elusive climate zones, and the recommendation of which grape varieties are best suited to each. In 1878 Hilgard welcomed a visit from Father John Bleasdale, who came from Melbourne to judge a wine and brandy competition in San Francisco. In Australia Bleasdale had already been preaching the gospel of cool climate for ten years.

Fog is a fact of life in California. It needed no University department to point out that the nearer you got to the ocean, the greater the chance of its towering white fog bank blotting out the sun. Its influence on inland valleys is much more subtle, but it soon began to be felt by grape-growers. One Judge Stanley, who owned land near Napa City, was ready in 1889 to tell the *San Francisco Chronicle*: "I consider that the lower end of the Napa Valley is the most suitable locality for grapes that will yield dry red wine… The district is within the range where sea air permeates the atmosphere. From this sea air the vines extract properties which increase the tannin in their fruit." In a word (though the judge used many) he specifically compared the Carneros district with the Médoc.

It was time to make comparisons with France and see how California was getting on. In that same year, 1889, they did, at the Exposition Universelle in Paris, and had no reason to be ashamed of their results. Of thirty-four medals or awards given to California entries for wines of various sorts, the Napa Valley won twenty. From that date on, justly or unjustly, it can be said to have assumed the lead in prestige, which it never lost through all the troubles that lay ahead.

bottled poetry Robert Louis Stevenson's romantic heart was stirred by the very name of the Silverado Trail, winding up the sunburnt side of the Napa Valley to the silver diggings on Mount St Helena.

"One corner of the land after another is tried with one kind of grape after another," wrote the author of *Treasure Island* in his one attempt at wine-writing. "So, bit by bit, they grope about for their Clos Vougeot and Lafite." The process he describes is if anything even more topical today than when he noted it. What were Schram's Schramsberg Champagnes like? How good were these proud medal-winners that were all to disappear? To Stevenson they were "bottled poetry" – so nothing has really changed.

CHAPTER 36

THE GOLDEN AGE

The Golden Age of wine-growing in Bordeaux and Burgundy in the nineteenth century is no fable. It is true that for a while in mid-century the owning of vineyards, especially in Bordeaux, was the most fashionable game in town, that bankers were ready to pay any money for famous properties, that vintage-time in the Médoc was a Champs Elysées of flounces and flirting. The image of that era has been assiduously cultivated through hard times since. It has stuck, at least in Bordeaux, largely because it gave rise to what could be described as the myth of the château.

At the end of the eighteenth century the leading properties of both Bordeaux and Burgundy had reached a fair level of technical competence based on centuries of well-learned lessons. They had almost completed the evolution of the style of wines they would be always be known for: especially among the reds of the Médoc and the Côte de Nuits.

Bordeaux still had some adjustments to make in its choice of grape varieties. The Cabernets Sauvignon and Franc and the Merlot were well-established but by no means universal. Petit Verdot and Malbec still played important roles, besides many minor varieties that have since all but disappeared.

In Bordeaux the end of Napoleon's wars brought no immediate relief – except that the customers did at least keep coming. Centuries of habit were not to be broken by even twenty years of fighting. Britain remained interested in only the very best wines; The Netherlands' interest continued, though mainly for cheap white wines and *palus* reds (or "cargo" wines), while Germany's purchases rose, until altogether it took a third of all Bordeaux's exports. A sad blow was the loss of much of the French colonial market that had been a mainstay of the eighteenth century, but in its place there began a small but growing interest from both North and South America.

An indication of the low state of the market was that the Bank of Bordeaux, newly opened in 1825, almost failed in 1830 and categorically refused stocks of wine as collateral for loans. The lack of credit gave the ever watchful merchants of the Quai des Chartrons more opportunities than ever for dictating terms to growers. The lead was taken by the powerful Nathaniel Johnston, backed up by Mr Barton and M Guestier – both of whom were able to buy themselves Médoc châteaux in the 1820s. (Guestier was known to growers as "Pierre le Cruel".)

Johnston accused the "first-growths" (Margaux and Haut-Brion in particular) of trading on their names with an 1834 vintage that was "no better than a 3rd or 4th growth". Growers' finances were so tight that in 1844 both Châteaux Margaux and Latour, looking for reassurance, signed ten-year contracts to sell their whole crop, good vintage or bad, at a preset price of 2,100 and 1,750 francs a *tonneau* respectively – which sounded reasonable until Château Lafite, under its most famous and spirited *régisseur*, Joseph Goudal, remaining staunchly independent, sold the 1844 crop for 4,500 francs – more than twice as much.

A contract with a *négociant* was more than a simple agreement to sell. Now that, for the first time, it was the merchants who were financing the growers, they made strict stipulations about how the estate was to be run, even down to the number of cultivations of the vineyard, the timing of manuring (once every nineteen years for a "first-growth"), the rate at which old vines should be replaced, and the Baltic oak that the barrels should be made of – with six hoops.

Goudal would have none of this. Luckily, in the long run, for all estate owners, he had the solid backing of enormously rich proprietors, the Vanlerberghe family (who had been described as "gun-runners" in the wars, and conducted operations through a London banker, Sir Samuel Scott). Goudal declared open war on the Quai des Chartrons merchants. He sold his excellent 1841 vintage at a colossal price over their heads – and on the condition that customers took some of the mediocre 1842 as well. Johnston was outraged and circulated his English customers, almost asking them to boycott Lafite. His idea was an orderly market – with the Chartronnais calling the tune. Johnston wanted to go so far as to accept orders only for "first-", "second-", "third-" or "fourth-growth" wines – the customer to leave it to his discretion whether he delivered Latour or Lafite; in other words for the Chartronnais to control the entire system and effectively abolish the carefully-nurtured notion of the individual *cru*, replacing it with an overall classification. (Heaven knows, said the proprietors, what the merchants would have got up to in their cellars.)

That there was a classification in place already there is no doubt. It did not become official until 1855, it covered only the Médoc (and Sauternes), and until the early nineteenth century it was more of a confidential consensus among the trade than an actual list. But ever since the early 1700s the brokers had been studying form – and it had been remarkably consistent. The "first-growths" were not only first in time; by and large, year after year, they remained first in quality. And the price differentials were enormous: in the eighteenth century "first-growths" sold for twice as much as "seconds", three times as much as "thirds" and four times the price of "fourths". Even granted that millionaires and their money are easily parted, the long-term consistency is impressive: such a consensus surviving from one generation to another can hardly all be done with mirrors.

The public first learned of the classification in Jullien's *Topographie*. He was such a confirmed classifier of everything that they may not have realized the significance of the ranking of Bordeaux. In his first (1816) edition, in any case, it was very simple, and evidently gleaned from the broker Lawton, who had briefed Thomas Jefferson on the top wines. Jullien distinguished between the "High" and "Low" Médocs, and gave what were to become almost the conventional characterizations of the four "first-growths" (Haut-Brion included). His descriptions still ring remarkably true today. He listed seven "second-growths"

Oak barrels at Château Margaux. Impeccable winemaking and a deep respect for the terroir keep the "first-growths" at the top.

(Rauzan and Gorce in Margaux; Léoville and Larose in St-Julien; le Clos de Brane-Mouton and Pichon-Longueville in Pauillac; and Calon in St-Estèphe). After that he was content to list the communes in order of quality with notes on the characters of their wines. On the quality of the top Médocs in general, though, he wrote both specifically and lyrically: their flavour, he said, reminded him of the smell of the best sealing wax, "and their bouquet shares the scents of the violet or the raspberry".

Jullien, the Parisian, was rapidly (in 1824) followed by a German Bordeaux *négociant*, Wilhelm Franck, who pushed the matter far further, naming a total of 408 properties in forty-one communes in the Médoc, and setting out four classes, growths, or *crus*. After the four "firsts", he listed only four "seconds", then eight "thirds", then eighteen "fourths".

Franck in turn was rapidly (in 1828) followed by a broker, Monsieur Paguierre, whose book was published in both French and English (in Edinburgh) at the same time. Paguierre's classification follows Franck almost to the letter. The chief interest in his book lies in his recommendations to growers on how to make the most suitable wine for each foreign market. His formula for red-winemaking is extraordinary. He proposes making a "mother-vat", a *mère-cuve*, in which the very best and ripest grapes are given a month-long maceration in *trois-six*, or double-strength brandy, while the rest of the harvest is trodden and fermented in the usual way. The contents of the *mère-cuve* "having finished fermenting" (in practice would they ferment at all, being pickled in spirits?) should then be added as a dose to each of the regular barrels. Evidently he was looking for extra strength and colour, but going about it in a most peculiar way.

As for foreign customers, Paguierre's experience tells him that the Dutch want natural wine so that they can mess it about in their own way at home, the Russians and Prussians want two- or three-year-old wine, racked clear of any lees, while the incorrigible British, still hankering after the kick of port and Spanish wines, are only happy with the traditional *travail* of adding Hermitage, Midi, or worse (he does not mention brandy) which makes their claret turn brown and dry with age. Powdered iris root helps the bouquet, he adds – and so does two fingers of "raspberry spirit" in each barrel. They expected the best growths to be kept no less than six years in cask. But when they were bottled (by their buyers) they were considered ready to drink.

More surprising than to find the top growths confidently classified are references already, in the 1820s, to a hierarchy in far greater depth, which is not elaborated on, but which extends downwards from the "*crus classés*" to "*vins bourgeois supèrieurs*", "*bons vins bourgeois*", "*petits vins bourgeois*", and even "*petits vins de Médoc paysans*".

So the brokers had already done their research and grading among what today are usually referred to as *petits châteaux*. By the fourth (1848) edition of Jullien he was even ready to coin this oft-repeated phrase: "These wines [the *crus bourgeois*] often acquire in maturity a degree of quality which makes them very difficult to distinguish from the fifth growths."

Even though business was slow in Bordeaux, one can feel a mounting public interest in this curiously constructed animal as list after list appeared. There was a consensus coming about which was unique in the world: a sort of perpetual auction in which properties were finding their relative values. The idea of grading the quality of land is logical enough, but in Bordeaux that was not what was happening. What was being classified was property – which inevitably includes the human element.

The book that brought interest to a peak is nowadays reverentially referred to simply as the Bordeaux Bible. It was a joint production by an English professor (and Freemason) named Charles Cocks and a Bordeaux bookseller called Michel Féret. In 1846 Cocks alone published *Bordeaux, Its Wines and the Claret Country* in English. It included the most comprehensive classification that had yet appeared, based, he said, on Franck's latest revision of his list, but augmented by his own researches, "price having appeared to me the best test of the quality supposed to exist in each wine".

Féret clearly pounced on this authoritative work and its writer, rechecked and slightly modified the list, and in 1850 brought out the first French edition, *Bordeaux et ses Vins, Classés par Ordre de Mérite*. Since then there have been fourteen more editions of *Cocks and Féret*, growing ever stouter, until today it lists nearly 8,000 properties.

Cocks must have been very close to the brokers. Had he lived one year longer, to 1855, he would have seen something very like his list appear as the official *Classement* by the Syndicat des Courtiers de Commerce, in response to a demand to the Bordeaux Chamber of Commerce from Napoleon III, as its contribution to the Paris Exposition Universelle of that year.

The key word which is missing from the Classement of 1855, or at any rate only appears on it five times, is the word "château". Seventy-four of the seventy-nine properties listed (fifty-eight red-wine producers, twenty-one white) appear as a simple name (Mouton, for example, or Langoa), followed by the commune and the name of the owner. To refer to the property the word *cru* or sometimes *clos* was commonly used, but château apparently only if a major building that justified the term existed (*e.g.* at Beychevelle) or had once existed (*e.g.* at Latour). It was the pretensions of proprietors, building themselves imposing residences in the full flush of the coming Golden Age, that brought the term château into common use.

From the 1850s on the Médoc began to acquire its familiar appearance: that of a series of large, vaguely historical-looking country-houses scattered among rolling parkland in which, instead of oaks and deer, there are vines, vines, and more vines. The golden years of the 1860s and 1870s gave the growers deep purses. It was a poor *vigneron* indeed who could not afford at least one turret tacked onto his farmhouse, to lend credence to the title château.

Joseph Goudal had had the wit to point out to his employers, when times were hard for his neighbours, that any land that Lafite bought from them immediately multiplied in value – because it became part of Lafite. They foolishly turned down several opportunities before, in the 1840s and for a considerable sum, buying the next-door patch called Les Carruades. But the principle is exactly correct and adds an almost mystical air to the notion of a *cru classé*: it can consist of single block of land, or several blocks, or indeed separate rows of vines all over the commune. So long as it belongs to its own tradition, as it were, all its wine can be labelled with its classed-growth name.

There is one document that finally tried to pin down what a château is – but not until 1942, and then without success: the name "château" (on a wine label) must be "linked to the existence of a particular *cru*, a specific vineyard that has been known for a very long time by the name in question, in accordance with its meaning and with local, faithful and reliable usage". Little, if any, of this relates to actual practice. The vineyard can even be exchanged for another (so long as that other is also classified – or apparently in some cases whether it is or not). There does not have to be any building on the property at all. The only word that really rings true is "usage": a château is

what it does. There is a word that fits it rather neatly: a brand. Though the number of *crus classés* has remained unaltered in the Médoc and Sauternes since 1855, the number of châteaux leapt from a dozen or two in all of Bordeaux, to 700 in 1874, 1,300 in 1893, and today stands at over 4,000.

The Golden Age arrived with the classification. On the face of it, times were not at all auspicious. A potent new fungus disease, oidium or powdery mildew, had appeared in Bordeaux three years before (having already decimated vineyards elsewhere in France) and was crippling or killing vines by the thousand. On the other hand, despite poor vintages shortage of wine made prices rise. It was also the very time when the gold-rushes of California and Australia fed a great deal of money into the world economy. And in 1853 the railway was completed between Bordeaux and Paris.

To Bordeaux, as a seaport, the railway was not quite such a revolutionary release from old constraints as it was in land-locked Burgundy – although steamships were a revolution in themselves. Where it helped most was in speeding travel to Paris and the northern markets such as Belgium and Germany. It brought Parisians to inspect this famous wine region. Having seen it, they wanted to own a part of it.

An account of the vintage at Beychevelle, the property of the banker Fould, sets the scene. Fould had married the daughter of a New Orleans cotton millionaire who had bought the baroque palace from "Pierre le Cruel" Guestier. After a vast lunch and cigars on the terrace the party strolled among the outbuildings to watch the harvesters at their cabbage soup (which was good, the writer noted, and full of bits of meat). Then rides or drives up and down the rows of vines – "*à côté de nous passe la calèche de la toute gracieuse baronne Gustave de Rothschild et de son mari... la jolie famille de M. Johnston... Duchatel... comte d'Aguado... Prince et Princesse Murat... les Ségur... les d'Erlanger... c'est le Faubourg St Honoré, ce sont les Champs Elysées prolongés, c'est Paris.*"

Where was the wine going, from this socially and industrially revolutionized Bordeaux? A very great deal (though

BELOW AND OPPOSITE These idealized, optimistic scenes of grape-picking and winemaking reflected the confidence of an age in which railways had given new markets for wine, and cities – and thirsts – had grown. Disaster, though, lay only just around the corner.

not of the best qualities) was crossing the Atlantic. Argentina, the land of beef and wheat, became Bordeaux's biggest single client in the years 1860–90, while the United States picked up the taste for claret (but not its English name) in the 1840s, rising to a peak in the 1850s, when for a whole decade it remained Bordeaux's best customer of all. It was the Civil War that ended this (since long-forgotten) era of American thirst, together with growing Temperance propaganda and the trend towards protectionism in America's trade policies. Later in the century California's growing production took up the slack.

By the 1860s, though, exactly the opposite was happening in Europe. A series of reciprocal treaties freeing customs barriers between nations started with the Prussian-inspired German Customs Union, the Zollverein, in the 1830s. Historically most significant for Bordeaux was the Anglo-French trade treaty of 1860. It led directly to the ending of the nearly two-centuries-old discrimination against French wine that had driven England to port. Suddenly the duty on French table wines entering Britain was one-twentieth of what it had been in 1815.

The British gave all the credit to the Chancellor of the Exchequer, William Gladstone. "Gladstone claret" was what they called the wonder of affordable Bordeaux. Between 1860 and 1873 the British (who had not by any means forgotten sherry, or anything else potable) multiplied their intake of French wine eight times. Very few statistics are needed to sketch the progress of the Golden Age. Bordeaux in 1858 (recovering from oidium) made 1.9 million hectolitres of wine; in 1862 3.2 million; in 1869 4.5 million and in 1874 and 1875 over five million.

As ever, the Médoc was in the forefront of these events. The story of St-Emilion and its neighbours in the nineteenth century is roughly parallel, though starting at a more modest level and remaining more closely knit, with less outside influence. "Stolid" is the word that springs to mind. Respectable Libournais families stayed put and steadily improved their wines as new ideas came along. Brittany and northeast France, Belgium and The Netherlands, continued to be their best clients. If there was any classification it remained a private matter among brokers and merchants; its possible publicity value did not occur to them – and journalists, it seems, did not spend much time in Libourne.

villages and vineyards It is easy to tell which of the communes of the Côte d'Or were accustomed to commerce in their wines under their own names and which depended on selling under what was effectively a generic title, such as Beaune. Where the village name stands alone, as at Volnay and Pommard, a market existed for wine under that name. Nobody, on the other hand, called for Aloxe or for Morey; all the renown of these communes was concentrated in its *tête de cuvée* or *grand cru*.

It was a logical step demanded by Burgundy's Golden Age to make the wines of the villages more saleable in their own right. From the 1860s the villages whose names rang no bells in themselves were permitted to attach the name of their most famous vineyard. Thus Gevrey became Gevrey-Chambertin; Morey, Morey-St-Denis from its *tête de cuvée* Clos St-Denis. The only district which did not adopt this practice was the Côte Dijonnaise, nearest to Dijon, where Brochon, Fixin, Marsannay, and Chenôve were well enough known as Dijon's local wines.

The difficulties of shipment in the Napoleonic wars had taught both the Libournais merchants and the growers a valuable lesson: that their wines improved with age much more than they had previously believed; it was worth investing in stocks to mature as they did in Bordeaux. St-Emilions, they found, would keep for twenty years. "Pomerols", wrote the *négociant* Beylot in 1829, "do not keep as long, but can be bottled earlier, and some have more bouquet than St-Emilions". He did not mention that St-Emilions were often still being used as a Hermitage-substitute for underpowered Médocs.

Whereas in the eighteenth century the wines of the Fronsac Côtes had been rated higher than Pomerols, in the nineteenth the situation was reversed. Fronsac suffered as an indirect result of the Revolution. The Richelieu family would never let its Fronsac pasture lands be planted with vines. When they were sold as *Biens Nationaux*, Libourne's bourgeois snapped them up as perfect virgin *palus* and made large investments converting them to vineyards. The Canon slopes across the river became unimportant in proportion to these productive fields – particularly as all wine prices in the 1830s and 1840s were at a low level. Fronsac's name came to be associated more with ordinary "cargo" wine than anything fine. Pomerol, in contrast, gained because of a change in farming practice. One of its earliest exponents was the editor of an influential but short-lived (1838–41) monthly journal for winegrowers called *Le Producteur*. According to his account, the immemorial custom on its plateau – ignored only by a few ambitious proprietors along its boundaries – was to alternate vine-rows with strips of plough for growing grain. It was impossible to manure these *joualles* without the vines taking their share of the extra nutrients. "It has to be admitted", wrote *Le Producteur*, "that the wine loses in quality what it gains in quantity."

It was, ironically, the apparent scourge of powdery mildew that did away with the *joualles* – and also with Pomerol's once-admired white wine. With vines dying all over France, the price of red wine rose to the point where even Pomerol threw aside tradition. It found itself making much better wine just in time to share in Bordeaux's Golden Age. Up to the 1850s Pomerol boasted one château: the very old estate of the de May family that had been known as Certan. In 1858 it became the first Pomerol property to be "Médocized" by a Paris banker, Charles de Bousquet. He added the inevitable slate-roofed tower, and confirmed the antiquity of its standing by calling it Vieux Château Certan. Its wine was rated the finest in the district.

Pétrus, the property of the Arnaud family, was cited among the good but not outstanding small estates. Old editions of *Cocks and Féret* illustrate the house with an engraving showing a turreted gateway that suggests an old manor, if not an actual castle. The modest house today shows not the slightest signs of any such thing, so perhaps the tower was a case of a *château en Espagne*. Pétrus remained in the Arnaud family until 1929, its hour of recognition still to come. Its name, however, is an example of what was happening in both Pomerol and St-Emilion: proprietors were looking for something snappier and more saleable than their rustic old handles. The Giraud family farm had the scarcely encouraging name of Trop-Ennuie, which could be rendered as "Too much trouble". Trotanoy, the new version, sold very much better.

Most of these adjustments were storms in teacups. One was considerably more: the breaking up of St-Emilion's only great estate of the eighteenth century – Figeac. Its inheritor, André de Carie-Trajet, with the great vineyard bequeathed to him from Vital de Carle, was one of few who despaired of wine-growing during Napoleon's wars and the blockades. Others sent their wine the difficult and expensive way north by road. Perhaps possessed by the idea of red-coated armies, he quixotically replaced half his vines with the dye-plant madder (a substitute for Mexican cochineal, which was blockaded out). By 1823 he was ruined; he died; his widow had to break up the estate. Figeac still exists, as one of the biggest and certainly of the best St-Emilion properties. But out of some of its best land, on the very boundary-line of Pomerol, the Ducasse family formed a new estate to which they gave the catchy name of Cheval Blanc. What could be more of a brand name than White Horse? From the 18505 onwards Cheval Blanc was destined to become one of St-Emilion's effective "first-growths"; sharing the honours of the gravelly plateau above the town with Figeac, but in the soft richness of its wine drawing nearer to a Pomerol. Ausone, Belair, Canon, and their neighbours meanwhile continued to dominate the limestone côtes around and below the town.

St-Emilion had missed a trick in the Exposition Universelle of 1855, which was the triumph of the Médoc. It did not make the same mistake in the 1867 Paris Exhibition. Thirty-seven properties collectively won a gold medal. But the renown of its wines beyond their traditional market, and their adoption as chic enough for Paris, really dates from the 1889 Exhibition, in which sixty of them collectively won the Grand Prix.

Nothing so dramatic as the nineteenth century apotheosis of Bordeaux happened in Burgundy. But then, you might fairly say, it never does. Big players are few in its slowly evolving story, and now that the church had been removed they were fewer still. In Chapter 27 we saw how a banker's money made in the wars held the Clos de Vougeot together for several generations, but the overwhelming tendency was for Burgundy's estates, already relatively small, to be divided and subdivided by a process in which the French laws of inheritance played (and still play) a major part.

The assumption on the death of a parent is that all the children inherit the property equally. Most estates today have formed themselves into business ventures to prevent the inevitable break-up that this entails. The Société Civile de Château Latour was the first such arrangement, set up by the descendants of Nicolas-Alexandre de Ségur. In the nineteenth century, when some of the best land in Burgundy changed hands, its fragmentation was accelerated by the *jeu des heritages*. Very few of the ancient *clos*, put together with infinite pains, survived intact – though here, as in most things, the Côte de Nuits and the Côte de Beaune evolved in different ways. Where there were more *têtes de cuvée* more money was involved, and there were fewer who could take part.

Was there not an opportunity here for new capital to start the process again, making new *clos* out of the broken-up mosaic? Certainly the merchant houses of Beaune and Nuits-St-Georges took every opportunity to create themselves estates. But it was too late to make a clean sweep: the best that could be done was a gradual accumulation as pieces of the jigsaw came onto the market. The biggest estate today is the size of an important Médoc château – but parcelled out all over the Côte d'Or; and the average size, taking all growers, big and small together, is a mere four hectares (ten acres) – also scattered.

The publication of Chaptal's treatise had given everybody a standard to work to, including such new or revived ideas as adding sugar to the juice and covering the fermenting vat. It was soon followed by many more detailed works dedicated to local conditions, but apart from giving empirical advice and building up confidence they did not alter much. Burgundy especially showed the resistance to change to be expected of an old establishment. The famous Dr Guyot, whose oenological advice was sought all over France in mid-nineteenth century, deplored the *immobilisme* of the Burgundian. Reactionary and secretive, it was said he was not concerned to know how things were done in the next village – but very concerned that the next village did not poke its nose into his cellars.

To Count Haraszthy, hurrying through looking for ideas for California, Burgundy seemed very primitive indeed: "Then, according to the size of the tank, from four to ten men, stripped of all their clothes, step into the vessel, and begin to tread down the floating mass, working it also with their hands. This operation is repeated several times, if the wine does not ferment rapidly enough. The reason for this, in my eyes, rather dirty work, is that the bodily heat of the men aids the wine in its fermentation." That same evening back in Dijon: "We partook of white wine that evening, as the process through which the red wine goes did not serve to increase our longing for the ruby coloured liquid."

If the idea of innovation as sacrilege was powerful among the simple, it is not difficult to understand why. Their special place in the world as Burgundian *vignerons* was the only thing special about a grinding life: it had almost mystical value and must not be disturbed. Where Burgundy did make adjustments, and not always happy ones, was in following too closely the taste of the clientele – doing precisely what Bordeaux had done for a century. An enquiry into such practices in 1822 found that *coupage* – "blending" is a kind word for it – had already become "systematic". If, as Chaptal had suggested, growers also added sugar, they were forcing the delicate Pinot Noir in just the way that deprives it of its unique perfume and tenderness. They were also making it easier to imitate. With the grapes of Bordeaux – already themselves a mixture – you can get away with a certain amount of "adjustment". Either burgundy is pure or it is nothing.

By the mid-nineteenth century, the prestigious slopes of the Côtes had become almost a monoculture of Pinot Noir, with perhaps some of its close relation, the Pinot Meunier, and

remaining plants and vineyards of Fromenteau and Chardonnay. What was to change, as the tide of prosperity at last (and not for long) reached the growers of less favoured sites, was the acreage of Gamay – a simple indicator of the demand for low-price wine within sales-reach of burgundy.

Burgundy's Golden Age was above all the era of the little man. It began to dawn with the Canal de Bourgogne, which was

oidium "Vine disease" was the name given at first to a mysterious malady that appeared in Bordeaux's vineyards in 1851. It was soon identified as a form of powdery mildew called *Oidium tuckeri*, of English origin, transmitted via Belgium to the vineyards of France. Its fungus spores spread with dreadful swiftness, encouraged by a cool damp summer, so that in two years the whole region was in a panic. A serious vine disease was something it had never had to face before. Countless descriptions, explanations, and proposed remedies were forthcoming. It attacked different vine varieties to different degrees in different soils. It killed the young shoots of the vines and halved the crops. A large reward was offered for a remedy, with the usual results: electricity was one of the first helpful suggestions.

The cure, suggested as early as 1852 but not widely believed or welcomed, was to dust the vines with finely powdered sulphur. Most proprietors were at first frightened of giving their wine a sulphurous taint, but the efficacy of the system, (and lack of alternatives) soon convinced them. By 1857 the practice was general throughout Bordeaux, and by 1861 the vines had returned to full health – at the expense of a regularly repeated dusting with sulphur.

Although the crisis was short-lived (and incidentally was at its height in the year of the Classification), some of its side effects were not. It stimulated a great deal of replanting, tending to favour the Cabernet and Malbec at the expense of the Merlot, and the Sémillon at the expense of the Muscadelle. It also gave the impetus to the planting of vines in France's new colony of Algeria – which was to have important consequences for the future.

Oidium, or powderly mildew, was the first serious vine disease to hit French vineyards. The cure, dusting the vines with sulphur, is credited to the Comte de la Vergne, whose *palus* vineyard at Ludon in the southern Médoc was badly affected.

opened to traffic from 1832. Paris was now as reachable from Beaune as it had been for a century from Beaujolais. But the moment of daybreak was the railway, which reached Dijon from Paris in 1851 – and for the moment went no further. This was the day that the downtrodden had been dreaming of. For a giddy decade Burgundy became the vineyard of the capital – and the plantations of Gamay spread wide out onto the fertile plain of the Saône, and up into the scrubby Arrières-Côtes behind the Golden slope. At last to be a Burgundian *vigneron* was to have all France – all Europe, even – at your feet. The fact that Burgundy was growing *vin ordinaire* did not discourage anybody; for a few brief years there was no competition.

Nor were the fine wines of the Côte d'Or forgotten in the rush. Their market expanded even further than the Gamay's – and much more permanently. In 1859 the Hospices de Beaune inaugurated the public auction of its wines: a totally successful piece of propaganda. In 1861, Dr. Lavalle's classification of the *têtes de cuvée* was ready for the Paris Exhibition, the German Zollverein, and indeed the British Empire.

But there was no reason for the railway to stop at Dijon. The advantage of being at the railhead was a purely temporary piece of luck. Once the tracks reached the Midi, Burgundy and all of France were open to the flood of cheaper (and sometimes riper) wines from the lower Rhône and the Languedoc. And meanwhile, without taking a ticket on any train, the phylloxera beetle was hopping, crawling, and winging its way northwards from where it had made its landing in the South.

CHAPTER 37

ZOLLVEREIN

With so much that is familiar already in place in our story – the Médoc firmly classified, Champagne sparkling, and Burgundy parcelled out among many of the families who are still tending it – there are still two nations to be created to fit together the map, and the wine-list, of modern Europe. Napoleon's adventures had sown the seed. But at the start of the nineteenth century Germany and Italy existed only in a geographical sense, and even that still far from clearly defined. As nations they were not yet even coherent ideas.

You could say the same of Italian wine – but not of German. If there is one region whose wine cannot have changed radically, even over the almost 2,000 years since its vineyards were first planted, it is the Rhineland, and more specifically its oldest wine-bearing tributary, the Mosel. It can never have made other than light white wines, ranging from thin and acid to ripely juicy. But if Germany's style of wine was settled long ago, its techniques, terminology, and even the regional distinctions that now seem set in stone, padlocked in place in a gothic dungeon of legislation, are all the fruit of the last 200 years – starting with the legendary late harvest at Schloss Johannisberg.

The Congress of Vienna set the scene. Napoleon had departed, but the Prussian army did not go quietly home. Europe was reorganized in an epic of hard bargaining, with Talleyrand in the French corner, and Metternich in the Austrian. Prussia was given a buffer zone along the French frontier, which included the Mosel, and the Mosel entered a period of unheard-of prosperity. Nature apparently approved, giving it the unprecedented number of six excellent vintages in the decade from 1819. And

Prussia cocooned its "own" wine region in a very comfortable arrangement of customs barriers that gave it privileged access down the Rhine, to northern Germany, to Prussia proper, to the Low Countries, and even to Britain. Between 1817 and 1840 the wine-growing population of the Mosel grew by thirty-eight per cent. Vines hugged the steep slopes from the river to the crest as they had never done before.

Their satisfaction was short-lived. The weather is rarely so kind to the Mosel as it was in the 1820s. The 1830s and 1840s saw a succession of terrible vintages. Equally seriously, Prussia began to put into effect its unconcealed ambition of dominating Germany, which it achieved by economic means. It made little sense to have to pay customs duties – the old curse of the wine-trade on the Rhine – simply because goods were transported from one part of Prussia to another via another German state. In 1834 Prussia lowered tariff barriers by agreement with Bavaria and Württemberg; then with Baden and Hesse in 1835. In 1838 almost the whole of Germany was united in the Zollverein, the Customs Union, from which Austria was conspicuously absent. Germany was on its way to becoming a single country – under Prussian control.

What effect did the Zollverein have on wine-growing? The Mosel was not alone in finding itself open to all comers. Economic unification – like the coming of the railways not long after – meant that there were winners and losers. To places where meagre wines had been grown for cheap local consumption (Prussia's own old vineyards around Berlin and Dresden came into this category) the Zollverein brought better and cheaper wines from the Rhineland.

As the French historian Gaston Roupnel pointed out, historically wine was originally grown where it was convenient; now it could be grown where it was best.

A t this stage we can visit the scene with André Jullien. By 1840 he had changed his mind about German wine: "… the dry and piquant flavour is generally displeasing to the French when they first encounter it… [but] it is far from being a coarse and corrosive acid." He now found it "fine and delicate". Nor does it "attack the nerves or trouble the reason when one has drunk too much". Jullien evidently studied his subject in depth. As for the bouquet, he found it "very aromatic, very distinct, and very smooth… equalling, if not surpassing, that of our best [French] wines". None of the German wines he drank, however, was sweet.

S chloss Johannisberg was the Emperor's personal reward to Prince Metternich for his services at Vienna. There is a distinct affinity between the selling strategy that Metternich

adopted and the Médoc's idea that a "first-growth" should make several distinct qualities of wine. Schloss Johannisberg was indisputably a "first-growth"; in Bordeaux it would have offered a *grand vin* and a second wine. But with the introduction of late harvesting a German cellar had a more complex set of alternatives; wines picked earlier or later, with more or less flavour, strength, and even sweetness.

For a diplomat of the *ancien régime* Metternich behaved with remarkable commercial acumen. He designated the different qualities of his wine by two different labels and several different coloured wax seals. The use of "château" labels was revolutionary, the grading system even more so. It formalized the practice of tasting and choosing the best casks in the cellar and settling on a price. In 1830 Metternich became so modern as to order that "no bottled wine from Johannisberg is to be sold unless the label is signed by the cellar-master". These concepts of grading and

of guaranteed authenticity were way ahead of their time; eventually they were to build into a system of legislation covering the whole of Germany.

By the start of the nineteenth century Schloss Johannisberg and the Steinberg systematically harvested as late as the season allowed. Ordinary growers still had to pick when they were told. It was a grave offence even to be found in a vineyard at all outside set hours announced by the church bells. Grapes are all too easy to pilfer. But the exceptional weather of the Comet vintage, 1811, gave even the humblest vintner a taste of nectar. In 1822 another harvest started to rot and shrivel on the vines while the sun still shone. The burghers could not bear to pick on the appointed date. The mayor of Eltville took their case to the ducal officers of Nassau; permission was given to wait for the rot to develop before starting the general harvest – and for the first time the majority of a vintage had the luxurious quality of a Spätlese.

The ruined castle at Landshut at Bernkastel on the Mosel. Vines are planted on the steep, suntrap slopes, while houses occupy the flat land.

Above all the Riesling showed its class over the earlier-ripening Sylvaner. Its wines, however sweet, maintained their piquancy, their vital nerve of fruity acidity. In normal harvests, and for ordinary wine, Sylvaner provided a great volume of a pleasant drink. But once late harvesting became legal, it fell back almost to the position of the Gamay in relation to the Pinot Noir.

Certainly by Metternich's time, probably before, the next logical step was taken. If a general late harvest made more potent wines, a selection of only the rotten bunches, kept apart from the rest, would make more potent wines still. "Auslese" was the term they coined (it means a picking out, or selection), inspired perhaps by the Austrian word *Ausbruch* for Tokaji. In other parts of Germany the word *Ausgelesen* began to be heard from the early nineteenth century on. As the century progressed, more Riesling was planted, and more care was taken, over repeated selections, sorting not only the rotten bunches from the merely ripe, but even the individual rotten grapes from within a bunch. The châteaux of Sauternes seem to have been perfecting the same technique at just the same time. Auslese came to mean selected bunches. Then about mid-century the word *Beeren*, meaning a single grape, was attached to the next degree of selection: a "Beerenauslese". Who coined the term and when it was first used does not seem to be on record. Château Yquem could be said to be a Beerenauslese.

At the time, and indeed until very recently, there was little, if any, uniformity in the way growers (even in the same district, let alone in different states) described their more and more carefully selected wines. Where Schloss Johannisberg and some other big estates initiated a system of good, better, and best (with stages in between where necessary), many growers

magyar orszag In the second quarter of the nineteenth century the vineyards of Hungary were larger than those of Italy or Spain. The little country took full advantage of its near-perfect climate for the vine. Tokaji apart, though, its winemaking and storage were still medieval. The best hope for its produce was to be bought as early as possible by a Polish merchant skilled in cellar practice.

Until 1848, when the Hungarians revolted against Austrian rule, progress was slow. The Austrians, with Russian help, crushed the revolution, but were forced to abolish serfdom, which gave Hungary the impetus it needed. The golden age of Hungarian wine started, and ended, only slightly later than that of Bordeaux.

Phylloxera attacked Tokaj in the 1880s, but grafting was rapidly organized and totally successful. Furthermore, Hungary possessed the ultimate weapon against phylloxera, its Great Plain, the Alföld, whose soil is pure sand. Once before, after the Turkish retreat, the Hungarians had colonized their little Sahara. In the 1880s, they discovered its potential for wine-growing without grafting.

Around Lake Balaton, and on the great Esterhazy estates at Mór, sandy soil was exploited, new grape varieties were introduced, and Hungarian wine renewed its ancient reputation with new vigour. And now the process is happening again, with Hungarian wine reinventing itself after decades of Communism.

THE GERMAN
CONFEDERATION

BALTIC SEA

NORTH SEA

Danzig

HOLSTEIN

Lübeck

Hamburg

Bremen

ELBE

HANOVER

Berlin

VISTULA

Warsaw

P R U S S I A

WESTPHALIA

RHINE

RHINE PROVINCE

NASSAU

HESSE

THURINGIAN STATES

SAXONY

ODER

Frankfurt

MAIN

LUXEMBURG

Prague

A U S T R I A N

BAVARIA

Munich

Vienna

WÜRTTEMBERG

BADEN

DANUBE

Budapest

SWITZERLAND

E M P I R E

▬▬▬ BORDER OF THE
GERMAN CONFEDERATION

were so carried away by their enthusiasm over their individual small casks of specially selected and reselected wines that they treated them almost as their children. It is no exaggeration: when there were only enough Beerenauslese grapes to fill a very small cask, a grower had been known to keep it in his bedroom or even his bed; fermentation might stop in the cool of the cellar and never restart.

There is no doubt that by the middle of the century the "first-growths" of the Rheingau had mastered the making of superlative sweet wines. We have the evidence of Count Haraszthy — for once (almost) at a loss for words. He and his son went to Kloster Eberbach (the abbey was then partly a prison) to taste the Duke of Nassau's Steinberger: "To describe the wines would be a work sufficient for Byron, Shakespeare or Schiller, and even those geniuses would not do full justice until they had imbibed a couple of glasses full. As you take a mouthful and let it run drop by drop down your throat, it leaves in your mouth the same aroma as a bouquet of the choicest flowers will offer to your olfactories."

At Schloss Johannisberg the wines "must be tasted to know their magnificence, for it is beyond the powers of description. These wines, like those of the Dukes of Nassau, are occasionally sold at public auction, but at such exorbitant prices that we poor republicans would shudder as much to drink such a costly liquid as if it were molten gold."

To winegrowers not in the stratosphere of the Rheingau the policies of the Prussians made almost as much difference as the weather. To the Palatinate it was the dawn of international (or even national) recognition.

Unlike most monarchs, the Palatine counts paid little attention to their wine-growers. Neither Church nor State was directly concerned. It was the country of proud, scattered, and usually disorganized gentry or local nobility without the means to make their voices heard, or their wines individually known. The Thirty Years War had decimated the region, and so had Louis XIV. Heidelberg Castle, once the seat of the counts, still lies in ruins as a memento of a French visit in the seventeenth century. But in the nineteenth the French made amends. In the words of the great historian of German wine, Dr Bassermann-Jordan, a man of the Palatinate, its winegrowers were "freed and awoken by the French Revolution". The region was even briefly a *département* of France under the name of Mont-Tonnerre. Fine wines had no local market, but the Zollverein gave them their opportunity, and a fortuitous land-tax survey by the Bavarian State in 1828 their specific identity. From the 1830s onwards the names of Deidesheim, Forst, Ruppertsberg, Wachenheim… – all the villages of the Mittelhaardt that had grown wine since Roman times without proper credit – found their place in the community of excellence. In 1841 the first Deidesheimer Auslese appeared and it became clear that the climate and soil of the region, geographically a northern extension of Alsace, are the most suited of all in Germany for the making of Spätlese and Auslese wines.

Alsace meanwhile was caught in the customs trap, excluded from the German market as part of France, which did not want its wine either. It was a painful situation for a region which "needed to export to avoid being drowned in its own wine" – and made worse by the dispirited planting of the heaviest-cropping, lowest-quality vine, the Knipperlé. At the same time Strasbourg became one of Europe's great brewing towns, so the danger of drowning was doubled. Where once Alsace supplied the Black Forest region of Baden across the Rhine (as well as distant markets both down and up the river), Baden began extending its own vineyards. From 1850 even Switzerland closed its borders to the wine that had for centuries been its staple. For Switzerland this meant a spate of creative and experimental planting, particularly in its oldest, warmest, and most fertile region, the Valais, which had had a spell as the

French *département* of Simplon, but had been reunited with its brother cantons in 1815. Such ancient alpine vines as Arvine, Amigne, and Humagne were elbowed aside to make way for Gamay, Sylvaner, even Pinot Noir and Riesling – but above all for Chasselas, or Fendant, which somehow seized the personality of the region to make a uniquely smooth and beguiling drink.

Switzerland's other principal regions on Lakes Geneva and Neuchâtel were already planted solid. We have the ubiquitous Haraszthy's report: "We arrived in Geneva [from Neuchâtel] after travelling eight hours continually among vine-yards… Not a spot as large as an ordinary brick-yard was left uncultivated, with the exception of where the old vines have been cut out to give the ground the necessary three years' rest."

When in 1870 France fell ignominiously to the Prussian armies, it seemed that Alsace would have its reprieve. This shuttlecock region was to be German again until 1918. But Germany regarded the vineyards of the Vosges rather as France did the Midi: never asking anything from it but a low price. In 1871 it represented more than a quarter of all Germany's vineyards and produced (this was the problem) thirty-nine per cent of German wine – unfortunately little of it of the keeping kind. "Furthermore", as the Alsatian Joseph Dreyer wrote, "the clash of personalities between the Alsatians and the Germans was irreconcilable. Each found the other's wine of inferior quality and did not hesitate to say so – with the difference, however, that the German was the buyer and the Alsatian the seller." It remained a sad story, with all but a few ignoring the potential of Alsace for wine of wonderful quality. Many growers who had done their best gave up in despair.

When Napoleon had marched in, Franconia was still been one of Germany's biggest wine producers. More than any, though, it was a domain of the Church, and thus the most affected by secularization. Würzburg reached its apotheosis in the age of the baroque. The "thick wreath of vines" of the Middle Ages still surrounded it; the Prince-Bishop's great Residenz dominated it; its vineyards supported two charity hospitals (one religious, one lay), each almost on the scale of the Hospices de Beaune. Germany's Romantic poets, Goethe and Schiller, took issue on the merits of the famous Stein and Leisten slopes overlooking the town (Goethe's choice was Stein).

Secularization is usually given as the prime cause of its decline – but that was not its effect on the Rheingau. In Würzburg the

trockenbeerenauslese Sweet wines were made whenever the grapes ripened to high levels of sugar, whether nobly-rotten or simply raisined by a hot autumn. No distinction was made, and the terminology was more imaginative than precise. When the word Beerenauslese ("selected grapes") was not emphatic enough to express the richness and rarity of the ultimate gleanings from the vines, *Goldbeerenauslese* and *Edelbeerenauslese* were available superlatives. Today's only legal term is Trockenbeerenauslese ("trocken" – literally "dry" – means that the grapes were shrivelled almost dry, either by rot or by heat). But even in the 1930 wine law this term had no legal definition.

Bavarian state took over the Prince-Bishop's domaine; those of the Julliusspital (the religious hospital) survive, as do those of the Burgerspital. Wine-growing declined in Franconia (as it did in more eastern parts of Germany that once had smaller, but thriving, vineyards) as a result of competition from other occupations – the Industrial Revolution, in other words – and the Bavarian tide of beer. Adverse weather in the nineteenth century has also been blamed and even the taste for tea-drinking. But whatever lowered the morale and profitability of its wine-growers, they were in no condition to fight the fungus plagues of oidium, and later mildew, when they arrived. Franconian wine today is an expensive luxury used, as it always was, by its own devoted citizens.

We left the Mosel in the 1840s struggling with the dreadful weather and the end of its protective Prussian cloak. What saved the Mosel was not the Prussians, but its own inherent quality: given decent weather, its increased plantations of Riesling made uniquely fine wine. Even in bad vintages, Mosel Riesling was excellent material for the rapidly-growing sparkling wine industry modelled on Champagne. By the 1840s steamers had shortened the journey time from Trier to Koblenz from two days to ten hours: the "railway effect", in a sense, came early. The 1850s provided three excellent vintages in a row, leading up, with perfect timing, to Gladstone's Budget that lowered British duties on light wines.

Most important of all, for all of Germany but especially for the Mosel, was the introduction of Chaptal's idea of adding sugar, suggested by the German chemist Ludwig Gall. It seems extraordinary that in this coolest of wine regions, with unripe, low-strength wine a regular problem, the idea had not been seized on before. The explanation must be that people were accustomed to thin wine (which in any case they used as an all-purpose drink, cold or hot and sweetened according to the season). Chaptalization – they called it "*Verbesserung*", or "improving" – gave them the possibility of saleable wine every year. It is enormously to the credit of the Germans that, unlike the French, they continued to prefer their wine natural, even if that meant drinking it pretty mean. As soon as a wine law was framed, in 1892, it made it mandatory to say whether a wine was natural (i.e. without added sugar) or not. That is still the basis of the German wine law – whereas the French long ago persuaded themselves that the systematic addition of sugar to raise the strength of their wine is none of the public's concern.

At first, of course, finding this new way to make their wine not only saleable, but also exportable, the traders of the Mosel over-encouraged sugaring. Good growers resisted. In the region of the Saar, above Trier, they did not give in until the 1920s. But politics once more turned in favour of the Mosel when the war with France in 1870 reminded the Prussians how strategically important their border region was. German prosperity now meant a national market. Wine merchants learned that by using sugar containing starch they could give their wine something approximately like the rich texture of an Auslese. In doing so they blotted out the delicate transparency of flavour which makes each good Mosel an individual. This struggle, between a gross commodity, cheap to produce and easy to sell, and what I can only call an intellectual one, with specific aesthetic appeal, in one guise or another has occupied the minds of growers, merchants and legislators ever since.

At this juncture, in the last decades of the nineteenth century, the temptation to produce volume at the expense of quality could hardly have been greater. Over the previous half-century the country's vineyard area had shrunk by as much as half, while the spending-power of the population, especially in the industrial North, had enormously increased. For the first time, Germany was a net importer of wine.

Not so much by intervention and diversification, as by training, legislation, and example, Prussia showed an admirable determination that quality was to be Germany's destiny. Without at first being precisely clear what it meant by pure wine, it declared itself in favour; then in a second law it allowed sugaring, but made any sort of "falsification" a criminal offence.

Perhaps the government's most effective move was to found a state wine school, still one of the world's most famous, at Geisenheim in the Rheingau in 1872, followed by model wine estates near Trier and on the Nahe. The idea of a model wine from a model cellar is perfectly characteristic of Prussian thinking. It allows us to ask the question: what was the ideal German wine of 1900?

It was a Riesling, certainly completely dry, unless it was a Spätlese. There was no ambition to make the type of fruitily fresh wine which is the fashion today – nor any means of adding and controlling sweetness, such as the twentieth century produced. High natural acidity and forceful flavour (the result of a harvest a fraction of the size a modern vine produces) was tempered by long aging in old oak casks, which also served to stabilize it perfectly. Such a wine would strike us as bold, austere, penetrating: an aristocrat, and an unbending one until it mellowed with age. Like a fine Pinot Noir from the Côte d'Or, its terroir would determine its precise flavours: its affinity with apples or peaches, slate or smoke or steel.

A Spätlese, on the other hand, would keep some natural sweetness, and an Auslese a great deal. The natural yeasts were not capable of finishing the fermentation to complete dryness, so the wine was stabilized with a dose of sulphur and left for time to do its work. After several years in cask the sulphur tang would disappear and the wine be totally stable, its sweetness again not fresh and fruity, but deep and satisfying. Such wines created connoisseurs by the very precision of their distinctions. "Intellectual" is the inevitable word.

To compare Prussia and Austria is the best way to emphasize the direction Germany had taken and the progress it had made in the nineteenth century. Within the Austrian Empire lay all the vineyards of Hungary, of the eastern Adriatic and the Tyrol. In total hectarage of vines the Empire had more than half as much as France, twice as much as the Italian states, and three times as much as Spain. Yet the only wine of "first-growth" standing it produced was Tokaji – indeed, all Vienna's best wines came from Hungary.

The shores of a windswept Lake Geneva. The Swiss vineyards reached their greatest extent, of some 34,400 hectares, in 1884; their current size is about one-third of that.

The liberal Emperor – "enlightened" is the usual term – Joseph II laid down in 1784 the simplest wine law of all: growers could only sell their own wine. Vienna's uproarious *Büschenken* and *Heurigen*, the wine-grower's cellar and his garden, turned into a perpetual party, celebrated to this day.

Happily we have an expert witness to the wines of the Empire on display. Henry Vizetelly was the official British judge at Vienna's Universal Exhibition in 1873, which claimed to be the first at which all the wines of the world were to be judged in competition together. Austria did not win many prizes.

"The wines of Austria", wrote Vizetelly "are as diverse as its population. At the extreme south [he is speaking of Dalmatia] they are so dark and fullbodied that when mixed with an equal quantity of water they are quite as deep in colour and as spirituous as the ordinary wines of Bordeaux… while in less favourable districts they are excessively poor and so sour as to rasp the tongue like the roughest cider. Many [these will be the Hungarians] have the luscious character of Constantia and the muscat growths of Frontignan and Lunel. Several, on the other hand, are disagreeably bitter [Tyroleans, perhaps?], others again are so astringent as to contract the windpipe while swallowing them, whereas a few of the lighter varieties possess the delicacy, if not the fragrance, of certain growths of the Rheingau. [Could these have been the Wachau contingent from the Danube?] It must be confessed, however, that although the specimens were remarkably varied and numerous, the better qualities were extremely rare."

CHAPTER 38

WHEN SORROWS COME

In March 1862 the Emperor Louis-Napoleon invited France's greatest scientist, Louis Pasteur, to the palace of the Tuileries to consult him on an extremely serious problem. Something was going badly wrong with France's wine, and at a time of unprecedented exports, boosted by the new gospel of Free Trade. An embarrassing number of bottles bought by reputable merchants and delivered to important foreign customers were turning out undrinkable. The good name of France, and of its most famous industry, was at stake. In the name of the Empire, said Louis-Napoleon, could the great *savant* investigate and report?

If it is surprising to read this, when France had been exporting wine without such problems (at least in such acute forms) for so many centuries, we should remember that the wines in question came largely from the 1850s, the period of the oidium crisis. One must suspect (although Pasteur does not refer to it) that the vines weakened by the disease were in turn producing disease-prone wine.

Pasteur's fame rested largely on his having discovered that fermentation is due to the action of yeast cells in reproducing. To find out why wines turned sour or vinegary he put samples of healthy wine under his microscope, along with wines with *tourne*, *pousse*, *graisse* – all the diseases that could make it undrinkable. Each slide was like a different cage in a zoo, peopled with entirely different, easily recognizable, microscopic creatures. It was only a step to identifying which of these bacteria was responsible for which wine disease. After a while, he said, he could tell by looking at a slide sample of a wine what it would taste like. His

breakthrough came when he proved that these bacteria, like all creatures, need oxygen to live and reproduce. Sealed in a test-tube without air, wine remained stable; with air its resident bacteria took over. The commonest, in fact the one which is present in all wine, is the vinegar bacterium. If wine is left exposed to air it will sooner or later turn to vinegar.

Pasteur's practical answer bears his name: pasteurization. It consisted simply of heating the wine in its bottle in a sort of *bain-marie* of hot water for long enough to kill the microbes or bacteria. He demonstrated that this could be done without giving the wine a cooked taste or otherwise affecting its ability to mature normally.

"When sorrows come, they come not single spies, but in battalions." Not a year after the scientist with the microscope had saved France's wine from spoiling, a foe appeared that threatened something far more drastic: literally to cut off the nation's wine supply at the roots. Within a quarter of a century the vineyards of France, and, via France, Europe – finally, some four-fifths of the vineyards of the world – were to feel like Pharaoh at odds with Moses and his God – for if seven is a biblical number, so is three. Oidium was the first plague. Its cure (or rather control) took only a decade. After oidium came phylloxera, and after phylloxera, mildew. They not only devastated all but a privileged minority of vineyards; they also altered fundamentally and permanently the way vines are grown. Wine, you might say, ended its state of innocence with the multiplied catastrophes that followed hard on its Golden Age. For many marginal vineyards it was the end. At the same time it put the strong in a stronger position than ever before. Nothing was to be the same again after the long struggle to protect and re-establish wine-growing in Europe – a process that in some cases took three-quarters of a century.

Pasteur needed a microscope to see the organisms that he brought under control. If you have good enough eyesight to see a pin-prick you can see a phylloxera louse without a lens. But it was still the minute size of this overactive animal that allowed it to escape detection. It had already been frustrating would-be winegrowers for centuries. Phylloxera was the culprit for the failure of Jefferson's, and every other eastern American's, imported vines. If they blamed the climate, the soil or more obvious bugs, it was because they never saw the real cause – nor did it ever occur to them that there might be an all-but-invisible pest to which the native vines had become immune.

It was the speed of steamships that brought phylloxera to Europe alive. Many must have set off on sailing ships, snug in bundles of American vine-cuttings or on the roots of potted plants being sent to Europe for ornament or experiment. None survived the weeks at sea. By the 1850s black-smoke-belching steamers had brought the passage down to nine or ten days. At the European port a train was waiting. Suddenly the tiny pest was in a larder that stretched to infinity. For it arrived just where the vines were thickest, at the mouth of the Rhône.

Bordeaux, Burgundy, Champagne, and the vineyards of old renown and new money were not alone in enjoying a Golden Age at this time. Between 1825 and 1850 the vineyards of the central *département* of the Languedoc, the Hérault, doubled in size. They were reacting to a popular taste for red wine that jumped by almost ten litres a head in each decade from 1848 to the 1870s. Very much to their advantage, too, was the boom, on northern farms that previously had grown vines, of cereals and sugar-beet to feed the surging urban population. When in the 1850s the Paris–Lyon–Marseilles railway reached the Languedoc from the industrial North the crisis of oidium had just passed in a cloud of sulphur dust. There was a gold-rush feeling in the air. Steamers from Sète were distributing tens of thousands of barrels to customers from Russia to America, but above all to the thirsty colonists in France's new acquisition, Algeria.

Inexorably the vineyard swept down from the hills to claim the fertile sweep of the coastal plain. Between 1850 and 1875 France added 202,500 hecatres (500,000 acres) to its vineyards; 131,625 (325,000) of them in the Languedoc. Cereals, olives, vegetables – every other crop was cast aside. Trade was free, money was easy, and Nemesis was standing in the wings.

The peculiar reproductive habits of the phylloxera need not concern us. They are complicated, but highly effective. A small import soon became a considerable population. Its effect on the vines was first noticed near Arles in Provence in 1863. Patches of vines, gradually spreading outwards from the country at the mouth of the Rhône, both east and west, were described as having "consumptive symptoms". They were acting rather like a patient with tuberculosis: their leaves withering and dropping, their new shoots without vigour, their fruit unripe. Three years after the symptoms appeared the vine was usually dead.

The habits of the phylloxera, as well as its size, made it a particularly hard villain to track down, because by the time the corpse was dug up for a post mortem, the culprits had moved on to feed from, and in due course kill, another vine.

The most striking aspect of the dead vine, when it was unearthed for inspection, was that its root system had virtually disappeared, and for no apparent reason. By 1866 a minority of proprietors in the affected zones (the numbers of the louse were just beginning to become significant) were voicing their concern, which was taken up by the agricultural press. The most active of these proprietors was the Montpellier stockbroker Gaston Bazille, father of the Impressionist painter Frédéric, who had invested heavily in vineyards. Bazille met the Professor of Pharmacy at Montpellier University, Jules-Emile Planchon, a man of many talents who had studied with the greatest of the Directors of Kew Gardens in London, Sir William Hooker. One of Planchon's many interests was entomology.

In July 1868 Bazille, Planchon, and assistants convened at a wine estate, the Château de Lagoy, near St Rémy, twenty-four kilometres (fifteen miles) from Arles, to get to the root of the mystery. A contemporary print shows them swarming among the vines, magnifying-glasses in hands, wearing top hats in the summer sun. There were flourishing, sick, and dead vines in

Pasteur was regarded as a national hero. He introduced asepis in surgery and discovered a vaccine for rabies. It is, however, the process of pasteurization that bears his name.

how to fake wine These times produced rich pickings for the unscrupulous. Chronic shortages (total French wine production fell by almost a half in the 1880s) pushed up the price of real wine inexorably. Wines previously considered fit only for vinegar or distillation now found a ready market, without coming close to making good the deficit. Apart from simply adding water, which *cabarets* had always done, the readiest answer was to fabricate wine from raisins, imported mainly from Greece and Turkey. Raisin imports before the crisis were only a few thousand tons a year (and were used mainly by *pâtissiers*). By the 1880s that figure had reached a million – mainly into such southern ports as Marseilles and Sète. A book published in 1880 in Marseilles was called simply *How to Make Wine from Raisins*. Twelve editions were called for within half as many years.

The alternative, simple way to produce fake wine was with beet sugar. Massive planting in the north of France had brought its price down to a very modest level. Chaptal would have turned in his grave to see the parody of his proposal in a *piquette* made of hot water poured on pressed grape skins and fermented with enough beet sugar to provide its entire alcohol content. This method doubled the amount of wine made from a given quantity of grapes. Figures are not available to tell us what proportion of the Frenchman's daily intake was produced like this.

---

the vineyard. For the first time they dug up healthy vines as well as affected ones.

What they saw, when they dug up an affected vine, was a seething mass of the tiniest aphids, mere pin-pricks individually but in such numbers that "the roots appeared to be varnished yellow". If this was the louse stage, Planchon realized, this insect must also have a winged phase of life. He soon found it, still needing a magnifying glass to see it: "an elegant little aphid with four flat, transparent wings". As an entomologist he recognized it as being similar to one that causes galls on oak leaves: *Phylloxera quercus*. Looking around at the dead vines, their roots entirely consumed by the incalculable numbers of the pest, he named it *Phylloxera vastatrix* – "the devastator". At this stage its origin was quite unknown; America was not even under suspicion – and indeed the majority of opinion was still that something so tiny could not possibly be the cause of vigorous plants dying wholesale.

There were good reasons to worry. By 1867 the symptoms had been spotted in the *palus* vineyards of Bordeaux. But nobody in France who was not personally and immediately affected was likely to be interested in a few dying vines, when the whole nation was moving (as they thought) into one of its hours of glory. The free-trading, liberal-thinking Empire of Louis Napoleon combined glamour and squalor, chic and corruption. Another Universal Exhibition in Paris in 1868 was to celebrate commercial triumph. In 1869 came the opening of the French-planned Suez Canal, and in 1870, infused with *folie de grandeur*, the Emperor decided on a trial of strength with Bismarck's Prussia. It was France's shortest and most inglorious war. Within weeks Prussia was besieging Paris, and withdrew only on payment of 1,460 tons of gold (raised from the public by government bonds at six per cent) and the transfer of long-suffering Alsace and Lorraine to Germany. No sooner had the Prussians left than the two-month revolution of the Commune gripped the capital. Lucky the

winegrowers of the South, one might well have said, whose worst problem was some dying vines.

With such general unconcern, the devastator had a flying start. Planchon and a growing number of associates had been working as an official Commission since 1869; yet in 1872 the Société d'Agriculture of the Gironde put up a prize of a mere 20,000 francs, scarcely enough to buy a second-hand carriage, for an effective remedy. The list of suggestions makes good light reading. Thousands of useless ideas came pouring in, ranging from burying a toad under each vine (this was borrowed from Pliny), to exorcism, to beating the ground mechanically until the pest was driven into the sea (or over a frontier).

By this time two principal lines of serious research were being followed: one the elimination of the pest; the other, somehow to find a vine which was immune to its attack. It was found that under certain circumstances the bug could be eliminated. If a vineyard could be completely flooded for a period the aphids would drown. Unfortunately the few flat vineyards where this was a practical proposition were the least valuable for the quality of their wine. A vineyard of more or less pure sand was also apparently immune: the louse could make no headway through its shifting grains. Both these solutions – the flooding and the sand – were an invitation to plant the flat coastal strip of the Languedoc. The Salins du Midi, the rich sea-salt extraction company which exploits the lagoons at Aigues-Mortes, beyond the marshy Camargue, found itself with an extremely profitable second string to its bow as the crisis deepened and more vineyards were destroyed. It planted the enormous, and hitherto useless, beaches with vines that give the most wine (and never mind the quality), the Carignan and Aramon.

In most vineyards the only hope of elimination was by chemical means: fumigating the soil. The chemist Baron Paul Thénard discovered that a substance called carbon bisulphide, made by passing sulphur vapour over red-hot charcoal, was extremely toxic to phylloxera – and to most other creatures too. Injected into the soil around the vines, it left nothing alive. In his early trials he was over-generous with the poison and killed the vines as well. The fumes made workers ill, and anyone standing downwind was at risk. It was also so inflammable that an explosion was a strong possibility.

Fumigation of one kind or another was widely used from the early 1870s onwards, right into the twentieth century; indeed until the 1940s there were vineyards in France where phylloxera was kept at bay by soil injection with an instrument like a giant hypodermic syringe, an inexpressibly tedious, and terribly expensive, operation.

A more effective alternative was watering the vineyard with a solution of sulphocarbonate of potassium (or sodium), but the gear that was required – pumps, miles of pipes, nozzles, and above all a huge amount of water – was either unobtainable or so hugely expensive that only "first-growths" could afford it. Some did, notwithstanding. Until the First World War a number of great vineyards in the Médoc were paying contractors to disinfect their soil every year, in addition to sulphuring against oidium and the tedious treatments that became essential when a second form of mildew became rampant in the 1880s.

The routine of growing wine had changed beyond recognition: from a simple, although labour-intensive, matter of pruning, cultivating, weeding, occasionally replanting, and gathering in the harvest, to a seemingly endless round of applying smelly substances to protect the vines from being consumed by insects and fungi. The alternative was to find a vine that resisted all these onslaughts.

The thought had first occurred during the oidium crisis: perhaps American vines might be resistant. Ironically enough, it may well have been the import of vines for oidium trials that introduced the phylloxera. It had simply not occurred to anyone, with the botanic gardens of the world excitedly filling up with exotic plants, that each plant has its pests, and that some of them might bring catastrophe in a new environment.

American vines had been tried in France before, in sailing-ship days. The foxy flavour of their wine had ruled them out. 1869 was the year when, from several directions at once, they began to look as though they might hold a solution. To credit the idea, or the work, to any single person is impossible; in the end scores of scientists were involved. But in that year Monsieur Laliman from Bordeaux noted that some imported vines appeared phylloxera-proof. At a congress at Beaune, Gaston Bazille suggested grafting: perhaps a French vine-top might "take" on an American root – he did not know then whether American roots would resist the pest or not. The theoretical proposition that they must came from another Montpellier scientist, Gaston Fouex, who was a keen follower of the still (in France) unfashionable Darwinism. He argued that if the phylloxera was a European insect it would long ago have wiped out the European vine; therefore it must be the native of a country where it could live its parasitic life without killing its host.

There were many questions to be answered before firm conclusions could be drawn. Assuming that grafting would work, and that French vine-tops could be united with American roots, would the flavour of the wine be affected? Which of the American species would take to the very different soils of Europe? Eastern America generally has acid soil; Europe's best vineyards just the opposite: alkaline soils, rich in lime. And which vines could most easily be propagated in the industrial quantities that would be needed?

Frenchmen in areas already affected would grasp at straws; any American rootstock was worth trying. Others, in regions the phylloxera had not yet reached, were highly sceptical about the whole idea. Chemical methods of control were much preferred by growers who could afford them. In the end they had the benefit of learning from others' mistakes; for phylloxera, outside the devastated south of France, was a drama played in slow motion. Ten years passed between its being reported in Bordeaux and reaching the best parts of the Médoc. It was not reported in Burgundy (in Meursault) until 1878. Inevitably a split developed between growers of Pinot Noir for fine wines, who dreaded losing their purity of flavour, and could afford to

fumigate, and Gamay-growers who wanted to graft and get on with it. It was nine years before American roots were allowed by the authorities, under pressure from the prosperous. As a result many American plants were smuggled in, not even to be grafted but to be used as *producteurs directes*. Even today it is possible to find a peasant grower in many parts of France who hoards a little supply of his strawberry-flavoured wine that he privately admits to liking.

As for Champagne, it was the last region of all to be attacked; not until 1901 did phylloxera appear along the Marne. But here the argument worked the other way round. The rich, having learned from the rest of France, knew that the best policy was a massive grafting programme. Small growers, who are the backbone of Champagne, saw it all as a plot to gain control of their vineyards.

If a forty-year crisis can have a critical moment it came in the 1880s. The scientists were polarized: chemists against grafters. At the International Phylloxera Conference in Bordeaux in 1881 the *sulphuristes* and the *Americanistes* presented their opposing points of view in heated debate. Whichever side won (and neither did conclusively), there were enormous physical problems to be overcome. George Ordish, the phylloxera historian, has calculated that there were about eleven billion vines in France. American roots for every one would need a length of two million miles of grafting wood, on to which 230,000 tons of French bud-wood would have to be grafted. These figures assume that all the grafts "took", and that all the roots were suitable. In practice, many of the early shipments of American vines intensely disliked the soil: it was not until after several years of laborious breeding programmes that truly compatible rootstocks for different sorts of soil, particularly alkaline ones, were created. That in the long run there would be distinct advantages in custom-made roots was too positive a thought for these dark days, for from 1878 the third of the Pharaonic plagues burst upon France with a suddenness and ferocity that eclipsed even phylloxera.

The enormous imports of American vine-wood had brought with them a new and voracious form of mildew, known as "downy" to distinguish it from the "powdery" oidium. Like

survivors of the plague Here and there among regions whose vines were wiped out by phylloxera there remain small patches which have unaccountably survived. One such is a few rows of vines in the port country, at Quinta do Noval; another, two small blocks of Pinot Noir at Aÿ in Champagne, belonging to the house of Bollinger. The Champagne vines are still propagated by *provignage*, or layering, which became obsolete when all vines theoretically needed grafting. Both the Nacional wines made by Noval, and the Vieilles Vignes Françaises made by Bollinger exclusively from "pre-phylloxera" vines, have a certain quality and depth of flavour that sets them apart. For port it is highly desirable, but the view of Bollinger's president is that Champagne from ungrafted vines (which produce small quantities of highly concentrated juice) is too "fat" for modern tastes. On this evidence, partly by helping to increase the crop, grafted vines seem to have given the wine of the twentieth century a lighter and more elegant touch.

oidium, it reduced the crop drastically and weakened the resulting wine. It took only four years for the Faculty of Science at Bordeaux to find a preventative: the famous "Bordeaux mixture", a combination of copper-sulphate and lime in liquid form that stains everything it touches brilliant blue. But the decade of the 1880s suffered acutely from ruined vintages, from farmers at their wits' ends trying to understand, to master, and to afford new remedies and routines, and, inevitably, from an unstoppable surge of faked and fraudulent wine.

For Spain, Portugal, Italy, all of France's competitors, the advent of phylloxera seemed at once a threat and an opportunity. In the long run their great gain was the encouragement to challenge France with quality wines. But France was the world's biggest producer and consumer of wine by such a margin that whatever happened to its industry affected everyone. Up to 1870 it had been a net exporter by a proportion of eight to one. By 1880 it was a net importer by three to one and in 1887, at the height of the crisis, imported twelve million hectolitres and exported two.

The immediate gainers by this reversal of France's role were the bulk suppliers of Spain and Italy. Although they too were reached by the aphid (Italy gradually from the early 1870s; Spain progressively from 1878) they went on a planting spree to provide dark blending wine to boost the pallid French production. France, meanwhile, having been attacked first, had discovered the solution, painful though it was. Its neighbours and rivals had the advantage of being prepared. They could begin grafting their vines as soon as falling production demanded it. The Italian government even discouraged treatment, to lower the surplus pouring from its vast new southern vineyards. Germany, with cool efficiency, at first seemed almost successfully to have denied the aphids a visa. By 1900 only 1.5 per cent of German vines had been attacked.

Algeria was the new recruit. At first France had looked on its new colony as a market for wine, not a supplier; in the 1880s this policy was dramatically reversed. Rather than import its needs from Italy and Spain, France would grow its own wine in North Africa. There were thousands of ruined wine-growers eager to emigrate. Algeria's vineyards (even in pre-French days the Algerians enjoyed their wine) multiplied ten times in the last twenty years of the nineteenth century, despite phylloxera, which found its way across in 1885.

I t has often been said (and was said very loudly at the time) that after phylloxera wines from even the best vineyards lacked something of the quality they had had before. It would be surprising indeed if nothing had changed. To isolate any one aspect as responsible, particularly grafting onto American roots, is to oversimplify the total revolution brought about by one deadly pest and two recurring diseases. Nor were they the only problems; two new parasites, the *eudemis* and *cochylis* grubs, added their nuisance value to the problems of every grower.

One natural reaction was to be over-generous with the fertilizer. Even in such austerely-controlled vineyards as the Médoc "first-growths", harvests surprisingly increased in the 1880s, when the vines were affected by both phylloxera and mildew. The soil-sterilizer sulphocarbonate was itself a fertilizer, but managers experimented with both organic and chemical compounds, trying to keep up the crop and to give vigour to the threatened vines. At Château Latour experiments were made with ground roast leather to put pep into the vines.

The aim of top-quality producers was to fight for the life of each vine and replace them individually as they died. A high proportion of old vines lies at the heart of the idea of a *grand vin*. Once a vine was dead, it could easily be pulled out of the ground with a simple pulley; there were no roots left to resist. Small proprietors took a deep breath and got it over with, uprooting their whole vineyards and replanting with grafted plants as quickly as they could. It is difficult to exaggerate, though, how hard the proprietors of great châteaux fought their losing rearguard action. Again, as in the 1840s, they were obliged to contract for several vintages to the Chartronnais, and the Chartronnais stipulated no grafting on American roots. This was as late as the years up to the First World War. In Burgundy it was not until 1945 that the old ungrafted vines of Romanée-Conti were pulled up.

The first two decades of the twentieth century proved to be the worst of all. The recently planted grafted vines were under attack by mildew in any humid weather, needing regular spraying at great expense. Now oidium returned to batten on the struggling young plants. At the same time the results of over-fertilizing inflated the quantity and diluted the quality. Prices fell, and even "first-growths" were losing serious money.

As if this were not enough, the impudence of the *fraudeurs* knew no bounds. If they were going to offer bogus Bordeaux or burgundy, why not go the whole way and label it with a "first-growth" label? Public reaction was only natural. Everyone had heard of the recurring plagues. What might the sulphur and the copper treatments do to the consumer? It is a familiar cry, and it gave the Scotch whisky industry its great opportunity. Suddenly the fashionable drinks were Scotch and mineral water. There was to be no general recovery of the prestige and profitability of wine for over fifty years.

T he final score of the half-century that followed the Golden Age in France is not easy to draw up. Most dramatically, it reduced the total area of vines in France by almost one-third; thirty per cent of what was destroyed has never been replaced. Whole regions where the vine was a marginal crop gave it up altogether. To counterbalance this the Languedoc replanted to excess. In 1875 it had seventeen per cent of France's vines; today it has twenty-seven per cent, and most of them on rich farm land which, in the graphic local phrase, *fait pisser la vigne*. Its decline from the hills to the plain can be plotted in its ever-increasing productivity. One acre (0.4 hectares) of vines produced three times as much wine in 1900 as in 1800, and today produces three times as much again.

The positive good that years of crisis did was to bring science into what was too often the hermetic ignorance of unquestioned tradition, and government into affairs it had generally been content to leave alone.

CHAPTER 39

RISORGIMENTO

Wine is even more central to the identity of Italy than it is to that of France. The name the Greeks gave to the peninsula was the Land of Wine. It has no single province where the vine is not at ease; and when the moment came, in the nineteenth century, for Italy at last to become a single nation, it was reforming landowners, men preoccupied with the agriculture of their respective provinces who, like sagacious senators of old, brought about the Risorgimento of their country.

To the creators of modern Italy, oidium and the Austrians were both deadly enemies. It was the warrior Garibaldi who persuaded the peasants to save their vines with sulphur. The stories of viticultural and political change are warp and woof in the epic of their doings.

That most impartial of reporters, André Jullien, wrote of Italian wine in the early nineteenth century in terms of disappointment more than condemnation: "The soil of Italy is famous for its fertility. Its climate and the long chain of mountains that stretch from the Alps to the foot of Calabria, offering in their length every variety of soil and situation favourable to the vine, seem to justify the name of Oenotria that the ancients gave it. One could believe that this country produces the best wines of Europe; but while the people of less favoured lands are busy choosing the best vines to suit their intemperate seasons, the Italians, accustomed to seeing the vine grow almost spontaneously, and everywhere give ripe fruit, never even try to maximize their advantages. Being sure of a sufficient crop, they neglect the care of their plants, even in the districts where the quality of their produce invites

attention… One can find dessert wines of extremely good quality, but those for daily consumption, which might be called 'mellow', cannot be compared with their equivalents in France. Most of them are at the same time sweet and sharp, often coarse, and even when they appear to have plenty of body and strength, travel badly and rapidly decline, even without having travelled. Their bad quality comes not only from neglect in cultivation, but even more from sheer bad winemaking."

Almost all Italian vines, Jullien goes on to say, are grown up trees, forming high curtains of foliage while the farmer plants his grain and beans below – in the words of Jules Guyot, the philosopher-scientist of French wine, "a liberty, equality and vegetable fraternity that destroyed three-quarters of their vigour and fecundity". It is precisely the method described by Pliny, still being faithfully followed at the time of the Napoleonic wars.

"What object has an Italian in labouring to improve that which cannot by improvement turn out of the slightest profit to himself? Trampled by the Austrian military, or by the feet of native tyrants, destitute of adequate capital, and weighed down by a vexatious system of imposts, what has he to hope for?" This, with the utmost sympathy, was Cyrus Redding, despairing over the Italy where the patriot bands of Carbonari were beginning to rise in liberal revolutions.

That the country was fragmented was not itself the problem: when had it not been since the fall of Rome? It was partly the very ease with which the ancient land of vines could find its sustenance that held it in a time-warp. Certainly atrocious government and exploitation played their part, but

there is also the question of geography to consider. Italy lies surrounded by lands that also grow the vine; where but in its own cities would its wine-growers find a market? Naples and Rome were its only substantial cities, and they both lacked the prerequisite for a healthy wine trade: a numerous middle class.

Italy did once have an export business. Venice in the fourteenth century had been one of the centres of the world's wine trade, creating "Greek-style" wine in the Veronese hills. The Florentine renaissance had seen a ripple, if not a flood, of international interest in flasks of Florence wine. And in the eighteenth century we have seen an English epicure working his way down the peninsula looking for, and finding, sweet and fragrant wines. If Italy had anything approaching a five-star wine in international eyes, it was Lacryma Christi from Vesuvius.

Italy and the outside world agreed that its wines fell into two categories: those from the tree-clinging vines which formed the great majority, and the staked vines that, just as they had done two thousand years before, marked out the areas of Greek influence. These were the wines, if any, that the world looked for from Italy: wines that were strong and sweet, or at any rate sweet, made in the Greek tradition. Exceptions to this rule were rare. Renaissance Florence undoubtedly drank good wine more or less in the Chianti style – though it was more famous for its strong Vernaccia and sweet Aleatico and *vin santo*. We cannot imagine the Medici, or indeed the Borgias, raising jewelled chalices, poisoned or not, of a thin and vinegary drink because it was the best their great estates could produce. The Antinori family is proud to have been selling Florentine wine from the fourteenth century; the Frescobaldi, too, whom we have met as bankers all over medieval Europe, traded in wine and textiles.

On the threshold of its independence Italy had no export market for anything but its sweet wines. Variety it certainly had; there were many hundreds, if not thousands, of local sorts of vine, and local ways of using them. But only rarely, even in the villas and castles of the aristocracy (including the aristocracy of the Church), was wine made with any care and knowledge, and it was not at that time the fashion for noblemen to offer their wine for sale at their palace doors.

Tuscany was where reform tentatively began, under the Grand Duke Peter Leopold, a Hapsburg by descent and a vassal of Austria in fact, but nonetheless a worthy successor to the long line of Medici Grand Dukes. His twenty-five years of rule, ended by the armies of the French Revolution, were notable for liberal policies – at least towards trade and the landowning class. Such families as the Capponi, Ridolfi, and Firidolfi-Ricasoli were, at least in theory, the Florentine equivalent of the Townshends and Cokes who were dedicated to modernizing their great Norfolk estates in England – with the crucial difference of the still-feudal Italian concept of the peasant bound to his plot. If Tuscany's land-holding system had been capable of reform, progress might have been made, but the deeply conservative peasants were accustomed to the *mezzadria*, the system of crop-sharing by which they never gained a greater share of their land. Even if their equally conservative landlords had wanted to change the system, the toilers would have thought it was a plot against their ancient tenure of the soil.

Napoleon's wars were over, Metternich had tidied up, and Tuscany was back in Austrian hands, when Baron Bettino Ricasoli inherited Brolio, the heavily indebted estate of his ancient family. To the Ricasolis the Medicis had been parvenues; they themselves were (and are) the true *noblesse d'epée*, tracing their lineage back to Lombard barons of the eleventh century. When the baron moved from Florence to his family's neglected estates (some say to put his beautiful young wife at a distance from the temptations of society), the reform of his property and its wine became his ruling passion.

In his researches he travelled through France and Germany studying every possible way of growing vines. He imported countless varieties, with an almost Haraszthyan hunger to try everything. Chianti Classico emerged from his experiments as the Italian equivalent of Pontac's "new French claret" – not, however, by adopting new varieties, but by rationalizing the old. Ricasoli finally narrowed his model down to the three Tuscan grapes that he found harmonized, to make what Pepys would have called a most particular flavour. He wrote of his findings that "Chianti wine draws most of its bouquet (which is what I aim for) from Sangioveto; from Canaiolo a sweetness that tempers the harshness of the latter without detracting from its bouquet; whereas Malvasia (which could be used less in wines that are to be aged) tends to accentuate the taste, while at the same time making it fresher and lighter and more suitable for daily use at table."

Alas, Ricasoli was denied the satisfaction of seeing his formula accepted as a fine wine by the world. In 1848 (the year of revolutions in Italy as in the rest of Europe) his countess died and his taste for his estates and their reform was swept away in his grief – and perhaps the new calling he found as a politician. In the 1850s oidium, the powdery mildew, struck, and the crop-sharing peasants, the *mezzadri*, abandoned the land in droves, flocking to cities or to America. The Brolio estate grew by 300 little farms as the *mezzadri* left their vines untended and their cottages to crumble.

Piedmont was the one other area of Italy whose landowners had traditionally, if not consistently, taken their wine production seriously. In the Middle Ages the nearness of Genoa had had its effect. Genoa, like Venice, had little land of its own but lived by and for the sea. Its hinterland, admittedly a stiff climb over the coastal Ligurian Alps, is the sheltered and fertile basin of Piedmont before the main body of the Alps begins: a basin only in a relative sense, as its Monferrato hills about the towns of Alba and Asti have steeper slopes and higher ridges than the hills of Tuscany.

Pietro de Crescenzi, author of the *Liber Ruralium Commodorum*, lived as a judge at Asti in the fourteenth century at the time when "Greek" wines were in high demand. The grapes here, he wrote, were left to overripen on the vines with their stalks half-twisted. Because this was impractical in high festoons among the trees, the vines of Moscato and Malvasia, newly introduced to make "Greek" wine, began to be short-pruned and staked. For centuries both kinds of vineyards continued side by side, *altinis et spanis*: proof that the growing of strong and aromatic wines was a specialized, and more profitable, branch of viticulture, practised by owners of land who did not have to subsist on what they grew. It is tempting to equate *spanna*, the name for a vine-stake, with the local name given in Novara to the Nebbiolo, the best of their vines.

References to the Nebbiolo as the grape of choice in Piedmont go back to the thirteenth century. It was to be joined by many others – red Dolcetto in the sixteenth century, white Cortese and red Barbera in the seventeenth – yet none of them is favourably mentioned in the early nineteenth century for anything but sweet wine. Jullien does not even consider the dry reds of the region. The King of Sardinia and his court imported their table wines from France, while much of the crude production of their tree-hung vines went to quench thirsts in neighbouring Milan, the capital of Lombardy and under Austrian control.

How often has the customs officer played the part of Messenger for some significant twist to our story? The Methuen Treaty, the Zollverein, and Gladstone's Budget are only three examples. It was the customs officer who blew the whistle for the Risorgimento. In 1833 the Austrian government had lowered duties on Piedmontese wines imported into its North Italian Empire of Lombardy, the Veneto, and Emilia in the Northeast. In 1846, under pressure from its wine-growers, notably the Hungarians, Austria doubled the tariff, and cut Piedmont off from its one export market. The following year Count Camillo Cavour, a landowner on the Ricasoli model in the Monferrato hills, who had been to England to study advanced farming methods, founded the newspaper called *Risorgimento*. In the same year King Carlo Alberti used the Agricultural Congress at Casal Monferrate to denounce the Austrians in terms that smacked of war.

Piedmont went into the war of 1848 alone, fought two battles against the veteran General Radetzky at Custoza and Novara in Lombardy, and lost. Carlo Alberti abdicated in favour of his son, Vittorio Emanuele II. Garibaldi, meanwhile, briefly succeeded in establishing a Roman Republic and became the country's hero. Cavour, now Prime Minister in Turin, was forced to turn to France for help as troubles descended. Napoleon III was to be his ally against Austria, and French wine science his aid as the invasion of oidium decimated the Piedmontese vines.

Sulphuring was known to control oidium, as Bordeaux had discovered, but who could persuade the peasantry to spray their vines, which sprawled in the tree-tops? The answer was Giuseppe Garibaldi, a son of Nice (then part of the kingdom of Sardinia) and so not only a national but also a local hero. When in 1856 only those growers who had used sulphur had any grapes to pick, Garibaldi's stock as a miracle-worker was at its height.

I n scarcely any part of Italy is "tradition" so revered, or so often given as the reason for this procedure or that, as in Piedmont. Yet hardly anywhere does tradition mean so short a span of time. In the Risorgimento years Piedmont's wines were reinvented, not by seeking to perfect an old formula but by hiring professional advice from France. The Marchese Falletti of Barolo did the recruiting, and Louis Oudart was the wine scientist he found. Cavour, with his own estate at Grinzane in Barolo, became his second client. The Frenchman found the Nebbiolo grapes superb, but could not understand why they were not fermented into a dry red wine. There was no inherent reason but bad wine-making: the fermentation died away but never finished, leaving the wine rather sweet and very unstable. Ripe grapes and a clean cellar were all that was needed. As the 1850s progressed the wine we know today as Barolo emerged: dark, potent, dry, and stable, with almost limitless potential to age.

Piedmont had no such thing until Falletti and Cavour commissioned Oudart's researches. If it could be done with Nebbiolo there were other possibilities for other grapes. Oudart set up his own establishment at Neive in Barbaresco, and the new King, an eager supporter of Cavour's reforms, dedicated his magnificent shooting-lodge and romantic retreat of Fontanafredda in the hills at Serralunga d'Alba, in the heart of the Barolo country, to making the revolutionary new wine.

Political considerations were next on this curiously interwoven agenda. Cavour's reforms included the roads and railways (which greatly helped the distribution of wine), the army, industry, and the financial system. In Turin he was laying the foundation of a workable Italian state.

The climax of the Risorgimento came in 1860. Ricasoli the winemaker was now virtual dictator of Tuscany – and he was fixed on union with Cavour. The southern half of Italy was now united to the Kingdom of Sardinia; Tuscany had voted for union as Ricasoli had told it to do. At this moment Cavour died, and Ricasoli became Prime Minister of the new Italy.

It remained only for Venice and the Papal States to fall for the Risorgimento for it to have achieved its aim. In the end it was the Prussians, defeating Austria in 1866 and France in 1870, who delivered the final pieces of the jigsaw – save for the Alto Adige, or Austria's Südtirol, which was to become Italian, not without mixed feelings, after the First World War.

For a few years in the 1860s, before the fall of Rome, Chianti should have enjoyed its hour of glory. Florence became the capital of Italy. The creator of Chianti was the Prime Minister. Royalty and embassies from all over the world were thronging Florence's cafés and its countryside. Alas, it seems they hardly noticed the local wine. This was the Golden Age of Burgundy and Bordeaux.

T he fact that there was now a united Italy did not, of course, mean that there was, or ever would be, a meeting of minds about Italian wine. Piedmont was to be the first province to make creative use of the new wine science on its grapes. From the Nebbiolo, in the footsteps of Barolo, the districts of Barbaresco and Gattinara created similar dark, powerful, tannic, and tremendous wines. Lesser grapes, Barbera, Dolcetto and Grignolino, made distinct, if not distinguished, dry reds. Freisa and Brachetto developed the hedonistic old idea of reds that

vermouth Turin, as an old capital city, has long enjoyed the advantage of well-established commerce and a substantial middle class, frequenters of cafés and leisurely social drinkers. In the eighteenth century the old alchemy of blending herbs, sweetening, and *eau-de-vie* became a commercial proposition making the fortune of Signor Carpano (whose recipe took the name of "Punt e Mes" – "point and a half" – from the Milan Stock Exchange). Others followed, perhaps the most famous being Messrs Martini and Rossi who, with a third partner, Signor Sola, bought another established company in 1864. The generic name for vermouth is the French for wormwood, or *Artemisia absinthium*, the bitter principle in the majority of such concoctions. The part of the old kingdom of Sardinia which is now in France, Savoie, shares the tradition with Turin, only making its vermouth (of which Noilly Prat is the most famous brand) drier and more herbal.

were sweet and fizzy and stained the table-cloth, while Carlo Gancia, at Canelli, invented a new role for the Moscato: not as "Greek" wine, but as the lightest and sweetest imaginable nursery-version of Champagne.

Despite the genial chaos of vineyards here as in every other part of Italy, Piedmont developed a different type of wine for each of its profusion of grape varieties. There appears to have been no calculated blending (as there might well have been, so close to Turin, the capital city of vermouth) to find an equivalent of claret or Chianti. Piedmont was a pioneer in naming wines by their grapes – or perhaps it was a throwback to the Middle Ages, when malmsey was malmsey, wherever it came from.

Doctor Cerletti was the director of Piedmont's new institute of oenology. He obligingly left a summing-up in French of the state of the Italian wine industry in 1889. It was a time of strained relations everywhere. France's gigantic appetite for supplies had provoked the planting of whole new regions where vines had never been grown before, and led to the fabrication of bogus wine as much in Italy and Spain as in France itself. Genoa was a principal centre of the trade.

Allowing for his understandable desire to present Italy in a favourable light, Cerletti gives plenty of evidence of the progress

A scene of foot-treading in Italy, photographed in the 1950s at Torgiano in Umbria, but typical of any time in the previous two millennia.

made in the generation since the Risorgimento. Phylloxera seldom reached epidemic proportions in Italy's far-from-mono-cultural landscape. It is easy to exaggerate the problem in the regions it did reach once the solution of grafting was known and tried. On balance it may often have been beneficial in making the wine-grower look again at his vines, and replant, when he did, with better varieties in better health.

The worst damage phylloxera did to Italy was indirectly, in the 1880s, before it had really taken hold, when it encouraged the notion that any sort of wine was saleable. The time was ripe for technical advance and the selection of the best vines. In most cases the opportunity was thrown away.

Cerletti described an Italy which was learning to bring down its vines from the treetops, and where the acreage of vineyards was increasing almost everywhere. The exception was the North, where only the modernizing Piedmont expanded its acreage. Liguria, Lombardy, and the Veneto made less wine – especially the Veneto, whose Austrian market had disappeared. By far the biggest increase was in Sicily and the South, where

Tuscany led the modern revolution in Italian wine, thanks to a handful of imaginative and strong-minded producers prepared to question their ancient traditions.

valleys that had never seen the vine were being planted, financed by foreign capital from France and Austria. In the twenty years from 1870 to 1890, the critical years for France, Italy's production of wine doubled – and most of the increase came from Piedmont and the South.

Of Piedmont, Cerletti reported that in the last thirty years, since the Risorgimento, the vines had been abandoned in damp valleys (where they suffered most from mildew) and concentrated on the hilltops, newly cleared of forests. The

emphasis, as always, was on reds, and the northern province of Novara, in the foothills of the main body of the Alps, was flourishing with such Nebbiolo wines as Gattinara and Ghemme. The sweet Moscato Spumante had become an industry, and vermouth, which he dated back to 1835, was exported all over the world. One of the great advantages of Piedmont, he claimed, was the abundance of good cold cellars where wine would stabilize and mature, to be bottled when it was ready to drink – often after ten or fifteen years in barrel. Strong southern wine was at this time entering more and more into the composition of these relatively expensive products, just as Burgundy and Bordeaux borrowed support from the natural potency of the Rhône.

Valpantena and Soave had a ready market. All the best wines of the Veneto were made of half-dried grapes in the Greek style: either strong and sweet as Recioto, or fully fermented as Amarone, in which a characteristic vein of bitterness joins the formidable alcohol content. These are surely the sort of wines the ancients cut with water.

Around Vicenza the name of Torcolato refers to the twisting of the grape-stems to concentrate their sugar. Each of the provinces had its approximate equivalent. In Treviso to the north of Venice it was Picolit; in most the umbrella term *vin santo* covered such heirloom wines, concentrated and rare, stored, often, in the conditions Pliny recommended, where extremes of temperature would hasten their oxidization. Up under the rooftiles was a favourite place – and still is.

Over the Apennines in Tuscany our guide of a century ago announces great advances since the Iron Baron's time: the addition of ten to fifteen per cent of Cabernet or Malbec to Chiantis to be aged. "Wines thus treated," he says, "have a savour and bouquet similar to Bordeaux." Who knows when the Cabernet grape was introduced to Tuscany? It was the vintages of Carmignano and Artimino, both of which "traditionally" add a measure of Cabernet, that André Jullien had singled out as some of the best of Tuscany half a century before.

Cerletti was writing just too soon to have heard of the enterprise of Ferruccio Biondi-Santi, a young veteran of Garibaldi's army, who in the warm south of Tuscany at Montalcino was reconstituting his phylloxera-struck vineyards. The traditional Moscadello had suffered badly from oidium and mildew. The young Ferruccio planted pure vineyards of Brunello (though still in the traditional Tuscan mixture with other crops). He took Barolo as his model, and looked for stability in a decade of barrel-ageing. 1888 was the first famous vintage of Montalcino, which rapidly became Italy's most sought-after wine.

Above all, Cerletti said, it was the Mezzogiorno that had been revolutionized. His book, for French consumption, does not mention that its speedy planting had been largely to supply the deficit caused by disease in France. It was French, German, Austrian, and Swiss capital that had turned the olive-groves of Apulia and the corn-lands of Sicily into a monoculture of the vine. These were not wines for drinking, he frankly admits. The heat of summer and their sheer strength makes it difficult to finish their fermentation. "Bulk wines produced by fascinating methods that are always inaccurate" is a contemporary description that rings all too true.

As the raw material for blending they were so dark and strong that winemakers in the North, whether of France or Italy itself, rarely resisted the temptation to add a tincture of this potent brew. In Italy, once France had enough (or too much) of its own (and Algeria's) wine for its blending vats, it was an unforeseen outcome of the Risorgimento that could set back the quality of its northern vineyards indefinitely. It had not been in Ricasoli's mind, nor Cavour's, that the old wine areas should face a great invasion from the South of duty-free, incredibly cheap, and formidably strong blending wines.

Only two areas of Lombardy have seriously to be considered: the Oltrepò Pavese, near Pavia, whose business was in supplying bulk wine to the merchants and restaurants of Milan (and which had no hesitation in buying southern wines to give them muscle), and the remote and individual Valtellina, which can almost literally be described as the south wall of the Alps. Here was yet another, and much the furthest north, of the pockets of "Greek" winemaking. Its dried-grape speciality, Sforsato or Sfursat, was customarily exported the very short distance to Switzerland.

Of the Veneto, the only thriving region was Verona. Oidium and downy mildew were rife in the humid climate to the north of Venice, but Valpolicella and its neighbours

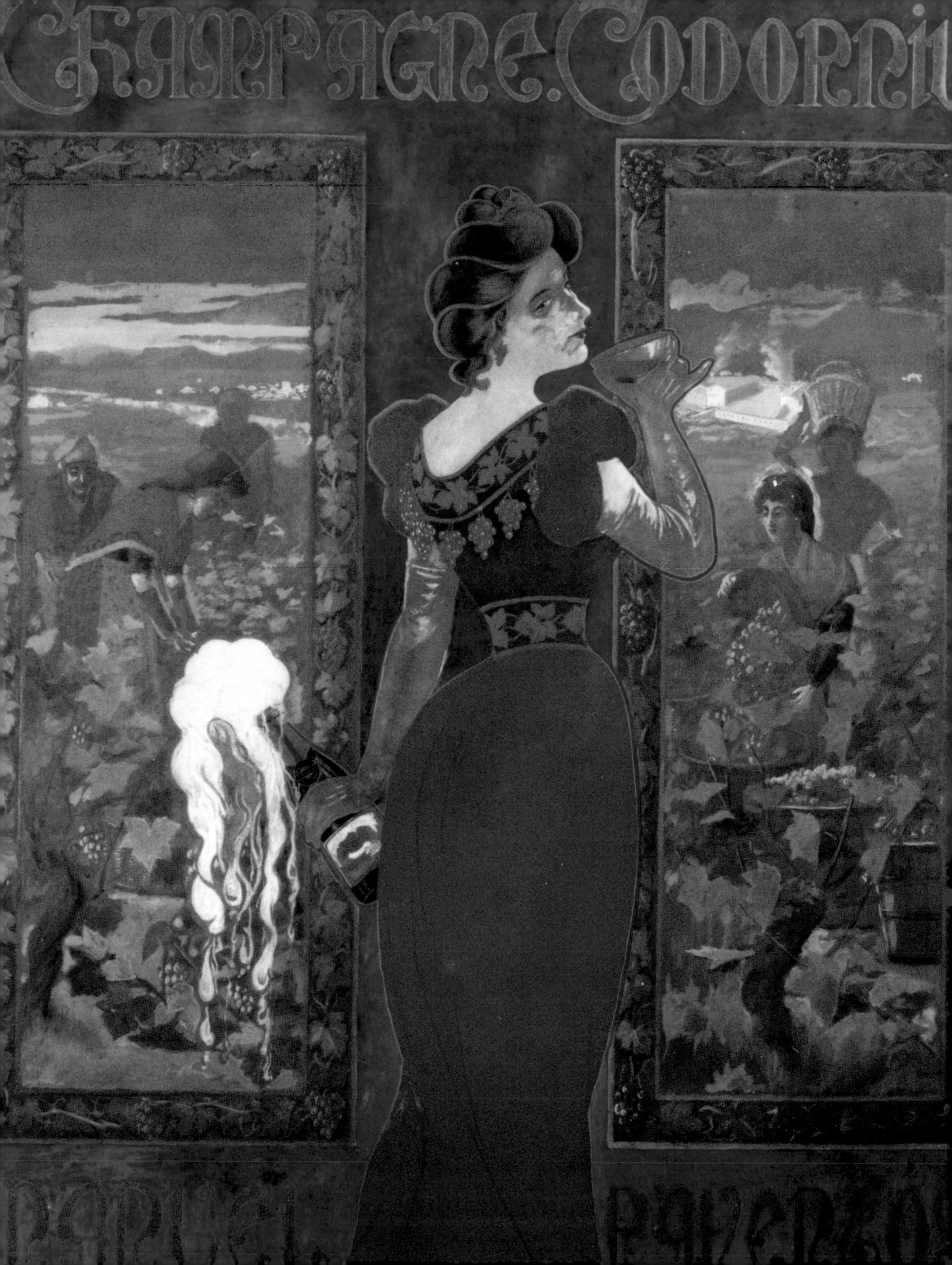
CHAMPAGNE. CODORNIU

CHAPTER 40

HISPANIC REVIVAL

Travellers in Spain in the nineteenth century, and those who drank Spanish wine at home, had very different impressions of Spain's capabilities. Nowhere, not even in Italy, was the distinction between wine for export and wine as daily sustenance so vividly clear. This is the wine the Spaniards drank, in the measured words of Alexander Henderson:

"Throughout the greater part of Spain, the peasantry store the produce of their vintages in skins, which are smeared with pitch; from which the wine is apt to contract a peculiar disagreeable taste called the *olor de bota*, and to become muddy and nauseous. Bottles and casks are rarely met with: and, except in the monasteries and great commercial towns, subterranean wine-cellars are almost unknown. Under such management we cannot be surprised that the common Spanish wines should fall so far short of the excellence that might be anticipated... or that the traveller, in the midst of the most luxurious vineyards, should often find the manufactured produce wholly unfit for use."

In defence of the *bota*, or leather bottle, it must be said that a well-used and carefully-tended one, never allowed to dry out or go thirsty (for they live on wine, and die without it), is a friendly and functional receptacle. Its purpose is not the same as that of a crystal goblet, but it perfectly expresses the place of wine in Spanish life, and certainly did not die out with the coming of glass. The real argument is not with the *bota*, but with the *borracha*, the whole animal-skin, as Richard Ford was at pains to point out (see "Wine Skins" page 224).

The distinction remained, though, between wines intended for export and those for local use. Of wines for export, by far the most important in the nineteenth century was sherry. In fifty years an industry had grown up that had overtaken port. In the view of many connoisseurs (especially, though not uniquely, in Britain) it was, or could be, the finest white wine on earth. Spain had no red to be compared with it; indeed, Spain's only red wine exports were of the inky variety used for blending – with one exception: Rioja was just finding its place as the luxury table wine of Spain, directly inspired by Bordeaux.

It was, as always, a case of the market setting the standards. When Valladolid was the capital, and Old Castile was the heart of Spain, the produce of the Duero basin, of Medina del Campo and Rueda, was proudly produced and proudly drunk. When the court moved to Madrid the great plain of La Mancha to the south became its supplier. Although the old Valladolid vineyards were still closer in distance, the Sierra de Guadarrama raised a formidable mountain barrier to transport. In La Mancha the towns of Valdepeñas and Manzanares won reputations for quality. The cellars of the Duke of San Carlos at Manzanares were said to produce "rich and racy" wines, while the best Valdepeñas was often compared with Burgundy – even, surprisingly enough, by Frenchmen. White Valdepeñas had a less favourable press, being compared with sherry of the second class.

The stumbling-block, as usual in Spain, was that a long journey over the parched plains of La Mancha was essential

LEFT The sparkling wines of Catalonia, which today go by the name of cava, were shamelessly using the name of Champagne in the 1890s. This advertisement for Codorniu reflects perfectly the spirit of the age.

to appreciate this nectar. According to Henderson, it was not to be judged by what taverns could offer in Madrid: "All these wines are normally transported on muleback in skins which impart to them their evil savour. Exceptionally wealthy citizens order them in little barrels…"

It was by this distinction, repeated presumably in every part of Spain, that the scent and flavour of barrels came to be identified unequivocally with the indulgence of the rich. Foreign merchants made use of barrels in Andalusia for their sherry and Malaga, and in Valencia even for their blackstrap Benicarlo on its way to Bordeaux for blending – the appearance of cowhides on the Quai des Chartrons might have been cause for comment. Aristocrats used them for their private supplies. Whatever potential Spanish wine might have would never be explored except around the coasts, in export areas, which were fundamentally two: Andalusia and the adjacent Valencia to the east and the Northwest, from Galicia along the Biscay coast.

Why was it that Catalonia, whose climate is so perfect for the vine, and which has Barcelona as an ideal port, played such a small part in exports until recent times? The answer lies partly in its often tragic history, caught between Spain and France, but perhaps more in its ominously named *rabassa morta*, a form of share-cropping, very much to the landlord's advantage, that held it rigidly in the Middle Ages until well into the nineteenth century. Catalonia was visible in the statistics, but mainly as a purveyor of *eau-de-vie*, with a footnote for the sweet and potent Malvasia of Sitges near Barcelona, and (until monasteries were secularized) for the celebrated black Priorato of the Carthusian house of Scala Dei, regarded more as a medicine than a drink. What revolutionized Catalonia's reputation for quality was the genius of the Raventos family who, in the 1870s, made the discovery that its native Parellada grape formed the ideal basis for sparkling wine.

T he Rioja, the Upper Ebro valley between Logroño and Miranda de Ebro, had been mentioned by enthusiasts at intervals since the Romans. Alas, the legions had not left their usual legacy of roads. Only a trickle of Rioja reached the outside world – despite the pilgrim ways to Santiago de Compostella passing through. The story of Rioja's first attempt to modernize, and how it was frustrated, is a sadly typical tale of Spain in the

eighteenth century. At length plans were laid to build the essential road to Logrono along the Ebro valley. In the 1780s the dean of Burgos and a native of Rioja, Don Manuel Quintano, travelled to Bordeaux to learn how wine could be made to keep.

Don Manuel's introduction to Rioja of Bordeaux methods, but above all of barrels, was an instant success – except with other winemakers. Cellar-aged wines were triumphantly exported to Cuba and Mexico and survived the voyage. But the authorities, instead of embracing the idea, reacted with petty envy by declaring that all Rioja must be sold at the same price. The cost of barrels and of three years' ageing was disallowed – even on appeal to the Council of Castile.

O idium was what woke the north of Spain from its torpor. Galicia on the north-west coast still maintained a moderate overseas trade with its Ribadavia, but the wines of Leon, the Duero, and Rioja rarely struggled further than the cities of the north coast. From 1850 the powdery mildew, imported from Portugal on American vines, laid waste the vineyards of the rainier regions. Rioja was affected, but Galicia with its grey skies was devastated. Many of its wine-growers had already emigrated; and in a region where rain falls intermittently all summer long, even sulphur could be only an expensive palliative: never a cure.

What Galicia lost by oidium, Rioja was to gain. Already it was almost the only supplier of the thriving port of Bilbão. It had supplies that France was desperate for. Even in the oidium years, and without a railway, the French came knocking at its doors for wine. In 1864, no sooner had the railway been built linking Logroño with Bilbão, Madrid, and the frontier at Irun, than news came of the phylloxera at work in France. Suddenly Rioja could sell the French all the wine it could make, and a fury of planting swept down the valley.

Its growers found that the vigorous Garnacha vine, the French Grenache, needed less spraying against oidium than their delicate Tempranillo (the name means "early one") – the secret of Rioja's fragrance and vitality. For bulk business it did not matter; there were great new warehouses in Bilbão where Rioja was blended in any case with Duero and La Mancha wines before joining the tide of wine heading for France. But there were more far-sighted landowners who looked beyond the sudden boom of an open French market. Either Rioja could become the concubine of France, to be forgotten once the French vineyards had recovered, or it could invest its unaccustomed income in offering France a challenge.

The same thought had evidently come to several Spaniards even before the oidium arrived. In Rioja it had a military and patriotic birth. Its sponsor was the Duke of la Vittoria, the former General Espartero and briefly Prime Minister of Spain, who had his own private bodega in Logroño, his home town. His *aide de camp* in the 1840s was the young Colonel Luciano de Murrieta y Garcia-Lemoine, who was born and brought up in Peru, in a family that owned a silver mine. General and colonel had both had been obliged to find exile in London. They were conservatives, Carlists, and on the losing side, in the civil war of

wine skins Richard Ford wrote: "The *Bota* is not to be confounded with the *Borracha* or *Cuero*, the wine skin of Spain, which is the entire, and answers the purpose of the barrel elsewhere. The *bota* is the retail receptacle, the *cuero* is the wholesale one. It is genuine pig's skin, the adoration of which disputes in the Peninsula with the cigar, the dollar, and even the worship of the Virgin. The shops of the makers are to be seen in most Spanish towns; in them long lines of the unclean animals' blown-out hides are strung up like sheep carcases in our butchers' shambles. The tanned and manufactured article preserves the form of the pig, feet and all, with the exception of one: the skin is turned inside out, so that the hairy coat lines the interior, which, moreover, is carefully pitched like a ship's bottom, to prevent leaking; hence the peculiar flavour, which partakes of resin and the hide, which is called the *borracha*. This flavour is peculiar to most Spanish wines, sherry excepted, which being made by foreigners, is kept in foreign casks."

succession that plagued Spain at intervals until the 1870s.

Evidently it was in London, where he lived for five years, that Luciano de Murrieta became interested in wine. On his way back to Spain he stayed and studied in Bordeaux. In 1850 he was back in Logroño, starting experiments with Bordeaux methods in the ducal vineyards and bodega. All the traditional methods had to go. The old Rioja way was treading and fermenting in shallow *lagos* like the *lagares* of the Douro. Many of the grapes remained uncrushed, fermenting by degrees in what today is known as "carbonic maceration": a process that was lengthy, hard to control, and woefully unhygienic. Murrieta's new method was rapidly crushing the grapes into deep vats to ferment, the classic *cuverie* of a Bordeaux château.

Like Quintano's, Murrieta's idea was not just to ship the wine in barrels as Bordeaux did, but to age it. There were no barrels to be had in Rioja. Even Bilbão could provide only little casks, much smaller than the Bordeaux models. At first Murrieta made do with quarter-casks to prove his point. Even within a year the hard young wine had smoothed and taken on new flavours that promised well. Rioja in future was to acquire its characteristic taste not just from its fragrant Tempranillo grapes but from ever longer ageing in oak. Oak, rather than grapes, became the immediately recognizable Rioja scent and even flavour.

The new Rioja, in a word, epitomized the wealthy Spaniard's idea of what good wine, red or white, should taste like: as far from the *borracha* as possible, limpid and lively, clean, light, and clear.

Modern vineyards in Chile. Spain was jealous of its colonies producing their own wine. They had to wait until independence in the nineteenth century.

Murrieta was not the first to build his own bodega; that credit goes to a man of greater means and rather different ambition. Don Camilo Hurtado de Amezaga, Marqués de Riscal, had fallen in love with Bordeaux. In 1850, he set about building a veritable château, or at least the working parts of one, over the river from Logroño in the province of Alava. Don Camilo must have been in Bordeaux at the same time as Don Luciano, but their ideas were not the same. One set out to perfect Rioja; the other to imitate Bordeaux.

Of Riscal's 202 hectares – no château in Bordeaux had half as many – he planted three-quarters with Rioja's grapes, one quarter with Bordeaux's, and even a little Pinot Noir.

At last in 1862 Riscal's wine was ready. Following the latest fashion in Bordeaux he refused to sell his *grand vin* (*reserva* is the Spanish term) in barrel, but bottled it in Bordeaux bottles wrapped in wire mesh and sealed: a publicity touch that the Médoc would not have been ashamed of. The moment of truth came in 1865, when he entered his wine in open competition in Bordeaux itself. For the ultimate test, this wine was Tempranillo pure; Cabernet in his eyes would have been less than a fair trial. It won first prize and disbelief that such a wine could come from Spain.

So close in time that precedence is immaterial, the third of what might well be called the original "first-growths" of Spain took shape, not in Rioja but in the once-famous region of the Duero. The idea of imitating Bordeaux was clearly in the aristocratic air, but only one stout-hearted landowner had the faith to plant Bordeaux grapes at well over 610 metres (2,000 feet) in country which bakes and freezes in a most un-Médoc manner.

The great estate of Vega Sicilia belonged to Don Eloy Lecanda y Chaves, who made the Bordeaux pilgrimage to buy his vines and his barrels with no encouragement or even curiosity from neighbouring vintners. He was, and long remained, the only one. If Vega Sicilia has a mystique no other Spanish wine quite shares, it comes partly from its eccentric geography but equally from its quite alarming horsepower. In an analogy with Bordeaux and its "first-growths" you would have to call Riscal the Lafite of Spain: at its best all perfume and silk. Murrieta is perhaps the Mouton: rich and resonant and deep. Vega Sicilia is the Latour, but Latour of a vintage that has raisined the grapes and fried the picking crews.

What these three great originals have in common, apart from ambition and success, is that all were conceived and operated well before phylloxera had arrived in France, and a decade before it became a crisis in Bordeaux. Rioja's rise to fame is often represented as an exodus of stricken winemakers across the Pyrenees. But that was a later phase of its development. By then the point had already been proved that Spain, after all, could make wine comparable to France's best.

Rioja's two "first-growths" did not remain alone for long. At some point in the 1860s Murrieta moved from the duke's to his own bodega. Curiously, the date is unrecorded, but he bought the 243-hectare estate of Ygay near Logroño, where the company is today, about a decade later, in 1872. By this time wine-growers all over Spain were in a state of euphoria. Phylloxera had swept though the Midi, and the French were on their knees for wine. Rioja certainly supplied its share of the dark anonymous fluid that most French wine merchants were looking for. Yet the bodega builders of this excited time took their lead from Riscal and Murrieta, aiming to sell oak-aged wine and build a market of their own on the proven quality of the region. Its best white grape, the Viura, turned out to be as capable of ageing to splendid distinction as its red. It also had just the freshness that makes the basis of good sparkling wine. All the raw materials were here to make a Bordeaux, a Burgundy and a Champagne for Spain.

By the end of the 1880s there were six large bodegas incorporating the new ideas, most of them built with French advice and some with French partners. But unlike Riscal they were not imitating anything specifically French, or even, by 1890, aiming at the French market. Spain by itself was market enough. Madrid, Bilbão, and overseas Cuba and Mexico were ready to buy everything they made. Rioja had locked on to a formula of its own, in which ageing in barrel played an ever increasing part. Perhaps the idea came from Jerez. Certainly it went far beyond anything that Bordeaux ever practised. To keep a wine, even a white wine, in barrel for twenty or twenty-five years was nothing exceptional – and not because sales were slack. A great vintage was one which could undergo such treatment and still keep the sweetness of fruit. These wines,

like no others, were built to be marathon runners, surviving not (like vintage port) by their heavy build, but by exceptional sinew and vitality. Apart from the remote and almost unobtainable Vega Sicilia, Rioja remained the only quality table-wine supplier of Spain for almost a century.

Phylloxera reached Rioja in the 1890s, wearing, it must have seemed for some, an air of retribution. Unscrupulous merchants had been using the good name of the region to sell wine fabricated with the very cheapest industrial alcohol from Germany. But Basque investments (the bourgeois of Bilbão saw Rioja as their own vineyard) and the continued presence of the French were a secure base. The stability of Rioja came partly from its very lack of exports – Spain was eighty per cent of its market – and partly from its profoundly bourgeois structure. From an early stage small wine-growers found the new barrel-ageing system beyond their resources, and contented themselves with simply growing grapes for the big bodegas. The current law only confirms what for a long time had been an established practice: only bodegas with a storage capacity of 750,000 litres, and at least 500 *bordelesas*, the Rioja term for the barrel it so profitably borrowed from Bordeaux, may export their wine with the seal of the regulating body, the Consejo Regulador.

We last caught sight of the wines of Spanish America almost three centuries before the emergence of Rioja, when the pirate Drake intercepted a galleon carrying wine skins from the new colony of Chile to the slightly older one of Peru. It had never realistically been within Spain's power to prevent her American colonies from supplying themselves with wine, rather than obediently waiting for vinegary supplies from the mother country. Yet even as late as the Napoleonic wars Madrid was doggedly sending futile orders to uproot vines and buy more wine from Andalusia.

On the other hand, while South America remained in the illiberal grip of Spain, there were no prospects of more than the most modest improvements. When, in the second two decades of the nineteenth century the colonies one after another declared their independence from the decrepit empire, it was the high coastal valleys of Peru which produced the most highly regarded wine in the greatest quantity.

The principal grape of Peru, as of Chile, was the Pais or Criolla, the same pious plant as that of the Mission of the Franciscans in California. But much preferred, both for sweet wine and as the basis of the local *eau de vie*, pisco, was the Muscatel. The poet Byron's grandfather, the Admiral Byron known as "Foulweather Jack", having survived shipwreck on Cape Horn and made his way half the length of Chile to Santiago, gave a glowing account of Chile's Muscat, which he found "full as good as madeira". It is uncharacteristic of André Jullien that his view of Chilean wines is contrary, to say the least, if not downright jaundiced. "They have the colour", he writes, "of a potion of rhubarb and senna, and their taste, coming from the tarred goatskins in which they are transported, comes close enough to these same drugs."

The pioneer in importing new and better vine varieties,

Don Silvestre Ochagavia Errazuriz, came from a Basque family that had first settled in Brazil. It is pure coincidence, but extraordinary nonetheless, that Chile's wine industry in the modern sense is precisely contemporary with that other Basque creation: Rioja. For it was in 1851, just as young Colonel Murrieta was making his first wines, that Ochagavia employed a French oenologist on his estate just south of Santiago to introduce the vines of Bordeaux, and also the Riesling.

The valleys of central Chile might have been planned for a great wine industry since the earth took shape. With fertile soil, bountiful sunshine, low humidity, and an infinite supply of water for irrigation – the snowmelt from the Andes – their vines were untroubled by disease, and from the start their vintages fermented without problems into powerfully fruity, healthy, stable, and transportable wines. The ruling elite of Chile in the nineteenth century was largely Basque in origin, mixed with not a little British and Irish blood. Most of the country's principal bodegas were founded in the river valleys around Santiago in the generation following Ochagavia's lead. As in Rioja, fine wine was made by a relatively small number of large bodegas.

If Ochagavia is credited with the role of a rather less frenzied Haraszthy in the history of Chile, his equivalent across the Andes in Argentina was almost Haraszthyan, at least in vigour and versatility. As a young man Don Tiburcio Benegas distinguished himself as a cool head in an emergency. In 1861 the old colonial city of Mendoza in the Andean foothills was destroyed by an earthquake. Its commercial and financial system seized up. Benegas, at the age of twenty-five, became the city's banker and restored its dislocated finances.

His interest in wine started with his marriage in 1870 to the daughter of a progressive landowner in the remote province. Meanwhile, on his own property of El Trapiche in the neighbouring province of Godoy Cruz (now San Vicente), he experimented with European vines imported both from Chile and directly from Europe. There was no doubt that with access to Buenos Aires the Andean foothills of Argentina could become one of the most prolific sources of good quality wine on earth.

The market would determine its style. Chile developed an idiom based on the ideas of Northern Spain, and heavily influenced by France. Without a great domestic market for quality wine it became the principal exporter in South America. Its tendency was to improve its already high standards. In Argentina the reverse happened. The great influx of Italian immigrants early in the twentieth century pointed the direction for its wine. It was to be rough and ready, sweet and tannic, plentiful and cheap.

Rioja vineyards near Haro are sheltered from the north by the Sierra de Cantabria. In the 1890s Haro's rail links made it an ideal centre for blending Rioja.

CHAPTER 41

FIFTY YEARS OF CRISIS

The vintages of 1899 and 1900 made, in Bordeaux, one of those famous pairs, like 1989 and 1990 – both excellent, each with its own style and character – that offer a glow of reassurance to lovers of wine, not to mention their producers. Nature was bountiful, and even those growers who were still struggling against phylloxera may have felt that the worst was over.

What Jeremiah would have foretold as the twentieth century opened that the wine industry would be on the brink of a depression that would be the longest and most severe in its modern history? The patches of clear sky in the first fifty years of the twentieth century were few and fleeting. Poor weather, war, slump, and intemperate fanaticism were all to contribute to Dionysus' distress. These were the labour pains of the world of modern wine. Modern standards of winemaking, of authenticity, and even of our very habits of appreciation and enjoyment, were to emerge from this long-drawn-out travail.

It is not surprising that (at least in France) it was hard for wine growers to grasp at this moment in history that their problem was simply too much wine. Recent memories were full of the risk, and often the reality, of whole vineyards being snuffed out. The fact that France had had to import huge quantities of wine was proof enough to a Frenchman that once it was self-sufficient again, all would be well.

Every nation from Morocco to Romania had acted independently on the same instincts and planted furiously. Inevitably prices collapsed. In the phylloxera years of the 1880s a hectolitre of wine in the Languedoc had fetched its grower

thirty francs. By 1900 the price was down to ten francs, while the grower's cost was fifteen.

It came as a shock for the Midi to discover that its wine was not wanted. Its growers looked for scapegoats – and in 1907, when the price had fallen to less than half the cost of production, they found a redeemer to lead them, as they thought, out of their misery.

Their singular choice was no ranting demagogue but a middle-aged farmer from Narbonne called Albert Marcellin. His rallying cries picked as the principal cause of their discontent an evil which, though obvious, showed how little he and his followers understood the real situation. They blamed the fabricators of fake wine – whose business had in reality collapsed even faster than their own.

A more realistic plank in their platform was protest against the chaptalization which enabled northern producers to offer them competition. In most of northern France phylloxera was still in full cry: growers were desperate for something to sell. To add sugar and water was, after all, permitted by the great Chaptal... and at this very moment the Chamber of Deputies in Paris was debating whether to tax sugar at fifteen francs per 100 kilos (the plea of northern deputies – in whose constituencies the sugar beet was also grown) or sixty francs, the demand of the South.

"*Vive le vin naturel*" and "Down with the poisoners" were the

LEFT The Champagne Riots of 1911, in which growers turned on merchants, came after four disastrous years of disease. Forty thousand military police were called in.

shouts of the crowds who gathered round Marcellin in alarming numbers at regular Sunday demonstrations in the spring of 1907, swelling from 80,000 in Narbonne in early May to over half a million in Montpellier in early June. They chose to ignore (or did not understand) the fact that they themselves were compounding the problem by importing potent Algerian wine to blend with the thin produce of their over-abundant harvests.

The Prime Minister, Clemenceau, was not known as "*le Tigre*" for nothing. He sent troops to Narbonne to arrest the ringleaders. Five protesters were killed in the resulting riot. Marcellin, who had consistently preached non-violence, went to Paris to talk to Clemenceau – walking unannounced, it is said, into the great man's office. He was ridiculed for it; but it worked. By the end of June the government had brought in a

law which provided for the first time in history for a census of how much wine was made each year, and how much was held in stock. It demanded a statutory "*Déclaration de Récolte*" from every wine-grower in the land. The law provided no control over how much might be made, but at least it gave the government a dipstick for the great sump which held so much potential trouble. Further measures brought in in September required a record of the use of sugar for chaptalization, and most fundamentally of all gave wine for the first time a legal definition, as being made "exclusively from the alcoholic fermentation of fresh grapes or fresh grape juice".

World War I provoked patriotic thirst. Throughout the war and the 1920s France's wine consumption rose. In 1900 it had been 100 litres a head; in 1926 it was 135. Naturally the growers seized the chance to plant more vines.

Once again euphoria was to be followed by a slump. This time, however, the government grasped the nettle. Algeria had more than doubled its production. The Languedoc was awash.

New Yorkers crowd a Park Avenue club to celebrate the end of Prohibition in 1933. "Champagne" – perhaps French, perhaps not – seems to be the order of the day.

And perhaps of more immediate concern was the post-war crisis that had left France's prestigious exporting wine regions bereft of customers. Not one of the nations that had bought Bordeaux, burgundy, and Champagne with such enthusiasm before the war had any money left to spend on luxuries. The Russian Revolution had removed one of France's most profitable markets – seemingly for ever. Germany, Austria, and Hungary were ruined by the war. Belgium would take years to recover. Britain, having bought as heavily as it could of the great mature Champagne vintages that had survived the war, made a virtue of necessity by persuading itself that much cheaper cocktails were more fashionable. Only the United States had money – and it had shot itself in the foot with the Eighteenth Amendment that brought in National Prohibition in 1919.

Decrees between 1931 and 1936 banned new planting, ordered the distillation of great quantities of wine, and obliged all *départements* that had indulged in the recent planting spree to pull up a proportion of their vines. Not only was France's total vineyard reduced by ten per cent by this measure, but the most popular (because most prolific) of the American-French hybrid vines planted after phylloxera, the Jacquez, the Noah, and the Clinton – names not mentioned in polite circles – were banned from the Déclaration de Récolte, which meant that growers might drink their wine if they chose, but were legally debarred from selling it. On the whole these measures were a success. They certainly amounted to a degree of government intervention in what might be grown where and by whom that would scarcely have appealed to Montesquieu.

But the time was ripe, because running parallel with the heavy political question of trying to balance supply and demand there had been, from the beginning of the century, a much more specific movement building strength. It concerned the right to use the world-famous names of the great wines: a matter which in the past had always been left to local authorities to police.

The first region to react in self-defence was, logically enough, the one that probably needed authenticating most urgently: Chablis. In 1900, seventy-nine Chablis producers formed a group to guarantee that, of all the millions of bottles labelled with the best-known name of all French dry white wines (or indeed all white wines of any sort), only theirs were the real thing. Their move, of course, made not the slightest impression on Californian, Australian, Spanish, or any other producers, who continued to sell whatever wine they liked as Chablis. But a stand had been taken. It meant that any of that minority of consumers who even cared if their wine was authentic or not was being offered a guide.

The Médoc followed, a year later, with a Union Syndicale de Propriétaires des Crus Classés du Médoc, a considerably more influential body which encouraged other regions to follow. The trend was clear enough for the government to back it with legislation. In 1905 it passed the law which was eventually to lead, thirty years later, to the system of *appellations contrôlées*. At this stage no definitions were even attempted. The law contented itself with a statement of principle against the fraudulent or deceptive use of names and descriptions.

The question now remained to be answered (and indeed to be asked): where do you draw the boundary line around a name? It was left to the local administration to decide what was (or was not) within the limits of Chablis or Champagne. In 1908 a new law more explicitly laid down that delimitations would be made by decree and following "local usage". Over the following years discussion was intense. In Bordeaux it raised the ancient question of the High Country wines. Often in the past they had been sold as Bordeaux when need arose. But now, as in the past, the influence of Bordeaux was greater than that of its scattered country cousins. In 1911 their status was finally decreed. Bordeaux meant the *département* of the Gironde alone. The High Country, including even Bergerac, was excluded.

Champagne was the cause célèbre of this administrative dilemma, but it was more than a matter of simple delimitation. It awkwardly combined with a situation similar to that in the Languedoc in 1907: real human distress over low prices and miserable living conditions. In 1908 the decree was published drawing the boundaries of Champagne. It included most of the communes of the *département* of the Marne; some in the neighbouring Aisne (whose wine the Marne growers described as "bean soup") – but none in the southern part of the province, the Aube, around Troyes where the medieval Champagne fairs had been held. Immediately the Aubois were up in arms. Were they not the true Champenois? – Only historically, came the reply from the Marne; the wine that bears the name of Champagne was born in the Marne valley, and Aubois wine cannot hold a candle to the great *crus* immortalized by Dom Pérignon. The government was indecisive, and appeared to favour the argument of the Aube.

More seriously, the vintage of 1910 was the last straw in a succession of four appalling years for all Champagne growers. To the battle with phylloxera, then at its height in Champagne (6,075 hectares of vines died in that year alone), was added a catastrophic year of rain and mildew when many growers made no wine at all. In 1911 the growers of the Marne, privileged or not, took to the streets against the merchants whom they believed not just to be pulling the strings of the administration but cheating them by buying bulk wine from outside the region altogether. Famous houses, the growers said, had been bringing in wine from Touraine and Anjou, the Midi, and even Germany and Spain. Prices were low because they, as well as the customers, were being defrauded.

The violence of their reaction went far beyond anything seen in the Languedoc four years before. Aÿ was the centre of the storm. This was no protest meeting, but a settling of old scores. Several thousand wine growers set upon the merchant-houses of the little town, broke down their doors, smashed their bottles, opened their barrels and let the wine flow into the streets. The homes of several merchants were similarly ransacked (though all agreed that the house of Bollinger in the centre of the town should be left untouched). Finally they set fire to houses and even vineyards (which were full of straw for frost protection). Firing the vineyards was inexplicable: it suggests that anarchists from outside the region must have been involved.

Champagne, as we have seen, is well accustomed to the sight of troops. This time it was a military police force that descended on it, 40,000 strong, to take up billets in every village of the region. A temporary compromise was reached by which the Aube was accorded the title of "Champagne – second zone", but before the government had had time to settle the issue it was not friendly troops that were parading though Reims and Epernay; it was Germans.

The Marne was the scene of two of the decisive battles of the First World War; in September 1914, when the German advance was checked in ten days of fighting among the heavy-laden vines, and in September 1918, when the Allies finally pushed the Germans from their positions and went on to victory. In the four years between, Reims was continuously in the front line, suffering more than a thousand days of German shelling beginning with the systematic bombardment and destruction of the cathedral in which the kings of France were crowned.

Reims would have ceased to exist during the war had it not been for its Champagne cellars, the great deep chalk-pits that lie under most of the city. They became an underground fortress, linked by tunnels, in which up to 50,000 troops lived. Astonishingly, the Champagne industry went on, even in this beleaguered barracks. More astonishingly still, the growers continued to tend their vines even among the trenches that criss-crossed the northern slopes of the "mountain" overlooking the city. They crawled like infantrymen through the white mud of winter to prune, and in the golden days of October they ran out to harvest with their usual songs. And 1914, 1915, and 1917 were all vintages of exceptional quality.

Scarcely was the Armistice signed in November 1918 than the government in Paris returned to the question of appellations – so rapidly, in fact, that before the Treaty of Versailles that formally ended the war was ready for signature, the concept of France's appellations contrôlées was formulated and included as a clause that the Germans were obliged to accept. How little mere geographical limits meant on their own was aptly illustrated not by a wine region but by something even more emotive to the French public: a cheese.

The scandal broke in 1925. Roquefort, that most piquant and creamy of cheeses, had duly been granted a delimited area of production in the mountains of the Aveyron, the southern central highlands of France. The court, however, had said nothing about its most vital characteristic: that it is (or should be) made of ewe's milk, not of cow's. Here was the problem in a nutshell. It was seized upon by Joseph Capus, Professor of Agriculture at Cadillac and member of the Chamber of Deputies for the Gironde. Capus saw for himself how the appellations of the great vineyards of Bordeaux were being used by unscrupulous (or indeed just stupid) growers for wines made by any methods from any grapes. It was not a question of ewe's

milk or cow's but of Cabernet or Noah. In 1927 Capus' influence added another law to the statute book, introducing the element that the Dukes of Burgundy had seen as fundamental four centuries before. The phrase the law employed might almost have been drafted by Philippe the Bold himself: "using grape varieties hallowed by local, loyal and established custom".

Capus was leading in the right direction. Eventually he would be recognized as the godfather of the appellation laws – le loi Capus is a phrase one still occasionally hears. But others were studying their regions in much greater depth, none more so than the owner of Château Portia, one of the most important estates of Châteauneuf-du-Pape, Baron Le Roy de Boiseaumarié.

The notion of terroir, now so emotively used to express the precise ecosystem of each vineyard, could be said to have sprung from this enlightened proprietor's proposals. It was he who in 1923 described the soil best suited to the thirteen grape varieties of Châteauneuf in terms of its natural flora of lavender and thyme. But just as important as the terroir were the cultural practices, the pruning, the maximum crop that would make good wine, the ripeness of the grapes, and the way they were handled in the cellar. These were the missing links in all the legislation that had gone before. Unless the appellation laws took each of the elements of wine quality as a separate and serious issue, they would be to no avail.

The law that eventually brought these elements together was largely Joseph Capus' work. It established, in 1935, the Comité National des Appellations d'Origine; a perpetual expert body to examine every aspect of each claim by a region for an appellation contrôlée. The processing of hundreds of appellations could now begin. After the Second World War the Comité became an Institut: the INAO, the governing body of the French world of wine and the model to which almost every nation looks as it struggles with its own version of the same intractable problem: how to legislate for something so variable as wine.

We have seen how adversity had created what might still be at the discussion stage without the conditions of the time. Perversity had its part to play as well. It was as the Great War ended, and the prospect of normality was rekindling spirits everywhere, that America produced the black joke of Prohibition. The best excuse of those who promoted Prohibition is that they had no idea what its consequences would be. Its net effect was to add more than half as much again to America's wine consumption. Production averaged over three-and-a-half million hectolitres a year over the thirteen years the law was in force, compared with two million hectolitres in the record pre-Prohibition year. Nobody knows how much wine was smuggled in from abroad (although the figure offered by the Champagne industry is over seventy million cases during the years in question).

The wine industry did not even have to go underground. Although it was strictly policed (at least a thousand enforcement officers were found guilty of extortion, conspiracy, perjury and other offences) it was still permitted to make wine for medicinal and sacramental use. Anyone could call himself a rabbi or indeed found a "church". Every drugstore sold medicinal wine, and every doctor would prescribe Paul Masson's excellent "Medicinal Champagne" for any patient suffering from an otherwise incurable thirst.

These legitimate exceptions, though, made up only perhaps five per cent of the wine that Americans drank during Prohibition. By far the greatest part was also made more or less legally, but under a gaping loophole in the so-called Volstead Act, the 10,000-word document that put flesh on the bones of the Eighteenth Amendment.

The loophole was a sentence in Section Twenty-nine. It read, in part: "The penalties provided in this Act against the manufacture of liquor without a permit shall not apply to a person for manufacturing nonintoxicating cider and fruit juices exclusively for use in his home…" – up to a limit of 200 gallons (909 litres) a year. "Nonintoxicating" apparently was too long a word for the millions of Americans who suddenly became home winemakers. A demand grew almost overnight for grapes in quantities never transported before. It was bad news for the wineries, but a bonanza for grape-growers, and for railroad companies. Within two years the price of grapes in California rose to three times its average before Prohibition as dealers filled every waggon they could find to rush them to the cities of the East.

The ideal, and the grape that was planted massively at the expense of better varieties, was the Alicante Bouschet – the red-juiced *teinturier* that Monsieur Bouschet had bred to lend colour to the pallid production of the Languedoc. So dark was its pulp and skin that after it had been pressed a second, and even a third, batch of "wine" could easily be made by fermenting sugar and water on the remaining *marc*. Its thick skin also survived the railway journey better than any other.

"Grape bricks" of concentrated juice were one solution, each one bearing a warning: "Do not add yeast or contents will ferment". A far more imaginative procedure was dreamed up by Paul Garrett, the creator of Virginia Dare: to use federal funds to "save the bankrupt grape industry" by making and marketing juice concentrate. What industry was more in need of President Hoover's farm-relief programme?

In 1930 "Vine-glo" was advertised – in terms which suggest a certain over-confidence, to say the least. Eight varieties were offered to the public: Port, Muscatel, Tokaji, Sauternes, Virginia Dare, Riesling, Claret, and Burgundy. Not only was the concentrate delivered to your home, but a service man came with it to start the fermentation, and came back again sixty days later to bottle and label the (presumably "nonintoxicating") wine – and more than likely bring another keg. So audacious a scheme attracted compliments from the highest quarters. Al Capone is reported to have banned Vine-glo from Chicago on pain of death. More seriously, a Kansas City court saw straight through the whole charade. But by this time the end of Prohibition was in sight. The next year, with Roosevelt's election as President, California became the first state to repeal its Prohibition laws, and from December 1933, in the depths of the Depression, the "noble experiment" petered ingloriously out across the nation.

I f there was rejoicing in the vineyards, it was to be short-lived. By vintage time Repeal had been imminent enough for wineries (most of which had not made wine for years) to wind up for action. They were to discover that the realities of restarting were less attractive than the idea. Most of the vineyards had been replanted with "shipping" grapes. Much of their equipment and cooperage was unusable, and many were inexperienced or rusty in even the principles of their craft.

Wines made in a hurry, some still fermenting, were rushed to the Christmas market. Bottles that had not turned to vinegar exploded in shop windows. Nothing could have persuaded the public more effectively that it was better off with the home-brew it was used to – on which, besides, there were no taxes to pay.

America had lost not only its wine industry, but also its taste for wine. Dry wines depend on good grapes and on reasonable skill in winemaking. Tastes vitiated by a dozen years of home-brew were looking for something sweet and strong. This was the way the industry had to go. The historian Leon Adams worked as a journalist in San Francisco through the whole unhappy period. "Most of the people in the industry thought of wine as a skid-row beverage," he recalls. "The bankers regarded wine as one by-product of the grape industry… Some growers, such as John Daniel of Inglenook, tried to secure larger loans to plant premium wine varieties – but grapes were grapes as far as banks were concerned."

In 1934, in the giddy aftermath of Prohibition, 800 wineries had licences, three-quarters of them new, in California. A few years later barely more than 200 were still in business. It was a desperately slow climb back, led by a handful of men whose faith was not to be shaken: true heirs of Jefferson, who believed that natural wine stands apart from all other beverages. Among them were the aristocracy who had survived: the firms of Krug, of Inglenook, Beaulieu, Wente, Martini and Paul Masson. Quietly getting on with their business of making low-

good years and bad As though in sympathy with the turbulence of the times, the weather in Europe in the twentieth century, up to the outbreak of World War II, left a trail of poor vintages to add to the wine-growers' problems.

Obviously there were wide variations from region to region, but taking Bordeaux, and more particularly the Médoc, as our sample, the first forty years of the century produced only eleven vintages that can be described as generally good, of which two, without qualification, were great.

The first nineteen years produced two extremely fine vintages: 1900 and 1906. 1920 and 1929 were the great vintages whose wines have reached pinnacles of perfection. In comparison, the forty years between 1940 and 1980 were generally successful at least twice as frequently.

One can argue that twenty-three vintages produced a clear majority of good or very good wines – although again only two vintages (1945 and 1961) can confidently be described in terms of the very highest praise. 1982, which may in time prove to be among the best of the century, falls just outside the forty years in question.

The record of the 1980s, though, with seven good or very good vintages out of ten, serves to stress that our immediate forebears were particularly unlucky.

priced wine in ever-increasing quantities in the Central Valley were three Italian firms, the future giants of the industry: the Franzias, Louis Petri, and the brothers Gallo.

A visionary journalist in the East, meanwhile, had germinated an idea that was to revolutionize the way California (and eventually a much wider world) thought and talked about its wines, the grapes it made them from, and the standards by which they could be compared and judged. Frank Schoonmaker asked the most fundamental questions from his suppliers in France, when he started a wine-importing business shortly after Repeal. Few Frenchmen at the time were aware of the vital importance of grape varieties. The law that made them mandatory for appellation wines was only six years older than Repeal. Carrying the thinking of Joseph Capus into his own selection of California wines, Schoonmaker abandoned the convention that borrowed a European name for every kind of wine. What, after all, in California, was the difference between a "Burgundy" and a "claret", a "Chablis" and a "Rhine"? One man's Rhine was another man's Sauternes. Instead, for his Selections made by Almaden, he named the grape variety involved (or dominant). His light-hearted back-labels gave a little vinous education, and initiated the revolution in the use of "varietal" names for most quality wines.

The woes of the wine grower in the 1910s, 1920s, and 1930s had one unpredictable result that has since stood him in good stead: the price of the finest wines came down to a level where they could be drunk by a much wider, and more inquisitive, range of amateurs than the plutocratic few they were designed for. The discussion of wine took on a new dimension as more palates became practised on wines of exceptional quality from different countries and regions. Up to this time, indeed, there had been gazetteers like Jullien's, but very little exposition of the properties and uses of different wines, or of its relationship with food. The great nineteenth-century gastronome Brillat-Savarin never mentions it.

RIGHT Prohibition's repeal captured in allegory by a Spanish artist. Several modern drinks companies owe their origins to the slaking of illicit American thirsts

les trois glorieuses Burgundy in the 1930s was in a sorry state, with sales so low that many non-resident proprietors, seeing no return on their investments, sold their vines, even in some of the Grands Crus vineyards. It was an opportunity that the working *vignerons* were never likely to see again, and life-times' savings were shrewdly spent on buying little parcels of the land they had worked for others. In an effort to promote sales and reawaken public interest, two leading citizens of Nuits-St-Georges, Georges Faiveley and Camille Rodier, had the inspiration of starting the Confrèrie des Chevaliers du Tastevin, which was inaugurated at a banquet at Clos de Vougeot in November 1934, on the eve of the annual auction of the wines of the Hospices de Beaune. The village of Meursault had initiated the "Paulée", a public lunch to celebrate the end of the harvest, in 1925. The three events, the banquet of the Confrèrie, the auction, and the Paulée de Meursault, taking place every year on the third weekend of November, became known as Les Trois Glorieuses, a promotional event that has stood Burgundy in good stead ever since.

Certainly there were wine books, of both the businesslike and the poetic kind. What was lacking was a voice that was personal and critical: a memoir of good and bad wines tasted, setting them in the context of the writer's (or the reader's) life. Colette wrote magically in this vein at moments. It was an Englishman, though, who is credited with launching the new genre: George Saintsbury, who had been both journalist and Professor of Literature, whose modest jottings, his *Notes on a Cellar Book*, opened the way in 1920 to the new critical and personal school.

The most prolific of all writers on wine from that day to this was André Louis Simon, a French expatriate in England, agent for Pommery Champagne from 1902 (when he was twenty-five) to 1932, who loved printer's ink almost as much as he loved good wine. In 1906–9 he published, in excellent English and at his own expense, the first three volumes of his *History of the Wine Trade in England* – the fruit of research that would have taken many historians half a lifetime. From the 1920s on the flow of his books and pamphlets was unending: all pithy, original and practical, yet with the irresistible trace of the Frenchman's oratory.

Around André Simon gathered a group of friends, wine merchants, and men of letters, who in 1931 founded a dining club in honour of George Saintsbury which still meets twice a year. Two years later, still during the Depression, several of the same friends founded the Wine and Food Society to proselytize in the name of "the art of good living": never wanton extravagance or elaborate meals; just what Simon called "honest wines and wholesome fare". The Society's quarterly journal helped to spread his gospel.

There is an English clubbiness about the books of Simon's friends that rarely seeks to look beyond the world of "classic" wines. H. Warner Allen, Charles Walter Berry, Ian Campbell, and Maurice Healy set the tone, reminiscent, sometimes, of Silas Weir Mitchell's old Madeira Party, or even the table talk of Oliver Wendell Holmes.

Yet Simon himself was acutely aware of the latent potential of the New World's wines. He travelled many times to America (first, as a Champagne salesman, to Chile in 1907: the wealth of Chile's nitrate mines gave it the highest consumption of Champagne per head of population in the world). On his arrival in New York in 1934 to found new chapters of the Wine and Food Society, a newspaper headline proclaimed "Europe's Greatest Eater With Us". The first American chapter was founded in New Orleans in 1935. Even at the age of eighty-seven André Simon was ready to investigate new ground. In 1964 he visited Australia and New Zealand, and was so impressed with Australian wine that *The Wines, Vineyards and Vignerons of Australia* was the penultimate book of his score of more than a hundred.

The essential unpretentiousness that made Simon the ideal interpreter of wine to the world is summed up in his modest definition of a connoisseur: "one who knows good wine from bad, and is able to appreciate the different merits of different wines". Many who have gone further have said too much.

CHAPTER 42

THE NEW WORLD CHALLENGES

Now that the New World's vineyards – Australia and California, New Zealand, South Africa, Chile, and Argentina – are giving us wines comparable to all but the very finest wines of France, it might seem their potential was never in doubt. But that is very far from the way it felt to André Tchelistcheff, a Russian émigré who came via France to the Napa Valley in 1937. He had been hired in Burgundy by Georges de Latour, the owner of the Beaulieu estate, to make the wines of his small private company, which had tottered through Prohibition with a sacramental licence.

Tchelistcheff had been working in France during the bleakest period of the 1930s, yet his first impression, he recalled, was of the startling crudity of Californian methods. Sulphur was thrown on the new-picked grapes by the bucketful until they were almost bleached; there was a mere vestige of a laboratory; when a fermenting vat grew dangerously hot (dangerous for the wine, that is) the only remedy was to heave in great blocks of ice to cool it down – a method which was not unknown, it must be admitted, even in Bordeaux. Stranger to him, and certainly less attractive, was the secrecy and suspicion that surrounded every operation. It was unthinkable to show your neighbour how you made your wine.

Thirty years before, Napa had been making wines that regularly won prizes in Europe. The old vineyards of Cabernet that had survived the rush to coarse varieties (there were about eighty-one hectares left) were producing wonderful fruit. But now there was virtually no market for good Californian wine, and scarcely any equipment to make it with. With a handful of

exceptions (nearly all discerning citizens of San Francisco and the surrounding cities), Americans continued to spurn the wines of their own soil. In New York, where fashions were set, it would have been eccentric, to say the least, to serve "domestic" wine. An enormous effort of will, and many years of research, were needed before Californian wines (and for California you can also read Australia throughout this period) were to become, and be acknowledged, challengers on an equal footing to the finest in the world.

Temperatures were the key. To a grape-grower, a Mediterranean climate is the recipe for an easy life, but the winemaker has to take a different view. The superiority of French and German wines was based on the matching of grape varieties to a relatively cool growing season, followed by the natural air-conditioning of cool autumn nights, followed by winter cold.

Arriving in California, Tchelistcheff was thunderstruck to see that wineries grew grapes for every sort of wine in the same vineyards. At Beaulieu there were twenty-eight different sorts of wine being made. The young Russian was a product of Capus' France, where appellations were all the talk. It seemed almost a moral outrage to plant Riesling and grapes for port side by side, and hopelessly optimistic to think that both should produce usable results. "Ecology", he recalls, "was known to us in Europe, but it was an absolutely foreign word here." Little by

LEFT Stainless steel took over the New World in the 1980s, making it possible to produce good table wines from regions that would previously have been too hot.

little that began to change, as wine growers listened to what the University of California at Davis (and Tchelistcheff) had to say, and as the merits of specialization were pointed out to them. But the distribution system still demanded a "full range" of wines to make up a brand, and it was not a good moment to tell your salesmen that your philosophy was different.

With hindsight it seems strange that the other crucial aspect of temperature, that of the fermenting tank, had not been tackled long before. The purpose of the buckets of sulphur was largely to prevent premature and precipitate fermentation, by which the wine lost all the flavour and perfume of the fruit, and rushed headlong towards becoming vinegar. It was certainly known that low temperatures do the same, far more effectively.

How to cool the vat in practice was the problem. Mr Brame in Algeria had bought a brewery cooling-system out of desperation in the 1880s, and from North Africa the idea found its way to Australia. But at this time there were only very few wineries that could afford this expense – or indeed that had the necessary water available.

As far as California was concerned, in the coastal valleys at least, and certainly in stone-built wineries or cellars, the hope was that the atmosphere would be cool enough to prevent disasters – and while vats were small in volume this was probably the case. The advice in the textbooks was clear: use a cold room or a cooling coil – or both. Yet in 1938 André Tchelistcheff was still resorting to blocks of ice. The general use of temperature- (and pressure-) controlled fermentation had to wait another twenty years, until stainless steel and electricity in large amounts became affordable. To most, in the 1950s, they were still a futuristic dream.

A dozen California winemakers were feeling their way towards quality in the late 1940s and early 1950s. There had been a handful of hopeful little start-ups: Mayacamas in the mountains between Napa and Sonoma; Buena Vista (restarted in 1943 in Haraszthy's old cellars); Martin Ray near Paul Masson in Santa Clara County, south of the Bay; and (an estate that was to become a miniature jewel, a sort of secret First Growth for white wines) Stony Hill at St Helena in the Napa Valley. Three or four of the old-established Napa wineries knew exactly what they were doing. Cabernet Sauvignons of the Beaulieu, Inglenook, Krug, and Martini vineyards of that decade have survived into the 1980s, and have matured into very handsome wines. But (and the "but" is not intended to be critical) they were wines in the vernacular style. It would have been hard to have mistaken them for French.

As for the white wines of the years after Repeal and before Renaissance, it was the Riesling that made the most distinguished bottles. Even when it was made strong and dry without cold fermentation the Riesling stood apart – just as it did in Australia. Picked at the right moment, it maintained its balancing acidity and aged beautifully. But again, nobody would have mistaken the wine for German.

This observation would not have bothered the winemakers.

Louis Martini, an Italian by origin, had a fully justified faith in his way of working with huge redwood tanks and large old oval barrels. Inglenook had a German winemaker who was very happy with the German-style barrels made of long-aged Baltic oak bought by the firm's Swedish founder. Even André Tchelistcheff, working for the one French-born proprietor among them, and the first to age his Cabernet in small oak barrels, did not flatter himself that he was making wine like Bordeaux. (For one thing he preferred American oak.) All aimed in their different ways at making irresistible wine from Napa Valley grapes – some more tannic, some less, some easy to drink young, some husky and demanding a decade in the bottle, but none in any sort of borrowed finery or modelled on Château Lafite or Château Latour.

This is where the Hanzell winery was different. Its founder was the former US ambassador to Italy, James D. Zellerbach, who had returned in 1948 with his wife Hannah and his fortune to a secluded upland valley just north of the town of Sonoma. During his time in Europe he had drunk much burgundy. Nothing had given him greater pleasure. So his retirement ambition was formed: to make wine as close to burgundy as he could get in California, by faithfully following every step of the Burgundian way of doing things.

He planted seventeen acres of Pinot Noir and Chardonnay (then a rare grape in California) on a slope not unlike – except in soil – the Côte d'Or, found a young winemaker, Bradford Webb, who was as dedicated to burgundy as himself, and installed temperature and humidity controls to match the atmosphere of a Burgundy cellar. He brought in new oak barrels from the *tonnelier* in Nuits-St-Georges, just as his favourite Burgundian proprietors did every year.

The story does not end happily for Mr Zellerbach. Not a vintage that he made through the 1950s quite measured up to his idea of great burgundy, and he died without knowing that his place in history had been won. His widow sold his last vintages in barrels at auction – fortunately to one of the most far-sighted and ambitious young men in the Napa Valley: Joseph Heitz. It was then, in 1960, that the word got out. Hanzell wines, but especially Hanzell Chardonnay, had the buttery, half-smoked aromas and flavours that up to then had spelt only Meursault, Montrachet, and Corton-Charlemagne.

Nothing could have revived the hopes of California more than this unexpected discovery. Proud as its winemakers were of their well-tuned wines, the realization that French flavours were within their grasp changed the morale of the industry almost overnight. In Chardonnay the French oak flavour is something tangible: easy to taste, simple to comprehend. Once you had learned to recognize the flavour, it could give the smack of quality, it seemed, to every wine. Heitz became the apostle of French oak, as much for his famous Martha's Vineyard Cabernet as for the Chardonnays and Pinot Noirs he had bought from Mrs Zellerbach. He had the audacity to charge $6 when the going rate was $2.5 or $3. In 1961 he opened his own winery, to add to the mere two dozen that were all the Napa Valley had still running. It was the valley's lowest point, with less vineyard area and fewer wineries than at any time since Prohibition. But from that moment on what had long seemed a huddle of eccentric craftsmen began once more to look like an industry.

Those first years of the 1960s are the turning point in modern wine history. A radical new idea was born in many places at once: that wine was not an esoteric relic of ancient times that was disappearing even in Europe, nor just a cheap way to get drunk, but an expression of the earth that held potential pleasure and fascination for everyone.

This was the era when the term "boutique winery" was coined, as dozens at first, and later hundreds, joined the rush to found their own. By 1970 there were 220 wineries in California; by 1980 more than 500. And the figures for Australia were not very different. Many were ephemeral; others have become landmarks, exploring new ideas, and making original contributions of hand-made wines that bigger companies' accountants will not allow them even to try.

True, tangible, and spectacular evidence that the Napa Valley was reborn came in 1966, with the launching of what has been its flagship ever since, the Robert Mondavi winery. Symbolically, it harked back to the spirit of the missions in the broad adobe arch of its facade. More significantly, when it was built it displayed the full glitter of the new technology: great stainless steel cylinders rearing up in the open air, their temperature monitored and controlled to the last degree by jackets of cooling fluid. It was a highly visible investment to challenge the leaders with technology that was state of the art (for once the phrase rings true), interwoven with old lessons learnt from France. Mondavi not only bought hundreds of barrels in France; he also tried every different type of oak and barrel-maker in as many combinations as that makes. His philosophy was empiricism to the point of mania. "There is everything to be learned," he said. He was bursting to experiment and discuss – and he carried California with him.

The vineyard figures tell the story. In 1965 there were 44,550 hectares of wine (as opposed to table, or raisin) grapes in the whole of California, most of them of inferior varieties and few in the best cool regions. Ten years later the figure had tripled, with many in the right places, many not; and with 9,720 hectares of Cabernet Sauvignon – but still only 4,050 of Chardonnay. Ten years later again the figure was only slightly higher, but there was an important shift towards the cooler coastal zones. While the Cabernet acreage had stayed about the same there were over 12,150 hectares of Chardonnay. Cool-climate Chardonnay, seasoned with French oak, had become the nation's favourite wine. But far more important, in 1980, for the first time in America's history, the nation drank more wine than spirits.

Wherever we have seen a revolution in taste, it has been the market that has pointed the direction. Specifically it was the long-awaited revival of Bordeaux in the 1950s that gave the

André Tchelistcheff wrote many of California's house rules. He came from Russia to work for a Frenchman in the Napa Valley in 1937.

signal – not just for Europe, but for the New World too. The 1940s had had four very good but small vintages: 1943, the famous 1945, 1947 and 1949. 1950 was a very big vintage, and a bargain even by the standards of the time. The Bordeaux of 1953 was seductive from the start. In 1955 prices were firmer than they had been for many years. Then came a killing frost in 1956, and three appalling years that made the baking summer of 1959 a talking-point, and its wine, in the crass phrase newspapers use, "the vintage of the century".

The tell-tale sign, if one had been reading the entrails, was that the phrase was taken up and repeated in America. The quality of a vintage made a headline, something it could not have done for forty years.

In California the lead came from the consumers of San Francisco. Leon Adams has pointed out that even during the years of Prohibition the people of northern California were able to make a better bath-tub brew. They could use real wine-grapes, Cabernet and Zinfandel, bought straight from good vineyards without suffering long journeys on a train. As the old Napa wineries had revived, rusty though they may have been, a trickle of good wine became a modest stream, at which a small but fascinated audience of prosperous young professionals in San Francisco and the cities round about had gathered to drink. Some, like the *parlementaires* of eighteenth-century Bordeaux, did more: they bought land and planted vines.

In Australia the new interest showed itself in the quickening pace at state and national competitions: the way the Australian wine industry has felt its own pulse since the agricultural shows of the Victorian era. Again, the enthusiasm was limited at first to a small group who could (or cared to) remember the interminable "bin numbers" by which most of the better wines of the long-established companies were known – just like the cask numbers that made German wine connoisseurs almost a secret society.

In both California and Australia, though, we must look at the mass market for the steps that made the 1960s the industrial, as well as the gastronomic, turning point. 1964 was the year that the Gallo winery at Modesto in the Central Valley, on the point of becoming America's largest, on the basis of such "pop" (i.e. sweetened and flavoured) wines as

Thunderbird, launched two landmark natural wines that assumed that Americans in very large numbers would actually like the taste. Chablis Blanc and Hearty Burgundy, although still clinging to borrowed French names, proved more than anything else that America was ready for wine as a clean, fruity, not quite dry, mealtime drink.

Australia's big companies went a slightly different way. By the mid 1960s they had the technology (the pressure tanks and coolers) in place to reinvent Australian white wine altogether. In place of the old burnt-out "dry reds" that, with port and sherry (and of course beer) were Australia's staples, they suddenly offered "Moselle", a Riesling- or Traminer-flavoured, and distinctly sweet, white wine. It was new German technology in the form of superfine filters that made it possible. It had been too risky before to leave unfermented sugar in the wine when it was bottled, but Seitz filters could clinically remove all trace of yeast that could possibly cause trouble. It remained only for Australia to adopt the "bladder pack", the plastic bag of three litres in a cardboard box with a tap, and all memories of fusty old bottles and corkscrews could be thrown aside. By the

The dramatic architecture of Robert Mondavi's winery, opened in 1966, is a Napa Valley landmark. The winery promised, and delivered, a revolution in Californian wine.

mid-1970s the word "wine", to most Australians, meant a white, fruit-juicy thirst-quencher as an alternative to beer.

What had changed, once and for all, regardless of country or culture or latitude, was that the fundamental lessons (among many others) had at last been learned: to choose grape varieties according to the climate; to control the temperature of the fermentation; and – to give wines a taste of luxury – to age them in French oak. Some of this was known in theory back in 1940; by 1975 it was known for certain everywhere.

One vital element remained a mystery, the one the French believe lies behind the ultimate quality of their wines: the influence of the soil. Still in 1980, in the hundredth anniversary issue of *California Agriculture*, an issue devoted to viticulture and oenology, not a single reference was made to the land itself, the soil in which the grape-vines have their roots.

California was ransacked for cool valleys to grow not just the fashionable favourites, Cabernet and Chardonnay, but the much less easily pleased Pinot Noir. A shrewd eye observed that the Willamette Valley in Oregon has a climate closer to that of Beaune than can easily be found in California. In 1965 David Lett began to plant his Eyrie Vineyard, and in 1970, with his first vintage, brought Oregon into the roster of quality wine regions. Washington State was just a whisker ahead. The university amateurs who called themselves Associated Vintners went commercial in 1967, encouraged by André Tchelistcheff, in retirement from Beaulieu and acting as mentor to countless hopeful wineries. The same year saw the first vintage of Chateau Ste Michelle, which has grown to be the biggest winery in the Northwest.

The same principles led Australia's vintners not just to re-examine where their grapes were planted, but also to realize that their traditionally narrow repertoire of varieties was by no means the best they could grow. If Max Lake was, in theory, going against the rules (though with remarkable success) by planting Cabernet in as warm a region as the Hunter Valley, there were the old Yarra Valley and Geelong vineyards in southern Victoria to be revived, virgin territory in southern South Australia to be planted, and a whole region south of Perth with a sea-cooled climate still unexploited for wine. South was one way to go; the other was uphill. In Pewsey Vale, high above the Barossa valley, Riesling found perfect cool ripening conditions, and even in warm northern Victoria growers have found the necessary cool nights by climbing to 762 metres and more. Coolest of all, with brilliant promise for Riesling, Chardonnay, and Pinot Noir, was Tasmania. But in 1958 it was a bold man who pioneered Hobart as a wine region.

Tchelistcheff had had no manual, and nor had any other of the pioneers of the new age. A manual was being written, though, in universities and research departments in a dozen countries. Students were being taught, and, more radically, teaching each other in ways quite foreign to the old way of doing things. Even academic hierarchies were crumbling in the torrent of new ideas and new questions.

The secrecy and suspicion that had kept even relations by marriage from sharing ideas could not survive the information revolution. What emerged was a sort of seething consensus, a vat of basic knowledge in full fermentation, its temperature rising, its fumes spreading, growing more potent by the day.

Its locomotive was a new international market, very different from the old national markets of the producing countries. They had been chauvinistic, inflexible, and unquestioning of quality or even authenticity. Wine was a commodity, part of the diet, set at different price levels for different rungs of the social ladder, but unlikely ever to grow in importance or volume. In the 1970s wine became for the first time a lifestyle choice for a new class of consumers: those with discretionary cash. They were first identified by supermarkets in Britain in the 1960s. Britain is a paradigm of these changes, and also an important influence on world wine opinion. What happened in Britain once again, as in the eighteenth and nineteenth centuries, set the agenda far beyond its shores.

The old assumptions (fine wines came from Bordeaux and Burgundy, via old London or provincial wine merchants) began to crumble in the early 1960s. In 1962 Parliament outlawed the retail price maintenance which had sustained an effective cartel. In 1964 another Act of Parliament permitted shops to sell alcohol within the hours when pubs were shut. Supermarkets were quick to take advantage of the novel liberalism. Where were they to find new supplies for new customers? At first they were conservative. Sainsbury, with Marks & Spencer and Tesco the leaders of the new High

degree-days Fitting the grape varieties to the climate was the first great undertaking of the University of California's department of viticulture and oenology, which had moved in the 1930s from Berkeley to Davis, inland near Sacramento. As far back as the 1880s Professor Hilgard had made the obvious distinction between the Coastal Ranges, where the ocean has a measurable effect, and the Central Valley, where it has little or none. Wasting no time after Repeal, in 1936 Albert Winkler and Maynard Amerine set out the principles of "heat-summation", or totting up the average temperatures of the days in the growing season when the thermometer is above 10°C (50°F). This wonderfully simple measure seems to work. At 10°C the vine is active and growing: What heat-summation does is to add up the temperatures of its active hours. It gives a direct means of comparison between vineyards across the world. The Médoc, for example, has about 2,500 "degree-days", or total degrees above 10°C during the growing season; the Napa Valley has a range from 2,340–2,610. Cabernet therefore should grow perfectly in the Napa Valley – and it does.

Little, if anything, is predictable in the choppy Coastal Ranges, where all depends on the cold sea air being vacuumed inland through gullies and over passes by the great hot updraught in the Central Valley. Sometimes a promising valley whose "degree-days" were a perfect match for Pauillac or Beaune turned out to be a funnel for howling gales on summer afternoons. But Winkler and Amerine's work has been text-book material now for over forty years, the equivalent of centuries in the history of European wine.

Street world of wine, did not launch a New World wine until 1970 (it was South African and white). It took it another seven years to offer its first wine from Italy.

But the move that broke the mould was, as usual, a political one. The British wine trade was snug within its immemorial customs until 1973. Established merchants with established customers knew what was expected of them. They were not too nice about adding a dash of a headier brew (as they added Hermitage to Lafite in the nineteenth century); even, it is said, bottling burgundy and Châteauneuf out of the same vat. Mostly, though, they practised cosy relations with suppliers, buying wines without the official papers that should go with them; sometimes to their customers' advantage in lower prices, sometimes not.

Averys of Bristol, for example, known for its excellent burgundy bottlings, admitted to operating in a parallel world where its Chambertin or Musigny was "unofficial" – and none the worse for it. But 1972 was the last vintage under the old rules. On September 1, 1973, Britain signed up for entry into the EEC. Whether the appellation laws were right or wrong, effective or ineffective, protected quality or merely producers, they had to be obeyed.

The scene was set for tectonic movement. But it was still slow in coming; wine-drinkers were conservative: resistant to learning new names, perhaps, more than new flavours. Australia, though, was lining up to serve. It was an ace.

There is no mystery about supermarket strategy: they compete on price, employing buyers with ways of persuading suppliers to accept less. To accept less, suppliers have to feel threatened – and in the 1980s in Britain, Australia was

the judgement of paris Nothing could have dramatized the millennium better than a tasting that was organized in Paris in 1976 by an English wine merchant, Steven Spurrier. He assembled a company of some of the best-respected wine-growers of Bordeaux and Burgundy, restaurateurs from Paris, and even the senior inspector of the Institut National des Appellations d'Origine, and offered them a range of French and California wines in unmarked bottles. California Cabernets were mingled with Médoc crus classés and California Chardonnays with grand cru and premier cru white burgundies.

In both groups, red and white, a California wine was judged best: in the Cabernet line Stag's Leap 1973 from the Napa Valley, with Château Mouton-Rothschild 1970 as runner-up, and in the Chardonnays, Château Montelena 1973, also from the Napa Valley, with a Meursault Charmes in second place. The other wines jostled closely in a finishing line that proved quite simply that their qualities, in expert French eyes, were approximately equal.

There was much disclaiming of the results (though not by the judges), saying (which is perfectly true) that the best Bordeaux and burgundy need longer to reach maturity and – more important to the tasters at the time – that the sheer ripeness of California grapes suggests to the French-trained palate an exceptional vintage. All this is beside the fundamental point. Whether or not the ultimate quality and value of the wines was precisely as they were found to be on that day, the principle was proven: after little more than a decade of experience with French techniques, Californians were able to match the originals they so much admired.

the threat. Much was made of this unregulated paradise for producers, contrasting it with the sclerotic old world where appellation-limiting regions, grape varieties, and the size of crops were supposedly hamstringing the whole wine industry. Australia was praised for its liberal attitudes that allowed grape-growers to irrigate their vines, and France ridiculed for seeing irrigation as another word for dilution. Australia meanwhile praised itself for making squeaky-clean, "fruit-driven" wines to precise parameters of scent and flavour. Any flavours not fitting the mechanistic model they described as "faults". The word "winemaker" has no European equivalent; nor did the job, that of a technically educated quality-controller. But nothing else will do for a market set to sell unprecedented quantities of consistent wine at apparent bargain prices.

There were other factors. In the mid-1980s the Australian dollar was drastically devalued. The perceived purity of high-tech wine was a powerful boost to sales, too, in 1985 and 1986, when Austria and Italy were both found guilty of adding substances (diethylene glycol and methanol, respectively) to mask the unripeness of wines with pretensions to quality. Nor did the fall-out from the explosion of Chernobyl raise confidence in European farm products.

To the British public, as so often the bell-wether when tastes in wine are changing, Australian wine had another overriding attraction: its names are in English. British bashfulness about pronouncing foreign names is legendary. French calls for facial contortions, Italian for enthusiasm, German for intense mental concentration. Australian gets no worse than slightly comical names from the aboriginal. Jacob's Creek proved the point so conclusively that ten years later there were Creeks, Valleys, Mountains, and Ridges on labels from countries where English is a foreign tongue.

Chile was the first emerging country of the old colonial world to throw its hat in the ring. It had long been the supplier of what are now called "premium" wines to South America, or rather to its urban sophisticates. Their taste was for wine "mellowed" by long ageing in wood, which in South America rarely meant oak, but antique wooden ovals of rauli, the southern beech of the temperate Andes. Over time, cleaned only by diminutive descendants of the Incas with scrubbing brushes, they acquired what might be called ancestral aromas.

Europe tasted the results politely, was intrigued by the story of vineyards so remote that phylloxera had never arrived, but was unimpressed. Chile had painful adjustments to make in the 1980s, pulling up and replanting half its vines, before the quality and clarity of its intense fruit flavours made an impression. And, just as in California thirty years before, it was the use of French oak that proved the decisive factor.

New Zealand was next, arriving on the international scene with dramatic, and wholly unexpected, éclat. The wines at a press tasting held at New Zealand House in London in 1984 made an extraordinary impression. A palpable buzz went round the room as the tasters encountered successful

New Zealand Sauvignon Blanc for the first time. Aromas only hinted at in familiar wines from the same grape in Sancerre and the Graves leapt from the glasses, a sensory assault that had journalists evoking gooseberries and melons with uninhibited relish. In a world where varietal character was at a premium, here it was in primary colours. New Zealand, in the high latitudes with hot days and cold nights, spelt out fruit flavours with almost painful precision. It fitted the inclinations of the turn of the century equally precisely.

Argentina's arrival on the scene was delayed by the political and economic shambles surrounding the Falklands War. Its wine industry, supplying most of South America's needs, was the world's fourth largest, and resolutely Italian in spirit. Large, wicker-covered containers of sweet and prickly red were the norm. Though its vineyards have rather different conditions from those of Chile they have the same advantages: low humidity, intense light, and a remarkable lack of the pests and diseases that bedevil European vines. In the ten short years since their arrival on the international stage they have brought the almost-forgotten Bordeaux grape, the Malbec, back into the limelight. Malbec was one of the building blocks of Bordeaux's fame. It fell out of favour for its relative proneness to rot, mildew, and frost, dangers (frost excepted) almost unknown in the Andes. Its quality and originality were key to Argentina's rapid success when it started to export to Europe and North America in the 1990s.

Latest on the stage in what has become a swelling chorus of excellent performers was South Africa, detained in isolation until the final decade of the twentieth century by its reactionary government. In a country where even the import of good grape vines was forbidden, there was little South Africans could do except produce bargain white wines from the grape they had fortuitously adopted, the Chenin Blanc of the Loire. They are certainly making up for lost time.

Christie's of London first auctioned wine in the 1700s. In 1966 Michael Broadbent (left) restarted its wine auctions, reflecting and encouraging a new interest in wine's intrinsic value.

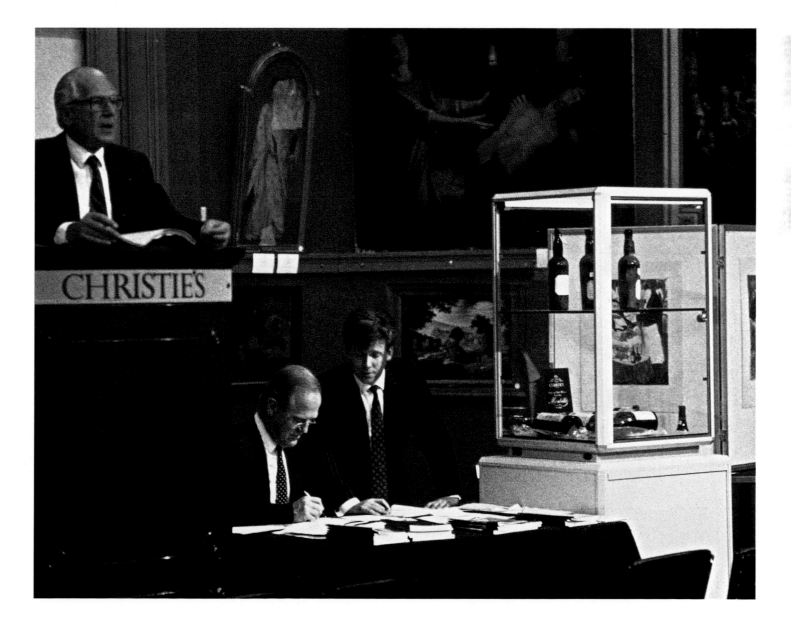

CHAPTER 43

THE OLD WORLD RESPONDS

In 1948 the French historian Daniel Halévy wrote an essay, "On the Acceleration of History", in which he demonstrates, with evidence, how time passes faster and faster. The pharaohs, he argues, had no sense of urgency in anything they did; the Egyptians lived in an eternal present. The rising of the Nile was the only relevant interval of time, and progress was a concept unknown to them. The Greeks measured time from the foundation of their cities; the Jews from the Creation. Christians anticipated an imminent Judgement Day. Nor did the Chinese conceive of progress; they ignored inventions (printing, for example, and navigation) which could have changed their lives.

Who first linked hope with scientific discovery to believe that progress was possible? Was it the alchemists, vainly trying to manufacture gold? Wherever it began, the belief that science could improve life without limit took over the western world. The pace of change was determined not by need but by discovery and invention – a process that inevitably accelerates. Whether or not time is shrinking, that is the practical effect of headlong scientific progress: the future happens at the same time as the present. We accept obsolescence without question, and become less and less able or willing to learn from the past.

Australia and California have never been captives of history; they were free to reinvent their old wine industries as they went along. It was a different story in a Europe that had spent most of the twentieth century tying itself to a more and more rigid code of regulations. In France, what began after phylloxera as moves to suppress fraud matured into the concept of *appellations contrôlées*. The Institut National des Appellations d'Origine was formed after World War II. It went much further than the mere policing of fraud, or even the drawing of boundaries between *cru* and *cru*; by degrees it came to regulate exactly what vine was planted where all over France. In 1990 its remit was made specific: so to limit planting that only geographical names would be necessary. The grape variety would eventually be mandatory. The control of detail by the state that defines France would make sure that everything that was not authorized was forbidden.

Its *fonctionnaires* have ideal material to work on: a land rich in traditions, many half-submerged, but real nonetheless – the inheritance of centuries of Gallic gastronomy. What is the genius that gives recipes and flavours equal ranking with historical monuments in French culture? How did the wines of such obscure corners as Fronton, or Tursan, or Menetou-Salon achieve definition and validity? The simple answer is that the French, even uneducated people shackled to the land, care about these things. The land is rich. Its farms produce more than the bare necessities, and on this surplus, however meagre, the national preoccupation with the table gets to work. And the bureaucrat moves in to codify the results. The wine-grower's every move is watched through binoculars from Paris.

The INAO can fine a farmer for even a tentative experiment in anything it has not prescribed (although, sadly, not for making and selling bad wine). While it takes the reasonable, and certainly historical, view that nothing would be gained, and confusion would be certain, if (for example) Cabernet were planted in the Côte d'Or or Pinot Noir in the Médoc, it also (for

example) bans Riesling from anywhere in France except Alsace. A grower in Limoux in the Midi in the 1990s planted a few vines of Riesling and Gewürztraminer, convinced that the cool conditions of the Limoux hills have potential for aromatic white wines. The INAO fined him and compelled him to pull them up, without right of appeal. Riesling is the prerogative of Alsace; in Paris, politics take precedence over progress.

At the turn of the twenty-first century winery design was becoming an art form. Spain has more than its share of these modern castles. Ysios in Rioja, by the architect Santiago Calatrava, is a notable example.

France's appellations evolved steadily over more than forty years into a crisply detailed schedule (to which minute details are regularly added; the mills grind exceeding small). Germany was slightly ahead in time, but far less ambitious in definitions. Its wine law of 1930 needed constant revision and clarification, and the 1971 version is widely regarded as doing even less that is useful for the consumer. Quality standards are still entirely self-policed. Portugal was the other country that in the 1930s granted a few historic regions *selos de origen*. All that happened in Italy and Spain was that the producers of the best-known wines formed associations to defend and promote their names. In Spain it was Rioja (in 1926) and Jerez (in 1933). In Italy Chianti was the inevitable test case.

The government in Rome would not be drawn into demarcating boundaries, but would agree only to legislate on the "special and constant characteristics" that Chianti should have. The producers of the central zone between Florence and Siena took the matter into their own hands. In 1924 they formed the Consorzio del Vino Chianti Classico, identified by a black rooster, to be followed three years later by their northern neighbours, who formed a rival Consorzio, with a cherub as its badge.

Anarchy reigned over the rest of Italy until 1963, when the government began its labour of Sisyphus, the task of agreeing the names, and framing the bye-laws, for the country's labyrinth of "traditional" wines. Were these traditions as soundly based as those of France? It is hard to say, as the wines on the whole were so badly made. But forty years later the job is still not finished and probably never will be. To induce a consensus among neighbouring farmers may take ten years of negotiation, to wrangle with the bureaucrats of Rome another five, and meanwhile events move on. By 2000 Italy had more than 220 Denominazioni de Origine Controllati, which specify exactly how much wine at what strength, pressed from what weight of

ABOVE The opinions of Robert M. Parker Jr. have influenced winemakers everywhere.

BELOW The Italian genius for design has spawned an infinity of new labels – but what is the wine?

which grape varieties in which demarcated zone, may bear the name of the DOC and also, something that France's appellation laws have never attempted – a full-frontal description of what the customer is to expect – the colour, scent, and flavour which constitute the "special and constant characteristics" of each wine.

Italy began its task either too late or too early; in any case, at the moment when tradition was far from being the first priority of a quickly-changing world. A DOC presupposes that whatever wines have been made in the recent past constitute the best a region can produce. It does nothing more than freeze the status quo. Which was more important, producers began to ask, the reassurance of an old name, a too-tight uniform hampering free movement, or the liberty of independence?

Different regions had different answers. Growers in Piedmont, for example, had a choice of excellent local vines perfectly suited to their vineyards. Nebbiolo is to Barolo what Pinot Noir is to the Côte d'Or. But in Tuscany, Baron Ricasoli's old recipe for Chianti was compromised by penny-pinching. Large amounts of white grapes were authorized in the blend, and the vine at the heart of it, the Sangiovese, had proliferated second-rate, over-productive clones that barely ripened. It was not regulation that was needed, but reform.

No one was better placed to show Chianti the way than the Marchese Piero Antinori. The Antinoris (their address is Palazzo Antinori, Piazza Antinori, Florence) have made Chianti for 600 years. He was not the first to have limited faith in the grapes of his ancestors. A Count Franchetti of Artimino, near Florence, had planted Cabernet Sauvignon in the nineteenth century, having married a Rothschild from Château Lafite, and their Carmignano blend of Cabernet with Sangiovese had even acquired its own DOC. Antinori agreed that Tuscany's principal grape was not well enough understood, or well enough selected, to make fine wine unaided. His solution was to Tuscanize

Cabernet Sauvignon, bringing it to the aid of over-light Chianti, but more boldly launching an unclassified wine with an overtly Cabernet character, Tignanello. The 1975 vintage of Tignanello, a blend of four-fifths Sangiovese with one-fifth Cabernet Sauvignon, set the pattern for what became known as "Super Tuscans". At the same time Antinori launched the first all-Cabernet Tuscan wine from his cousin's seaside property at Bolgheri, Sassicaia. Now the question was why had no one planted in this favoured spot before? (The answer: no one lived there; the Maremma coast was plagued by pirates and malaria).

A wider question was where did such unregulated but superior wines fit in to the system. Legally they had to be sold as *vini da tavola* – the humblest rank in the book. The law looked an ass as their prices shot past DOC levels. Italians are not bashful about ambitious, even flamboyant, pricing. It was for the market to approve the new Super Tuscans. It emphatically did. And Chianti found itself the country cousin of innumerable new-age blends from ancient cellars, usually scented with Cabernet and invariably with expensive French oak.

Where the market led the law had to follow, creating, in 1992, the new category, more lightly policed than DOC, of Indicazione Geografica Tipica, or IGT. It was not too proud, either, to give such a mould-breaking estate as Sassicaia a DOC of its own. Meanwhile Chianti profited from Tuscany's mended reputation and fortunes: in heavy high-shouldered bottles of near-black glass, Riservas could claim prices undreamed of in the old *fiasco* days. It was reprieve for Sangiovese, already ennobled in the form of Brunello di Montalcino. Not Cabernet but French oak, heavy bottles, and ambitious marketing soon appeared all over Italy, sometimes accompanied by better wines, sometimes not.

At the same time in Spain something similar happened. The house of Torres in Catalonia had a big business and a broad perspective, shipping wines in bulk to North and South

ABOVE: LEFT Piero Antinori was the driving force behind the revival of Tuscan wines in the 1970s and 1980s.
RIGHT Robert Mondavi (left) and Philippe de Rothschild turned friendship into the first Franco-Californian joint wine venture, Opus One.

America. The Torres brand, rather than an appellation, was its sales point. Torres took the initiative, first by bottling and establishing a label worthy of respect, then by planting Cabernet and Merlot to follow the international trend of the 1960s. When Torres Gran Coronas Cabernet 1970 was judged the equal of Château Latour of the same excellent vintage, it might have seemed inevitable that international varieties would repopulate the vineyards of Spain.

It did look, for a while in the 1980s and 1990s, as if a tsunami of Cabernet and Chardonnay was about to engulf the world's wine-drinkers. They were the grapes of choice in all the New World's emerging wine countries (even Australia flinched from its habitual Shiraz, though New Zealand pressed ahead with Sauvignon Blanc and Oregon with Pinot Noir). For such countries as Portugal and Greece, and those who were marooned behind the Iron Curtain, with a baggage-train of traditions and grape varieties which they had never fully exploited or even understood, and perhaps only half-believed in, there was a sore temptation to plant what was most in demand. Nor did the new mass consumer market look for anything more challenging.

What seemed an equal risk, at least to those who see diversity as important, was the ubiquitous advance of new wine technology. By the end of the twentieth century there were few winemakers, in either the New World or the Old unaware of wine science: the physical and biological grounds of their art, and the controls available to improve, or at least to change, the wine they were making. The new position was dramatized by the invention, in September 1987, of the "flying winemaker", an Australian technician employed in his down-time (the Australian vintage being six months away) to supervise production in a French winery, rather as a pilot joins a ship to navigate into port – except that the pilot brings local knowledge, the flying winemaker scientific training. The first was Nigel Sneyd, flown to Bergerac, to the growers' cooperative of St Vivien et Bonneville in Montravel, by Tony Laithwaite, an English wine merchant devoted to France who saw nothing but opportunities in the latest technology. Sneyd made 5,000 cases of an unoaked dry Sémillon. It won a gold medal at Mâcon the next year.

Flying winemakers introduced Australian winemaking disciplines. The first thing their French colleagues noticed was a doubling of their water bills as every corner of the premises was hosed down twice a day. As little as possible was left to chance. The litany of their precautionary controls starts with hygiene, then seeks to eliminate any deviation from a master-plan. The grapes must be picked at a precise degree of ripeness, protected from oxygen, if necessary by inert gases, pressed at low temperatures, preferably in a closed press, and fermented with selected and artificially cultured yeast. If oxygen is needed to mould the molecules, it can be bubbled in in controlled quantities. If enzymes are required, they can be added at the right moment. Acidity can be adjusted, and oak flavours added. New research adds new possibilities of control every year.

The more you control, on the other hand, the more you must decide. The Bordeaux oenologist Emile Peynaud once said: "The winemaker's ultimate goal is to do nothing." But only the most privileged producers are in the position where they have no adjustments they want (or perhaps dare) to make. Winemaking on biodynamic principles carries this attitude to extremes. For the others the choice becomes bewildering.

It is always the market that decides. To Goethe it was clearly polarized. The rich, he said, want the best wine; the poor, a lot of wine. The information age, though, has brought a third force into the market; the middle-class wine buff, more demanding than either those who can afford to drink famous growths regularly or the mass who, in the time-honoured phrase, know nothing about wine, but know what they like. Professional men, doctors in particular, led the way. By the 1950s the London wine trade saw the need for similar qualifications and inaugurated the Institute of Masters of Wine, under the auspices of the medieval Vintners Company. The MWs, as they were soon called, rapidly generated a body of scholarly knowledge. And to satisfy critical, knowing consumers a new service industry evolved, starting in the 1960s with new ways of writing about wine in books,

magazines, and in merchants' lists. Journalists discovered a market for any information, even the most arcane, that gave a wine, and its producer, a distinguishable profile.

I t started with grape varieties. Proud proprietors of Bordeaux châteaux were at first surprised when journalists asked them what grapes they grew. Some could not even answer the question without research. With quizzing, self-doubt set in. Were the old oak fermenting vats up to it? Would stainless steel be better? Each decade since the 1960s has seen new questions. Harvest dates, thinning the crop on the vines, concentrating the must, the choice of yeast, the length of maceration, and the choice of barrels have all become topics of moment.

We have seen how the taste of oak in wine became something desirable in California in the 1960s. Up to then, in France, it had been something to avoid – or at most incidental in the early stages of fine wines. "First-growths" chose barrels from the Baltic precisely because they gave the wine the least flavour. The role of the barrel, they believed, was neutral storage with the perfect degree of oxidization, while the wine matured ready for bottling. A new generation of American, then of Australian, and finally of European tasters saw it differently. Rioja had been transformed by barrels in the nineteenth century. Now the vanilla flavour found in the oak of certain French forests became the hallmark of every fashionable wine. (A few preferred the sweet taste of American oak chosen in Rioja.) By toasting the inside of the barrel, coopers found, they could give any wine a caramel flavour – a plan taken up with enthusiasm by producers eager to attract attention to otherwise unremarkable products. Better still, with the price of barrels steadily rising, and their original function all but forgotten, they could hang a bag of oak chips in a steel tank for the seasoning effect, and who would know the difference?

The world had never seen such open competition before, between different countries and regions growing the same grapes, using the same methods, and aiming at the same markets. It was neatly dramatized by the American critic Robert Parker Jr, who in the 1970s devised a scoring system for wines based on the American High School formula of points out of 100, discounting the first fifty points. A numerical appraisal needs no translation. His eloquent tasting notes tend to be overlooked; dealers and collectors can play with the numbers on their computers. If his system tends to favour strong wines of rich flavour and obvious personality it is because they stand out in comparative tastings. In a thirteenth-century Battle of Wines conducted by the King of France the sweet wine of Cyprus beat all comers.

The French and German wines that served as models were historical accidents, evolving where the soil, climate, and the demand were most propitious. If all the best came from areas where conditions were marginal, it was because slowly ripened grapes have most flavour, and cold weather during fermentation preserves it. But science is there to prevent accidents. If it can reproduce these conditions, by advanced techniques of cultivation in the vineyard and by air-conditioning the cellar, presumably there is only a residual advantage in possessing the historic original.

the euro effect   The European Union has had a profound effect on the evolution of the wine industry through its massive "transfers" of money from North to South. The quality of many wines from Portugal, Spain, southern Italy and Greece has been transformed by these political investments. The apparent miracle of fine wines suddenly appearing from parts of Europe previously known (if at all) for blending wine has a simple explanation: billions of euros from the pockets of Europe's more prosperous citizens, their potential consumers. Very few complaints have been heard.

The theme of the twenty-first century is no longer imitation, or even emulation. It is fashioning new idioms. Cabernets from California and Chile, Australian Riesling, New Zealand Sauvignon Blanc, Argentine Malbec are as confident as claret on the world stage. Bordeaux, meanwhile, reconsiders. The cult of "garage" wines is an ironic take on the very notion of the château; they are untraditionally big wines from little properties. Perhaps by the end of the century claret made in the traditional style, lean and long-lived, will be considered a period piece: the Chippendale of the wine list. What other classics can be certain to survive in their present form? Champagne and Chablis, red burgundy, the peerless Rieslings of the Mosel, perhaps vintage port, Barolo… it is not an endless list.

When we followed James Brydges, the opulent Lord Chandos, down to his cellar at the start of the eighteenth century, we found him collecting wines from all over France and Italy, with a special penchant for anything sweet. For an equivalent three centuries later (Chandos was entirely pragmatic) consider a list published in *The Wine Spectator*, naming The Top 100, "the most exciting wines" of 2003. Twenty-five, of which seventeen were red, were from California or Washington State. Fifteen were from Italy, largely Tuscany and Piedmont, of which one was white. There were ten red Bordeaux, nine reds from southern France,

A modern winery reflects the globalization of wine. This is Terra da Vino in Barolo, Italy: it could be anywhere on any of five continents.

eight French whites, seven Spanish reds, seven Australian reds, six German whites, four Chilean reds, three ports, and three each from New Zealand and South Africa. And one from Argentina.

The vitality of the world of wine is the concluding message of this book. Never before has it had so many admirers, or critics, as at the turn of the twenty-first century. From being the daily drink of a handful of Mediterranean nations, and an exotic luxury to the rest of the world, it has become a subject of intense worldwide interest, competition and comparison, an industry comparable in some ways with fashion, with the great difference that for all the style and glamour of its market image, its roots are in the earth.

For no critic should forget, as he dallies with epithets, sipping his barrel-fermented Chardonnay, or rates one precious bottle half a point behind another, that wine is one of the miracles of nature, and that its 10,000 years of partnership with man has not removed that element of mystery, that independent life that has made men think of it, alone of all our foods, as divine. Farmer and artist, drudge and dreamer, hedonist and masochist, alchemist and accountant – the wine-grower is all these things, and has been since the Flood.

INDEX

noble rot/mould *see* botrytis
Noilly Prat 220
Noir de Pressac *see* Malbec
Noirien 73, 74
Nuits-St-Georges 149, 162, 177, 179

O

Ochagavia Errauriz, Silvestre 226–7
Offley Forrester & Co. 174
oidium (powdery mildew)
  see diseases
Omar Khayyam 17, 55–56
Ondenc 50
Opus One 247
Ordish, George 213
Osborne, Mr 193–4
Osborne, Thomas 170
Ottoman Empire
  Austria and 126
  Cyprus 84, 94
  grapes 15
  Hungary and 125
  Islam 56
  Spain and 100
  Venice and 84, 100
  vineyards 58
  wine drinking 22, 56
  wine trade *82, 83,* 100
  winemaking 13, 16, 58
Oudart, Louis 218
Ouvrard, Julien-Jules 149

P

Paguierre, M 198
Pais *see* Mission [grape]
Palomino (Listan/White French) 95, 171
Pape Clément 79
Parellada 224
Paris 51, 152–4
  cabarets 152–4
  droit d'entrée 152, 153
  French Revolution 152–3
  guingettes 152, 153
  Siege of 180
  smugglers 152–3
  vins de France 63, 75, 78, 112, 154
Parker, Robert M. Jr *246,* 248
Pasteur, Louis 210, *211*
Pedro Ximénez 95, 164, 171
Penfold, Christopher 185
Peninsular War 165, 169, 170, 172, *175*
Penn family 187, 189
Penning-Rowsell, Edmund 78
Pepys, Samuel 107, *109,* 161
Percival, Robert 132
Pérignon, Dom 112–17, 177
Perrier, Joseph 178–9
Perrier-Jouët 180
Persia 15, 17, 55–56, *57,* 58, 131
Peru 91, 226
Pesquera 89
Petit Verdot 108, 143, 196
Petit Vidure *see* Cabernet Sauvignon
Petite Sirah 143, 195
Petri, Louis 234
Pétrus 143, 200–1
Peynaud, Emile 248
Philippe d'Orleans 117
Philippe the Bold of Burgundy 73, 74
Philippe the Good of Burgundy *70, 71,* 73–74
Phillip, Arthur 181
Phoenicians 15, 57
phylloxera *see* diseases
Pichon, Jacques François de 140
Pichon-Lalande 140
Pichon-Longueville 140, 198
Picolit 221
Picpoul 154
Piedirosso 39

Pijassou, Professor 140
Pineau 73
Pineau de la Loire 101
Pinot Blanc (Morillon) 114
Pinot Gris (Fromenteau/Beurot) 73, 74, 114, 148, 154, 201
Pinot Meunier 114, 201
Pinot Noir [grape] 74, 112, 114, 146, 147, 150, 154, 192, 201, 207, 213, 225, 238, 241, 247
Pinot Noir [wine] 208, 238
pisco 226
Planchon, Jules-Emile 211–12
Plat, Hugh 106
Plato 27
Pliny 36, 39, 40, 50, 67, 156, 212, 215
Pluche, abbé 114–15
Pol Roger 179
Poland 59, 125, 126, 127, 140, 162, 188
Pombal, Marquês de 123
Pomerol 200
Pommard 162, 200
Pommery & Greno 179
Pompeii 36, *38,* 40, 48
Pontac(k) 108, *109,* 111, 145, 162, 163
Pontac family 107–8, 109, 111, 145
port 90, 98, 102, 111, 118–23, 127, 129, 162, 163, 164, 165, 172–5, 200, 223, 249
  ageing 174, 175
  Australian 184, 185
  barcos rabelos 120, 121, 122
  brandy, adding 122, 123, 168, 174–5, 182
  Douro 102, 111, 119, 120, 121, 169, 174, 175
  Douro Wine Company 123, 172, 174–5
  elderberry juice, adding 174, 175
  feitorias 119, 123, 136, 172
  Factory House, Oporto 172
  lodges 122, 172, 174
  "portoport" 121
  "priestport" 121
  quintas 172–4, 175
  shippers 172–3, 174, 175
  sweet 171
  tawny 172, 175
  Upper Douro *118,* 119, 120, 121, 122, 123, 172–4
  vintage 172, 174, 249
Portugal 172–5
  Alentejo 89
  Azores 111
  Black Death 89
  Britain and 89, 90, 109, 111, 119–23, 132, 134–6, 161, 162–3, 164, 165, 169, 172, 174, 175
  Carcavelos 123
  civil wars 174
  cork 106
  exploration 90, 119, 136
  France and 121, 165, 171–2, 214
  Islam 54, 57, 89
  lagares 67
  Lamego 120
  Lisbon 102, 111, 119, 120, 121, 123, 161
  Madeira *see* main entries
  Miguelites 174
  Minho 119–21
  Monção 119, 121
  Netherlands and 102, 120, 121
  Oporto 102, 111, 119, 120–1, 122, 123, 165, 169
  Oporto Factory House 172
  Pinhão 120
  port *see* main entry
  quintas *see* main entry
  Reconquista 89, 90
  selos de origen 246

Spain and 89, 91, 111, 119, 121, 123, 135, 172, 224
USA and 136
Viana 119
vineyards 57, 89, 121–2, 123, 133, 165, 169, 172–4, 247
  feitorias 119, 123, 136, 172
  oidium 224
  phylloxera 213, 214
  ramo 123
wine measures 120
wine trade 89, 109, 111, 119–23, 134–6, 161, 162, 164, 165, 169, 172–4, 214
winemaking 134, 135, 136, 174
Also see specific grapes/wines
Postup 84
Pramnian 25
Prignac 145
Priorato 69, 224
Prohibition 231, 232–3, *234, 235,* 237, 239
Prosecco 84
Prošek 84
Protos 89
Prussia 126, 194, 208
  Austria and 203, 218
  Belgium and 203
  Britain and 203
  France and 140, 178, 180, 198, 203, 207, 208, 212, 218
  Netherlands and 203
Pury, de, family *182,* 186

Q

Quintano, Manuel 224
quintas *118, 119,* 172–4, 213

R

"Rainwater" 136
Rákóczi family *124,* 125, 126
rancio 162
Rauzan, Pierre de 140
Rauzan-Gassies 140, 198
Rauzan-Ségla 140, 198
Raventos family 224
Ray, Martin 238
Recioto 221
Redding, Cyrus 168, 175, 215
religions, wine and 28–34, 42–45
  Babylonian 16–17
  Bacchanalia 32–34, 42, *46, 47,* 51
  Christianity *see* main entry
  Cistercians *see* main entry
  drug use 30
  Druids 46
  Egyptian 22
  Greek *see* Dionysian cult
  Islam *see* main entry
  Judaism *see* main entry
  Puritanism 96
  Roman (Imperial) 32–34
retsina 25
Reynell, John 185
Rhenish *see* France: Rhineland *and* Germany: Rheingau
Ribadavia 89, 224
Ricasoli, Baron Bettino 217–18, 221
Riesling [grape] 51, 74, 153, 156, 158, *185,* 195, 205, 207, 208, 227, 237, 241, 245
Riesling [wine] 156–8, 185, 208, 238, 249
Rioja 34, 48, 89, 224–5, 226, *227,* 246
Rioja [wine] 89, 223, 224, 225, 226, 227, 246, 248
  Ygay 226
Riscal 225, 226
Riscal, Marqués de 225, 226
Rivero, J.M. 170
Rivesaltes 142

Rocheret, Bertin de 117
Roederer 176
Roman Republic/Empire
  Britain and 50, 51–52
  Carthage and 35–36, 48
  Galen 40
  fall of 52–53
  Gauls (France/Germany) and 35, 37, 40, 41, 46–53, 75
  religion and wine 33–35
  Spain and 37, 40, 48
  vineyards 57
  wine drinking 36, 39, 40
  winemaking 13, 15, 36, 38, 39, 40–41, 50, 156
  wine trade 12, 35–36, 37, 40, 46, 48–50
  Pompeii 36, *38,* 40, 48
Romanée-Conti 143, 149 150, 177, 214
Romania/Romaney/Rumney 83, 92
Roth, Adam 184
Rothschild, Philippe de 108, *247*
Roupnel, Gaston 204
Rozier, abbé 150
Rüdesheimer 155
Ruinart family 117, 176
rum 164
Ruskin, John James 172
Russia
  France and 154, 176, 177, 178, 198, 231
  Hungary and 125, 126
  vineyards 126
  wine drinking 58, 177, 178
  wine trade 58, 59, *82, 83,* 125, 154, 177, 178, 198, 231
Ryrie, William 186

S

Sabine 40
sack (*saca*) 94, 111, 161, 163, 164, 170
  Canary 93, 95, 134, 135, 161, 162, 163, 164, 169
  Palme 162
  sherry 93, 94, 134, 164, 169
St-Brise 145
St-Denis 200
St-Emilion 200
St-Evremond, Marquis de 117
St-Julien 140
Saintsbury, George 234
Salisbury, Lord 161, 162
Sangiovese (Sangioveto) 217, 246, 247
Sansevain, Jean-Louis 191
Sassicaia 247
Sauternes 101, 108, 144, 145
Sauvignon Blanc [grape] 51, 195, 243, 247
Sauvignon Blanc [wine] 243, 249
Schiller, Friedrich von 207
Schloss Johannisberg 158, 159, 203, 204–6, 207
Schoonmaker, Frank 234
Scotland *see* Britain
Scuppernong [grape] 187, 189
Scuppernong [wine] 189
Ségur, Nicolas-Alexandre, Marquis de 143, 201
Sémillon [grape] (Green Grape) 131, 144, 192, 195, 202
Sémillon [wine] 248
Sercial 135
Serra, Junipero 190
Serres, Olivier de 65, 67
Setinum 40
Sforsato/Sfursat 221
Shakespeare, William 94, *95,* 96, 97, 134
sherry 48, 89, 92–95, 163, 168, 169–72, 179, 200, 223, 224, 246
  ageing 170–1

ACKNOWLEDGEMENTS

Mitchell Beazley would like to acknowledge and thank the following for providing images for publication in this book.

2 Private Collection/www.bridgeman.co.uk/Roger Perrin/Artist: Leonetto Cappiello © ADAGP, Paris and DACS, London 2004; 6-7 Scala, Florence/Galleria Palatina, Florence, Italy; 9 The Art Archive/Museum der Stadt Wien/Dagli Orti (A); 10 Prado, Madrid, Spain/Giraudon/www.bridgeman.co.uk; 16 akg-Images/British Library, London; 17 Art Directors/M Barlow; 19 Photo12.com/Institut Ramses; 20-21 The Art Archive/British Museum, London; 22 Werner Forman Archive/Schimmel Collection, New York; 24 The Art Archive/Heraklion Museum/Dagli Orti; 27 akg-images/Soprintendenza Archeologica, Potenza; 28 Worcester Art Museum, Massachusetts, USA/www.bridgeman.co.uk; 31 Staatliche Antikensammlungen und Glyptothek, München; 33 Corbis/Yann Arthus-Bertrand; 34 Polish Archaeological Mission/Paphos Museum; 38 The Art Archive/Dagli Orti; 41 Corbis/Jonathan Blair; 43 Bayerisches Nationalmuseum, München; 45 John Rylands Library, University Library of Manchester; 47 National Museums of Scotland/www.bridgeman.co.uk; 52-53 Corbis/Sandro Vannini; 55 Werner Forman Archive/Museum für Islamische Kunst, Berlin; 57 Courtesy of the Arthur M Sackler Museum, Harvard University Art Museums. Promised gift of Mr and Mrs Stuart Cary Welch, Jr. Partially owned by the Metropolitan Museum of Art and the Arthur M Sackler Museum, Harvard University, 1988. Photo credit: Allan Macintyre. Image copyright: © 2004 President and Fellows of Harvard College; 58 Kunsthalle Mannheim; 60 British Library; 62 jonarnold.com/R Butcher; 63 akg-images/Staatsbibliothek zu Berlin Preußischer Kulturbesitz; 64 By permission of the British Library/Roy 14E VI fol 17; 66 Österreichische Nationalbibliothek, Vienna, Austria/Alinari/www.bridgeman.co.uk; 69 British Library; 71 Château de Versailles, France/www.bridgeman.co.uk; 72 Photo12.com/ARJ/Bibliothèque municipale, Dijon; 73 Corbis/Bo Zaunders; 76 By permission of the British Library/Roy 14E IV fol 232 Min; 80 Scope/Jean Luc Barde; 82 Octopus Publishing Group/Jason Lowe; 86 Scala, Florence/San Martino dei Buonomini, Florence, Italy; 88 Scope/Jacques Guillard; 90 Aldus Archive; 93 By permission of the British Library/Add 15217 fol 33; 95 New York Historical Society, New York, USA/www.bridgeman.co.uk; 97 The Art Archive/British Museum/Eileen Tweedy; 100 akg-images/Museum of Fine Arts, Budapest; 102 Archives municipales de Bordeaux; 104 Corbis/Burstein Collection; 105 Courtesy of the Warden and Scholars of New College, Oxford/www.bridgeman.co.uk; 106 alamy/Justin Kase;108 Collection Particulière Cliché Musée D'Aquitaine, Bordeaux, France - tous droits réservés; 109 BURDIN S A; 110 Hugh Johnson; 113 Musée Condé, Chantilly, France/Lauros/Giraudon/www.bridgeman.co.uk; 115 Sonia Halliday Photographs; 116 From 'A History of Champagne' by Henry Vizetelly; 118 Claes Löfgren/winepictures.com; 120 Harvey Wine Museum, Bristol; 122 Mansell Collection; 124 Patrick Cronenberger; 126 Heeresgeschichtliches Museum, Vienna; 127 John Lipitch Associates; 128 Cape Province, Republic of South Africa/Ken Walsh/www.bridgeman.co.uk; 130-131 With thanks to Lowell Jooste at Klein Constantia Estate; 135 The Art Archive/Francesco Venturi; 137 Scope/Jacques Guillard; 139 Patrick Cronenberger; 141 Scope/Michel Guillard; 142 Hugh Johnson; 144 Scope/Michel Guillard; 147 Hugh Johnson; 148 "Livre de commande de tissus" Maison Bouchard Père et Fils, Beaune, France; 151 Photo12.com/ARJ; 153 Bibliothèque Nationale, Paris; 157 Kunstverlag EDM Von König GmbH & Co KG; 158 Janet Price; 161 © Copyright The British Museum; 163 Christie's Images, London/www.bridgeman.co.uk; 166 Harvey Wine Museum, Bristol; 168 The Institute of Masters of Wine Library/Guildhall Library; 170 Gonzalez Byass; 173 The cellar at Bodegas Domecq's La Mezquita Winery, Jerez/Allied Domecq Wine UK Ltd; 174 Christies; 175 Courtesy of the Director/National Army Museum, London; 177 From 'A History of Champagne' by Henry Vizetelly; 179 Photo RMN - L'Hoir/Popovitch/Musée National de Céramique, Sèvres; 180 akg-images; 183 Scope Features/Jean Luc Barde; 184 & 185 Tahbilk Winery & Vineyard; 188-189 Corbis/Ted Streshinsky; 193 California State Archives, Sacramento; 194 akg-images; 197 Patrick Cronenberger; 198-199 Private Collection/Archives Charmet/www.bridgeman.co.uk; 202 André Hampartzoumian; 204-205 Root Stock/Hendrik Holler; 209 Pierre Sauter/Musée Historique de Lausanne; 211 Mary Evans Picture Library; 219 Fondazione Lungarotti/Torgiano Wine Museum; 220-221 Corbis/Todd A Gipstein; 222 Codorníu Group/J Rocabert; 225 Octopus Publishing Group/Jason Lowe; 227 Corbis/Michael Busselle; 228 The Art Archive/Dagli Orti (A); 230 Corbis/Bettmann; 235 The Art Archive/Dagli Orti (A); 236 Octopus Publishing Group/Jason Lowe; 239 Corbis/Ted Streshinsky; 240 Avis Mandel; 243 Christie's Images; 245 Ysios Winery, near Laguardia, Rioja Alavesa/Allied Domecq Wine UK Ltd; 246 top Corbis/Raymond Reuter; 246 bottom Hugh Johnson; 247 left Scope/Jean Luc Barde; 247 right Robert Mondavi Winery; 249 The Cellar of Terre da Vino in Barolo/Terre da Vino.